THE COMPLETE GUIDE TO
SHARPENING

THE COMPLETE GUIDE TO
SHARPENING

Leonard Lee

The Taunton Press

Taunton
BOOKS & VIDEOS

for fellow enthusiasts

First printing: January 1995
Printed in the United States of America

A FINE WOODWORKING Book
FINE WOODWORKING® is a trademark of The Taunton Press, Inc.,
registered in the U.S. Patent and Trademark Office.

The Taunton Press, 63 South Main Street, Box 5506,
Newtown, CT 06470-5506

Library of Congress Cataloging-in-Publication Data

Lee, Leonard.
    The complete guide to sharpening / Leonard Lee.
        p.   cm.
    "A Fine woodworking book"–T.p. verso.
    Includes index.
    ISBN 1-56158-067-8
    1. Woodworking tools.   2. Sharpening of tools.   I. Title.
TT186.L43   1994   94-37677
684'.08'028 – dc20   CIP

■ To Lorraine, who not only makes it all possible, but so enjoyable

ACKNOWLEDGMENTS

Some years ago, Tom Hurley of Toronto and I set out to write a book on sharpening but (through no fault of Tom's) got mired down along the way. Very little of the prose from that earlier effort survived to be included in this book, but some of the photographs did as well as a variety of jigs that Tom had developed or modified to make shop sharpening easier and more accurate. These photos and jigs are most evident in the chapters on drill bits and saws, although there are several elsewhere in the book as well. Thank you, Tom, for permission to use this material.

Of all the other people whose contributions should be acknowledged possibly the first should be the hundreds of customers over the years who asked "Why?" They provided the reason to write.

A number of people were instrumental in enabling me to write. Peter Sewell of the National Research Council of Canada patiently and cheerfully photographed dozens of tools and stones through an electron microscope. This was critical to understanding materials and processes. Dorothy Liberty of Forintek (Ottawa) provided key library services. Sandy Stewart (Mississippi Forest Products Laboratory), Vincent Farengo (Everlast Saw Company) and Roger Comer (Eagle Carbide) took turns educating me about carbide cutting tools. Norm Franz of Vancouver and Bill McKenzie of California and Australia were generous with answers, advice and photographs, a small portion of which is presented in Appendix 1. The Canadian Conservation Institute took a number of photographs under some time pressure.

On the editing side, Jerry Glaser applied the whip of precision to many technical matters, as well as making available a wealth of material from his library. Brother Bob answered dozens of grammatical questions, and Peter Chapman at The Taunton Press helped substantially with sequence and flow while excising many lumpy passages and smoothing others. Donna Curtis typed everything, sometimes through the fourth or fifth revision, but always cheerfully.

On the business side, the staff at Lee Valley Tools and Veritas Tools frequently took up the slack caused when I dropped normal duties to play author. To all of those above and those unintentionally missed, I offer heartfelt thanks.

On the home front, I was an indifferent companion at the best of times as the book was being written, and variously testy, distracted or too busy to be fit company at the worst of times. For tolerating all of this plus three other decades of my aberrant activity, I thank my wife, Lorraine.

And, finally, I owe the most to my parents, William and Winnifred Lee, who spent most of their lives ensuring that their children would have the opportunities that had been denied them. From a hardscrabble homestead in northern Saskatchewan they saw their children through all the education that could be absorbed, while they denied themselves all the luxuries of life and some of the basics. This is a debt that can never be repaid, only acknowledged.

CONTENTS

INTRODUCTION

Woodworkers tend to believe that the only thing separating them from the masters of the craft is another piece of equipment. Since this widely held belief has provided me with a living for many years as president of both a tool-manufacturing company and a tool-retailing firm, I should not even attempt to change it. But from time to time a missionary zeal seizes us all, and I am so seized with the relationship between sharp tools and good woodworking.

Although good sharpening technique alone is not sufficient to make you a master of the craft, it can allow you to maximize whatever innate skill you have. For truly talented woodworkers, it can elevate their work to a level from which they would otherwise be forever barred; only sharp tools can create the crisp detail and fine joinery that their minds are capable of conceiving and their hands of constructing.

I became interested in sharpening for two reasons. First, I mistakenly thought that it was the only thing separating me from the masters because I owned almost every conceivable tool, and, second, I was embarrassed by the endless stream of customer questions that I could answer only hesitantly. Pride is a great motivator.

The specific event that triggered a decade-long analysis of sharpening materials and techniques was the introduction of Japanese water stones to the Western world. Like most woodworkers, I was an oil-stone user and initially looked askance at these oriental intruders: they were just so untraditional. Besides that, they seemed to wear much faster than Arkansas stones, another reason to mistrust them. But they gave wonderful results. In the coarse grits they cut faster than anything I had used before, and in the fine grits they gave a better finish than any other stone. Why? What made them so effective?

Fortunately, I found a scientist at the National Research Council of Canada who had the two necessary ingredients to help unlock the mysteries: boundless curiosity and tremendous skill in using an electron microscope. As fast as I could provide the stone samples and chisels sharpened on them, he photographed them and helped interpret the results.

Within a year, we had covered the Japanese stones, the Arkansas stones and a wide selection of Western man-made stones, as well as a selection of honing compounds. Many of the mysteries of sharpening stones were unlocked. But how could this information be applied to creating a durable edge of the correct shape? I wish the answers were as straightforward in this area as they are in the field of abrasives, but they aren't. Maintaining the keenness of an edge depends on many factors, the main ones being the technique of the user, the material being worked and the nature of the metal in the tool. All will be dealt with in this book.

The first five chapters cover theory and equipment; the rest of the book deals with various tool groups by category. Throughout, emphasis is on the most effective combination of edge shape and keenness for each tool. Overriding all is the nature of the work required of each tool, because edge shape flows from this requirement.

I hope to convince you that sharpening can be done competently and economically by anyone. You can even make some of your own sharpening equipment. But most important, I hope this book will make your woodworking more enjoyable by removing yet one more barrier between you and mastery of the craft.

CHAPTER 1
THE MEANING OF SHARPNESS

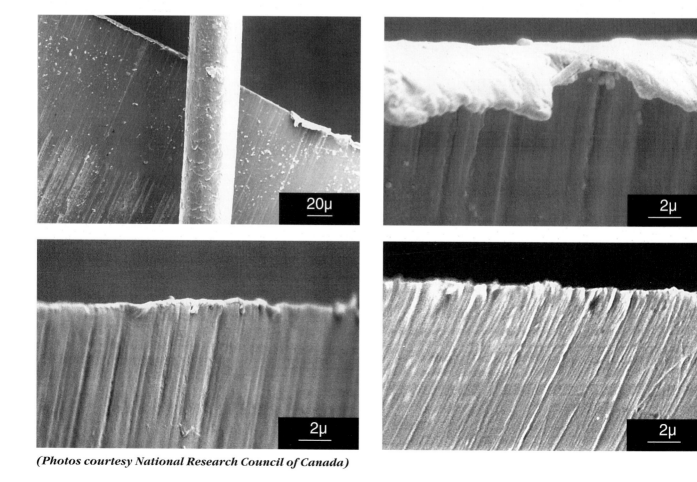

(Photos courtesy National Research Council of Canada)

In the last 2,000 years, Western civilization has used at least three standard references for sharpness. For the first 1,500 years, the standard was a serpent's tooth. As serpents went out of vogue, the expression became "sharp as a tack," a modern equivalent of the serpent's tooth. For the last 100 years or more, both "sharp as a tack" and "sharp as a razor blade" have served as standards in everyday speech. Since there is little call for tools that just puncture wood, both the serpent's tooth and the tack can be set aside as standards in woodworking. The razor blade makes a more useful reference standard.

SHARPER THAN A RAZOR BLADE?

Back in the 1970s, the question of sharpening received a lot of attention in woodworking circles when Japanese water stones were introduced to the West. There had been little new in bench stones since man-made stones had taken most of the market from natural stones some decades before. Debate raged over the effectiveness of these new Japanese stones that used water instead of oil to clear away swarf.

Top left, a standard craft razor blade and a human hair; top right, the same razor blade at increased magnification; bottom left, a Wilkinson Sword razor blade; bottom right, a chisel sharpened on a 6000x water stone then honed with chromium-oxide honing compound. The difficulty of using a human hair for comparison is that it is huge in relation to the details that we want to look at. Accordingly, the photomicrograph showing the hair and craft razor blade is shown at a reduced magnification. If it were shown at the same magnification as the other three, the diameter of the hair would be almost the width of the page. The bar in the bottom right-hand corner of each photomicrograph gives the scale in microns, indicated by the Greek letter µ (1 micron equals one millionth of a meter).

As both an amateur woodworker and a seller of sharpening equipment, I was interested in the new stones and tried out a wide variety of them. I found that they not only cut quickly but that the finer grits seemed to give an even better edge than the natural Arkansas stones that I had been using. But it seemed to me that some comparative standards were necessary to underpin these trial results or it would forever be a matter of opinion.

It occurred to me that a good standard of comparison would be a razor blade. Could you actually sharpen a chisel or plane blade as sharp as a razor? Fortunately, I was able to interest a scientist at Canada's National Research Council in the question. Dr. Peter Sewell, an expert in laser technology, was very skilled in the use of an electron microscope. He agreed to photograph a series of edges sharpened on different stones, both natural and man-made. The results were fascinating.

Early in the game, Peter photographed some razor blades. At the time, Wilkinson Sword razor blades were giving Gillette a hard time in the market, so a Wilkinson blade was photographed as well as one of the standard craft razor blades, the single-edge type suited to freehand use. The photomicrographs of the two blades showed a substantial difference in edge refinement (see the photos on the facing page). The craft blade had a great wire edge that looked like a cresting wave. The Wilkinson blade had a much better defined edge, but even this had a wire edge in places.

And so the fun began. Peter photographed a hair from his head for size comparison, and then he photographed dozens of chisel tips that we sharpened in exactly the same manner on a variety of stones. To minimize the variables, we used chisels of the same type and size that came from a single factory run at Marples. In this manner, we tried to eliminate the effect of different alloys and different hardnesses. To our surprise and pleasure, we found that a number of our test chisels were in fact sharper than razor blades. One is shown here; a greater variety is shown in Chapter 4.

All of this proved that, with basic modern equipment, every woodworker could produce edges sharper than at least the two razor blades photographed. But anyone who has used a razor blade to cut wood knows its limitations. It can be used for incised cuts only; even slight lateral pressure will cause the edge to crumble or even snap the blade. There has to be some relationship between the sharpness and shape for different uses.

THE IMPORTANCE OF SHAPE

Sharpness for a cutting tool could be defined as two surfaces meeting at a line of zero width. That might be fine theory but could result in bad practice. To be effective, a cutting tool not only has to have an edge of zero width, but the angle at which the two surfaces meet must accommodate the intended use of the tool and the material from which the tool is made. The intended use part is straightforward. Most people know what they intend to use a tool for or they wouldn't bother sharpening it. Metallurgy presents a more difficult problem. Seldom do we know the specific alloy of a tool and, even if we did, it would mean little to most of us. But we usually know whether the tool is made of tool steel, high-speed steel, or carbide. These and other categories will be covered in more detail in the chapter on metallurgy (see pp. 18-27), but the vast majority of woodworking hand tools are made of high-carbon tool steels so we will deal only with them for the moment.

Despite the wide variety of tool steels used to make chisels and plane blades (chrome vanadium, tungsten vanadium, D-2, etc.), they all function within a narrow performance band as far as brittleness is concerned, and brittleness is a basic concern when you are shaping an edge.

A razor blade is shaped to cut hair, not wood. The steel can be very hard, very thin and sharpened at a very acute angle. It need only cut small-diameter pieces of presoaked protein. A woodworking chisel made from the same type of steel at the same hardness would need to be thicker (for strength and rigidity) and sharpened at a more obtuse angle; otherwise, it would never withstand the forces that it would be subjected to. We could use exactly the same abrasives on the chisel and get the same keen edge as the razor blade (better, I hope); the only difference would be the angle at the junction of the two meeting surfaces.

This is a roundabout way of leading you back to the proposition that a reasonable definition of sharpness should include not only the keenness of the edge but also the suitability of the shape of the edge considering both the nature of the steel and the intended use of the tool. Therefore, throughout this book the word "sharpening" will be used to describe what are really two different activities—giving the edge keenness and giving it shape.

To illustrate the importance of shape, consider a length of steel with a cross section like an isosceles triangle,

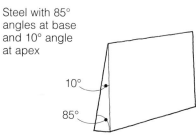

Steel with 85° angles at base and 10° angle at apex

10°

85°

with base angles of 85° and an apex angle of 10°. If all three sides were carefully ground and honed to create three perfect edges, which edge would you least want to have dropped on your finger? The three edges might be equal in keenness but not in effect.

And so it is with woodworking tools; keen edges that do not consider other factors are of limited use.

UNDERSTANDING SHARPENING

To sharpen woodworking tools effectively you have to understand how to shape an edge that will cut cleanly and repeatedly while staying keen. In turn, this requires an understanding of:
• the physics of severing wood fibers (see Chapter 2);
• the strengths and weaknesses of different alloys (see Chapter 3); and
• which abrasives will cut the fastest and still give you the quality of edge you need (see Chapter 4).

With a basic knowledge in each of these areas, you can confidently select and sharpen tools to perform any woodworking task. More important, once you have a grounding in each of these areas, you can get the most value out of your tools. You will select them more intelligently, use them more efficiently and sharpen them more quickly than you did before. You will also use a lot less sandpaper when you get to the finishing stage of any project.

SHAPE AND FUNCTION

Most people ask questions that are impossible to answer when they are in search of sharpening information. One such question is, "How should I sharpen an ax?" The answer depends on how the ax is to be used. If it is going to be used as a felling or notching ax, it would be sharpened one way. If it is for splitting firewood, it would be sharpened another way. But even more basic in this case is the design of the ax. It is impossible to sharpen a felling ax to split wood effectively; the basic shape is wrong. A splitting ax is equally bad for felling. Each ax is shaped for its individual function and does not become interchangeable through any magic of sharpening technique. One is designed to sever fibers and the other to divide them. Their basic shapes reflect these facts (see the photo on the facing page).

If an ax happens to be "dual purpose," it can be biased to perform one function better than the other but it will always lack the core property to perform either function well; it will lack proper body shape. Fortunately not all

tools are as intractable as axes. Many general-purpose tools can be shaped to meet a specific need.

So the first consideration in sharpening is always, "Can I shape this tool to do what I want it to do?" To answer that question you need an understanding of wood and how it reacts to a cutting edge, the first of the three basic knowledge areas. Knowing how wood reacts will let you select the most effective edge shape. For example, if you want to shape a chisel to chop mortises in hardwood, you will know that the wood will exert substantial bending force on the tip of the chisel. The bevel angle you select will reflect that knowledge.

But there is no need to extend that bevel angle all the way to the back of the blade. You want a strong edge, a chisel that will not flex, yet a wedge shape as slim as possible so that it will penetrate a reasonable depth with a single mallet blow. If you need a 35°

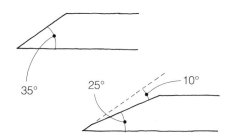

35°   25°   10°

bevel angle to stop edge crumbling or folding, rather than grind the entire chisel tip at 35°, you can grind the chisel at a basic angle of 25° and put a 35° angle on only the last 1/16 in. or so. You now have a chisel that holds an edge well, is just a bit more flexible, but penetrates more easily. You have changed the way the tool works. Just how much change you make in it depends on your personal technique and on the metallurgy of the chisel.

METALLURGY

As three quick examples of the importance of metallurgy, consider:
• a traditional Japanese chisel, high-carbon-steel-hardened to Rc62, laminated to a wrought-iron base;
• a high-carbon-steel Western chisel hardened to Rc58-60; and
• a chisel alloyed to reduce brittleness and to increase ease of manufacturing. It might have both chrome and vanadium in significant quantities as well as carbon.

The Japanese chisel will take a wonderfully keen edge but will need a beefy bevel angle (35° to 45°) to prevent crumbling. A high-carbon steel hardened to Rc62 is relatively brittle as woodworking tools go (see pp. 36-37 for a discussion of hardness scales), so the bevel should be continued at the same beefy angle at least to the lamination line to benefit from the damping action of the wrought iron. To a great extent this negates any advantage of a double bevel because the chisel would not be driven into the wood past the first bevel in normal use.

The high-carbon-steel Western chisel will be less brittle at Rc58-60 (and will probably not take quite as keen an edge) but might still need a steep bevel angle for some distance back from the edge to give the edge sufficient strength.

The alloy chisel, being able to flex more without failure, could be shaped for better penetration and still hold its edge. As the three examples show, unless you understand how each alloy type reacts to the forces experienced, it is impossible to design the most effective, yet durable, tip without a lot of experimentation.

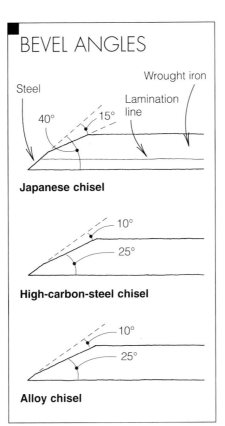

BEVEL ANGLES

Japanese chisel

Steel — 40° — 15° — Lamination line — Wrought iron

High-carbon-steel chisel

10° — 25°

Alloy chisel

10° — 25°

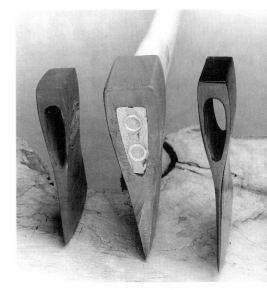

The three axes shown here (from left to right, a dual-purpose ax, a splitting ax and a felling ax) illustrate that there is more to sharpness than a keen edge. Equally important is the basic shape of the tool: the angle at which the cutting surfaces meet must accommodate the intended use of the tool.

ABRASIVES

Finally, to arrive at the desired edge shape efficiently, you need a general understanding of abrasives and the techniques of using them. You want to be able to sharpen quickly, using coarse abrasives for shaping and fine abrasives for honing, but if you use the wrong abrasives or the wrong technique, you could end up with a keen edge that has been fatally flawed in the process of creating it.

The most common error in shaping a high-carbon-steel tool is to overheat it, thereby softening the edge. Regardless of how well you then hone that edge, it will degrade quickly in use. You will have ruined it with your technique. A less common error, but equally damaging, is to use a hard abrasive on a sensitive steel. Traditional Japanese chisels, for example, are among the hardest chisels (at Rc62 or more) that most woodworkers will encounter. They cannot be treated as casually as their Western cousins because they are more brittle. You can actually cause minute fractures in the steel by shaping

them on a power grinder or on a diamond bench stone. (In general, only soft stones are used with Japanese chisels.) The edge might appear to be perfect after honing, but the tiny fractures would cause it to chip quickly in use.

So, a definition of sharpness has to include all four factors: the material to be worked, the metal in the tool, the technique of the user and the suitable use of abrasives.

In view of all this, a sharp tool can be defined as one that has a keen edge that will hold its shape in repeated use for a given material and technique while producing a good surface finish on the wood. Throughout the remainder of this book, the themes of tool composition, intended use (both materials and technique) and suitable abrasives will occur repeatedly. That is what sharpening is all about.

CHAPTER 2
THE PHYSICS OF SEVERING WOOD FIBERS

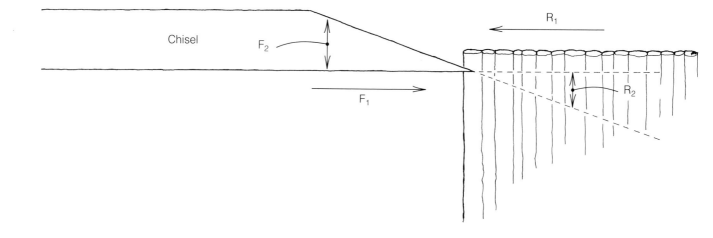

I know. You want to go directly to tool sharpening without having to go through a course in physics. Well, you can do that if you wish, but if you read this chapter you will do a lot better job of sharpening anything that cuts wood because you will understand how wood reacts to cutting tools, dull or sharp.

THE NATURE OF WOOD

For a good understanding of the nature of wood, I can recommend no better book than Bruce Hoadley's *Understanding Wood* (The Taunton Press, 1980). This very readable book is a classic in the field, and a virtual necessity for anyone who intends to do any serious woodworking. The material that follows is an over-simplification of the structure of wood, but it is sufficient to describe the major factors at play when wood and cutting tools interact.

To start the oversimplification, consider wood to be a bundle of straws held together by glue. The straws are cellulose and the glue is lignin. This could be a fairly loose, fragile bundle (like some species of cedar) or an extremely strong, rigid bundle (like cherry). The primary differences between the two are the amount of force required to separate the fibers and how readily the fibers will crush or tear when a cutting force is applied to them.

If you remember your high school physics texts, the assumption was often made that there was zero friction in a process. I'm going to ask you to accept the same assumption now, because taking friction into account at this stage adds many complications without adding much information. Ignoring friction, therefore, the approximate forces at play when you begin to cut end grain with a chisel (see the drawing on the facing page) are as follows:

F_1 = the force required to begin to cut fibers

F_2 = the force required to begin to raise the chip

R_1 = the resistance of cell walls to being severed

R_2 = the resistance of the chip to being lifted

These represent the equilibrium forces just before the wood begins to be cut. As soon as the force applied to the chisel becomes greater than the resistance of the wood, cutting starts.

HOW WOOD REACTS TO CUTTING EDGES

Wood can be cut many ways in relation to both grain and annular rings. The force required for different cuts can be quite different. A landmark study in the cutting forces in woodworking was the doctoral thesis of Eero Kivimaa presented to Finland's Institute of Technology in 1950. Using a knife sharpened to the industry standard of the day and cutting Finnish birch at 12% moisture content, he got the results shown in the drawing below.

Cutting end grain (A in the drawing) requires nearly three times the force that it takes to cut parallel to the grain (B). In turn, it takes more force to cut parallel to the grain (B) than it does to cut cross grain (C). These forces change with different woods and different moisture contents, but the ratios hold well over most temperate wood varieties. Recognizing the difference in these forces becomes as important as the different hardness of the species that we use. We know that it will always take more force to cut end grain than parallel grain or cross grain. Combined with this difference is the different way fibers react as we try to cut the three different ways.

END-GRAIN CUTTING

If we look at the cutting action a bit more closely, we begin to see the relationship between edge shape and what is going to happen to the wood. Consider one fiber being cut. The chisel is a wedge passing through the fiber, virtually prying the fiber apart. As it

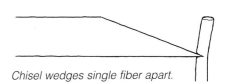

Chisel wedges single fiber apart.

enters the fiber wall, the fiber begins to bend because the chisel is wedging it apart on one side while the other wall is still intact. If the wood is sufficiently elastic it will tolerate this division without tearing. But wood is not very elastic. It can be compressed much more readily than it can be stretched. Even in steam bending, when the fibers are at their most flexible (softened with water and the lignin in a plastic state), most fibers can be extended less than half of one percent before rupturing.

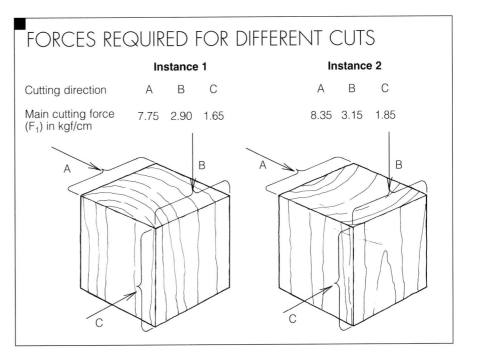

FORCES REQUIRED FOR DIFFERENT CUTS

Cutting direction	Instance 1			Instance 2		
	A	B	C	A	B	C
Main cutting force (F_1) in kgf/cm	7.75	2.90	1.65	8.35	3.15	1.85

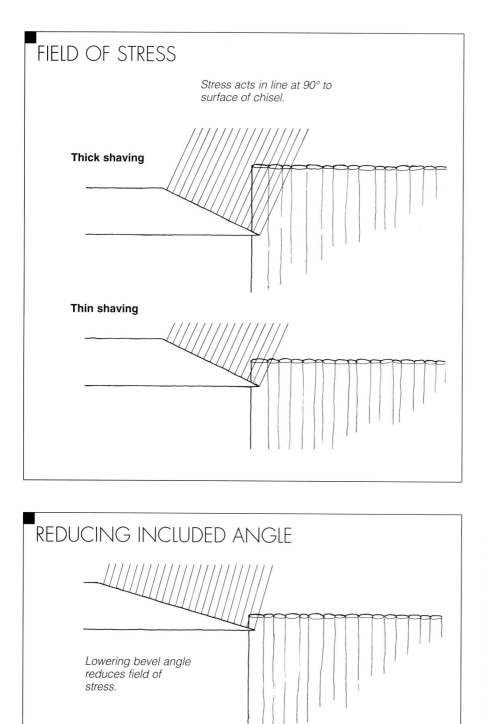

FIELD OF STRESS

Stress acts in line at 90° to surface of chisel.

Thick shaving

Thin shaving

REDUCING INCLUDED ANGLE

Lowering bevel angle reduces field of stress.

Wet or dry, the stresses at the cutting plane become so great that the fibers begin to tear apart. The phenomenon we like to think of as cutting becomes, if we are lucky, a controlled tearing process. If we are unlucky (and the intent of this chapter is to tell you how to control your "luck"), it becomes a series of uncontrolled tears that can leave a very rough surface.

But the process is actually more complicated than what has just been described. Wood is a bundle of such fibers all glued together with lignin. What we do to one fiber affects the surrounding fibers. If we consider the fiber immediately behind the one being cut, it is being subjected to stress before the blade even reaches it. So is the one behind that. We have a chain reaction affecting a number of fibers.

It quickly becomes apparent that we want an edge shape that will cause the minimum amount of tearing stress as the blade passes through the wood. There are several ways we can reduce the stress.

The most obvious one is to make the wedge more efficient by reducing the included angle (see the bottom drawing at left). Since the bending stress acts in a line at 90° to the surface of the wedge, if we reduce the bevel angle we restrict the field of the stress. In this example, we would reduce the field to a single fiber. This solution would be fine if we had tool steel that would not bend or break at such a low bevel angle, but the practical limit for a chisel is about 15° for end-grain work in most hardwoods. Even though reduction of the bevel angle reduces the force component needed to lift the chip (or, conversely, the resisting force of the wood tending to bend the chisel tip downward), it is not a simple relationship; the practical limit is governed by the thickness of the chip, the nature of the wood and the steel in the chisel. If the bevel angle is lowered too much, the edge will break or fold, effectively dulling the chisel.

A dull chisel creates a whole new set of problems. Fibers start to crush instead of being cut. These immediately create a false edge that is more rounded (duller) than the actual edge. Instead of being severed, fibers flatten and are stretched on both sides of the cutting plane. Highly uncontrolled fiber breaking takes place well below the cutting line. The crushed fibers build up ahead of the edge until the density is increased

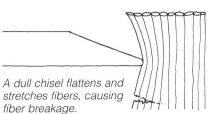

A dull chisel flattens and stretches fibers, causing fiber breakage.

to the point that they are finally severed. The process immediately starts again, and you get a "cheesy" surface that shows this repeated pattern (see the photo at right).

You can do four things to make end-grain cutting easier. First, you can keep the edge of a chisel as keen as possible (see Chapter 6). Second, you can take lighter cuts. When you reduce the chip thickness enough, the telegraphing of stress to adjacent fibers is minimal since the field of stress has been restricted to very few fibers. The chip also breaks more easily since a shorter section of cell wall is involved; it presents less resistance than a longer section. The cut almost becomes like shaving off a series of whiskers, since the shaving breaks very frequently.

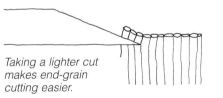

Taking a lighter cut makes end-grain cutting easier.

Third, you can keep the included angle (or bevel angle) of the chisel as low as possible consistent with edge retention. This is a matter of trial and error with a tool. You start with a low bevel angle and increase it only if you get edge failure. The failure is quickly evident by the scratches on the end grain (as shown in the photo at right). Keep increasing the angle by honing at a higher micro-bevel angle (see p. 62) until the edge holds its shape.

Fourth, you can skew the chisel. Instead of cutting directly across the grain, hold the chisel askew the path

The two outer wood samples show the effects of an imperfect chisel edge. The cheesy surface at left was produced by a dull chisel; the scratched surface at right by a chisel with edge failure. The middle sample shows a cleanly cut surface. (Photo by Susan Kahn)

SKEWING THE TOOL

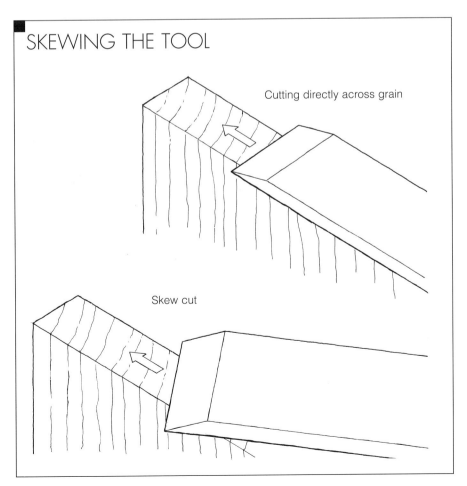

Cutting directly across grain

Skew cut

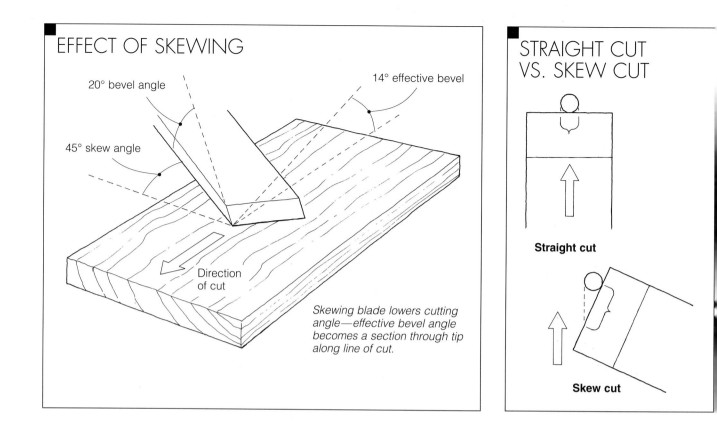

EFFECT OF SKEWING

20° bevel angle

14° effective bevel

45° skew angle

Direction of cut

Skewing blade lowers cutting angle—effective bevel angle becomes a section through tip along line of cut.

STRAIGHT CUT VS. SKEW CUT

Straight cut

Skew cut

of travel. This has exactly the same effect as lowering the bevel angle, because it lowers the cutting angle. If you have a chisel with a 20° bevel angle, by rotating the chisel 45° and taking a skew cut, you will get the same cutting action that you would if you had lowered the bevel angle to 14° (see the drawing above). If you skewed the chisel even more, say to 60°, you would get a cutting angle of 10°.

But, you may ask, "Why doesn't the edge fail at this cutting angle?" It does not fail because exactly the same amount of distortional force is being applied over greater blade width. Consider the drawing at right above, showing a chisel cutting a single fiber: one cut is square across the fiber; the other is in the same direction, but with the chisel skewed so that the force of severing the fiber is distributed over much more blade.

In the straight cut, the resistance of the fiber to being cut is concentrated on about one fifth of the chisel edge. In the skew cut, the same force is distributed over half of the blade. In fact, there is *less* distortional force per unit of blade length with the skew cut than with the square cut. This leads directly to one of the little-known facts about tool technique—a blade used at a skew can be sharpened at a lower angle than a blade used to cut squarely across the wood, and the skewed blade will still retain its edge. This is part of the magic of the "slicing" cut (see p. 14) that is widely talked about but little understood.

Taken in combination, the above explanation of forces also leads to one of the basic tenets of tool sharpening. A chisel should always be sharpened at the lowest bevel angle consistent with edge retention. Such a chisel will cause the least tearing and leave the smoothest surface in every instance, except when cutting against the grain in parallel-grain cutting.

PARALLEL-GRAIN CUTTING

As we know from experience (and as Kivimaa showed in his study), cutting parallel to the grain is easier on tools than cutting end grain because it takes less force. The reduced cutting force means that the opposing force acting on the tool is similarly reduced. The distortional forces on the tool are lower. But the process is similar. Where we were aiming for controlled tearing with end-grain cutting, we now have to concentrate more on controlled splitting. The objective is always to cut, not split, but the wood often will not cooperate.

First of all, because the forces are more moderate, parallel-grain cutting immediately implies lower cutting angles. But chip formation in parallel-grain cutting is quite different from chip formation in end-grain cutting. There is a tendency for running cracks to develop in the chip, a problem that is

PLANING AND BLADE DIRECTION

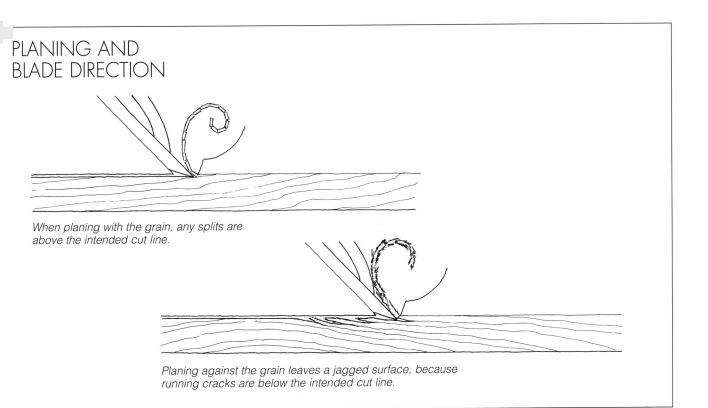

When planing with the grain, any splits are above the intended cut line.

Planing against the grain leaves a jagged surface, because running cracks are below the intended cut line.

not present in end-grain cutting. For this reason, you should always plane "with the grain," that is, when the grain is rising up and away from the direction of cut.

Because parallel-grain cutting is associated more with planes than with chisels, a plane will be used as the cutting tool in this explanation. When you are cutting with the grain, planing is easy. The wood may split in front of the blade but the splits are above the intended cut line and do not cause a problem. The split runs into the waste wood and actually helps chip formation. The shaving comes away as a linked series of broken chips as fibers are cut until a crack develops (see the top drawing above). Then the crack runs out until the chip becomes thin enough that it breaks, or until the shaving is levered up on the cap iron causing the chip to break just at the mouth of the plane. This process is all very easy and pleasant. All you have to worry about is keeping a keen edge on the plane blade.

THE WORK OF DR. NORMAN FRANZ

Most woodworkers take plane-bed angles for granted; it does not occur to them that changing the cutter angle might contribute more to a smooth surface than honing the blade. Nearly 40 years ago, Dr. Norman Franz of the University of Michigan studied how shavings were formed, using a care-fully controlled cutting process and a high-speed camera. Among many other things, he found that the type of wood surface generated by planing could be changed by changing the cut-ting angle. Appendix 1 on pp. 229-234 covers some of the highlights of Dr. Franz's work.

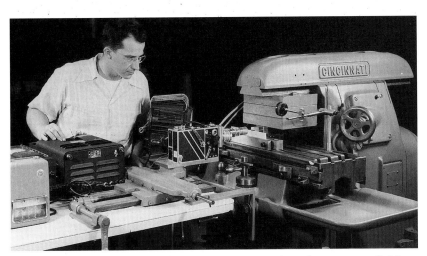

Dr. Norman Franz and his apparatus for recording the process of chip formation.

CHIP BREAKING

A cap iron on a plane is also called a chip-breaker. Cutting against the grain, it is important to break the chip into pieces as short as possible. The longer the chip, the rougher the finish will be because it will break deeper below the cut line. To get the best chip-breaking action, you should:

1. Keep the blade as sharp as possible so that it cuts into the fibers instead of just wedging them apart.

2. Keep the cap iron close to the cutting edge. This forces the most rapid change in direction of the chip, causing it to break sooner.

3. Close the mouth of the plane to just greater than the thickness of the chip to reduce the length of the levered portion of the fiber. The front of the mouth is holding the fiber down and the blade is lifting it. The closer they are together, the shorter the broken pieces will be.

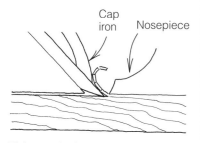

Tight mouth, fine shaving, close cap iron

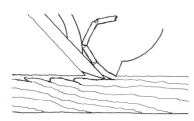

Wide mouth, coarse shaving, cap iron set back

4. Take thin savings. A thin chip breaks more readily than a thick one. It also lets you keep the plane mouth narrower.

5. Where possible, skew the plane.

Since true parallel grain almost never exists in the real world, we can move from planing with the grain to planing against the grain. The transition will be through that very small amount of parallel grain that does exist in real woodworking, associated as it always is with one of the other two types.

Planing against the grain is never fun. Wood fibers are always more willing to divide longitudinally than be severed transversely; as Kivimaa has shown, about three times as willing. As a result, planing against the grain becomes a process of controlling the running cracks that begin at the blade edge and follow the grain to some point below the intended cut line. As the plane moves forward, the chip is pried up by the blade and cap iron until the chip breaks, partially beneath the cut line. The result is a finish with a series of jagged fiber breaks (see the bottom drawing on p. 11). Since it is virtually impossible to plane against the grain and get a silky finish, the objective becomes one of getting the least rough finish possible.

One obvious solution is to close the mouth of the plane so that the chips will break more frequently and leave a smoother rough finish (see the sidebar at left). If the plane has an adjustable nosepiece, it should be brought back

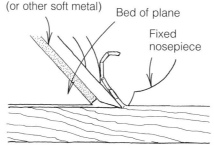

so that there is just room for a shaving to pass between the blade and the front of the mouth. If the plane has a non-adjustable mouth, a sheet of brass or soft iron can be fitted under the plane blade to bring the blade forward as far as needed to tighten the mouth (as shown in the drawing above).

Of course, taking a lighter cut helps as well. The thinner the shaving, the more easily it breaks. Similarly, the thinner the shaving the tighter you can make the mouth of the plane. The tighter the mouth, the more frequently the shaving is broken and the shorter the running cracks will be.

But the best solution is to tighten the mouth, take a light cut *and* skew the plane. By skewing the plane you materially change the forces at work as you sever fibers. Consider how the fibers are arranged when you are planing against the grain. It is really just a variation of end-grain planing. The fibers are at an angle to the surface not 90° to be sure, but still presenting themselves partially in cross section. A close-up of a portion of the surface would look something like the drawing below. By straight planing you are plucking up the fiber ends, creating the running cracks that are then broken off to create a rough finish. But if you skew

When planing against grain, fibers are at angle to surface.

Planing direction

the plane, part of the force on the fibers becomes lateral to the grain not in line with it.

As with the skewed cut in end grain, the force of severing the fiber is distributed over greater blade width, but in this case the fiber is lifted less because it is being forced up a ramp of lower slope (see the drawing on the facing page). The distance A is twice as great as the distance B. The effective cutting angle in the skewed cut is only half the cutting angle in the straight cut, so there is less tendency to create a running crack. More important, the lifting or wedging force on the fiber is now acting at an angle to the grain, not parallel to it. Instead of plucking up the tip of the fiber, the blade enters the fiber from the side, creating a lateral force as well as a longitudinal force.

STRAIGHT CUT VS. SKEW CUT

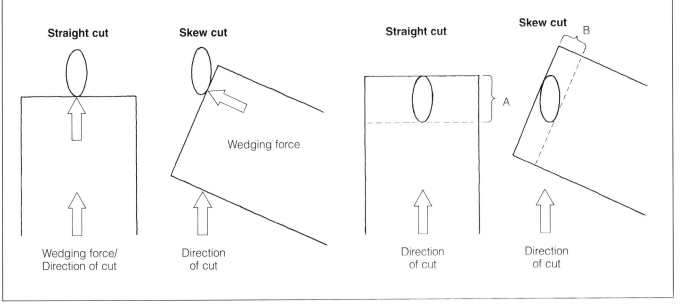

Straight cut

Wedging force/
Direction of cut

Skew cut

Wedging force

Direction
of cut

Straight cut

Direction
of cut

Skew cut

A

B

Direction
of cut

Not only is the fiber not plucked up, as it is in straight planing, but the fiber is actually being held in position by part of the cutting edge as the blade passes through it.

In practice, the forces do not conform to theory as predictably as they do in the other examples given in this chapter. A lower bed angle in the plane is indicated, but as the bed angle is lowered, the relative forces change; there is more compressive force on the fiber and less lifting force. But at the same time, the lower angle encourages fiber separation since it is now reducing the angle at which the fiber is bent. The fiber is less liable to break and more liable to develop a running crack. But the more the blade is skewed to the angle of the grain, the more the splitting tendency is reduced. The forces become lateral to the fiber, forcing it against adjacent fibers rather than lifting it. It requires a great deal of experimentation to determine just when the combination of forces changes in your favor to give a cleaner cut. This is an area requiring much more research (see the sidebar at right).

THEORY VS. PRACTICE

I fell in love with the tight-mouth, light-cut, low-bed-angle theory but found that it did not work as well on wood as it did on paper. This might have been because too little research was done or that it was done poorly. One of the test planes used is shown below. It had an alarming tendency to grain-follow. This could have been for several reasons (e.g. wide mouth, flexible blade, etc.), but even a finely tuned #60½ low-angle block plane showed a similar tendency in certain grain configurations.

To date there has not been an opportunity to do the sort of controlled testing that would indicate whether the theory is flawed or whether it just has limits. Meanwhile, I strongly recommend that you read Appendix 1 on different chip types and keep your cabinet scrapers handy.

This low-bed-angle plane was developed to test the theory that a skewed blade gives a cleaner cut when planing against the grain.

SKEWED BLADES IN CARVING

There are many instances when skewed blades are used in carving, but often the carver does not realize that it is the change in forces caused by skewing that produces the desired result.

Fred Cogelow, a top North American carver from Willmar, Minnesota, designed a set of skew gouges for working difficult grain. He designed them to allow limited cutting against the grain, since it is nearly impossible to cut with the grain on larger pieces without getting into awkward tool positions or awkward rotation of the piece being worked. As is necessary with skew chisels, the gouges are available in pairs, one left-hand and one right-hand. These gouges, as well as some designs of chip-carving knives, show the direct application of skewed blades to carving.

Making a roll cut with a gouge

For a smooth finish, carvers will often roll a gouge as they push it through the wood. Anyone who has ever carved end-grain basswood knows how effective a roll cut can be. Instead of forcing the gouge directly through the fibers, the rolling action is a dynamic way of skewing the blade, effectively reducing the cutting angle, reducing the force per unit of blade width and reducing fiber tearing. It is not at all obvious, but the roll cut is a skewed-blade cut.

Making a slicing cut with a knife

Using a knife on the same end-grain basswood, carvers know that they get a smoother finish if they draw the knife across the wood with a slicing cut. Once again, the geometry of the skewed blade is at work. Just like the roll cut, the slicing knife cut is exactly the same as skewing a plane or a chisel in use. In this case, the amount of skewing is much greater but the effect is the same.

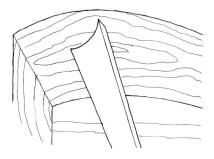

Skew gouge cutting across grain (leading edge of gouge on right)

Rolling a gouge has the same effect as skewing a blade.

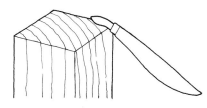

Drawing a knife across the grain with a slicing cut is a method of skewing the blade.

A roll cut (at left on the end-grain surface) produces a much smoother finish than a straight cut (at right).

CROSS-GRAIN CUTTING

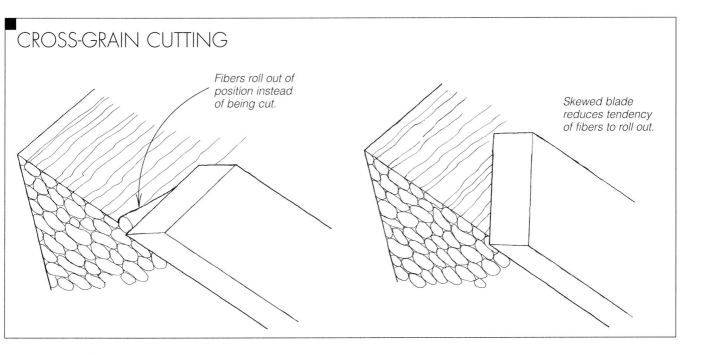

Fibers roll out of position instead of being cut.

Skewed blade reduces tendency of fibers to roll out.

CROSS-GRAIN CUTTING

The results of a skewed blade are much more apparent and much more easily controlled when cutting across the grain. If you have ever tried planing directly across the grain, as you might when making raised panels, you know that there is a tendency for the fibers to roll out of position rather than being cut. The result is a reasonably level but rough finish.

When planing directly across the grain, the plane blade is applying both shearing and lifting forces on a fiber. In fact, the fibers react in groups, not as single fibers. Instead of only a single fiber being sheared or rolled out of position, a bundle of fibers will be affected, breaking away where the cell walls are weakest. When entire groups of fibers break away, the break line often will dip well below the intended cut line; this is the cause of the rough finish.

But when a blade is skewed, not only are the total forces acting on a single fiber or bundle of fibers reduced, but the direction of the forces changes to act partly parallel to the fiber instead of completely transversely. Skewing the blade reduces tearout, but there is also another helpful factor at play. As the blade moves across the wood, the

fibers are actually being held in position by one part of the blade while another part of the blade continues to cut them. The smoothness of cut is further enhanced by a tight mouth and a low cutting angle, the same as with end-grain cutting.

But the skewed blade is the most important factor in this instance. It is for exactly this reason that a skew chisel pares tenon cheeks more smoothly than does a square chisel and that panel-raising planes have skewed blades.

CLEARANCE ANGLES: A CASE OF APPLIED PHYSICS

As described earlier, fibers deform a certain amount before they submit to being cut. In the case of end-grain cutting, the deformed fibers tend to right themselves as the cutting edge passes. For this reason, there is always a recommended clearance angle for plane blades (see the drawing on p. 16).

The amount of clearance required is governed by many factors: the nature of the wood, the depth of cut, the sharpness of the blade, whether or not the cut is end grain or cross grain, and so on. You will read and hear all sorts of conflicting advice on appropriate clearance angles for bench planes; I have seen recommendations from as low as 3° to as high as 15°. While I am a fan of low clearance angles because they allow lower cutting angles, I am not going to enter the fray by making a flat declaration that any particular angle is best because there are too many variables at play.

The main factor to consider is that you need enough room to accommodate fiber springback or you will find your plane porpoising in use, making a series of scalloped cuts. Consider an end-grain cut with a low-

TOOL GEOMETRY

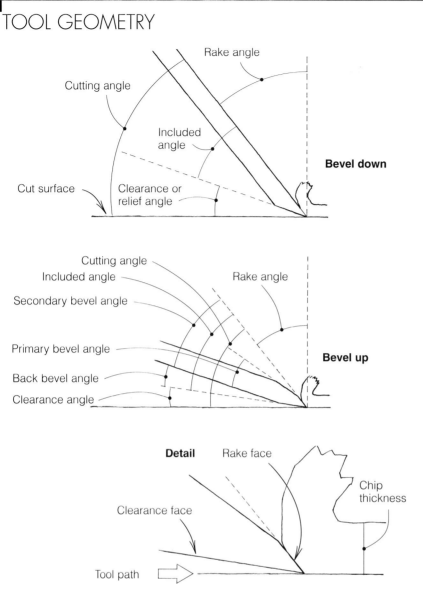

Rake angle

Cutting angle

Included angle

Bevel down

Cut surface

Clearance or relief angle

Cutting angle
Included angle
Secondary bevel angle

Rake angle

Primary bevel angle

Bevel up

Back bevel angle
Clearance angle

Detail Rake face

Chip thickness

Clearance face

Tool path

Cutting angle The total included angle of the cutting tip plus any clearance or relief angle. The complement of the rake angle.

Rake angle The angle between a line drawn normal to the cut surface and the rake face of the cutter. Always the complement of the cutting angle.

Included angle The angle formed by the rake face and clearance face of a cutter tip.

Clearance/relief angle The angle between the clearance face and the cut surface.

Primary bevel The basic grind angle of a tool.

Secondary bevel A bevel at a slightly steeper angle than the primary bevel next to the cutting edge. A micro-bevel is a very narrow secondary bevel.

Back bevel A bevel on the clearance face equal to the included angle minus the secondary bevel angle (or minus the primary bevel angle on a cutter that has no secondary bevel).

angle block plane. The fibers are bent forward slightly before they are cut. When they then spring back, they return to a level that is slightly higher than the line of cut (see the drawing on the facing page). A heavy cut increases fiber distortion, causing the fibers to bend more before being cut. When they spring back, they spring back to a higher level than they would with a light cut. For light cuts therefore you can live with a smaller clearance angle.

It is not just fiber springback that causes blade porpoising: Blade distortion contributes to it as well. Just before fibers fail (i.e., are cut), there is maximum stress on the blade. The resistance of the fibers to being cut causes the blade to flex into the wood, essentially taking a deeper cut than intended. When the fibers fail, the blade straightens at the same time as the bent fibers straighten. The two activities are reinforcing in nature.

A related factor affecting the amount of springback is the basic cutting angle. As shown in the drawing on the facing page, the cutting angle is 37° (the 12° bed angle plus the 25° bevel on the plane blade). The reason for developing the low-angle block plane in the first place was to have a plane that had a lower cutting angle than standard bench planes, which are usually 45° (Common pitch) or 50° (York pitch). As shown earlier (p. 8), the lower cutting angle creates less stress on the fibers so they will deform less.

Standard bench planes are all used with the blade "bevel down," so the cutting angle is always the bed angle. But block planes are normally used with the blade "bevel up." This leaves a lot of latitude for tinkering with cutting angles. We don't have to accept some arbitrary cutting angle (like 37°), but can raise it or lower it if we want to.

A lower bevel angle is usually functional for planing many softwoods (cedar, pine, etc.). If light cuts are taken, a good plane blade will support a 20° bevel angle. This will lower the cutting angle to 32°, and cause less fiber distortion and less springback. In many woods this lower bevel angle and reduced springback leaves more than enough clearance at 12°.

FIBER SPRINGBACK

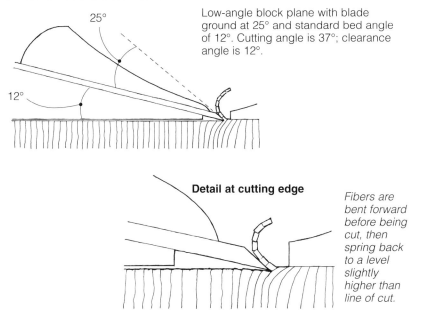

25°

12°

Low-angle block plane with blade ground at 25° and standard bed angle of 12°. Cutting angle is 37°; clearance angle is 12°.

Detail at cutting edge

Fibers are bent forward before being cut, then spring back to a level slightly higher than line of cut.

SETTING ANGLES: THE 1-IN-60 RULE

No honing guides currently available readily allow you to put **5°** of bevel on anything; the angle is beyond their range. This is not a problem, however. If you want to set an angle of less than **20°**, use the basic rule that a **1°** angle subtends an arc of 1 unit at a radius of 60 units. The 1-in-60 rule is close enough for many purposes, particularly sharpening at low angles. You'll find that a 10-unit rise in 60 units is about **9½°** and a 20-unit rise in 60 units is about **19°**.

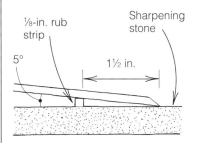

⅛-in. rub strip

Sharpening stone

5°

1½ in.

If, for example, you want a **5°** back bevel on a blade, simply place a rub strip ⅛ in. thick at a point 1½ in. back from the blade edge. A scrap of steel or even hardwood attached with double-faced tape will serve. Using the rub strip as a guide, you can confidently stone a back bevel on the blade knowing that you are within minutes of **5°**. The back bevel does not have to be very wide — somewhere between ⅟₆₄ in. and ⅟₃₂ in. is fine — but it should be as finely honed as possible.

This rationale automatically leads us to another easy modification. Let's assume that the plane blade is not the best on the market and we experience some edge folding or crumbling at a 20° bevel angle. Rather than increase the bevel angle, we can reduce the clearance angle, not by changing the bed but by putting "back bevel" on the blade. As explained in the sidebar at right, it is a simple matter to put a 5° back bevel on the blade, which will substantially increase edge strength without affecting the forces on the fibers during cutting. All we have done is use some of the unnecessarily large clearance angle.

You will find that you can easily live with this reduced clearance angle on woods that have little springback (any dense, fine-grained hardwood). But on these woods you may find that you may have to beef up the basic bevel a bit to retain your edge. Even if you do, you can still end up with a 5° advantage over an unmodified blade. With a good blade used on softwoods with a light cut you will probably find that you can sneak a few more degrees off the

primary bevel onto the back bevel, keeping the total included angle at the edge the same but further lowering your cutting angle.

This whole discussion of relief angles has completely avoided recommending any one angle, because bevel angles and relief angles are a function of what sort of blade you have, what woods you usually work and how aggressively you attack them. With an understanding of the interaction between fibers and the cutting edge, though, this is the typical sort of problem you can solve for yourself, customizing your tools to suit your work. Now, aren't you glad you didn't skip this chapter and go straight to sharpening something?

CHAPTER 3
METALLURGY

Once mankind learned to control fire, the development of metal tools was almost inevitable. Nearly 5% of the earth's crust is iron, and, sooner or later, some tinkerer was going to melt the right rock.

The progression from iron tools to steel tools was more complex. There are many varieties of iron ore in the world, but most of them contain numerous contaminants that would frustrate a tool maker. The principal iron ore is hematite (Fe_2O_3), the ore of the great Mesabi Range bordering Lake Superior. The main contaminants of hematite are oxygen, sulfur, phosphorus, silicon and carbon. Carbon combines with the oxygen, and the addition of lime during the smelting process encourages the sulfur and phosphorus to combine with the slag for easier separation, leaving a reasonably pure cast iron at 3% to 4% carbon content.

But the most historically significant iron ore in the tool business is magnetite (Fe_3O_4). A hard black stone with natural magnetic properties, it is the richest and purest ore. It has an iron content in excess of 60%, is free of sulfur and contains little phosphorus. Although it occurs in significant quantities in Norway and North America, the great magnetite ore body in northern Sweden was the first to be developed, and it was iron from this source that made Swedish steel famous. Iron from this ore, first converted to wrought iron and shipped in that form, also underpinned the fame of Sheffield steel. Modern metallurgical techniques can overcome the problems of lower-grade ores (such as hematite), but the European edge-tool business depended almost exclusively on the pure Swedish wrought iron in the 1700s and 1800s.

WHAT IS STEEL?

Basic steel is a combination of iron with a small percentage of carbon. Mild steel has 0.15% to 0.25% carbon, medium-carbon steel 0.25% to 0.50% and high-carbon steel above 0.60%. Most tool steels are in the range of 0.80% to 1.20%. For centuries, carbon was the only alloying element commonly used with iron. The primary problem in the early days was ridding the iron of unwanted elements, not searching out new ones to add. In common usage, plain carbon steel is not called alloy steel, even though it is an alloy of carbon and iron. The term "alloy steel" is normally reserved for iron with two or more alloying elements (such as chromium, tungsten, etc.).

Iron alone is relatively soft. It does not hold an edge well, wears quickly and has little resistance to bending. But the addition of a bit of carbon to iron has a marvelous effect. The carbon combines with the iron to form hard carbide platelets (Fe_3C) cemented together in a matrix of iron. The combination is resistant to wear and to bending.

Carbon is normally added when the iron is liquid; a melt will be charged with the appropriate amount of carbon (usually in the form of high-carbon steel) for the steel type being made. But early steels were not made by adding carbon to a melt; they were made by a type of case hardening, a process whereby iron bars were packed in charcoal, heated in an airless chamber, and the carbon in the charcoal was absorbed by the iron. The steel had to be packed in an airtight chamber because in the presence of air the charcoal would burn. The iron would also oxidize to form ferrous oxide (FeO). In short, it would rust. Although case hardening is an antique process, it is still often used today when a very hard surface is needed on thin stock that must still retain shock resistance (for example, on beading-tool blades). The unhardened core retains toughness in support of the hardened cutting surface.

■ SECOND-CLASS STEEL

There is ample evidence that the British colonies had more than "taxation without representation" to be concerned about in the 1700s. Sheffield had an unwritten policy of shipping low-grade steel to the colonies while it supplied domestic manufacturers with the better-quality steel made from Swedish wrought iron. There is also evidence that even the finished products shipped to the colonies contained lower-quality steel. It could just as justifiably have been chisels that were dumped in the Boston harbor that fateful day rather than tea.

MAKING STEEL FROM IRON

Although crude forms of steel have been made for 3,000 years, controlled methods date back only to the 1600s. The earliest controlled method was the cementation method. Swedish wrought-iron bars, interleaved with charcoal, were packed in earthenware boxes, sealed and placed just above a furnace in a tall chimney. The iron was heated to a bright yellow, kept there for a week and then allowed to cool very slowly (to keep it from hardening) for another week. The bars were then cut up, brought to a welding heat and forge-welded together. In this layering process, the uneven carbon content was minimized. Only the very pure iron from the Swedish magnetite ore made this process practical; otherwise, impurities would have ruined the steel.

In 1856, Henry Bessemer built the first furnace that could purify otherwise unusable iron by blasting air through the molten iron to burn off impurities and excess carbon. The price of steel dropped by 75%. The Bessemer process was quickly followed by the open-hearth process (which allowed better carbon-content control) and then the various electric furnaces that contributed to the even finer control needed for alloy steels. The use of tungsten to develop high-speed steel was discovered in 1868; manganese steel was developed in 1888, and stainless steel in 1913.

On many old tools you will find the declarations "Cast Steel" or "Silver Steel." These are leftovers from the early days of steelmaking.

Cast Steel

In the early 1700s a British clockmaker, searching for a better steel for clock springs, discovered that if he took steel made by the cementation method and melted it in a crucible, he had steel of far greater consistency. In essence, by melting it, he ensured that the carbon would be evenly distributed in the steel. In turn, this allowed him to make much more predictable clock springs. They had no soft spots. The process quickly spread among other craftsmen, and steel treated this way became known as "Cast Steel" or "Crucible Steel."

Silver Steel

This mark is most commonly found on old handsaws. One of the most irritating problems with early saws was the difficulty of keeping the steel bright, clean and relatively frictionless in a kerf. Plain carbon steels rust quickly, as anyone who has left a carbon-steel tool outside during a shower knows. The other problem was dealing with the constant trade-off between hardness and toughness. If the blade was hardened to the point that the teeth stayed sharp for an extended time, the steel was usually too brittle, causing the blade to crack or break under stress. When it was discovered that adding a percentage of chromium to high-carbon steel not only increased the hardness and toughness but also gave the steel a bright silvery finish that improved rust resistance, the alloy was quickly dubbed "Silver Steel" by some enterprising vendor. Needless to say, there was no silver in the alloy.

HEAT TREATMENT

Just as critical as the carbon content of steel is the heat treatment it receives. It has to be heated, forged, hardened (quenched) and then partially softened (tempered) in a very controlled manner to ensure fine grain, good distribution of carbides and toughness. In some respects the heat treatment process is more important than the alloy itself.

The same is true in the sharpening of tools. You can have the finest chisels in the world but still ruin them with bad grinding technique. If you overheat an edge when grinding, it will turn blue. The blueness is evidence of two things. First, it indicates that you have burned the thin edge. The heat will have freed the carbon to combine with oxygen. You will now have iron, not steel, at the tip of your chisel. Second, just adjacent to the burned part, you will have annealed a section of the tool, reducing hardness so that it will no longer hold an edge. What you do next is very important. If you ignore the blue band, go ahead and hone the tool, carefully lapping off the blue mark, and pretend that nothing happened, you will be like the majority of woodworkers and will deserve the bad service that tool will give you from that day forward.

If, on the other hand, you quietly remonstrate with yourself for a moment then go back to the grinder and, taking care not to overheat the tool, grind it

TO QUENCH OR NOT TO QUENCH?

As a general principle, quenching tools during grinding is a substitute for good technique. The drawing below shows what happens to a quenched tool.

1. Tool at room temperature before grinding. The thin edge heats and cools very rapidly in comparison to the main blade body.

2. As the tool heats up during grinding, it expands.

3. If the metal were perfectly elastic, this is what the tip would look like as it first hit the water and the thin tip cooled more rapidly than the rest of the blade.

4. But metal is not perfectly elastic, and as it shrinks, tiny cracks are created in the edge.

5. When the entire blade has cooled, the cracks may become invisible but they will be there.

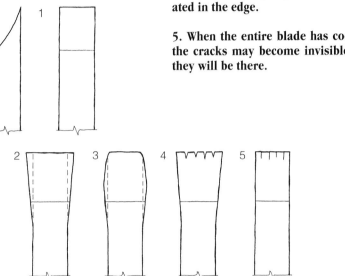

Dotted lines show normal width at room temperature.

ALLOYING ELEMENTS

Chromium
Increases high-temperature strength and shock resistance; increases hardness through formation of chromium carbide; reduces tendency to warp during heat treatment.

Cobalt
Increases red-heat hardness of high-speed steel; refines the grain; increases tensile strength.

Manganese
Increases hardness, tensile strength and resistance to wear.

Molybdenum
Increases hardness and tensile strength; makes steel easier to machine.

Nickel
Increases toughness, hardness and corrosion resistance.

Silicon
Increases hardness, tensile strength and elastic limits.

Tungsten
Refines the grain; increases heat, wear and shock resistance as well as tensile strength.

Vanadium
Used only in combination with other elements (often chromium) to increase hardening ability, refine grain and resist softening on tempering.

---

back to sound steel, you will have grown immeasurably as a craftsman. While I may have mildly overstated the case, there is no question about what you should do with a burned tip. Be brave, take the extra ten minutes to grind out your error, and learn from your mistake.

ALLOYING ELEMENTS

You will frequently see tools that are marked with the main alloying elements. For example, a chisel might have "chrome vanadium" or "tungsten vanadium" etched on the blade. Without getting into the endless arguments about the qualities of different alloy steels, some of the reasons for adding various elements besides carbon are presented in the chart at right above.

Obviously there is considerable overlap in alloying characteristics. In addition, the percentages used are interdependent. Two or more of these alloying metals could be used in carefully controlled ratios to impart special qualities. Equally important, the optimum qualities of any alloy can be realized only if the heat treatment is carefully controlled. More than one craftsman has made bad furniture from perfectly good lumber. So it is with steel; only competent treatment of the alloy will result in a good tool.

THE SPARK TEST TO IDENTIFY METALS

When there were few alloys on the market, a spark test was a quick and accurate way to identify iron and basic steel types. With the hundreds of alloys now used in tools it is much less reliable, but it can still be used for rough classifications in many instances. It is still an effective testing process with older chisels and plane blades. The spark patterns shown are those that would be generated by grinding a tool on a powered dry wheel.

Wrought iron
Long yellow streaks, becoming leaflike
in shape before expiring

Mild steel
More variety in streak length, with smaller
leaves and some sparking

Medium-carbon steel
Almost no leaf, some forking, great variety of
streak length, sparking nearer the wheel

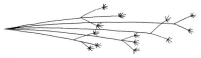

High-carbon steel
No leaf, bushy spark pattern, forking and
sparking starting very close to the wheel; less
bright than medium-carbon steel

Manganese steel
Small leaf before streaks fork to form sparks

High-speed steel
Faint red streaks forking at the tip

Stainless steel
Bright yellow streaks with a small leaf end

ALLOYS OF PARTICULAR INTEREST TO WOODWORKERS

Of the thousands of alloys in everyday use, only a few dozen are of specific interest to woodworkers. And of these few, some of the key ones are not steel but more modern metals developed to make edges as durable as possible.

High-speed steel (HSS) Alloys that will cut at high speed and high temperatures are particularly valuable in motor powered cutting tools like drill bits. When it was discovered that tungsten alloys were air hardening (i.e., they required no quenching), the use of these alloys quickly spread to tools requiring "red-heat" strength. Typical tungsten alloys are T1, M1 and M2 (see the chart on the facing page).

Such high-speed steels are more costly to make and to machine than plain high-carbon steel, but they are truly the woodworker's friend. They are tough, durable and forgiving. Every time you remove a high-speed-steel bit from a scorched hole in a piece of cherry, you should be thankful that modern metallurgy has triumphed over your bad technique. The bit lives to cut again. A carbon-steel bit would have to be tossed.

Just as all tool steels are not created equal, neither are high-speed steels. There is a continuing trend to the use of high-speed steel in woodturning tools, but the difference in alloys is substantial. Some tungsten-based HSS tools have as little as 8% tungsten, others 18% or higher. In general, higher tungsten content reduces wear in use. This means longer periods of time between sharpenings.

Stellite Stellite is not a steel alloy, since it has no iron in it. A typical stellite composition is:

Cobalt	50%
Chromium	33%
Tungsten	10%
Molybdenum	5%
Carbon	2%

Tantung "G" has similar ratios of these elements and also includes up to 1% iron and 2% to 7% columbium. Extremely wear-resistant, both stellite and Tantung "G" are used in cutting tools and for other surfaces where wear resistance is important. Some high-quality knife-sharpening steels are made from stellite. This is a case where terminology has been overtaken by technology: There is no steel in a stellite "knife steel."

Tungsten carbide Tungsten carbide (which is strictly a compound, not an alloy) is increasingly important in woodworking tools as woodworkers look for tools that will hold an edge indefinitely in difficult conditions. Fine powders of tungsten carbide and cobalt or nickel are mixed together with binders, heated and hydraulically pressed into molds of various shapes. The shapes can vary from the tiny balls in the tips of ball point pens to the solid rods used to make some router bits.

Like steel, there is a near-infinite variety of tungsten-carbide compositions. Other components such as titanium carbide and vanadium carbide can be added to the mixture to achieve shock resistance, machinability, and so forth. The trade-offs are usually between the hardness and wear-resistance characteristics and the resistance to shock. Developments are so rapid in this field that it would be futile to describe the various compositions; they are superseded almost monthly by ever more versatile composites that have finer grain structure, greater shock resistance and lower price. At one time, a rough rule of thumb was that edge-durability ratios of plain high-carbon steel to high-speed steel to tungsten carbide were 1:10:100, but these ratios become a rougher measure every day. For example, the new micro-carbides with very fine grain structure and as little as 3% cobalt can outlast regular tungsten carbide in some cases by a factor of 10. (See Chapter 14 for more detail.)

Much as with steel, it is possible to make a poor-quality tungsten carbide cheaply; high-quality carbides are more costly. While price is never a wholly reliable guide, it is one of the few

ALLOYING ELEMENTS FOR HIGH-SPEED STEEL

	T1 Tungsten	M1 Molybdenum	M2 Molybdenum
Carbon	0.72%	0.80%	0.82%
Manganese	0.25%	—	0.25%
Silicon	0.25%	—	0.25%
Chromium	4.00%	3.75%	4.25%
Tungsten	18.25%	1.50%	6.25%
Vanadium	1.15%	1.15%	1.90%
Molybdenum	8.75%	—	5.00%

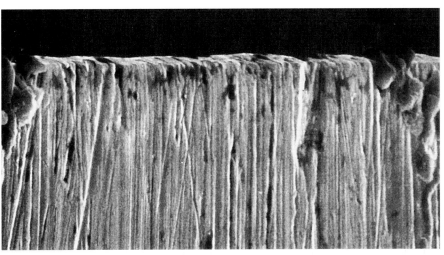

Although this blade looked mirror-bright to the naked eye, rust had started to form and was visible as bulbous clusters under an electron microscope. (Photo courtesy National Research Council of Canada)

indicators you can use in this field unless you are willing to make a detailed study of the subject.

Stainless steel Most woodworkers do not appreciate how quickly rust can degrade an edge. Even when no rust is apparent to the naked eye, it can be quietly destroying a good edge (as shown in the photo above). The only place most woodworkers will come across stainless steel is in some carving knives (for example, sloyd knives).

Even there, it is sometimes used to clad a steel core rather than being used for the cutting edge itself.

Makers of kitchen knives are particularly concerned about rust because knives are used to cut high-acid materials (fish, citrus fruit, etc.) that aggressively attack steel. One of the

favorite alloys of knifemakers is 440C stainless. It has six alloying elements:

Carbon	1.00%
Manganese	0.50%
Silicon	0.40%
Chromium	17.50%
Molybdenum	0.45%
Nickel	0.20%

When a tool-steel alloy has a chromium content greater than 10% (and usually less than 18%) it is referred to as "stainless." In fact, it is not stainless, only stain resistant. Over time, any stainless tool steel will rust to some extent. The time required is just much greater than it is for plain carbon steel.

Laminated steels Brought to welding heats, steels of different compositions (or iron and steel) can be welded together with pressure. Traditionally this was done by a blacksmith. The materials would be brought to welding heats at the forge, one metal would be placed over the other on an anvil and struck with a hammer to merge them. Before steel became a mass-produced product, most edge tools had steel edges and wrought-iron bodies. The price of steel dictated that it be used only where absolutely necessary in a tool.

There were advantages to this process. In plane blades, for example (or plane "irons" if you prefer, a term that indicates their origin), the iron backing dampened vibrations. The dead blade improved performance, reducing chatter in use. With axes, a worn cutting edge could be replaced, regenerating a tool that was otherwise sound. Tips of plowshares could be replaced with the same economy.

But the greatest advantage of the process was that an alloy that was ideal for a cutting edge (hard, wear resistant but probably brittle) could be limited to that part of the tool. The rest of the tool could be made from a material more suited to the structural strength required.

The process has been widely used in Japan for centuries and is still in use today. Traditionally, Japanese chisels had wrought-iron bodies with steel faces. They are still made that way today, although mild steel is used more often than wrought iron.

Top: These Japanese plane blades clearly show their structure. A thin layer of steel has been welded to a much thicker layer of wrought iron. The unused blade at right shows the typical hollow grind of a Japanese blade. (Photo by Susan Kahn)

Above: The weld line on the ax at left is clearly visible. The ax at right has been whacked on the poll one too many times, distorting the cheek and causing the iron/steel weld to fail on one side. Both are turn-of-the-century heads.

A JAPANESE BLADE MAKER

There are still a number of traditional plane-blade makers active in Japan, although mechanized methods have supplanted most of them. Some of these blade makers have been classified as national treasures, the embodiment of history.

Their workshops are invariably small with a tiny furnace/forge in one corner and a low-mounted anvil on a block of wood in the center. The other necessities of the craft are within easy reach of the craftsman, who usually sits on a small pillow by the anvil.

The shop arrangements vary, but the one constant is that you are sure to find a huge ship's anchor or length of anchor chain just outside the shop. Wrought iron, with its excellent rust resistance (because of the incorporated slag fila-

ments), was prized for anchors and anchor chain. The old anchors and chains are now raw material for blade makers. It is hard to think of a more awkward form for the raw material. When the craftsman needs wrought iron, he has to hack it from a giant anchor weighing several tons or from a chain link that can be 5 in. thick. There is much to be said for the infinite variety and shape of rolled stock available to today's Western blade maker.

SEMI-MODERN CHISEL MANUFACTURING IN JAPAN

Iyoroi chisels are among the best made in Japan. They are manufactured in a small factory on a farm near Miki City. The owners, Mr. Iyoroi and his wife, live in the farmhouse near the factory. When three of us came to see the factory one day, Mr. Iyoroi, a gentle and slightly formal man, then in his 80s, welcomed us and suggested that we first see the plant and then have tea with him and his wife. As we left the house, he took us on a short side trip to a small outbuilding to see if the family duck had laid an egg that day. It had, and we took the egg back to the house before continuing the tour of the plant.

The inside of the plant was the Japanese equivalent of a Dickensian workhouse. Workmen squatted next to completely unguarded grinders with open pulley drives. The air was filled with the noise and dirt of industry. About a dozen men were engaged in the various processes of chisel making.

Steel rod was being cut, heated, forged, hammered, shaped and ground. But the most remarkable operation of all was the process used to incorporate the steel face in the laminated chisels. Forged chisel blanks were heated white hot at the tip, a sprinkling of flux was put on the recess for the steel blank, then a workman holding the hot blank in a pair of tongs with one hand would place the steel bit on the flux with his other (bare) hand. The bit and blank were then put in the open-faced furnace to bring the bit to a welding heat (somewhat lower than the blank), then forged together on an anvil with a few heavy blows followed by a series of tune-up taps on the sides and faces. The worker's thumb and the two adjacent fingers of the hand used to place the steel bit on the blank had only vestigial finger nails. The tips of the fingers had been killed back from years of exposure to intense heat whenever he placed a steel insert on a chisel blank.

Returning later to the house, we had tea, Mr. Iyoroi thanked us for our visit, and gave each of us a beautiful set of boxwood-handled carving tools made in his factory. No tools that I own today bring with them more vivid recollections in use than those carving tools.

Mr. Kozo Iyoroi. (Photos this page by Shiro Tanaka)

SPECIAL PROCESSES

In the search for ever longer tool life and more time between sharpenings, some unusual processes are being used to influence tool wear. These include supercooling, impulse hardening, laser hardening, titanium-nitride coating, diamond coating and magnetic fluxing.

SUPERCOOLING

Although little discussed today, in the 1980s there was great interest in the effect of supercooling on tools. Drill bits, saw blades (particularly saw chain) and even chisels and plane blades were being treated by supercooling. Some wild claims have been made about the effects of supercooling, but there is evidence that it was effective in many instances. Much like the proponents of the magical power of pyramids, however, the supercoolers often asked people to take the process on faith.

The known effect of supercooling is that it can convert austenite to martensite. Since martensite is much harder than austenite, supercooling can improve both the strength and wear characteristics of an alloy. For it to work, however, there must be austenite present in the first place, which is not the case with all tools. It has proved to be most effective with stainless-steel alloys where austenite is normally present.

IMPULSE HARDENING

Most commonly used on jigsaw blades and handsaws, impulse hardening is a localized hardening process that hardens only the part of the tool that experiences wear. It is possible to make saws with very hard teeth (Rc60-70) while leaving the body at Rc40-50 as required for toughness. In conventional impulse hardening, a saw blade (hand, jig, band, etc.) is induction-heated and

then immediately quenched with a blast of air or water. The impulse can be from $\frac{1}{10}$ of a second to 5 seconds, and the hardening depth ranges from 0.020 in. to 0.100 in. There is usually some distortion involved.

A more sophisticated process using very high frequency pulses for much shorter times (1 to 100 microseconds) permits greater localization and shallower penetration (0.002 in. to 0.020 in.), still yielding extreme hardness on the wear surface but a softer and tougher core. It can be done with virtually no distortion.

You can usually tell which process has been used by the amount of discoloration of the blade. With high-frequency pulsing, only the top half of a tooth will be discolored. In regular impulse hardening, the entire tooth and a strip of the saw body will be discolored.

An interesting sidelight of the very high frequency process is that the steel can be heated so rapidly and in such a thin layer that it also becomes self-quenching. There is no need for a blast of air or water because the adjacent steel mass rapidly cools the heated film. The cooling can be so rapid that the film is not really a solid but a super-

cooled liquid. The rapidity of the process prevents crystal growth and the layer is homogeneous, quite different from ordinary steel. It can be as hard as Rc70 and very resistant to wear. The process is roughly comparable to making plate glass, which is also a super-cooled liquid, not a solid.

Done well, impulse hardening can create very fine grain steel that can outlast conventionally hardened blades by a factor of 5 or more. It is a standard process now with most bandsaw-blade makers.

Impulse-hardened teeth are not usually intended to be resharpened (although it can be done with diamond files) because sharpening can remove the hardened surface, particularly in the case of high-frequency pulsing.

AUSTENITE AND MARTENSITE

For several reasons, I have consciously avoided describing the exact chemical and physical transformations that take place in steel alloys during heating, hardening and tempering. The first reason is that it is difficult to explain succinctly. The second is that the process is tangential to woodworking; even if you knew the process intimately, it would have little practical application in a woodworking shop.

But having used two terms that are explained nowhere else in the book, I owe you some explanation of them.

Steel is heated to an austenitic state so that the carbon and other alloying elements become dissolved and can permeate the structure. The purpose of quenching is to convert austenite into much harder martensite. To maintain fine grain structure, quenching often must be done at a rate that leaves some austenite in the steel.

Cold treatment, sometimes as little as -76°F (-60°C), can convert the remaining austenite to martensite. The process is particularly effective with stainless alloys that have a high chromium content.

LASER HARDENING

Very controlled hardening of steel can be done with lasers. Unlike impulse hardening, which requires induction coils to be shaped to fit either side of the tool tip to be hardened, a laser beam can be focused on any surface, anywhere. By controlling the beam energy and duration, very precise hardening is possible. Much like high-frequency impulse hardening, lasers can be used to create very localized films of super-cooled liquid steel.

TITANIUM-NITRIDE COATING

Cutting tools are often surface-coated by a physical or chemical vapor-deposition process that creates a hard surface film. Titanium nitride is one such finish. It is particularly effective in metal cutting since it reduces the crater wear caused by the chemical interaction at the high-temperature interface of the tool and the material being cut. For woodworking tools, it is effective for its other properties, which are its hardness (30% or more greater than high-speed steel at Rc62) and its very low coefficient of friction.

DIAMOND COATING

For decades diamonds have been used on the tips of various tools, drills in particular. They were sometimes imbedded in a softened tip (so that they looked like chocolate chips in a cookie) and sometimes held in place with a metallic coating. Both processes required relatively large diamond crystals to be effective.

Currently researchers are working on a new diamond-coating process that holds much promise for woodworking. The process is one whereby diamonds are cultured right on the cutting tool. The crystal formation can be controlled so that crystals are aligned (adjoining and abutting), to create a virtually continuous smooth film. The different coefficients of contraction and expansion between the diamonds and the substrate have yet to be overcome, but a ceramic substrate is showing promise. It is probable that such diamond-coated router bits will be available at competitive prices in a very short time.

MAGNETIC FLUXING

Magnetic fluxing involves placing a tool (usually a cutting bit) in a small chamber that is bombarded with pulsed waves of magnetic energy. The tool actually vibrates momentarily until it is stress relieved. Increased tool life from the process has ranged from 30% to nearly 200% as reported by users.

The process is based on the principle of magnetostriction—the change in length of a ferromagnetic material when it is magnetized. The crystalline structure of steel is a latticework of separate magnetic dipoles; as the tool is magnetized, the dipoles are aligned causing the material to grow or shrink slightly. The rapid fluxing (developed by Innovex of Hopkins, Minnesota) changes the magnetic field unequally in the tool. The process begins at the surface and then permeates the tool, a sort of tidal wave of magnetostriction, creating shear forces within the tool that serve to equalize concentrations of residual stress. The process is similar to work hardening.

An interesting sidelight of this process is that some cutting-tool users have long recommended magnetizing tools because it increases the modulus of elasticity of the tool, extending its life. So whether or not you give your cutting tools the high-tech treatment, you may want to use a simple electromagnet to magnetize them for the benefit that the process gives. For tools like twist drills that will be used for cutting iron or steel, it is not a good idea since it causes chips to cling to the tool. However, for drilling non-ferrous metals or for woodworking, it would not cause this problem.

CHAPTER 4
ABRASIVES

The search for abrasives parallels the development of man's metallurgical skills. Before iron was discovered man had little need for abrasives. In the Stone Age, the best edge tools were made from flint, which was chipped to form a sharp edge. In the Bronze Age, tools made of copper and copper alloys were beaten to the required edge; this was readily done because they were malleable. To resharpen, the tools were hammered into shape. But iron tools (and later, steel) required some abrasive method of refining a forged edge and restoring it again after dulling.

NATURAL VS. MAN-MADE ABRASIVES

For most of modern history, only naturally occurring abrasives such as sandstone were used to sharpen tools. Only in the last hundred years have man-made abrasives come into common use, and only in the last fifty years have they been predominant.

Historically, abrasives for sharpening came in two basic forms: grinding wheels and bench stones. The wheels came in all sizes but in one predominant shape, a transverse section of a cylinder. Bench stones were most commonly rectangular slabs but also included dozens of specialized shapes for sharpening tools other than chisels and plane blades. The shapes and their uses will be covered in Chapter 5; in this chapter, the abrasive particles themselves will be examined.

BENCH STONES

Although natural grindstones have been supplanted by man-made stones almost universally at both lower cost and increased efficiency, the replacement of natural bench stones has been slower and more grudging. Partly this is for reasons of tradition and partly it is because the advantages of man-made bench stones are not as clear-cut as they are with grindstones.

Two water-bathed natural-sandstone grinders. The smaller one at right is a typical 'settler's' wheel, later featured in early Sears catalogs. The treadle-operated wheel has a well-designed stand with a splashboard and a hook-and-eye connection for the water trough so that it could be easily emptied after use.

There is not much argument about coarse bench stones. It is generally accepted that you get the best combination of cost, efficiency and predictability with man-made silicon-carbide and aluminum-oxide stones compared to the various sandstones that were once used. But in the area of finishing stones people who use Arkansas oil stones, Welsh slate, Belgian water stones or natural Japanese water stones would often rather fight than switch.

This historical attachment has led to the curious phenomenon where several current bench-stone manufacturers try to replicate as closely as possible the natural stone they are replacing. This is the case with the Arkansas Perfect stones now on the market, and also with the finer

Japanese water stones. In the case of the Arkansas Perfect stones, the manufacturer grinds up natural novaculite and reconstitutes it to make the stones. In the case of Japanese water stones, the manufacturers adopted a resin bond (see below) to best mimic the soft bond of the natural Japanese stones. While they came close, I think that anyone who has ever used a top-quality Japanese natural finishing stone will tell you that no man-made stone feels quite the same. There is a softness to the abrasive action that is not replicated in the artificial stones.

WHAT MAKES A GOOD STONE?

Although all stones are abrasive to a certain degree, humans quickly discovered that some worked better than others, and the interminable argument about what makes the best sharpening stone began. Then, as now, the search probably included the five factors basic to selecting a sharpening stone: the size, shape, hardness and toughness of particles, and the type of bond that holds the particles to each other.

Particle size The size of particles in a stone is basic to the speed of abrasion. Within limits, larger particles remove larger chips of metal. Smaller particles remove smaller chips and give a finer edge. It is important that particle size be consistent so that abrasion results are predictable.

Particle shape Obviously, spherical shapes are not ideal for abrasion. Highly angular shapes are. Although early humans would not have known the shape of a particle, they would have known that a specific stone cut faster than some other stone that gave an equally fine edge. Particle shape would have been chosen intuitively.

Hardness The abrasive particle should be substantially harder than the material to be abraded. If not, it will become worn and rounded, unable to perform its function.

Toughness A particle can be so fragile that it may not survive long enough to become worn at all. Particles must have a reasonable level of shock resistance or they will too readily fracture in the abrasion process.

Bond The way particles are held together to form a stone is critical to the functioning of the stone. If particles are held in place too solidly, the surface of the stone will eventually be worn smooth and the abrasion rate will be reduced dramatically. If the bond between the particles is too fragile, particles will constantly be torn from the face of the stone and the stone will lose its shape and wear out very quickly.

HOW BIG IS A GRAIN OF SAND?

Some readers may remember the Monty Python skit about small rocks floating. It was probably a similar real-life situation that finally led geologists to agree on a classification system for particles found in nature that most of us call dirt and stones. The standard particle sizes are metric; approximate inch sizes are given for those who are more comfortable with the imperial system.

	Limiting Dimensions	
Particle Classification	**Millimeters**	**Inches**
Boulder	256 and larger	10 and larger
Cobble	64 to 256	2½ to 10
Pebble	4 to 64	5/32 to 2½
Granule	2 to 4	5/64 to 5/32
Very coarse sand grains	1 to 2	0.040 to 0.080
Coarse sand grains	½ to 1	0.020 to 0.040
Medium sand grains	¼ to ½	0.010 to 0.020
Fine sand grains	⅛ to ¼	0.005 to 0.010
Very fine sand grains	1/16 to ⅛	0.0025 to 0.005
Silt particles	1/256 to 1/16	0.00015 to 0.0025
Clay particles	1/256 and smaller	0.00015 and smaller

SANDSTONE

The reason that sandstones were the stones of choice for everything except fine honing for so many years was that they most ideally combined all of the above features. Sand deposits can have amazingly consistent particle sizes. As an example, there is a deposit at Ottawa, Illinois, that is so consistent that it was used over the years for various standards. Even today, it is still the standard material used in the "sand drop test" to determine the durability of applied finishes. This deposit not only has particle-size consistency but shape consistency as well.

But sandstone generally is not a consistent product. First of all, "sand" is descriptive of size, not composition. You might have a sand that is made of feldspar or a sand that is made of quartz. The sandstone that was used for grinding was usually quartz crystals that had been bonded together in nature by something else. The sandstone might have been formed when a bonding agent such as calcite was leached from overburden and deposited between the particles, cementing them together.

The variety of possible particle sizes, from 0.0025 in. to 0.080 in. (see the sidebar above), the angularity of the particles and the variety of bonding agents can create a wide variety of sandstones. The larger particles with a hard bond make a sandstone suitable for rough grinding of iron; smaller particles with a softer bond would be suited to the fine finishing of steel. The regularity of particle shape tends to be much more consistent than the bond, and, unfortunately, at 7 on the Mohs scale (see p. 37), quartz is only as hard as very hard steel. As an abrasive, natural sandstone eventually proved inadequate to the metallurgical developments of the 1800s.

Washita stone

Soft Arkansas stone

Hard Arkansas stone

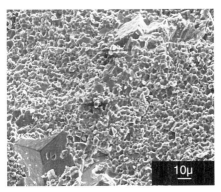

Black Hard Arkansas stone

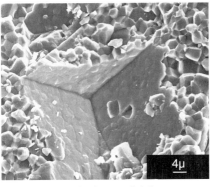

Anomaly in Black Hard Arkansas

*Natural Japanese water stone
(Photos courtesy National Research
Council of Canada)*

OTHER NATURAL ABRASIVES

The other natural abrasives did not lend themselves at all to power grinding, either because they were too fine or too weak structurally to be turned at any speed, but they were suited to use as bench stones. Among such bench stones both Welsh slate and Belgian water stones were used for fine finishing of steel edges, but the stone that dominated the bench-stone market for more than a century was the novaculite deposit in Arkansas.

The Arkansas stones were given various names, which has led to more than a little confusion over time. It is generally accepted that (from coarse to fine) they are graded Washita, Soft Arkansas, Hard Arkansas and Black Hard Arkansas. But anyone who owns one of the old Norton Lily-White Washitas can tell you that it is better than any Hard Arkansas marketed in the last twenty years. Similarly, the translucent Hard Arkansas that was traditionally used for surgeon's stones was extremely consistent, would give

a very good finish and was generally held in higher regard than the Black Hard Arkansas. Over time, as the best parts of the deposit were mined, grades have become unreliable. It is very difficult to find top-quality Arkansas stones on the market today. Most that are currently sold have variable hardness and visible inclusions in the stone.

The highly regular shape of the novaculite particles is both a blessing and a curse. Viewed under an electron microscope, you can see how they nest together in a very tight and regular matrix. The photomicrographs shown above were taken ten years ago. Even then Arkansas stones were of highly variable quality. The Washita stone appears to have a particle size about the same, on average, as the Soft Arkansas and the Hard Arkansas stones. In fact, both the latter have at least one particle larger than anything seen in the

Washita. Only the Black Hard Arkansas is clearly of finer grain. The regularity of particle size makes for a consistent abrasion pattern, but the tight nesting causes a problem: Worn particles are not easily released and the rate of abrasion is reduced appreciably. If you have ever lapped an Arkansas stone, you will know that a freshly lapped stone cuts much faster than one that has been used for a while. You can get a good edge on a well-used Arkansas stone, but it takes a while.

A further problem with the very tight nesting of the particles is that some of the bond lines are stronger than others and it is possible to get a large number of particles acting like a single particle. The photo in the center of the bottom row shows such a configuration in a Black Hard Arkansas stone. This is a freshly broken stone that reveals this anomaly, but you can sometimes see it with the naked eye in a bench stone. I have found this anomaly only in Black Hard Arkansas, not in any of the other

Arkansas stones. The first time I went looking for it was when I found that I was getting what appeared to be a very deep random scratch in an edge that I was honing. After cleaning the stone thoroughly I saw that light was reflecting from one spot in the stone. Since the facets on novaculite particles are so small that you could not normally see light reflect from any single particle, I examined the stone under an inspection scope and found an anomaly similar to the one photographed.

The photomicrograph at bottom right on p. 31 shows the structure of a natural Japanese water stone. Again the particle size is quite regular, but it is of completely different construction—it looks like a piece of flaky pastry. Unlike the particles in the Arkansas stones, the particles in Japanese water stones are not tightly nested. Neither are they as large. The shape does not look particularly aggressive, but it is, and the stone cuts quickly for such a fine finish.

This particular chip came from a stone owned by Toshio Odate, author of *Japanese Woodworking Tools: Their Tradition, Spirit and Use* (The Taunton Press, 1984). I have no doubt that it is one of the top-quality Japanese water stones. Although I did not use this particular stone, I have used other Japanese natural water stones and they have a wonderful feel to them. The cutting action is really quite soft, and I believe that they are uniquely suited to the very hard blades that are used in Japan.

CHISELS SHARPENED ON VARIOUS STONES

All of the chisels shown here but one (photo 1) were lapped on an 8000x stone to a mirror finish on the face before honing the bevel. This distorts the results somewhat by making the chisels whose bevels were honed on the coarser stones look better than they would if both the face and the bevel had been done on a coarse stone.

So that you can appreciate what a difference this makes, the first photomicrograph below shows the bevel of a chisel that was honed and then finished on a strop charged with green compound. It would have had an excellent edge except the face of the chisel had not been lapped. The intersection of the grind marks on the face with the finely finished bevel leaves the chisel with a very jagged edge. The photo gives some indication of how irregular the edges would have been on some of

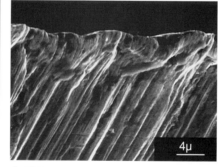

1. Bevel honed and stropped on green compound (face of chisel not lapped)

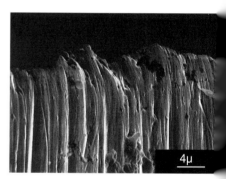

2. Bevel honed on a 400x aluminum oxide oil stone

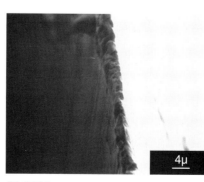

6. 800x water stone

7. 1200x water stone

11. 8000x water stone

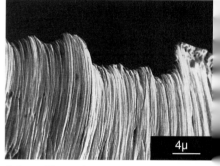

12. 8000x water stone honed with chromium oxide

(Photos courtesy National Research Council of Canada)

the coarser stones if the faces had been lapped on a coarse stone rather than finished first on an 8000x water stone.

The comparisons of the chisel edges are quite straightforward. The photos are shown at the same magnification, with the exception of photos 11 and 12, which are at about half the magnification of the others. Photos 13, 14 and 15 are repeated from Chapter 1 for comparison. Most photos were taken at an angle of 70° to the normal in order to capture as much of the chisel edge as possible. Photo 9 is photographed at 80° to the normal, which shows about twice as much chisel edge as the others but begins to cause focusing problems as well.

Photos 11 and 12 are exceptional in that they sight along an edge that was first honed on an 8000x water stone and then finished by stropping on a hone charged with chromium-oxide compound. Because of the sequential shots, this chisel could not be gold-plated before photography (as were all the others), thus the much greater glare in the photographs. Nonetheless, it very adequately shows the refining effect of stropping.

As a final point of interest, there is rust forming on the edge of the chisel in photo 4 (upper right-hand corner) and in photo 8 (both upper corners).

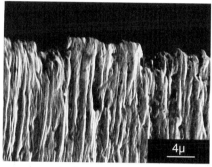

3. Soft Arkansas oil stone

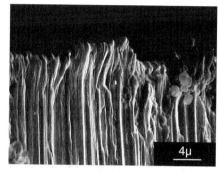

4. Hard Arkansas stone

5. Black Hard Arkansas stone

8. 6000x water stone

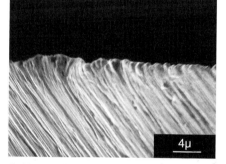

9. Natural Japanese water stone

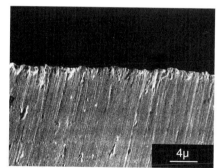

10. 8000x water stone

13. Standard craft razor blade

14. Wilkinson Sword razor blade

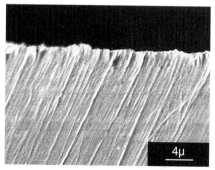

15. 6000x water stone honed with chromium oxide

THE IMPORTANCE OF BOND

Of the five factors important to abrasive performance (particle size, shape, hardness, toughness and bond), the most critical over time has been bond. For centuries, sandstones were the only powered grinding wheels used because they were the only ones that would both hold together under centrifugal force and still release particles at a controlled rate to prevent glazing.

The common thread that runs through the development of decent man-made grindstones and bench stones is the problem of developing a suitable method of bonding particles together. The significance of this is highlighted by the fact that natural diamond was being used as an abrasive in the gem industry in the 1600s but did not become significant in the tool industry until this century when better bonding methods were developed. The same is true of some of the natural abrasives that were so significant in the last century.

Emery (imported from Asia Minor and Greece until a deposit was found in Massachusetts in the 1850s) is basically aluminum oxide, but it is contaminated with a fairly high percentage (25%) of iron oxide as well as lesser quantities of other material. Although widely used at one time, emery was so variable in particle size and structure that it was normally ground and sieved before either being applied to a soft metal wheel or a leather-covered wheel for surface finishing.

Similarly, corundum (first brought from India in 1825), which was nearly pure aluminum oxide and had better cutting properties than emery, suffered from the same problem. It was sometimes fixed on cast-iron wheels with glue, but the most successful bond was the resin bond that had been used in India. Of very limited strength, this was usable only in powered wheels of small diameter. The first real breakthrough in bonding was with the development of wheels using vulcanized rubber as a bond. For some types of wheels (notably the Cratex line) this bond is still used today.

But the development that led directly to most modern grindstones was the work of Sven Poulson, a Massachusetts potter, in the 1870s (see the sidebar at left). He fired a mixture of emery and clay to create the first vitrified-bond wheel. It was this process on which the Norton Company was founded.

THE MOVE FROM NATURAL TO ARTIFICIAL

By this time corundum had almost entirely replaced emery for grinding, but good corundum was scarce and expensive. Silicon carbide was developed in 1891 and artificial corundum (aluminum oxide) in 1897. By 1910, both abrasives were highly developed. Aluminum oxide was particularly successful, completely replacing emery and natural corundum in wheels. Because the nature of crystallization could be controlled, aluminum-oxide abrasives for a wide range of grinding purposes were developed.

It is important to note that not all aluminum oxides are created equal. The basic raw material for making aluminum-oxide abrasive is bauxite. The highest-quality bauxite yields the whitest and highest-quality wheels. You will often find that cheap aluminum-oxide wheels have a fair percentage of brown particles in them.

Man-made diamonds It is only in the last thirty years that man-made diamonds have become significant in tool sharpening. Diamond dust had been used for centuries in gem cutting and various lapping processes, but the generally prohibitive cost had prevented its use in grinding wheels. But in the last thirty years both DuPont and General Electric have developed methods of making diamonds. DuPont uses an explosive process that creates tremendous pressure to convert a mixture of carbon and metal powders to diamond crystals. General Electric uses a crystal-growing process of quite different technology.

The primary difference between the two processes is that the DuPont process creates polycrystalline diamonds whereas the General Electric process creates monocrystalline diamond. The difference is significant. In the DuPont process a micro-crystalline aggregate is formed where the individual crystals are of angstrom size, that is as small as 0.0001 microns. They can be composed of just a few atoms, are highly faulted and are not 100% dense. Such diamond makes an ideal lapping compound since the aggregate breaks down in the lapping process creating ever-finer abrasive. The General Electric diamond, on the other hand, is monocrystalline and, like natural diamond, does not fracture as readily.

Except for lapping, diamonds have to be held in a metal backing; there are three ways to hold them. They can be soldered in position, as is usually done in making single-point wheel dressers (see p. 43). They can also be held in position physically by pressing them into a copper or aluminum base until the metal is crimped around them thereby trapping them. But the holding method you will normally see, particularly in diamond files of all types, is where the diamond is held to the metal backing by a nickel-plating process.

You will generally find that the monocrystalline diamond is appreciably more expensive than the polycrystalline. Wheels, bench stones and files made from single crystals are worth the extra money. The crystals are subject to wear and fracture over time but at a far slower rate than the poly-crystalline diamond, which crushes quickly in use and continues to fracture until only the tiniest monocrystals are left. A general rule of thumb is that monocrystalline is best in bonded form and polycrystalline is best for lapping.

LAPPING AND POLISHING COMPOUNDS

There are many instances when you want an abrasive that is not solidly formed like a wheel or a bench stone. Lapping compounds are used between two surfaces; they tend to bed in the softer one and abrade the harder one. Polishing compounds are used just a bit differently: The compound is applied to a backing and then used to abrade something else. As a rule, lapping is used where flatness is paramount; polishing is used where speed and fineness of finish are most important.

Silicon carbide, aluminum oxide and garnet are all used as general industrial lapping compounds, but a wood-worker need be concerned only with silicon carbide since it is the best for cast-iron and hardened-steel alloys. Aluminum oxide is used for mild steel, stainless steel and bronze. Garnet is used as a non-imbedding compound with glass and plastics.

Among the range of polishing compounds used for honing and stropping, only a very few apply to the sharpening process. These can be broken down into those for medium polishing and those for fine polishing.

The medium polishing compounds include black, red and white rouge, tripoli, quartz and levigated alumina. All except red rouge and tripoli have some application. The black and white rouge can be used to polish medium-hard materials, and the quartz and levigated alumina can be used on hard materials. The tripoli and red rouge are unsuitable for sharpening. Specifically, red rouge is for soft materials like brass and is not a good choice for hardened steel blades.

Among the fine polishing compounds, there are really only two that apply—tin oxide and chromium oxide. Pumice is used on soft metals, trichromium oxide on stainless steel and aluminum, and cerium oxide for optical glass. Tin oxide and chromium oxide can both be used across a range of metals and a range of hardnesses. Chromium oxide cuts the fastest and is definitely the best choice in a honing compound. For increased speed of

SIZING DIAMONDS

In diamond mining a great deal of non-gem-quality material is mined. Called bort, this has been used for centuries in lapping processes and in a more limited manner in grinding wheels and wheel dressers. Coarse bort is separated by a sieving process exactly the same as that used for other types of grit. The separation of lapping grades (everything that passes through the finest sieve) is done by a very unusual process. All of the fines are mixed with a high-grade olive oil, stirred and allowed to stand for five minutes. The oil is then poured into another container, and the material that has settled out is given the grade of the finest of sieves that was used.

Next begins the process of separating the various grades of diamond dust for lapping processes. The oil is stirred again and left to stand for ten minutes, after which it is poured into another container and everything that settled out in that ten minutes is labeled #1 lapping compound. The process is repeated according to the following table to get the other grades.

Grade of lapping compound	Settles in
#1	10 min.
#2	30 min.
#3	1 hr.
#4	2 hr.
#5	10 hr.
#6	until oil is clear

The process is not really one of sizing (although it tends to work that way for natural diamond because it is so blocky in shape) but rather a process that separates particles according to their mass and relative surface area. The same principle is used for water- and air-flotation systems for grading other abrasive particles.

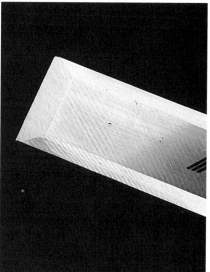

A hardness tester is used to determine the relative hardness of various tool steels.

The depth of the dimple in the surface of the tool (right) indicates the hardness of the steel.

cutting, chromium oxide is sometimes mixed with very fine aluminum oxide as well. The aluminum oxide is harder and cuts more aggressively.

HARDNESS SCALES AND TESTS

Just as hardness is important in polishing compounds, so it is in all sharpening activities. You need adequate hardness differential between the abrasive and the tool being sharpened or you will get poor abrasion. Anyone who has tried honing a carbide bit with an aluminum-oxide stone knows the problem well.

The oldest hardness scale still in use is the Mohs scale developed by Friedrich Mohs in 1826. Based on the susceptibility of a material to being scratched, Mohs ranked ten materials from talc to diamond on a scale from 1 to 10, with talc at 1 and diamond at 10. The primary problem with the Mohs scale is that it is not consistent in any respect except the order of hardness of the materials. It has since been augmented by various tests that show relative hardness of materials so that you can determine not just whether one material is harder than another but also exactly how much harder.

There is still some complication in this field, however, because a whole series of different hardness tests are now in use, each suitable for specific materials. It is necessary to provide some correlation between the testing methods to make them useful.

For woodworking tools, the most commonly used test is the Rockwell Hardness Test. The Rockwell system uses a variety of scales (A, C, D, 15-N, etc.), but the most common is the C scale, indicated by the "Rc" or "HRc" you frequently see in literature on hardness of steels. The C scale test is based on the depth of penetration of a shaped diamond under a load of 150 kg into the surface of steel. You may have seen the telltale dimple that such a test leaves in tools (see the photo at left).

Other tests are Brinell (which measures penetration of a hardened steel ball at a load of 3000 kg) used on softer steels and Knoop (which uses an elongated diamond). Since the Knoop hardness is more applicable to minerals, it is combined with Rockwell C and Mohs in the table at right. It is apparent from the table why aluminum-oxide stones are not very effective on carbide bits. It is equally apparent why diamond wheels are used to sharpen all the carbides.

UNDERSTANDING GRINDING WHEELS

Only in recent times has a standardized international code been developed for grinding wheels. Although the quality of abrasive and the consistency of manufacture can still vary among various makers, you can have some confidence that stones with the same code will function similarly. And, unexciting though the subject may be, you need to know something about the composition of grinding wheels or you will inevitably ruin tools attempting to grind them on a standard bench grinder using no coolant.

To start with, the stones that come with the standard bench grinder can be put to better use as patio stones than for grinding chisels and plane blades. They are almost inevitably coarse, hard stones that will quickly burn any woodworking blade. You can use them to sharpen lawnmower blades or clean up your welding, but you shouldn't even think about grinding tools with them. It is those stones that have given dry grinding a bad reputation.

The following explanation of grinding-wheel codes will help to explain many of the recommendations that come later in the book. In the example on p. 38, a Norton code has been used. The only difference between this code and the code you will find on a wheel made by any other company is the "38" at the beginning and the "BE" at the end. The central part of the code is according to the ISO (International Standards Organization) code for grinding wheels.

RELATIVE HARDNESS OF SELECTED MATERIALS

Substance	Mohs	Knoop	Rockwell C
Talc	1		
Gypsum	2	32	
Magnesia	-	370	38 (cabinet scraper)
Apatite	5	430	42 (handsaw)
Nickel	-	557	51 (hand scraper)
Feldspar	6	560	
Most chisels, plane blades	-	690-776	58-62
Japanese chisels (laminated)	-	776-822	62-64
Quartz	7	820	64
Chromium	-	935	68
Zirconia	-	1160	
Berylia	-	1250	
Topaz	8	1340	
Garnet	-	1360	
Tungsten-carbide alloy	-	1400-1800*	
Zirconium boride	-	1550	
Titanium nitride	9	1800	
Chromium carbide	-	1820	
Tungsten carbide	-	1880	
Tantalum carbide	-	2000	
Corundum	-	2000	
Aluminum oxide	-	2100-2440	
Beryllium carbide	-	2410	
Titanium carbide	-	2470	
Silicon carbide	-	2480	
Aluminum boride	-	2500	
Vanadium carbide	-	2520	84
Boron carbide	-	2750	
Diamond	10	7000	

* In a matrix of cobalt or nickel; includes C1 to C4 grades.

38 A 80 - H 8 V BE

38 A 80 - H 8 V BE

Norton symbol

The first number indicates the type of aluminum oxide that Norton used in this stone. Norton uses a number of other types as well but is reluctant to explain them to consumers.

38 **A** 80 - H 8 V BE

Abrasive

A = Aluminum oxide
C = Silicon carbide
D = Diamond
There are many codes for abrasives, but these are the ones of interest to woodworkers.

38 A **80** - H 8 V BE

Grit size

Grit size can range from 8 to 500. The band from 60 to 120 is used in basic tool grinding.

38 A 80 - **H** 8 V BE

Grade

Wheel grade is indicated by a letter from the following ranges:

ABCDEFG	HIJK	KMNO	PQRS	TUVWXYZ
Very soft	Soft	Medium	Hard	Very hard

A wheel is make harder by increasing the amount of bonding material. This reduces the volume of the pores and makes the abrasive particles more resistant to release. The wheel lasts longer but tends to grind hotter because it retains more worn particles than a softer wheel; this reduces the cutting rate and increases friction when grinding tool steel.

38 A 80 - H **8** V BE

Structure

Structure describes the grain spacing.
0 1 2 3 4 5 6 7 8 9 10 11 12
Dense —————————————————> Open
In general, an open structure is cooler cutting because of entrained air and reduced friction. It also has reduced tendency to glaze. A dense structure is more durable but is hotter in use and more subject to glazing.

38 A 80 - H 8 **V** BE

Bond

The most common bonds are:
V - Vitrified (tool grinding)
B - Resinoid (high speed, rapid metal removal)
R - Rubber (high-pressure grinding)
E - Shellac (where an elastic bond is needed)
M - Metal (used with diamond and boron nitride)

38 A 80 - H 8 V **BE**

Bond modification

An optional manufacturer's designation for some modification to the basic bond; in this case it indicates a modification to the basic vitrified bond.

Norton grinding wheel, code 38A80-H8VBE. (Photo by Susan Kahn)

The stone used as an example (38A80-H8VBE) is the best all-purpose stone for dry grinding in a wood-working shop. It cuts quickly with minimal friction but excellent abrasion. For very light grinding where a fine finish is important, such as with carving tools, a 100x or 120x stone can be used but the rest of the code should be the same. It is important to have a relatively soft bond and open structure.

SEEDED-GEL STONES

For more aggressive grinding, such as reshaping of high-speed-steel turning tools, the new SG (seeded gel) stones from Norton work well. The grit in these is an aggregation of submicron particles. The sieved grits are actually made up of many small particles much like polycrystalline diamond versus monocrystalline diamond. They, too, are self-dressing wheels in that particles will fracture under pressure rather than load up, but they are designed for greater grinding pressures than would be normal in grinding chisels and plane blades. These wheels also grind hotter because they are not available in a bond softer than "I." But this is less of a problem with high-speed steel, which has excellent red-heat hardness and can take higher grinding temperatures than regular tool steels without deteriorating.

The polycrystalline particles in the SG wheels are available in four concentrations: 100%, 50%, 30% and 10%. The balance would be standard 38A grit. The recommended concentrations for HSS turning tool grinding would be 50% or 30%. The codes for these would be, respectively, 5SG80IVS and 3SG80IVS in 80x and 5SG100IVS and 35SG100IVS in 100x.

CHAPTER 5
SHARPENING EQUIPMENT

For the purposes of this chapter, I'm going to assume that you want to sharpen tools as cheaply and quickly as possible. If cost is irrelevant to you and you have more money than you know what to do with, I will be glad to put on my tool vendor's hat for a while and quickly bring you to greater economic equality with your fellow man. If, on the other hand, you are the sort of person who insists on making all of your own tools, be forewarned that this chapter actually recommends buying some things. If you have ever tried to make a file, for instance, you will understand completely.

The second general bias throughout this chapter is that more time will be spent on simple sharpening equipment than on complex equipment. The basic principle here is that if you understand how to arrive at predictable results on simple equipment it will be an absolute breeze for you on equipment that has all the bells and whistles. Accordingly, the complex and costly will briefly be considered, and then more time will be spent on simpler equipment since it usually requires better technique because of the absence of jigs and fixtures.

POWERED SHARPENING EQUIPMENT

As is common in many areas, powered equipment does not necessarily do things better it just does them faster. In sharpening, powered equipment is most useful when you want to remove a great deal of material. This could be grinding back an entire edge to eliminate a nick, major reshaping of an edge to lower the bevel angle, or restoration of an edge deformed by bad honing technique. Most of this equipment can also be used for honing, an activity that can include minor edge shaping as well as general refinement—what you do when you are stropping, polishing or buffing. Incidentally, all of these terms are not mutually exclusive; just as grinding is basic edge creation or restoration, honing is edge refinement, which can be achieved in various ways including polishing, buffing and stropping.

Motorized wet grinders are available in vertical-wheel and horizontal-wheel designs. Note that the tool rest on the vertical-wheel model can be raised so that the tool being ground can slope downward, to prevent water from running down the blade.

GRINDERS

Grinders are usually separated into two categories, wet and dry. A wet grinder uses water to cool the edge being ground as well as remove swarf from the wheel to prevent glazing. A dry grinder is dependent upon the wheel bond structure to reduce heat buildup and prevent glazing. The boundary line between the two types can be a bit fuzzy. Some wet grinders use a transfer roller to pick up water from a reservoir and apply it to a rotating wheel. These might more accurately be called damp grinders. Similarly, some dry grinders are modified to have a fine mist of water directed at the edge of the tool being ground. These might also be called damp grinders.

These indistinct models highlight the basic problems with the two types. A wet grinder can be dirty and inconvenient if there is anything less than excellent water control when using the machine. However, the great advantage is that it is possible to remove material quickly without fear of overheating the tool and drawing its temper. Dry grinders are inexpensive, clean and compact but carry with them the constant risk of overheating an edge.

Wet grinders Nothing is safer than a wet grinder for shaping a cutting edge, whether it is a knife, a carving tool, a plane blade or a hatchet. With an ample supply of water, the edge stays cool and the stone is clear of all swarf, giving a very even cutting action. Wet grinders come in both horizontal-wheel and vertical-wheel styles (see the photo above). Since it is nearly impossible to get hand-powered wet grinders any more, I'll deal only with the much more common motorized versions.

Most horizontal-wheel wet grinders are made in Japan. Both coarse and fine wheels are available, although a single 800x (i.e., 800-grit) or 1000x wheel will accommodate virtually all shop grinding. Horizontal-wheel wet grinders are delightful to use in that you never burn a tool, but they are also disconcerting in some aspects. First, because the process is so smooth and quiet, you are lulled into thinking that metal is being removed slowly, which is not usually the case. Resin-bond wheels cut very quickly, and you can take 1/16 in. off the end of a chisel in a deceptively short period of time.

A freestanding commercial tool rest, grooved to accept sliding jigs and drilled for rotating jigs, mounts directly to the bench in front of a dry grinder (left). The tool rest in the photo at right is a shopmade fixture with a tilt mechanism and a jig slot.

Because they were originally developed for sharpening knives, horizontal-wheel wet grinders often have inadequate jigging for woodworking tools. This combined with the fact that most of them have flutter in the wheel makes them more suitable for freehand grinding than jigged grinding.

It is possible to take out the wheel flutter by truing the wheel with a single-point dresser (see p. 43), but then the wheel will usually run true only in a single shaft orientation. If you remove the wheel from the shaft and replace it, you will have to rotate the wheel to exactly the same spot it was at when trued or flutter will still be a problem.

None of this is very significant when sharpening knives, and the wet grinder can be a real pleasure with both knives and carving tools. Used with carving tools, though, it quickly gets a scalloped surface that reduces its usefulness for chisels and plane blades.

There are a variety of vertical-wheel wet grinders on the market, but some have wheels too small for use in sharpening woodworking tools (small wheels will undercut the bevel too much). A minimum acceptable wheel size is 6 in. diameter (8 in. or 10 in. is preferable). These grinders often have lateral wobble, which, although disconcerting, is not critical to their function at low rpm. Much more critical is what is called "hop," the lack of concentricity around the axis. Hop can be removed readily with a diamond-point wheel dresser.

As with almost all grinders, you should look carefully at the versatility and accuracy of the tool rest. It should be a stable, easily adjustable rest that is parallel to the face of the wheel. Another consideration for a vertical-wheel wet grinder is the position of the rest. With a bathed-wheel grinder, the tool rest must be mounted high enough that any grinding being done has the bevel as the lowest point so that the water will run off the tool back onto the wheel, not down the blade. (On wet grinders that use a transfer roller to pick up water from the trough and apply it to the wheel, water running down the blade of the tool is not a problem.)

Vertical-wheel wet grinders frequently come with vitrified-bond wheels, which are slower cutting than resin-bond wheels but also wear more slowly. Resin-bond wheels are available for many vertical grinders, as they are for horizontal grinders.

Of the two types of wet grinder, I prefer the vertical-wheel style, primarily because it is much easier to maintain a true wheel and also usually easier to build specialized jigs for. A horizontal-wheel grinder produces a flat grind, which I prefer to the hollow grind of a vertical wheel (see pp. 61-62), but the very low speed of a vertical-wheel grinder lets you safely use the side of the wheel where flatness is critical.

Dry grinders While there are some horizontal-wheel dry grinders, they are almost all for industrial use and beyond the budget of the average woodworker. The grinder that is most commonly found in woodshops is a vertical-wheel, double-spindle bench grinder for either 6-in. or 8-in. wheels. These are inexpensive and versatile machines, though virtually unusable as they come from the store.

The first problem is that the grinder will come with wheels that are totally unsuited to grinding chisels and plane blades or any hard, high-carbon tool steel. The grinder will probably have one fine and one coarse silicon-carbide wheel. Both wheels will have very hard bonds more suited to cleaning up castings or welding spatter than to sharpening tools. These wheels can be used for rough grinding but certainly not on any tool that you care about. I would restrict them to lawnmower blades and shovels. As recommended in the previous chapter, the best all-purpose wheel you can put on such a grinder is an A80H-8V (see pp. 37-39).

The second thing that has to be done with these bench grinders is either to replace the entire tool rest or remanufacture the one that comes with the grinder. Since the vast majority of these tool rests are not fixable, it is easiest to build or buy a freestanding tool rest that you mount in front of the grinder (see the photos on the facing page).

With the right wheel and a good tool rest, a dry grinder becomes a real workhorse in a shop. To my mind, it is second in usefulness only to a good belt sander.

Truing and dressing grindstones Truing a grindstone is the process of creating or restoring the stone to the shape you want. New stones are seldom perfectly true, and you should be prepared to true one as soon as you buy it. Although some abrasive manufacturers sell very hard abrasive sticks for truing wheels, a diamond dresser is both more accurate and easier to use.

The most common reason for having to true a stone is that it is out of round. To true such a stone, clamp a single-point diamond dresser (a ¼-carat model costing about $15.00 should outlast you) between two pieces of wood or in a grinding jig. The tip of the dresser should just touch the highest point of the wheel at an angle anywhere between 10° and 15° below the center point of the wheel, but never less than 5°. Angling the dresser in this manner will protect the diamond from destructive shocks.

Turn the grinder on and slowly traverse the face of the wheel, using the jig to control projection of the dresser (see the drawing on p. 44). For a second pass, tilt the dresser up until it is taking a cut of 0.001 in. or 0.002 in. (about the thickness of this paper).

GRINDER ACCESSORIES

Whether you buy a tool rest, make a tool rest or remanufacture the one that came with the bench grinder, as a bare minimum you want the following three features:

1. The face of the tool rest should be at 90° to the running plane of the stone at all settings.
2. The tool-rest table should be lockable in a variety of angular settings.
3. You should have a grinding guide in which you can clamp tools and slide them back and forth across the tool rest for grinding.

There are a number of specialized grinding guides and jigs that you can buy or make; these include jigs for radius grinding of skew chisels (see p. 127) or grinding of lathe gouges (see p. 124). But these are peripheral accessories; all you really need are the three core functions listed above.

A jig that clamps the tool and can be slid across the tool rest is essential for accurate grinding. Shown here are a commercial jig (left) and a shopmade jig (right). (Photo at left by Susan Kahn)

To true a grindstone, clamp a diamond dresser in a grinding jig and pass it across the face of the rotating stone. (Photo by Susan Kahn)

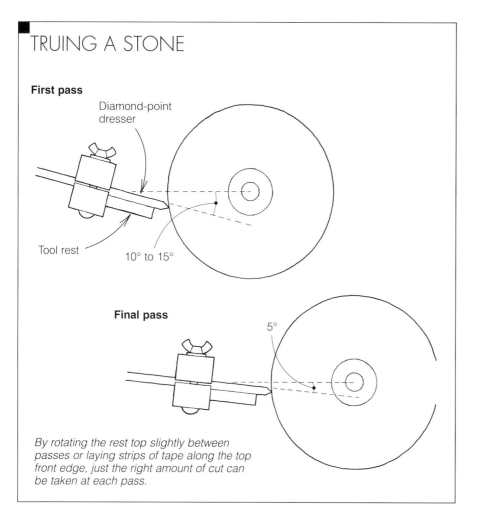

TRUING A STONE

First pass

Diamond-point dresser

Tool rest

10° to 15°

Final pass

5°

By rotating the rest top slightly between passes or laying strips of tape along the top front edge, just the right amount of cut can be taken at each pass.

Tools for dressing grindstones include a diamond dresser (which can also be used for truing stones) and star-wheel dressers. The cutters of the star-wheel dresser at right have been worn through frequent use and are long overdue for replacement.

Traverse the wheel again. Repeat the process until you have a perfectly shaped wheel or until you have reached the 5° angle. If you have reached 5° and the wheel is still not true, reset the dresser below 10° (but not more than 15°) and start again. This will give you a square-faced wheel parallel to your tool rest.

A grindstone needs to be dressed to restore its cutting ability, usually after it has been glazed through carelessness. This can be done with a star-wheel dresser or a diamond-point dresser (see the photo below). A star-wheel dresser is most applicable with hard wheels; it leaves a coarse, aggressive surface. I prefer a diamond point because it can be used both for dressing and for truing wheels. You will find that the only time you have to dress an A80H-8V wheel is when someone has misused it (for example, grinding brass or aluminum). Otherwise, it does not glaze and the only servicing it needs is occasional truing.

BELT SANDERS

The belt sander is probably the most underrated sharpening tool in the woodshop. It can be used for virtually any job where you might normally use a bench grinder and for a wide variety of jobs (such as knife sharpening) that a bench grinder cannot adequately perform. The entrained air in the belt combined with the length of the belt makes for cool cutting, but not so cool that you should not be careful of tool temperature. On a belt sander you have a choice of a long flat area, a convex area or a slightly concave area on which to sharpen. Each has its use at different times. If you wish, you can even add platens of greater convexity for specialized hollow grinding, which is something that knifemakers often do (see the drawing on the facing page).

Belts are relatively inexpensive and available in a wide variety of abrasives and grits. You can use belts as coarse as 60x for rapid stock removal and work up the range to very fine honing belts, which are now available as fine as 16,000x. Alternatively, you can buy a leather belt and charge it with honing compound for fine finishing.

A belt sander makes an excellent sharpening center. The narrow, 1-in. belt sander is ideal for sharpening knives and carving tools, while the 3-in. belt-sander attachment is handy for tools like axes and hatchets.

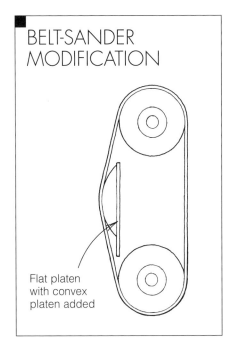

BELT-SANDER MODIFICATION

Flat platen with convex platen added

Much like bench grinders, most belt sanders suffer from inadequate tool rests, but it is even easier to build a suitable rest for a belt grinder than it is for a bench grinder because the work area is normally above the motor and unhampered on either side.

SANDING DRUMS

Sanding drums, which are inexpensive and available in a wide range of diameters (usually ½ in. to 4 in.), are ideal for sharpening in-cannel gouges, scoop adzes and cornering tools.

You can mount the sanding drum in a drill press (or in a hand drill clamped in a vise) and bring the tool to the drum, or put the drum in a flex shaft and bring the drum to the tool. For fine work, like small gouges, I prefer to use the sanding drum in a flex shaft and fix the tool in a vise. For something like a scoop adz, it is easier to have the sanding drum in a drill press.

A sanding drum mounted in a drill press is a handy tool for sharpening large in-cannel gouges (left). The sanding drum can also be mounted in a flex shaft (above). (Photo at left by Susan Kahn)

CHARGING A FELT WHEEL

Putting the initial charge of honing compound on a felt wheel is not easy. A new wheel is fuzzy and will tend to throw compound all over the shop rather than accept it. To complicate matters, the binders in bars of honing compound tend to dry out over time, so any bar that has been sitting on a store shelf for months will be less likely to stick to the wheel.

Professional polishers call this initial charging process "building a head." They use various methods, but a common one is to spray the rotating wheel lightly with diluted animal glue or fish glue. This creates a sticky base for the compound. Unless done very carefully, I find that this can harden the wheel too much. I prefer to singe the wheel* to remove the fuzziness then dress it with a bit of hard fat or mineral oil. It will then take a charge more readily. Once the wheel has been well charged once, it will readily accept subsequent dressings.

*Do this exactly the same way you would singe a chicken after plucking. You don't know how? Ask your grandmother.

Charging a felt buffing wheel with honing compound.

A shaped felt wheel is ideal for honing the inside of gouges and parting tools.

As with belts, sanding-drum sleeves are available in a wide range of grits and are inexpensive and effective. Used with a light touch, there is no reason ever to overheat a tool.

FELT BUFFING WHEELS AND BOBS

The use of felt wheels developed from the need to put a fine edge on a tool quickly. Until very recently, it was impossible to buy ultra-fine abrasives in belt or power-stone form. Since felt wheels could be charged with any one of a variety of fine abrasives, they became popular substitutes for fine-grit bench stones.

Basically you want to avoid the normal buffing wheel (which is made of cloth) and use a solid felt wheel instead. If you do use a cloth wheel, you need to put large stiffening flanges on either side; otherwise, it will be too soft to use with any sort of control. Even with flanges the wheel will round bevels, destroying the ideal geometry of the edge.

To call these buffing wheels is really a misnomer (buffing implies restoring or enhancing a surface by removing oxides or making a surface more consistent). A felt wheel, once charged with abrasive, will actually hone, removing material as it refines an edge. Charged with a good honing compound, it will remove material quite quickly. The mirror finish that is left by a fine compound has lulled people into using such wheels for polishing brass. Big mistake. It will leave a fine finish but strip off a substantial amount of brass in the process.

Felt wheels come in a range of densities, and only the harder wheels are normally used in honing tools. For carving tools, a shaped wheel is available, which is particularly handy for dealing with the inside of parting tools and gouges (see the photo at left).

Bobs are small, shaped-felt heads, usually mounted on an ⅛-in. diameter (or smaller) shank for use in a flex shaft. They are used for gouge flutes, in-cannel gouges or similar hard-to-hone shapes. They are charged in exactly the same manner as a felt wheel (see the sidebar above).

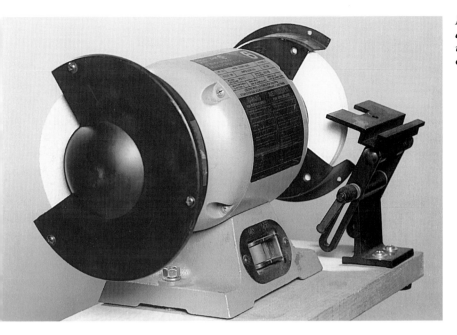

Mounting a grinder on a swivel base allows you to work with a grinding wheel and a buffing wheel running in opposite directions.

Felt-wheel setup Here, I would like to concentrate on the standard 6-in. felt wheel with a square face. The first consideration with this wheel is that it should be mounted so that it turns away from you at the top. This is just the reverse of the normal bench-grinder setup. You have at least four choices here. You can get accustomed to doing everything on the bottom half of the wheel and have it turn toward you, or you can mount your bench grinder on a swivel base so that you can rotate the whole grinder through 180° and lock it in position. This lets you have the grinding wheel on one end turning toward you at the top and, when rotated, a felt honing wheel rotating away from you at the top. But since either of these methods may be illegal where you live, I cannot actually recommend them to you. Check your local legislation to see what is allowable.

The third alternative is to have your grinder on an island stand where you can easily work on either side. This way you can have wheels properly shielded and still running in opposite directions. As a fourth alternative you can use a completely separate unit for buffing.

BENCH STONES

Although you can do everything from initial shaping to final honing with bench stones, very few people today would turn to a bench stone to restore an edge that had hit a nail. Some form of power grinding is normally used for major metal removal, and bench stones have been relegated to the work of edge refinement. Both natural and man-made bench stones come in a wide range of shapes and sizes.

NATURAL BENCH STONES

There are only two groupings of natural bench stones regularly available in North America: the Arkansas stones and the natural Japanese water stones.

The Arkansas stones were described briefly in the previous chapter. As a rule, the older the Arkansas stone, the better the quality. You can often find old Arkansas stones at flea markets; they may have to be trued but this is a small price to pay to get a good-quality stone. It is still possible to buy new Arkansas stones that are of good quality, but it is unusual to find any in bench-stone sizes. They are now usually only found in the smaller shaped stones. If you are convinced that a natural Arkansas bench stone is what you want and you cannot find

one at a flea market, I recommend that you contact a dealer in antique tools. Dealers frequently get stones as part of lot purchases of tools.

Good-quality natural Japanese water stones are getting scarce as well, though you can still buy them from retailers specializing in Japanese tools. The best indicator of their scarcity is the price you will have to pay for a decent stone: A good stone will cost you several hundred dollars; a top-quality stone can cost $1,000 or more. Clearly, you need to be quite certain that you want a natural water stone before spending this kind of money. There is no question that a very fine natural water stone has a wonderful feel to it, but I would consider one only if I were using top-quality Japanese chisels and plane blades on a regular basis.

GRADING NATURAL JAPANESE WATER STONES

Fred Damsen (The Japan Woodworker) has done more than anybody I know to introduce traditional Japanese tools and Japanese water stones to the North American market. Fred describes the grading process as one of sniffing, scratching, tapping and spitting. It isn't exactly a voodoo art, but it is close to it.

Fred says that the primary features to look for are water-absorption rates and apparent material consistency. The fineness of the stone, as well as its porosity, particle shape, bond, and so on, are known to the miner. The wholesaler who buys from the miner will also have a good idea of the value of the stones from different mines. The final price will be struck in negotiation between the two. The stone then passes through the marketing chain with that relative price intact. As a consumer, it is very difficult for you to differentiate between stones, and there are no easy tests. Your best assurance of good value and a good stone is the reputation of the person selling the stone to you.

MAN-MADE BENCH STONES

Man-made bench stones can be entirely man-made, as is the case with a silicon-carbide stone, or they can contain a natural abrasive (novaculite, corundum, etc.) that has been crushed, sieved and rebonded to give the desired shape, particle consistency, bond and structure.

Oil stones The two most common man-made oil stones are silicon-carbide and aluminum-oxide stones with vitrified bonds. Although these stones are available in a fairly wide range of grits, most woodworkers use only the coarser grits. Both of these stones are fine for fairly rapid stock removal, but there are much better choices for fine honing.

As you can see from the photo-micrograph of a Fine India (400x) stone at left below, the vitrified bond almost totally masks the abrasive particles. The bond overwhelms the abrasive particles. Such a stone cuts slowly and glazes quickly. Compare the structure to the Japanese water stone in the photo at right below.

For very hard steels and for high-speed steels a silicon-carbide stone is suitable, otherwise an aluminum-oxide stone should serve well for virtually all of your steel edge tools. A 90x stone is a good choice in either style for rapid material removal.

Water stones Man-made water stones from Japan first came into the North American market about twenty years ago. Although they are still not well known in the handyman market, they are probably used by 90% of professional cabinetmakers. With only minor exceptions, most of the Japanese stones have a resin bond, cut very quickly and wear more rapidly than Western stones. To my mind, they can be forgiven their tendency to wear rapidly, because of the speed of cut and the very consistent particle size in the stones. I find that an 800x resin-bond water stone cuts more quickly than a 90x aluminum-oxide oil stone. (The only time a 90x stone might cut as fast as a water stone is when the stone is brand new or just after it has been lapped.) Worn and rounded particles remain locked in position in the oil stone, but spall off a water stone at a controlled rate.

Looking at the photo at right below you can see a structure that is porous and does not mask the abrasive edges of the particles. There are globules of resin in sight, but they act only as a bonding agent since they are softer than steel and would be quickly removed if they came between a blade and an abrasive particle. In addition, a water stone gives a far finer degree of finish for the same cutting rate. In the very fine ranges, such as the 6000x or the 8000x Japanese stones, there is no comparable Western man-made stone.

20μ   4μ

The vitrified bond of an aluminum-oxide (Fine India) oil stone (left) gives the stone a quite different structure from that of a resin-bond Japanese water stone (right). (Photos courtesy National Research Council of Canada)

Reconstituted stones I find that Arkansas Perfect stones, which are reconstituted novaculite (see p. 29), function much like the natural Arkansas stones. The photomicrographs at right show a Washita and a Hard Arkansas stone in reconstituted form. They are more porous than the India stone shown in the photo at left on the facing page, but otherwise the particles are similarly masked. I do not recommend them.

Diamond stones As the hardest of all materials, diamond can be used on steel of any hardness, on carbides and, equally important, on other abrasives. This last point may sound odd, but a diamond stone is useful to have if only to flatten all your other stones.

Traditionally, diamond stones have been available only in relatively coarse grits (600x or less), but this is changing as ever-finer grits are demanded to touch up carbide cutters. 1200x diamond hones and files are now available.

Two things to look for in diamond bench stones are monocrystalline diamonds and a flat substrate. The vendor should be able to tell you whether the diamond is mono-crystalline or polycrystalline type (see p. 35); you can check the flatness of the substrate yourself. You can expect to pay about twice as much for a good monocrystalline stone as you would for a polycrystalline stone, but you can also expect it to last much more than twice as long.

Ceramic stones Ceramic stones are a variation of vitrified-bond stones. Normally sold only in very fine grits, they are used for honing rods in knife sharpeners and other specialized shapes where structural strength is necessary. They cut well when new but have such a hard bond that the abrasive particles become rounded in time, and since they cannot dislodge the cutting action is reduced. To remain effective over time these should be lapped or refaced regularly. A good job for a diamond stone.

HONING OILS, HONING WATERS

The primary purpose of a honing oil is to keep a stone from glazing. It should provide enough lubrication to keep metal from bonding to the stone, but it should not mask the abrasive action. The honing oil also acts as a flushing agent to clear dislodged abrasive and metal chips. It should be a non-drying (or non-curing) oil that will not clog the stone. A light mineral oil is most commonly used, although something like diesel fuel will also serve.

With stones that have an open structure and a soft bond, glazing is caused primarily by crushed abrasive particles packing the pores. With such stones, water is all that is required as a flushing agent. Since many such stones also have resin bonds, only water should be used because many oils will attack the resin bond.

Some people like to use soapy water (instead of oil) with oil stones. A vitrified bond is impervious to almost everything except hydrofluoric acid, so it will not damage the stone. I have not experimented with this and cannot comment. But I would caution you never to use anything but water with water stones. People who have stored their water stones in antifreeze in the winter have found to their regret that some antifreezes dissolve resin bonds.

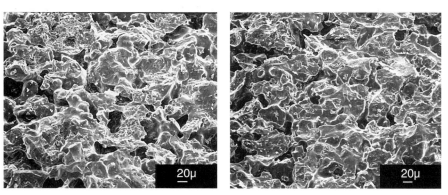

Reconstituted Washita (left) and Hard Arkansas (right) stones have a masked structure similar to that of an aluminum-oxide stone. (Photos courtesy National Research Council of Canada)

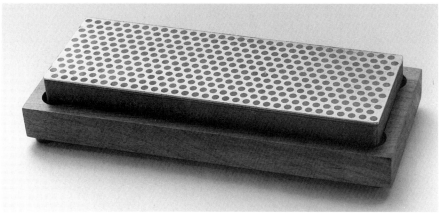

A monocrystalline diamond bench stone is a good stone for basic sharpening and excels as a tool for truing other bench stones.

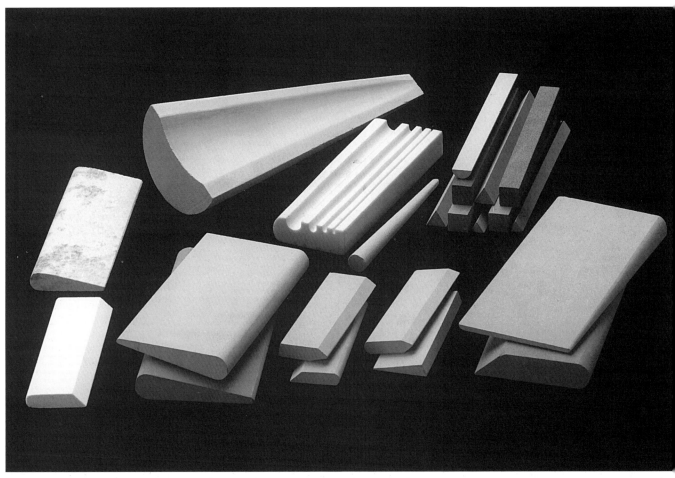

Shaped stones, available in numerous profiles and abrasives, are nowadays used primarily to sharpen turning and carving tools.

Lapping a bench stone on plate glass with loose silicon-carbide grit serves to flatten the stone as well as remove any glazed layer. (Photo by Susan Kahn)

SHAPED STONES

There are too many shaped stones on the market to do an adequate job of describing them all. There are gouge cones, slipstones, round, triangular and square-section stones. They are available in natural Hard Arkansas, resin-bond aluminum-oxide water stones, vitrified-bond aluminum oxide and silicon carbide, and an increasingly large number of diamond-coated shapes.

To a great extent, power-sharpening equipment has rendered many of these stones obsolete. In addition, many of the special shapes they were designed to sharpen are now made from tungsten carbide, and they are only sharpened with diamond. The ones that have continued to retain some popularity are the gouge cones among turners and the slipstones among carvers. Both are now available in either water stones or oil stones. With slipstones, resin-bond water stones are preferable but, just like the bench stones, they need more care since they wear more rapidly. The one place where the natural Arkansas still has a clear advantage is with stone files of the type used to touch up combination plane blades and filed edges like auger-bit chippers or two-man crosscut saw teeth. Water stones are too soft in these uses, and vitrified-bond stones are not available in fine enough grits.

KEEPING STONES FLAT

Eventually stones wear from use. If they wore evenly there would be no problem, but they tend to wear most in the center; eventually a stone becomes so dished that it is impossible to hone a straight edge on it.

The easiest and fastest way to flatten any bench stone is to use a coarse diamond bench stone. If you can afford one, it is a wonderful luxury. For the poor and the parsimonious, there are several other alternatives. Silicon-carbide paper on a sheet of plate glass works well, although the stones will quickly dull the sandpaper. Loose silicon-carbide particles on plate glass with a bit of water or WD-40 will also work as a lapping medium. It is even more effective if a hard plastic like Mylar is backed with plate glass and silicon-carbide particles put on the Mylar. They will bed in the Mylar and abrade the stone. On the plate glass alone they tend to roll around a bit too much, and the process takes longer.

Particularly with Japanese water stones, it is possible to true a finer stone with a coarser one. As an example, an 800x water stone can be used to true a 6000x or an 8000x stone. Using the stone with a circular rubbing motion, you can be reasonably sure that the coarse stone will stay flat as it is abrading the finer stone. You should be aware, however, that stones rubbed together will normally wear until they have mating surfaces. These surfaces will always be flat if you are using three stones in rotation. If you have only two stones to rub together, you can get mating surfaces but one might be concave while the other is convex.

WHAT SIZE STONE?

Although it can be tempting to buy cheaper, small bench stones, I recommend that you buy a stone that is at least 2½ in. wide by 8 in. long. You will find that the common size of 2 in. by 6 in. will often be too small. It is not only too short for an easy honing action in many instances, but it is too narrow for any blades wider than 1¾ in. I would prefer to own fewer stones and have them a decent size.

Whatever method you use to lap stones, it's a good idea to flush them completely since it is possible to get contamination from the lapping grit or the coarse stone that was being used. This is not a particular problem with coarse bench stones but is very much a concern with fine finishing stones, particularly those with a resin bond because particles will imbed in them more readily than in vitrified-bond stones. Fortunately, your fingers are sensitive enough to detect a rogue particle in one of your finishing stones.

Storing stones Another way to contaminate a stone is to store it badly. All stones should be kept in covered containers. Oil stones are usually kept in fitted wooden boxes; water stones are best kept submerged in a covered bath, unless they have wooden bases. Wooden-base stones may be stored upside-down in a shallow bath, keeping the wood well clear of the water, or they can be stored dry. It is generally best to keep water stones wet so that they are ready for immediate use (a dry

stone can take several minutes to fill) and to avoid the salt deposits that can accumulate in the pores if you have hard water and allow stones to dry out between uses. You will find that very fine stones (6000x and finer) function well with just surface water on them, so they can be stored dry if desired.

One exception to these general recommendations is that water stones should never be allowed to freeze unless they are completely dry. A wet stone will burst when frozen. As a further word of caution to innovative woodworkers who think they can store stones in antifreeze, most antifreezes attack resin bonds.

HONING GUIDES

I recommend the use of honing guides with chisels and plane blades for two reasons: speed and accuracy. A good guide should let you select a honing angle, clamp the tool firmly at that angle for shaping a basic bevel, and then let you make a small angular adjustment for fine honing of a secondary bevel or micro-bevel. In addition, you should later be able to set the tool at exactly the same angles again when you need to resharpen it.

A system that lets you do all this will remove the least metal each time you have to sharpen a tool. Since metal removal is a function of time when you are honing, such a system is also therefore the fastest. Equally important, it provides the accuracy you want for maintaining bevels at their optimum angles.

There are only two honing guides on the market that meet these criteria, the Eclipse guide and the Veritas guide. At this point I am reminded of the qualifier that a publisher sometimes puts at the end of an opinion column in the financial press. It runs something like this: "Columnist X may own stocks or bonds discussed in this column." I declare such a conflict with the Veritas guide, but since I used an Eclipse guide for a decade before the Veritas guide was developed I think that I can deal with it as an old friend.

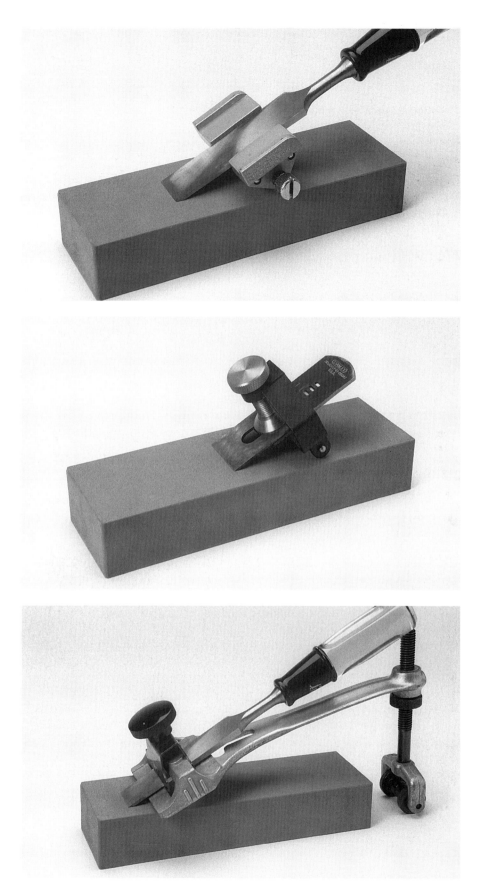

The Eclipse guide (see the top photo at left) is a side-clamping design that clamps firmly but cannot handle skew chisels, spokeshave blades or butt chisels at normal honing angles. The Veritas guide (middle photo at left) is a top-clamping model that clamps firmly (a hair less so than the Eclipse) and can handle skew chisels, spokeshave blades and Western butt chisels at normal grind angles but not Japanese butt chisels. It does not clamp very narrow chisels as well as the Eclipse, but, once clamped, they are easier to hone because of the wider and more stable roller on the Veritas. For different reasons, it is easy to get a tip off-square on a narrow chisel with either guide if care is not taken. On chisels wider than ¼ in., the Veritas guide holds blades so that they hone true; the Eclipse guide has a narrower roller with enough play in it to be a problem.

Finally, the Veritas guide has a cam roller that lets you adjust the bevel by 1° or 2° without unclamping the tool. With the Eclipse you can achieve the same effect by sliding a piece of plastic or metal under the roller. It restricts the range of travel of the guide, but since it is only necessary when honing a micro bevel it is more of a nuisance than a limitation.

The Veritas guide is best used with the Veritas angle-setting jig (see the top photo on the facing page). So is the Eclipse. The setting jig has a pentagonal disc with five bevel angles on it from 15° to 35° at 5° increments. To set the bevel angle on a blade, the blade is clamped loosely in the jig, rolled up to the setting jig and then clamped tightly only after adjusting the blade until it is flush with the beveled face of the jig.

One serendipitous feature of the Veritas jig is that it automatically adjusts itself on a skew chisel. When the skew is set flush in the angle jig, with the cutting edge tucked into the join of the pentagon and the base, and a loosely clamped guide is allowed to slide down the chisel until the roller hits the base of the setting jig, it will automatically orient itself correctly. Just plain luck. It wasn't designed to do that.

The side-clamping Eclipse guide (top) and the top-clamping Veritas (middle) are two of the most effective honing guides available. The General guide (above) is a dependable tool but does not provide good angular control. (Photos by Susan Kahn)

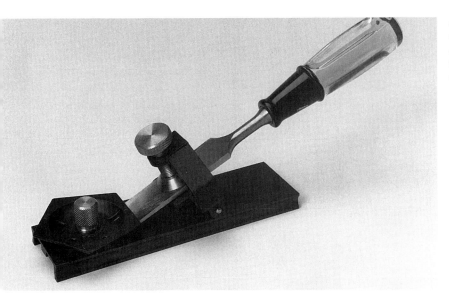

A commercial angle-setting jig, which can be used with either the Veritas or Eclipse guide, allows accurate setting of bevel angles from 15° to 35°. (Photo by Susan Kahn)

Before leaving the subject of honing guides, brief mention of the General guide is in order (see the bottom photo on the facing page). This is a workman-like guide that is suitable for occasional do-it-yourself use but unsuitable if you want good angular control. There is no easy way to set honing angles, never mind returning to them exactly when it is time to resharpen. But the General guide is quick to set up and allows you to use shorter stones because the roller runs on the work table, not on the stone.

WHY USE A MICRO-BEVEL?

The primary reason for using a micro-bevel is that it saves honing time. If you want a 25° bevel angle on a tool and you grind the bevel at 25°, you then have to hone the entire bevel in order to get a keen cutting edge. On a very fine stone, like an 8000x, this can take quite a while and wear away a lot more stone than if you grind at 24° and put on a 1° micro-bevel with a half-dozen strokes on the stone. The fine finish on the whole bevel makes no difference in cutting, it is only the last few thousandths of an inch that is important to the edge. (For more on micro-bevels, see pp. 62-63.)

SETTING ANGLES ON AN ECLIPSE GUIDE

If you want to use a wide range of angles with an Eclipse honing guide, you have to make a special setting gauge. The guide's instructions tell you how to set 25° and 30° by measuring blade projection from the guide, but this is both limiting and cumbersome. It is easier to spend a bit of time and make a setting gauge so that you can put the tool tip against the stop and slide the guide up to the gauge edge before clamping.

This same system will work with the Veritas honing guide if you do not have the Veritas angle-setting jig.

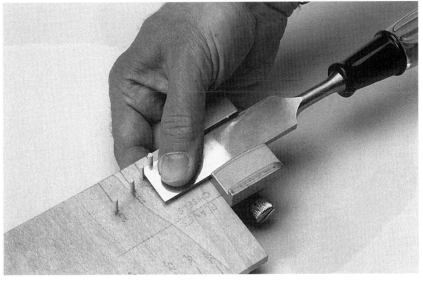

This shopmade angle-setting gauge for use with the Eclipse honing guide allows setting of bevel angles from 20° to 35°. (Photo by Susan Kahn)

STROPS

The word "strop" is used ambiguously nowadays. Originating with the leather barber's strop, it was both verb and noun. Lately some writers have used it to describe any fine sharpening operation, whether or not the edge being sharpened is being passed in a trailing stroke (a "stropping" action) over the abrasive. But not here. To me, stropping always means the use of a trailing stroke, and a strop is something that could be accidentally cut with a leading stroke.

A strop is used to touch up an edge. Although a variety of materials can be used for strops, with very few exceptions the strops are normally charged with a stropping compound before they are used. This is certainly the case with strops made from cloth or wood, but not always the case with strops made from leather.

LEATHER STROPS

Many leathers contain a natural abrasive. Under a microscope it appears to be some kind of silica. Until recently, natural leather strops were in common use in barber shops. But the traditional barber's strop is not the type that would normally be used in woodworking, because it is too flexible. Flexibility was no problem for a barber, because a straight razor was hollow ground on the sides to maintain just the right geometry for stropping on a taut belt. In woodworking it is more normal to fix the leather to a firm backing such as a piece of wood in order to minimize bevel rounding during the stropping process. The leather is also normally charged with a chromium-oxide compound. It then makes an excellent strop for all kinds of edge tools, especially knives.

While not exactly strops, leather belts are available for some belt sanders. These are usually charged with a buffing and honing compound such as chromium oxide and are very effective with knives and carving tools.

WOODEN STROPS

The least publicized and probably the most useful strops of all are ones made of wood. A good chromium-oxide compound (one that has a small percentage of fine aluminum-oxide particles in it as well as chromium oxide) applied to a piece of wood makes a potent sharpening device. As an example, I no longer use slipstones with carving tools. Taking a simple gouge as an example, I do the basic sharpening with a power system and all the honing with wooden strops (see Chapter 9). Using a soft wood like basswood or pine, you cut a groove in the face of the scrap with the gouge that you want to hone and you then have a perfectly formed strop for the bevel (see the photo below).

Turning your attention to the edge of the piece of scrap, you also cut it with the gouge but to match the inside of the gouge. It takes only seconds, and you now have a strop that is matched perfectly to the tool that it is going to be used on. You will find that the wood is very easy to charge with chromium oxide and that the strop will cut quite quickly. More important, unless you are particularly careless, you readily avoid bevel rounding using strops like these.

The potential for wooden strops is obvious. Pieces of wooden dowel can be charged with compound; V-shaped pieces of wood can be used for honing the inside of parting tools. But the true magic of it all is that you can use the blade that you want to hone to form the piece of wood to shape. In seconds, you can make a wooden strop that is perfectly matched to any shape of tool you have.

FILES

In sharpening, files are usually used for basic shaping. They are often followed by similarly shaped honing stones. Files are limited to tools that are relatively soft, usually Rc50 or less—tools such as handsaws, scrapers and axes. On tools like chisels or plane blades files are not only ineffective but will also dull very quickly.

Files that look alike can be dissimilar in use; the difference in performance usually reflects the difference in quality. A well-made file starts with a smoothly ground blank made from annealed steel. Sharp chisels are used to raise the file teeth before the file is hardened. If the blank is not smooth, the file teeth will be ragged and irregular. If the chisels are not sharp, the file teeth will have slightly rounded tops (like cresting waves) caused by the deformation of the blank as the chisels enter at an angle to raise the teeth. A well-made

Cutting a groove in the face of a softwood block with a gouge produces a perfectly formed strop for honing the bevel of the same gouge. (Photo by Susan Kahn)

file looks smooth on the uncut portion and feels smooth along a single-cut ridge. It will also have sharply defined edges on all teeth. If it is not carefully hardened, the fine tips will lose some of their carbon allowing them to dull quickly.

It is getting increasingly difficult to find good files. Nicholson has always made good files but it has reduced its range substantially in the last decade. Most of its files are now sold under the Black Diamond brand, but at one time the company sold under all of the following brands, which can still often be found in old hardware stores—McClellan, K&F, Great Western, Superior, Eagle, J.B. Smith, Beaver, American, Arcade and Globe.

Files come in a bewildering array of shapes, sizes and cuts. While it is always pleasant to be able to chose from a wide variety, you really need only a very few files to handle 95% of all the sharpening jobs in your shop.

MILL FILES

Mill files, so named because of their early use in filing circular saws in lumber mills, are absolutely indispensable in any shop. If you can afford only one, an 8-in. file is your best choice. It is the best compromise of fineness versus rapid stock removal. If you can afford them, a 6-in. file is handy for fine work, including jointing fine saws, and a 10-in. file is ideal for heavy stock removal in relatively soft steel that you might encounter in axes or many gardening tools. But an 8-in. mill file (bastard cut) is just about the handiest file you can have in the shop, and all the rest of those listed below cannot approach it in general usefulness.

The one thing you will notice in common with all the files discussed below is that the mill file is a single-cut file. In the Rc range from approximately 35 to 50, single-cut files remove steel fastest with the least clogging. They also wear more quickly than double-cut files.

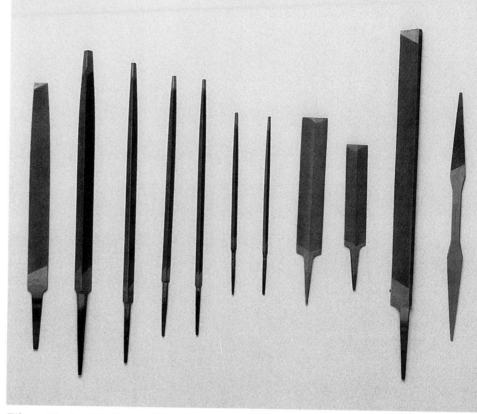

Files with specific sharpening applications include (from left to right) an 8-in. mill file, six triangular handsaw files, two feather-edge files, a Great American crosscut file and an auger-bit file. (Photo by Susan Kahn)

TRIANGULAR HANDSAW FILES

Specifically for sharpening handsaws, triangular files are of limited usefulness for anything else in the shop except sawtooth bits. These are tapered files and are graded as regular, slim taper, extra-slim taper and double extra-slim taper. If you are uncertain about what file to use for a given saw, you should use one that has a flat that is at least double the length of the face of tooth that you intend to file. This is to ensure that you get three usable pairs of filing surfaces on each file (see p. 148).

At one time there was a saw file made called a Double Ender, which was tapered from the center toward both ends and was cut from the ends toward the center so that it gave six intersections. These files were about 7 in. long and, since you normally use only about a 3-in. stroke, it was like having two files.

WEB-SAW FILES, FEATHER-EDGE FILES

When Swede saws were popular, the file of choice for the cognoscenti was a web-saw file, a file no longer in production. Actually they were for use on any saw that had tooth tips more acute than 60°. Naturally, since they are no longer available, I attribute far greater utility to them than they ever probably had.

But they have an Eastern cousin, the feather-edge file, which is now fairly widely available in North America. This is the file that is used for sharpening Japanese saws, all of which have tooth tips more acute than 60°. Feather-edge files are a little thinner in the body than web-saw files but have the advantage of being available in a safe-face version as well as in a full-cut version. The safe-

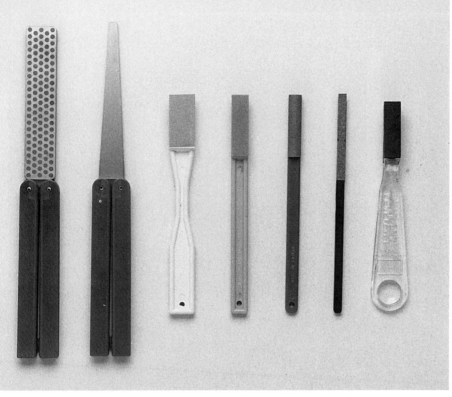

Diamond hones and files, shown here in a range of configurations and grit sizes, are used to sharpen tungsten-carbide-tipped tools. (Photo by Susan Kahn)

useful. Boron carbide is normally in block form glued to another type of backing. Diamond files are usually only available up to about 600x (although a 1200x file has just been introduced), and boron carbide up to 400x. A 400x boron carbide gives a finish about equal to a 600x diamond.

SANDPAPER

Sandpaper, dealt with in passing under belt sanders (see pp. 44-45), is an excellent sharpening material used on shaped backings of different types. A 600x wet/dry silicon-carbide paper mounted on a block of wood still makes an inexpensive fine stone for a chip carver. Combined with a simple stropping block with chromium oxide, it can be a complete sharpening system for someone.

Similarly, PSA-backed sandpaper can readily be attached to a wooden dowel for use with gouges. With a shaped surface, a spray-on adhesive and the right type of grit of sandpaper, you can make a sharpening device of almost any shape you want.

MICRO-FINISHING ABRASIVES

There are newer, finer abrasives coming on the market rapidly. One of the most impressive is the micro-finishing line from 3M. The regularity of the grit size and the aggressiveness of cut are exceptional. Probably most impressive in the line is the 0.5 micron chromium oxide on 3-mil Mylar. It will put a mirror finish on an edge faster than a stone that is five times as coarse. Considering that it is a 16000x abrasive, it is amazingly aggressive.

I believe that the effectiveness of the Mylar-backed abrasive is a result of the electrostatic charging process that 3M uses when bonding particles to the

face version is cut on only one side, which means that if you accidentally slither off whatever you happen to be filing, the back of the file will not do random damage to anything it encounters. This is a very desirable feature when you are first getting accustomed to the intricate geometry of Japanese saws. Again, these are excellent fitting files.

GREAT AMERICAN CROSSCUT FILE

These files are certainly on the endangered species list and will probably not be manufactured much longer. A specialized type of saw file, it has a rounded back for gumming out between teeth. Between them, a feather-edge file and a chainsaw file will do the same job.

AUGER-BIT FILE

Specifically designed for sharpening auger bits, this file has one end cut on both faces but not cut on the edges; the other end is cut on the edges but not on the faces. It is designed this way so that you can file the chippers of an auger bit without marking the screw point or the lip. Similarly, you can file the inside of a spur without scoring the chipper. Although this file has a highly specialized purpose in sharpening, its greatest usefulness around the shop is for those dozens of fitting jobs where you want to be able to dimension one surface without affecting an adjoining surface. Perfect examples are when you want to file the inside bevels of a corner chisel, or dress off a high spot on a plane bed without scoring the cheek.

DIAMOND FILES, BORON-CARBIDE FILES

Only two types of abrasive deal effectively with tungsten carbide: diamond and boron carbide. Diamond files come in a variety of configurations, but a flat file is probably the most

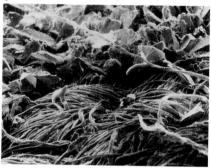

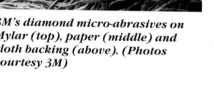

3M's diamond micro-abrasives on Mylar (top), paper (middle) and cloth backing (above). (Photos courtesy 3M)

Mylar. The particles are all standing up like iron filings on a magnet when they are glued in place. These microfinishing abrasives are available in belt, roll, disc and sheet form (the last two with or without PSA backing).

Because of the flatness of Mylar and the very regular application of grit, these leave a finer finish than similar grit on regular paper or cloth backings. To give an indication of the flatness of Mylar film, compare the three photos above, which are from 3M's diamond abrasive line.

With this discussion of abrasives and sharpening equipment behind us, the boiler-plate section of the book is complete. As Peter Drucker, the management guru, observed, sooner or later all planning must degenerate into actual work. We are at that point now.

CHAPTER 6
CHISELS

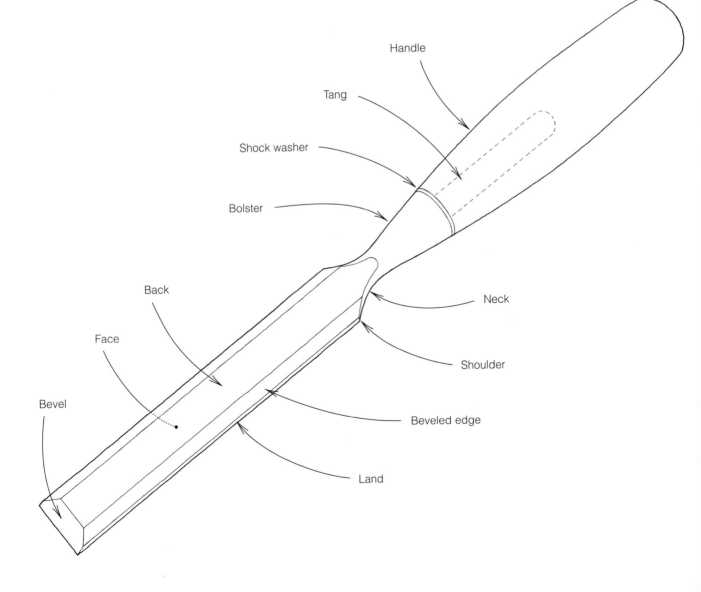

Handle

Tang

Shock washer

Bolster

Back

Face

Neck

Shoulder

Bevel

Beveled edge

Land

Somewhere in the mists of time man discovered that a wedge-shaped rock could be used to divide things. It was probably only a matter of days before he found that it was also a handy little prying tool, and probably only a matter of minutes after that when he damaged the tip prying something that really needed a bigger rock. The pattern for the use and abuse of chisels was set early in the tools' history.

GENERAL SHARPENING PROCEDURES

Chisels do not come from the store ready to use. Most have been ground to a basic shape, a few have been honed, none have been lapped and almost all have been dipped in lacquer to prevent rust. The first thing to do to your new chisel is to remove the lacquer.

REMOVING THE LACQUER

Lacquer must be removed from the face of the chisel and the bevel. On all except mortise chisels, it is not mandatory to remove the lacquer from the back and the sides, but my preference is to strip it all off up to the neck. Otherwise, you have scuffed lacquer on part of the tool, which not only looks ugly but also can give you a false sense that the tool is still rust-proofed. Lacquer thinner or paint stripper can be used to remove the lacquer. Be sure the thinner does not get on the handle, since it can soften some plastics and will strip lacquer off wooden handles.

LAPPING THE FACE OF THE CHISEL

In the condition it comes from the factory, the face of the chisel will have grinding marks on it, as shown in the top photo at right. If you did not first lap the chisel but devoted your attention only to the bevel, regardless of how well you honed that bevel, it would still be intersecting with a grooved face and the resulting edge would be ragged. So the first thing you have to do is remove these grind marks and make the face of the chisel as smooth as possible (as explained below).

A chisel comes from the factory with grinding marks on its face (top). These marks must be removed to create a sharp edge and to flatten the face (above).

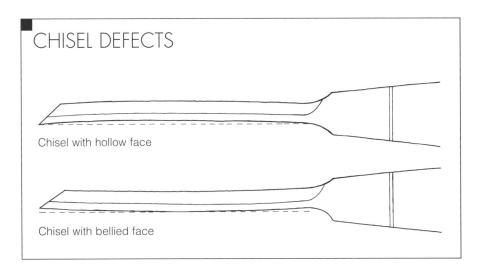

CHISEL DEFECTS

Chisel with hollow face

Chisel with bellied face

There is a second reason that lapping may be necessary; the face of the chisel may not be flat. Although a slight hollowness can be accepted in a chisel face, it cannot have any belly and still function well. A chisel with a belly in it should be returned to the vendor.

FIXING A CHISEL
WITH A BELLY

There are times when you have no choice but to fix a bellied chisel. If the chisel needs a great deal of work, I would start on a belt sander with a 120x belt. This assumes that you have a nice flat platen to work against as you hog off the bulk of the material on the belt sander (being ever conscious of the steel temperature). Check your work frequently by lap-ping the chisel briefly on the stone. The lap marks will tell you immedi-ately where the high points are and how much you still have to remove.

These are guerrilla tactics but quite effective. You will find that you can do most of the straightening on a sander without taking off steel that you do not want to remove.

TRUING THE SIDES
OF A CHISEL

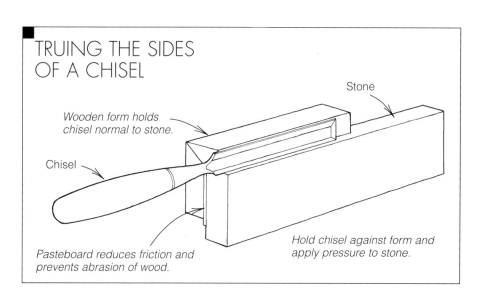
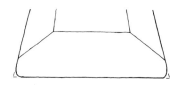

Wooden form holds chisel normal to stone.

Chisel

Stone

Pasteboard reduces friction and prevents abrasion of wood.

Hold chisel against form and apply pressure to stone.

To lap a chisel, hold two fingers on the back of the tool while rubbing it back and forth on the stone. With a narrow stone you may need to skew the chisel to the line of travel to get most of the face on the stone.

If that is not possible, initial flattening can be done on a belt sander (see the sidebar at left). Only when the face is very close to flat should you start work-ing it with stones.

Most chisels made today are ground reasonably well. Two types that you should immediately be suspicious of are chisels that have been hand ground (several German styles) and chisels that have been polished. Hand-ground chisels are almost never flat, square or straight. Polished chisels almost invariably have the sides rounded and

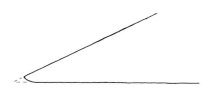

the face dubbed next to the bevel. The rounded sides (above) prevent you from getting a flat, full-width cut; the dubbed face (below), if uncorrected,

would mean that you would constantly have to tilt the chisel up to get it to cut. You would then have poor control of the tool.

To fix the dubbed tip, you usually have to grind about $1/16$ in. off the bevel. Lapping the chisel face will show when you have removed enough material. To true rounded sides, you can use a belt sander or dress them back on a stone. It is best to do such dressing on the edge of the stone, because you can quickly wear a groove in the stone when repeatedly rubbing a narrow edge in the same spot. The drawing at left shows a simple setup for truing the sides of a chisel as well as squaring the sides to the face.

For lapping most chisels you can start with an 800x or 1200x stone and then go directly to a 6000x or 8000x stone. This is one time you want to be absolutely sure that your stones are flat (see p. 51), because it is a fair amount of work to lap a chisel and you do not want to have to do it more than once.

It is not necessary to get the entire face of the chisel flat. Just as you can tolerate some hollowness fore to aft, you can tolerate some hollowness from side to side. If you have a chisel that is slightly hollow from side to side, you can stop lapping it as soon as you get the face to approximately the same configuration as most Japanese chisels, which are ground hollow on the face (see the bottom chisel in the photo at right). You do not have to be concerned that the edge will eventually reach the hollow portion. In the normal sharpening process the hollowness will slowly be eliminated as you remove a small amount of metal each time you sharpen.

If you are using a water stone, you can save yourself some time if you stop flushing your stone and let the crushed abrasive particles accumulate as you are approaching a satisfactorily lapped face on the coarse stone. This will slow the sharpening process by reducing the depth of scratch that the stone puts in the chisel, but the lost time will be more than made up when you move on to the fine stone. It will take you less time to refine the surface, because the scratches left by the preceding stone are shallower than they would have been from a flushed stone. This technique, which is frequently used with water stones, is a way of changing the effective grit size of a stone to your advantage.

SHAPING THE EDGE

There are two basic activities to shaping the edge of a chisel: setting the basic bevel angle and then honing it. The guiding principles you use here are that the bevel angle should be the lowest possible one consistent with edge retention in intended use, and that you want to spend the minimum amount of time resharpening. Under each chisel type discussed later in this chapter, there will be recommended basic bevel angles, as well as exceptions to the general process that I am about to describe.

Most Japanese chisels (above) are ground hollow on the face, whereas Western chisels (top) are ground flat.

Hollow grinding For at least the past twenty years, various cabinetmakers have recommended using a hand or power grinder to put a hollow bevel on a chisel so that it can be rapidly honed. The basic principle is that you clamp the chisel in a simple jig that can be slid back and forth on the grinder tool rest to grind a regular hollow from one side of the blade to the other. When you then hone the chisel, only the very front and the very back of the bevel will ride on the stone. This makes it possible to hone blades without using a

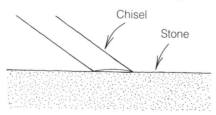

honing guide, since it minimizes the tendency of the blade to rock during honing.

While I am all for a method that reduces sharpening time, hollow grinding often does so at the expense of a strong edge. The undercutting of the bevel weakens the edge. Equally bad, if you hollow-grind at an angle that will give you the necessary edge strength, you have to hone at a higher

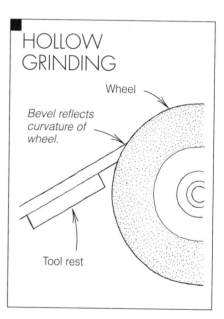

HOLLOW GRINDING

Wheel

Bevel reflects curvature of wheel.

Tool rest

HOLLOW GRINDING

Hollow grinding creates a smaller real bevel angle than the apparent bevel angle. The effect is accentuated as blade thickness increases and/or as grinding-wheel diameter decreases. The table shows the effect for a limited number of examples.

Bevel angle	Grinding-wheel diameter	Reduction in bevel angle caused by hollow grind		
		⅛-in. blade	¼-in. blade	½-in. blade
20°	4 in.	5.24°	10.53°	21.44°
	5 in.	4.19°	8.41°	17.00°
	6 in.	3.49°	7.00°	14.10°
	7 in.	2.99°	5.99°	12.05°
	8 in.	2.62°	5.24°	10.53°
30°	4 in.	3.58°	7.18°	14.48°
	5 in.	2.87°	5.74°	11.54°
	6 in.	2.39°	4.78°	9.59°
	7 in.	2.05°	4.10°	8.21°
	8 in.	1.79°	3.58°	7.18°

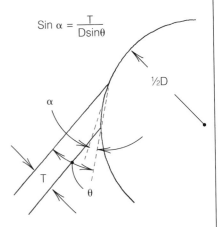

$$\sin \alpha = \frac{T}{D \sin \theta}$$

If you want to calculate the angular reduction (α) caused by hollow grinding at an apparent bevel angle (θ) for any blade thickness (T) and given wheel diameter (D), use the formula shown in the drawing above.

angle than is desirable for the best cutting action.

The problem is not nearly as acute if an 8-in. grinding wheel is used, but most shops are equipped with 6-in. wheels, which, in time, become 5-in. wheels or even smaller. The undercutting is a major problem with small wheels.

There is really nothing wrong with hollow grinding, but it should be limited to about half the bevel—the half farthest from the cutting edge. As an example, if you want to put a 25° bevel on a chisel, you can remove 2° or 3° more from the back half of the bevel to reduce your honing time substantially. For strength, you have only to worry about the front half of the bevel (with

the exception of laminated chisels, which will be dealt with later). What you do with the other half of the bevel

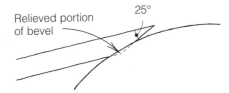

will affect rigidity, but it will not materially affect edge strength.

Removing 2° or 3° saves time in sharpening on bench stones because you have to deal with only the first half of the bevel. As this lengthens with repeated sharpenings, you can periodically relieve the back part of the bevel on a grinding wheel or belt sander.

Micro-bevels The best way to avoid a weak edge and still reduce your sharpening time is to use micro-bevels. A micro-bevel is a narrow secondary

bevel at an angle slightly higher than the primary bevel. As an example, if you want to put a 25° bevel on a chisel, you would shape the basic bevel at 24° on a coarse stone and then hone on a fine stone at 25°. You need only a very narrow bevel on the fine stone, because the efficacy of the cutting action is determined only by the bevel angle and the edge keenness for any given chip or shaving thickness. Such a narrow bevel might only be ¹⁄₆₄ in. wide (see the top photo on the facing page).

The sole purpose of a micro-bevel is to get the finest possible edge in the shortest period of time. There is absolutely nothing wrong with grinding and honing the entire bevel at 25° if you wish to. The time it takes to do this though is substantial, and the performance difference is usually not detectable.

FRICTION ON THE BEVEL

Back in Chapter 2, I asked you to accept the assumption that there was no friction in the cutting process. Well, Dr. Norman Franz did not ignore friction in his work (see Appendix 1), and he found it to be a significant factor at low rake angles (high cutting angles). But he also found that surface roughness of the tool was relatively insignificant if the roughness was grinding serrations parallel to the path of travel of the escaping chip.

Since most of the sharpening procedures recommended here result in grooves being parallel to the path of travel of the escaping chip or shaving, and since we are dealing with high rake (low cutting) angles, we can still safely ignore friction.

Adding a micro-bevel at an angle slightly steeper than the primary bevel both strengthens the edge and reduces sharpening time.

For best control when honing freehand, hone with the blade askew the direction of travel on the stone.

For good angular control, you need to use a honing guide (see pp. 51-53 and the photo on p. 64). All of the honing guides are compatible with the micro-bevel technique. The Veritas guide has an integral cam in the roller for quick setting of micro-bevels, but the same technique can be used with all other honing guides with some sacrifice in their function but without having to unclamp the chisel from the guide. All you have to do is form the basic bevel on a coarse stone and then, when you switch to your fine honing stone, slide a flat piece of material of credit-card thickness under the roller. With a couple of honing guides, like the Eclipse, the range of travel is then limited to the distance between the roller and the point where the edge touches the stone. With guides like the General, there is greater range of movement.

Honing technique I recommend using a honing guide because you need good control of chisel bevel angles if you want to get maximum performance out of your chisels. Chisels work best when ground at the lowest possible included angle consistent with edge retention. Freehand honing does not give you that sort of control.

However, like everyone else, I do lots of freehand honing. I have a selection of chisels that are the true orphans of the tool world; they might be too soft, not straight, or rust pitted—maybe all three! Whenever I have to fix something like the barn door or the garden gate, I cheerfully grab one of these chisels, put a quick edge on it with the belt sander, touch it to the felt

buffing wheel and go off to work in wood where dirt and nails lurk. But I would not do that with my bench chisels. I want them in top condition.

I keep a couple of 30° bevel chisels for cutting end-grain oak or similar destructive woods and the balance are shaped for softwoods or hardwoods, all with the honing angles marked on the tool somewhere: 15° for one paring chisel, 18° for another, skews at 20°, a great gathering around 25° and a few mortise chisels in the 30°s.

If I honed those chisels freehand, all the bevel angles would creep up and none would be as finely tuned nor work as effectively as is the case now. If you are determined to do all your honing freehand, all I can suggest is that you hone with the blade well askew the direction of travel on the stone. This gives you the best shot at good angular control.

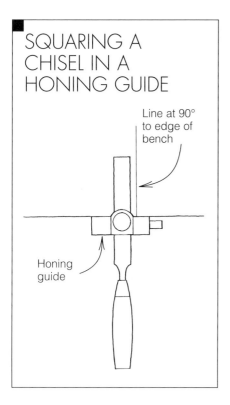

Line at 90°
to edge of
bench

Honing
guide

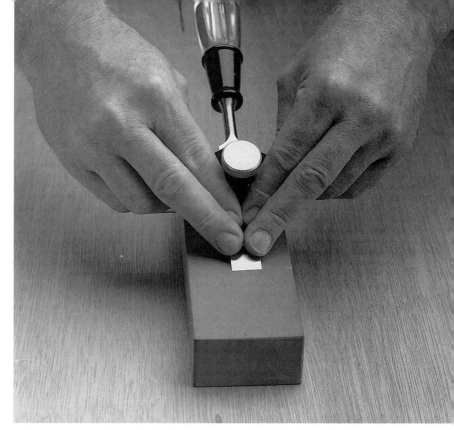

When using a honing guide, keep finger pressure well forward on the blade with thumbs hooked behind the guide. Use the whole surface of the stone for even wear.

When using a honing guide with a bench stone, there are only a couple of things that you have to be alert to: You should have the chisel set in the guide at the correct angle, and it should be set squarely. There are numerous ways to set the angle, and the instructions with your honing guide should tell you how to do it. It is an easy matter to square a chisel in a honing guide, since virtually all guides can be held against the edge of a bench while the chisel is aligned with a mark at 90° to the edge of the bench (see the drawing above).

When you are shaping the main bevel, you do not have to worry about forming wire edges. You just lean into your work and try and use as much of the stone surface as possible so that you keep the stone reasonably flat through even wear. Always keep finger pressure well forward on the blade with only your thumbs hooked behind the guide (see the photo above). The honing guide should be carrying almost no weight. It is only there as a guide and should have only enough weight on it to keep the roller in firm contact with the stone. As you work, flip the stone end for end every so often to be sure that you are giving it equal wear in all areas.

Once you have formed the basic bevel you have to exercise a bit more care. The first thing you should do is give the face of the chisel a few lapping strokes on the fine stone. This will remove or bend back any wire edge that has formed. You then go about forming your micro-bevel, which should only take a half-dozen strokes on the stone. Next take two or three lapping strokes on the face, and then take one or two more strokes on the micro-bevel using pressure only on the forward stroke. This sequence will eliminate wire edges. To check your work, run the newly sharpened edge along the tip of a thumbnail; if it feels frictionless, the edge is ready. If you feel any roughness, retrace your steps in the process to a point that will let you correct the problem.

When the chisel eventually becomes dull again, you do not have to repeat all the steps. The lacquer is off, the face is lapped, all you have to do is touch up the bevel. Depending on the dullness of the chisel, this might mean using only your finest stone to rehone the micro-bevel. Usually it is faster to go back to a coarser stone (800x to 1200x), renew the primary bevel and put a new micro-bevel on the chisel. Then follow the sequence from that point on.

RUST NEVER SLEEPS

A key to preserving the sharpness of tools is the prevention of rust—not just the visible rust that noticeably pits a blade but the slight rusting that comes from testing a blade with your thumb or finger. Rust like this, although visible only under an electron microscope (see the photo on p. 23), is already causing deterioration of the keen edge.

A pitted blade edge. (Photo by Susan Kahn)

Where rust pits intersect the edge of the blade, you get a blade nick. Some old tools that have been allowed to pit deeply are hardly worth restoring. Unless the face of the tool can be brought to a mirror finish, the same as the bevel, you will continue to have problems when repeated sharpenings cause the receding bevel to encounter craters in the face.

WHEN TO RESHARPEN?

There are several ways to tell when you need to resharpen a chisel. One is when you notice a difference in use. If the wood seems to be getting harder, check the chisel. Another is to look at the edge under a good light. A sharp edge reflects no light. But the most usual indicator is when you see scratches on your finished work. You know immediately that you have a damaged edge.

Fixing nicked chisels If you have seriously nicked a chisel, you may have to remove a fair amount of steel to eliminate the nick. You can do this with a coarse bench stone, but you should be prepared to spend a fair amount of time at it. Even aggressive bench stones take quite a while to work past a nick. It is faster to use a wet grinder, a dry grinder or a belt sander. In the case of the last two, you have to be very careful not to burn the tool or draw the temper.

If you are using a belt sander or a dry wheel, set your bevel angle either with the platform of the tool rest or by setting the projection of your chisel from the edge of the rest. In either case, use a simple grinding jig, which you can make or buy. With a belt sander, use only a coarse belt (80x is fine). With a dry grinder, use a soft-bond, open-structure wheel (such as an A80H-8V, see pp. 37-39 for details). With either, use a light touch and check tool temperature often. Both cut quickly but can overheat an edge.

For a very deep nick, the best approach is to mark a line across the chisel using a square and marker pen and grind back to the line. I first grind the edge square, right back to the mark, then re-form the bevel. This lets you work a bit faster with less danger of burning the edge, since you get good heat dissipation from the blunt edge to the main body of the tool. Heat dissipates more slowly from a thin section.

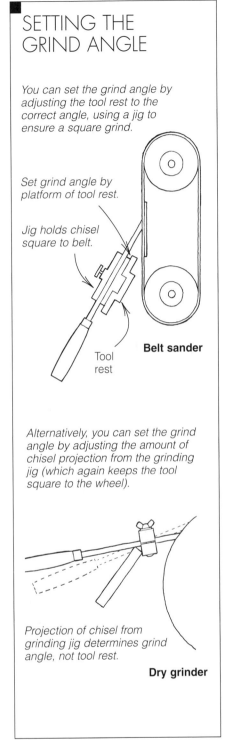

SETTING THE GRIND ANGLE

You can set the grind angle by adjusting the tool rest to the correct angle, using a jig to ensure a square grind.

Set grind angle by platform of tool rest.

Jig holds chisel square to belt.

Belt sander

Tool rest

Alternatively, you can set the grind angle by adjusting the amount of chisel projection from the grinding jig (which again keeps the tool square to the wheel).

Projection of chisel from grinding jig determines grind angle, not tool rest.

Dry grinder

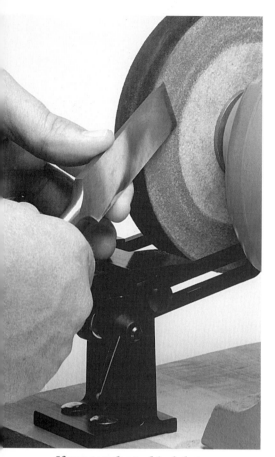

Do not try to grind material off too quickly. Check blade temperature frequently against the back of your hand, and when the blade starts to get warm cool it down by laying it on a slab of metal, which will act like a heat sink. This is better than dunking the tool in water (see the sidebar on p. 21). When you have formed the bevel, revert to your bench stones for the final steps.

BUFFING OR STROPPING CHISELS

Some woodworkers touch up their chisels between sharpenings on a felt buffing wheel or a leather belt on a belt sander; either would be charged with a buffing compound first.

There is nothing wrong with either system as a quick fix, but I recommend that you never buff the face of the chisel. Almost invariably you destroy the flatness. Similarly, you will find that you are not saving time at all if you round the bevel. I also recommend

If you touch up chisels between sharpenings on a felt buffing wheel, use only the side of the wheel to minimize bevel rounding.

using only the side of the felt wheel to minimize bevel rounding. The bevel rounding caused by a leather belt on a belt sander is negligible if good technique is used (i.e., honing only over the platen where the leather can flex the least, and honing only at a smal incremental angle increase). This method is all made even easier if a micro-finishing belt (see pp. 56-57) is used on the belt sander instead of a leather belt. There is no flexing, and the flat joins even eliminate bumping.

UTILITY BEVEL-EDGE CHISELS

Woodworkers who own only one style of chisels usually have bevel-edge chisels, the workhorses of the shop. This makes it a bit difficult to recommend sharpening angles, since the chisels will see use in all types of wood and in all activities from paring to mortising.

Usually a 25° bevel angle is adequate for these chisels, except in the smaller sizes. As you may have noticed, you will more frequently roll the edges on narrow chisels than on wide ones.

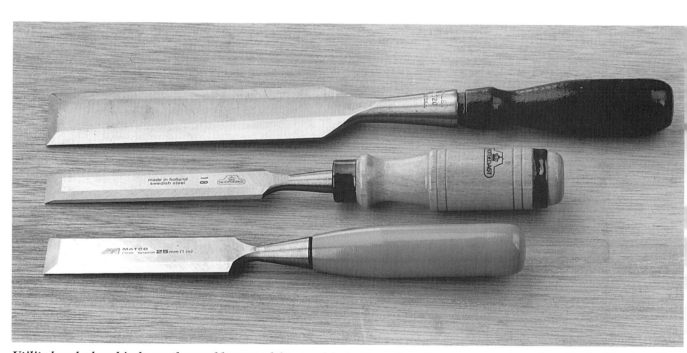

Utility bevel-edge chisels are the workhorses of the woodshop. At one time they were mostly socket chisels, like the old Stanley chisel shown at top. Now they tend to be tanged chisels, like the Dutch-made, Scandinavian style in the center or the ubiquitous plastic-handled type shown at bottom.

The reason for this is fairly straight-forward. Assume that you are going to do some light mortising with a 1-in. chisel and a ¼-in. chisel. If you use mallet blows with the same force on the ¼-in. chisel as on the 1-in. chisel, the ¼-in. chisel will be subjected to four times the deforming force as the 1-in. chisel (see Chapter 2). Since we all tend to forget that the force of mallet blows should be modified according to the width of chisel we are using, we frequently overstress narrow chisels. Accordingly, it is a good idea to put a higher bevel angle on narrower chisels (30° is appropriate). Such narrow chisels are seldom used for light paring so this steeper bevel angle is justified for edge retention.

If you have only one set of chisels you might even consider putting a bevel angle as low as 20° on the largest chisel, remembering that if it is used for any light mortising, the mallet blows should be light as well. Since the largest chisel is most frequently used for paring this will give you the greatest versatility in a single set of chisels. If you never use your bevel-edge chisels for mortising and you have other

chisels specifically for paring, you should be able to put a 25° bevel angle on all of them and be quite happy.

PARING CHISELS

Paring chisels are usually the same basic design as bevel-edge chisels, except that the blades tend to be a bit thinner and longer. Square-edge paring chisels are less common than bevel-edged ones but seem to be preferred by shipwrights. Possibly this is because shipwrights tended to use square-edge chisels in all of their other activities. Cranked-neck paring chisels (no longer common) are for use on large, flat surfaces where an offset neck is needed to prevent handle interference with the surface.

Since paring chisels are almost invariably used with hand pressure alone and not with a mallet, they are not subjected to the same forces as other chisels. In addition, as their name

implies, paring chisels are usually used for very light cuts. As a result, they can be sharpened at bevel angles of 20° or less. For very fine work, a 15° bevel angle is not unusual. Otherwise, the general sharpening procedures described at the beginning of the chapter apply.

For information on sharpening slicks, very large paring chisels used in timber work, see pp. 74-75.

MORTISE AND FIRMER CHISELS

Mortising is just about the toughest test of a chisel edge. Cutting end grain subjects the chisel edge to nearly three times the force of parallel-grain or cross-grain cutting. The bevel angle on a mortise chisel has to be more obtuse than on other types of chisels to withstand these forces. For softwoods, mortise chisels should have a 30° bevel angle; for hardwoods, a 35° bevel angle. These recommendations are averages only. The steel in your particular mortise chisels may let you get away with somewhat lower bevel angles, or it may be relatively brittle and

Paring chisels, shown in straight and cranked-neck designs, can be sharpened at relatively low bevel angles. Most people associate the term 'paring' with small, light chisels, yet there used to be much larger and heavier (but still slim) styles used in some trades—chisels like the shipwright's socket paring chisel shown at top.

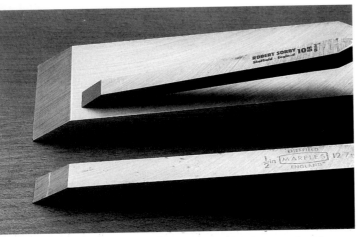

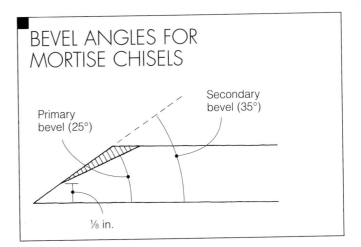

BEVEL ANGLES FOR MORTISE CHISELS

Primary bevel (25°)

Secondary bevel (35°)

⅛ in.

Mortise and firmer chisels require fairly steep bevel angles in order to withstand the force of cutting end grain.

ORIGINS OF THE MODIFIED TIP

For a long time after first modifying a mortise chisel for better penetration, I was quietly smug each time I used a modified chisel. I honestly thought that it was an original idea.

But when I was digging out some photographic samples for this book, I came across an old set of Greaves mortise chisels that I had bought many years ago because they were such good examples of their type. All of them still had their labels and were

little used. The largest one had a wired handle to contain a crack; the great weakness of that style was the design of the handle and the lack of a shock washer. The handles were almost guaranteed to split in use.

However, you might be able to see the modified tips on some of them and the generally low bevel angles on all of them. I have been much less smug since noticing this and much more concerned about my memory.

Greaves mortise chisels.

require somewhat higher angles. Your guide is edge failure; start at a low bevel angle and increase it only as much as required to prevent the edge from folding or chipping.

"Firmer" is a term used to describe utility chisels of sturdy build. They normally have square edges and since they are frequently used for mortising, they are lumped in here with the general recommendations for mortise chisels.

For speed of sharpening and best penetration, I recommend a primary bevel of 25° and a secondary bevel of 30° or 35°, as required, extending back to about ⅛ in. of blade thickness (see the drawing above). It is apparent that a chisel of this shape will penetrate more deeply than one that includes the hatched area. The wedging action is reduced.

The edge has a strong secondary-bevel angle extending well back; the only concern is the effect on rigidity. The reason mortise chisels are as thick as they are is only party to provide the rigidity needed to counteract the force. As the tip is deflected by the reactive force of the wood, a beefy blade is needed to keep the chisel from bowing and vibrating. But most mortise chisels are of deeper cross section than needed for rigidity. The extra depth is for alignment of the tool in the mortise. The minor modification of relieving the bevel angle detracts very little from overall blade rigidity; it is usually not noticeable in use.

If you are constantly working softwoods like clear pine, the extension of the secondary bevel can be reduced from 1/8 in. to as little as 1/16 in of blade thickness. In fact, with clear pine you can also reduce the tip angle to less than 30° with most chisels.

SQUARE AND UNSQUARE MORTISE CHISELS

Most mortise chisels sold today have a rectangular cross-section. Some, particularly those made in Germany, are tapered from the face to the back, sometimes as much as 1/16 in. in total. The chisel is tapered to reduce friction in the mortise and to allow minor directional changes as mortising progresses. Good work can be done with either style, and the choice is largely a question of personal preference.

Unfortunately, mortise chisels are among the worst made of any modern chisels. Manufacturers do not seem to realize what the critical aspects of a mortise chisel are, and it is common to find blade sides that are not straight and that form an angle greater than 90° with the face of the chisel. Neither condition is acceptable.

If you have a chisels with these defects, you have no choice but to correct the faults before you use them. You can use a belt sander or disc sander to remove the major portion of the metal and finish off by lapping on a bench stone.

Few people actually use mortise chisels today since there are so many other ways to remove most of the wood from a mortise that it is possible to dress out the remainder with just about any chisel. Given this reduced market, I do not expect to see mortise-chisel manufacturing improve in the near future.

HOW DESIGN FEATURES GET LOST

The first time I visited the Sorby factory in Sheffield, England, in the 1970s, I asked the works manager why they were the only manufacturer to round the back of the bevel on their mortise chisels. He looked at me quizzically, drew himself up and said something like, "We have been doing that, man and boy, for the 40 years that I've worked here." Although that was not the answer I was looking for, I dropped the subject.

Thinking about it weeks later, after I had returned to Canada, I realized that rounding the junction between the bevel and the blade back would make it easier to lever waste out of a mortise. That particular part of the chisel is used as a fulcrum in the process and rounding it would prevent the corner from digging in.

I should have said something to Sorby at the time because the next year their catalog showed all mortise chisels with a sharp intersection between the bevel and the back. A useful design feature had been lost because nobody knew why it was there.

The old-style Sorby mortise chisel, with rounded bevel back, is shown in front of a standard mortise chisel.

MORTISE CHISELS

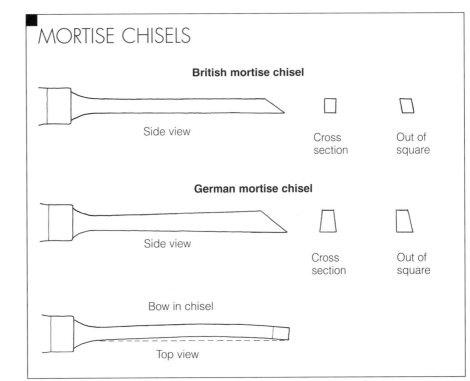

British mortise chisel

Side view

Cross section

Out of square

German mortise chisel

Side view

Cross section

Out of square

Bow in chisel

Top view

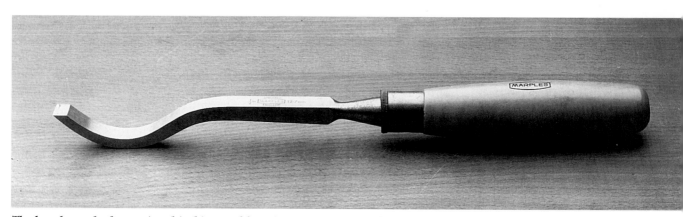

The bevel on a lock-mortise chisel is roughly in line with the axis of the handle.

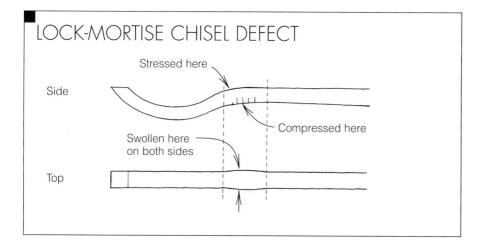

LOCK-MORTISE CHISEL DEFECT

Side

Stressed here

Compressed here

Swollen here
on both sides

Top

LOCK-MORTISE CHISELS

As the name implies, lock-mortise chisels are used for levering waste out of the deep mortises required to install door locks. They are essentially scraping chisels not cutting chisels and are usually ground and honed with the bevel approximately in line with the handle. Just like standard mortise chisels (and possibly for the same reason), lock-mortise chisels are almost invariably badly made.

They are usually made by bending square stock freehand. When you bend square stock, the steel is stretched on the outside of a curve and compressed on the inside of the curve. This causes a problem at the transition point from straight blade to curved blade. The sharp directional change creates two "hips" on the back of the chisel, and most manufacturers do not grind these off completely. Some manufacturers do not even seem to realize that the hips are a serious problem because they become the widest point on the chisel preventing it from entering the mortise past this point.

The hips can be ground off quickly on a belt sander or worried off on a coarse bench stone. This part of the chisel must be no wider than the face of the chisel. Whether or not you like using honing guides, this is one chisel that has to be sharpened freehand. It is easiest to clamp the chisel in a vise, bevel up, and hone the bevel in line with the axis of the handle. The actual bevel angle is not critical, it is the angle that the bevel makes with the handle that determines the chisel's effectiveness. Some lock-mortise chisels have quite a pronounced curve in them, while others have a relatively shallow curve. The latter will work deeper mortises.

SKEW CHISELS

Skew chisels are actually a variant form of paring chisels, though they are usually square-edged not bevel-edged. They are most effective in end-grain cuts and in paring the cheeks of tenons. Wooden-plane makers prized these chisels for working the beds of planes, since the square-sided skew would let them work next to the cheek without undercutting it, while at the same time avoiding the choppiness that could result from using a square-edged chisel on a plane bed. A skew chisel will not suddenly dig in, the way a square-end chisel will. For similar reasons skew chisels are ideal for paring the cheeks and shoulders of tenons. To understand their usefulness on tenon cheeks, refer to Chapter 2 on cross-grain cutting.

Skew chisels are usually sharpened with a bevel angle of 20° or less. Depending upon the equipment you have available, it can be a tricky process. Side-clamp honing guides are of no use with skew chisels, so you must either sharpen them freehand or use a top-clamp honing guide such as the General or Veritas guide (see the photo below). With either guide it is important that the cutting edge be exactly parallel to the transverse axis of

the guide. This is not as easy to achieve as you might think. It is simple with square-edge chisels because you can set the bevel angle first and then fine-tune the squareness afterward. With a skew chisel you have far more opportunity to go wrong. And this is one case where you do not want to solve the problem with applied geometry.

If you are using the Veritas honing guide and angle jig, you will find that the best way to set the honing guide on a skew is to have it on the blade loosely as you set the blade in the angle jig and then just release the honing guide. It will slide down the blade and automatically align itself correctly.

If you are using the General guide, concentrate on getting the cutting edge of the skew chisel exactly parallel to the front edge of the honing guide (90° to the path of travel) and then adjust the tilt angle as required.

Skew chisels, available in left- and right-hand pairs, are specifically adapted to cutting end grain.

With the skew chisel held in a top-clamp honing guide, keep the cutting edge parallel to the transverse axis of the guide as you hone back and forth on the stone. (Photo by Susan Kahn)

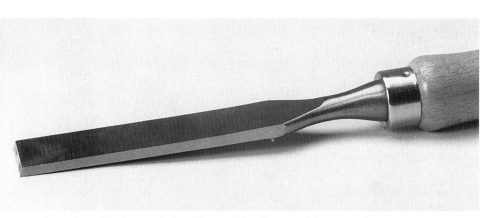

Scraping chisels, traditionally used in plane making, are sharpened at very high bevel angles, which increases control and prevents inadvertent digs in the work surface. (Photo by Susan Kahn)

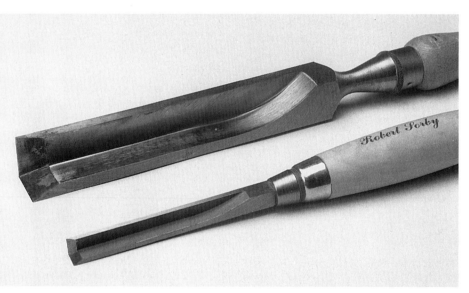

Corner chisels, shown here in 1-in. and ³⁄₈-in. sizes, are used to clean the corners in mortises. (Photo by Susan Kahn)

SCRAPING CHISELS

Scraping chisels are almost never used any more, but at one time they were used by plane makers to make fine-tuning cuts on plane beds. They are a fitting chisel for end-grain work. Scraping chisels were traditionally sharpened at a 90° bevel angle, but looking at the research results of Dr. Norman Franz (Appendix 1) an argument could be made that they should have been sharpened at a 70° or 75° bevel angle. Either way, a high bevel angle increases control and ensures that there are no inadvertent digs. Maybe these forgotten tools will enjoy a resurgence.

CORNER CHISELS

A corner chisel is used to clean the corners in mortises or hinge gains. Large ones, usually 1 in. on a side, were very popular with wheelwrights, who called them "bruzzes."

These are truly the chisels from hell when it comes to sharpening. I used to think that sharpening a V-tool used in carving was difficult, but it is child's play compared to doing a first-class job on a corner chisel.

The first thing you have to realize with the corner chisel is that it has two faces not one. Both have to be lapped until decently flat and then polished. Turning your attention to the inside bevels of the chisel you will normally find one of two things. If it is a new chisel, the manufacturer will probably not have risked sharpening it well and you will find a square edge, but one that is very blunt. If it is a used corner chisel, the edge is likely to be fairly keen but it will probably neither be straight nor at 90° to the spine of the chisel. The first thing you will have to do in this instance is grind the end of the chisel square. When this is done you will now have reached the state where the used chisel will be exactly the same as the new chisel, a good square end but blunt.

For reasons known only to the world's corner-chisel manufacturers, I have always found corner chisels to be fairly soft, almost never harder than Rc58. Many antique ones are as low as Rc54 or Rc55. This means that they can readily be filed, and a file is unquestionably my first choice of sharpening tool for a corner chisel. You have the necessary control to sneak up on a sharp edge without overshooting it.

You should use a safe-edge file (see pp. 55-56) for the job; otherwise, you will cause yourself some problems in the corner. Although an auger-bit file has one end where the edges are safe and another end where the faces are safe, it is a bit small for most corner chisels. I recommend that you grind the edge off a 6-in. or 8-in. mill file and use it instead. For a chisel too hard for a steel file, you can use a diamond file. You'll almost certainly have to do some work on the edge of the diamond file, because the file face seldom comes out to the edge of the supporting backing plate. You'll have to dress the backing plate flush with the file edge.

A 30° bevel angle is fairly standard with corner chisels, though you will find antique ones with higher bevel angles. I suspect that this was partly an insurance policy on the part of the original owner who wanted to be absolutely sure that an edge didn't fold in use, and partly the tendency to increase bevel angles to save sharpening time. Given the nature of use of a corner chisel, it would seem that 30° should be about appropriate. I have used them only in softwood and 30° was fine. In testy woods like oak, 35° might be necessary.

Once the inside of the chisel is filed, it should be honed with a file-shaped stone, as fine as can be found. To finish off the tool, put some green buffing compound on the face of a stick and use it on the two bevels just as you would a file.

It is important to keep the two cutting edges at 90° to the spine of the tool. If they are swept backward, the heel of the tool will constantly be forcing its way through wood that is not yet free to be released. With the wings square or with slight forward sweep the wood will release freely. But realistically, if you get two straight edges that cut well, just leave the thing alone. Be glad you didn't get a hook in the corner.

Use a safe-edge mill file to sharpen the inside bevels of a corner chisel. (Photo by Susan Kahn)

JAPANESE CHISELS

The traditional Japanese chisel is quite different from its Western counterpart. First, it is a laminated chisel with a very hard steel face (Rc62 to Rc64) laminated to a soft-steel or wrought-iron back. The use of very hard steel requires the soft back both for the damping qualities and to provide an element of toughness that the steel face alone would not have. Second, a traditional Japanese chisel has a hollow face for faster sharpening and to make it easier to maintain flatness. Japanese chisels are sharpened in the same manner as Western-style chisels but normally require higher bevel angles to avoid edge chipping.

Most traditional construction, cabinetry and interior trim in Japan is with softwoods. To avoid crushing of the fibers it is necessary to have particularly keen chisels, but there is no great toughness requirement since they are subjected to little distortional force from the softwood. The use of a very hard high-carbon blade makes sense

Traditional Japanese chisels, which have a hollow face (left), are usually sharpened at higher bevel angles than Western chisels. (Photo by Susan Kahn)

THE STEEL USED IN JAPANESE CHISELS

When people talk about traditional Japanese chisels, you may hear them say that the chisels were made from "white" steel or "blue" steel. Alternatively, they might say "white paper" steel or "blue paper" steel. These are not technical standards but refer to the color of the labels that Hitachi uses for some of their commercial grade steels. Among Japanese manufacturers, these become "Blue Label #1," "White Label #2," and so on. Both types are high-carbon steels in the 1.0% to 1.2% carbon range alloyed with silica (0.1% to 0.2%) and man-ganese (0.2% to 0.3%). The "blue paper" steels also have chromium (0.2% to 0.5%) and tungsten (1.0% to 1.5%) added for toughness. Japanese manufacturers routinely produce chisels from these steels in the Rc62 to Rc64 range, substantially harder than any Western-style chisels.

For the soft-steel back, they use a very low carbon steel (0.06%) with a bit of silica and manganese (both at 0.2%). The highest-quality tools still use wrought iron from old anchors or anchor chain as the backing material.

---

under these circumstances. The high-carbon steel will take a very fine edge if the brittleness can be tolerated.

If you intend using traditional Japanese chisels for Western hard-woods you are going to have to use higher bevel angles than you are accustomed to. For most purposes, an extra 5° should be sufficient, but for mortise chisels you may need as much as 10° more than you would use on a Western chisel.

It is perfectly acceptable to use the same micro-bevel sharpening system that you use normally, but I would not recommend relieving the back half of the bevel as earlier recommended for Western chisels (see p. 62). Neither should you use a modified tip on the mortise chisel, unless you make sure that the lowered angle is well back into the soft steel. Most Japanese chisels that I have used will take a wonderfully keen edge, but they are far more prone to edge crumbling than other alloys. Woods of inconsistent hardness (such as end-grain oak) can cause very

rapid edge degradation. A pin knot can take out a piece large enough to make you weep.

With successive sharpenings the hollow face is going to get ever closer to the cutting edge. You do not want it to get much closer than ⅛ in. or you risk weakening the edge, particularly on a mortise chisel. You have two choices. You can lap the back of the chisel to effect the necessary recession of the hollowness, or you can try the Japanese method of tapping it out with a hammer. I use the lapping method for two reasons. First, I have not found the hollow face to be a discernible advantage in use and therefore am not concerned about reduction of the hollow through lapping. Second, I cannot bring myself to use a steel hammer on a chisel blade because I am convinced that I would do more evil than good.

But for those of you who are seized with the karma of Japanese tools, I can recommend two excellent books that will explain the process of hammering out the hollow: *Japanese Woodworking Tools: Their Tradition, Spirit and Use* by Toshio Odate (The Taunton Press, 1984) and *Japanese Woodworking Tools: Selection, Care and Use* by Henry Lanz (Sterling, 1985).

SLICKS

A slick is a very large paring chisel that is always used two handed, usually with shoulder pressure as well (see the top photo on the facing page). Traditionally, a slick was held much like a lance, the primary difference being that the butt of the handle nestled just below the shoulder and the tool was guided with the off hand. Because slicks are used for paring cuts, they almost never have a bevel angle higher than about 25°.

Slicks are sharpened in two different ways. For dovetail work in logs where the paring is almost invariably with the grain, the slick is sharpened with a square tip. For more diverse work, which could include lap joints and notches, a slick is usually sharpened so that there is a slight crown to the edge. On the 3-in. slick shown in the bottom photo at left on the facing page, the blade is crowned nearly ⅛-in. at the center. The amount of crown can vary according to personal taste.

There are two reasons for crowning the edge. First, a slight crown makes the slick versatile in use. Light paring cuts can be made that use nearly the entire width of the blade but still clip the end fibers, preventing any splintering and leaving a very smooth finish. Second, a crown makes the tool more control-lable. The crown tends to keep the blade cutting directly in line with the applied force. It is much like a shallow gouge; it tends to maintain a cutting line through self-centering forces.

Most slicks (except Japanese ones) are soft enough to be filed. It is fairly straightforward to shape the edge of a slick with a file, but I strongly recommend that you file from the back of the bevel toward the front. You end up with a wire edge, which you could avoid if you filed in the opposite direction, but you also get to keep ten fingers intact.

Slicks for paring lap joints and notches are typically ground with a crowned blade. (Photo by Susan Kahn)

A crowned blade leaves a very smooth finish when cutting cross grain.

To file a regular crown I recommend filing the edge squarely back to a marked line, then filing the bevel until the edge is sharp. It is easier to achieve a fair curve the first time this way, rather than trying to strike the bevel and curve simultaneously.

The square-tipped slick would be sharpened in basically the same manner as any square-ended chisel. The only difference would be that it might be easier to bring the stone to the tool rather than vice versa. You can work the edge from whatever position you feel most comfortable. My preference is to have the edge of the tool just sticking over the edge of the bench and use the stone in a rotary motion.

Do not attempt to flatten the entire face of the slick. The vast majority of older slicks actually had a slight bend (or belly) in the blade about halfway along. Whether this was done intentionally or accidentally is uncertain. There is no question that some relief is needed for a slick to function easily, but the few users still around tend to be a bit vague on the reasons.

In any event, you will probably find it useful to sharpen your slick with a slight crown to the edge. The dead-square tip can be difficult to control, but once you get accustomed to using a slick you will be pleasantly surprised at how quickly your skill develops and by the versatility of the tool in any large-timber work.

CHAPTER 7
PLANES

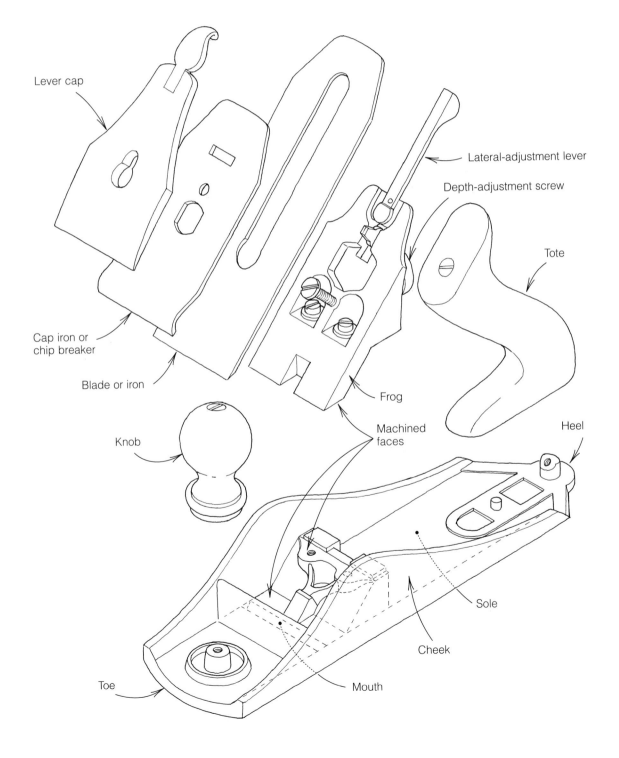

Lever cap

Lateral-adjustment lever

Depth-adjustment screw

Tote

Cap iron or
chip breaker

Blade or iron

Frog

Knob

Machined
faces

Heel

Sole

Cheek

Toe

Mouth

I doubt that there is any hand tool more satisfying to use than a finely tuned plane with a perfectly sharpened blade. The ease of use, the consistency of results and the general feeling of craftsmanship generated create one of the magic moments of woodworking.

Sharpening the blade perfectly is a relatively easy task compared to the fine tuning. The production process that is used for most bench planes today seldom creates an end product that is ready for use even if it came with a sharp blade—which it usually does not! When you buy a new plane you are usually getting a collection of parts that can only be converted into a fully functioning tool with a fair amount of thought and a substantial amount of work.

TUNING A PLANE

There is little point in sharpening the blade well if it is not going to be seated well on the bed of the plane or clamped in place in a manner that will minimize flexing of the iron in use. A quick checklist to put the plane in reasonable working order would include the following steps:

1. Strip off the lacquer First, remove any lacquer from the plane blade, the sole of the plane and the sides. It is only there to make the plane look good and prevent it from rusting until it is sold. After stripping, you can wax any parts you won't be abrading. The wax will prevent rusting and reduce friction.

2. True the sole With the blade in the plane and the lever cap in position tightened for use, lap the sole of the plane until it is flat. Lapping can be done in a variety of ways, but the most practical method in a small shop is to use silicon-carbide grit on a cast-iron lapping plate, or on a fairly firm plastic sheet such as Mylar fixed to a sheet of plate glass with spray adhesive.

Moving the plane in a figure-eight or circular motion, lap the sole with silicon-carbide grit on a sheet of Mylar-faced plate glass.

LAPPING THE SOLE

When the sole of a plane body is being milled (or ground), the plane is clamped on the cheeks. The clamping pressure causes the sole to arch outward. When the clamps are released after machining, the finished sole is almost invariably hollow. A bit of hollowness is of no great concern, but there are three places where you must be certain that the sole is dead flat after lapping—both tips and the front of the mouth, as shown below.

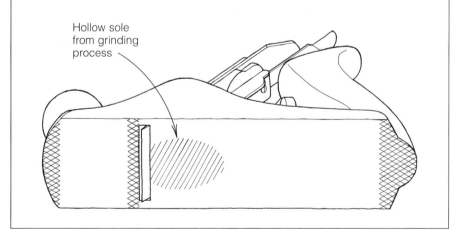

Hollow sole from grinding process

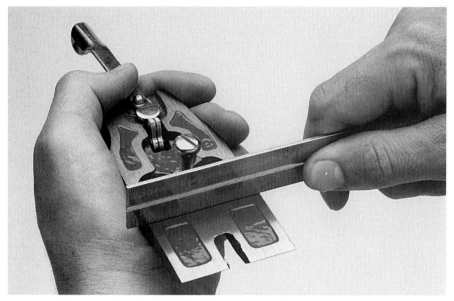

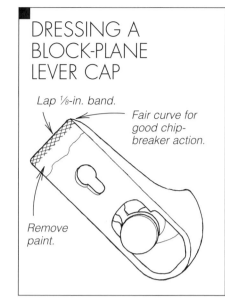

Lap ⅛-in. band.

Fair curve for
good chip-
breaker action.

Remove
paint.

Use a straightedge to check that the machined surfaces of the frog are true.
Check diagonally as well as transversely. (Photo by Susan Kahn)

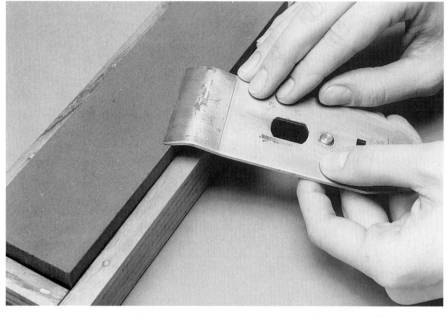

Dress the tip of the cap iron on a stone, with the opposite end of the iron held
about ⅛ in. below the level of the stone.

The dressed cap iron should fit tightly across the width of the plane blade.

Start with about a 90 grit and do not move to a finer grit until the sole of the plane is flat in all critical areas. (Change to a finer grit only to get the degree of smoothness that you want on the plane's bottom.) Use a slightly circular or figure-eight motion in lapping to keep the grit evenly distributed under the sole. Take care to keep the pressure directly down on the plane with no tendency to tilt it.

Having the blade and lever cap in position and tightened introduces the permanent forces that the plane will experience. With these forces in place as the sole is being trued, you have some assurance that the sole will be flat when you really need it to be flat, that is, in use.

3. True the bed The bed is everything that the blade rests on, including the frog and the machined surface adjacent to the mouth. The machined surfaces of the bed should be in a single plane from top to bottom and side to side. This may require some adjustment of the frog (if it is adjustable) or filing of the bed, with frequent test fittings of the blade using machinist's dye or carbon paper to indicate high spots.

This is exactly the same process that dentists use to test and then modify a new filling to suit your bite. With a plane, f you paint the blade with machinist's dye, the dye will transfer to the high points of the bed when the blade is pressed into position. If you use carbon paper, put the carbon side next to the bed before positioning the blade.

4. Dress the lever cap The first ⅛ in. or so of the lever-cap bottom should be lapped on a stone so that it will create a single line of contact with the cap iron, or with the blade itself on those models that do not have a cap iron. This is important since the lever cap has to fit well to tension the blade in the plane, minimizing chatter in use.

On a block plane, the lever cap also serves as a cap iron and should fit snugly to the blade across its entire width. To dress it, scrape the paint off the last ¼ in. of the bottom of the lever cap near the tip and lap a band about ⅛ in. wide on it (see the drawing on the facing page). You should also fair the curved tip so that shavings will slide over it smoothly.

5. Dress the cap iron The cap iron, or "chip breaker," should be dressed across its width at an angle that is just slightly less than one that would make it parallel to the plane blade. This will ensure that the nose of the cap iron fits tightly to the plane blade; if there are any gaps, shavings will inevitably lodge between the cap iron and the blade, choking the mouth of the plane. This dressing can easily be done freehand (see the middle photo on the facing page).

As long as the unground tip of the cap iron is held ⅛ in. or more below the level of the stone being used to shape the tip, you will have the right geometry to give you a tight fit. After the cap iron has been dressed and fastened to the blade, it should meet the blade all across the tip and be slightly canted away from it toward the arch (see the bottom photo on the facing page).

SHARPENING THE BLADE

Just as you would do with a chisel (see p. 59), the first thing you do with a plane blade is remove any lacquer or paint and lap the face of the blade. Lapping can be done on a medium stone (800x to 1200x) followed by a fine stone (4000x to 8000x). Unlike when lapping a chisel, you do not have to be concerned about the entire blade being flat at the perimeter. Any slight hollowness or belly in a plane blade is compensated for by the clamping pressures between the lever cap and the blade. Your primary concern is just to get a good smooth surface on the face of the blade near the cutting edge before turning your attention to the bevel.

After choosing the bevel angle (see the discussion of specific types of planes for recommended angles), I strongly recommend that you use a honing guide (see pp. 51-53) for the bevel-shaping process. The guide lets you apply greater pressure while holding the exact angle you want, and you get better results in less time than with freehand honing.

As with chisels, I recommend putting the basic bevel on the blade at 1° less than the micro-bevel (see p. 62). Basic shaping on an 800x stone and finishing on a 4000x to 8000x is suitable.

CHOOSING A BEVEL ANGLE

Choosing a bevel angle is a nearly limitless discussion area because of the nearly limitless combination of plane types, wood types and cutting processes. Many aspects will be covered under the various plane types detailed in the rest of this chapter, but the first major division is between those planes where the blade is used bevel down (the vast majority, including all bench planes) and those planes where the blade is bevel up—the block planes and low-angle special-purpose planes.

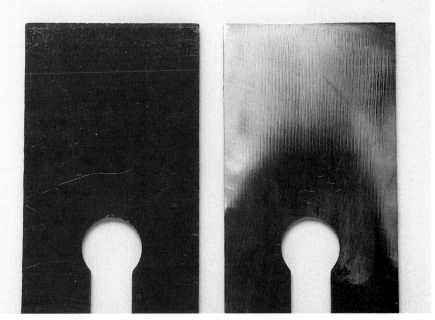

A plane blade before (left) and after lapping (right). (Photo by Susan Kahn)

Bevel-down planes as a group represent an exception to the general rule that blades should be sharpened at the lowest angle consistent with edge retention, because the bevel angle has no bearing on the cutting angle. A sturdy edge is wanted, and a basic grind angle of 30° to 35° will give you good blade stability and the least chatter.

Turning to blade shape, the general rule of thumb for standard bench planes (#3 to #8) is that the blade be sharpened square across unless you intend to be working wood wider than the blade; in this case, you would either round the blade corners, crown the blade or do a bit of both, depending on your intended use.

SMOOTHING PLANES (#3, #4½, #5½)

The #3 smoothing plane is usually used for the final smoothing of large flat surfaces. It is not used to take off much material, so it should be set for a very fine shaving. You want to the corners of the blade to be slightly rounded, so that overlapping passes of slightly different height will not have a distinct overlap line nor will you get any fiber tearing as would be the case with a square-edge blade.

Whether or not you use a honing guide, it is a fairly simple matter to put a straight basic bevel on a smoothing-plane blade and then bias the process first to one corner and then to the other to round off the last ⅛ in. or ¼ in. of blade. The rounding does not have to be substantial, since the plane will be used only for very light finishing cuts.

The #4½ and #5½ are planes designed for hogging off wood in the smoothing process. In normal use it is not enough to just round the corners of these blades, the entire blade should be crowned by 1/32 in. to 1/16 in. This can be done with a honing guide putting "English" on one side and then the other, but it can be difficult to get enough curvature this way. One easy solution is to keep a worn stone specifically for sharpening such blades. Such an out-of-true stone can be used only for the bevels and never for lapping. A better alternative is to use a simple jig to grind the crown, as shown in the sidebar on the facing page.

An adjustable mouth is desirable in any plane, but particularly in smoothing planes. The plane at top, of current German production, has a sliding insert in front of the mouth. The old smooth plane in the middle has an adjustable nosepiece much like modern block planes. The steel plane at bottom relies on a movable frog to open or close the mouth.

BENCH PLANES

Virtually all bevel-down planes have bed angles of 45° or 50°. In the areas of greater specialization, 45° bed angles are commonly used for soft-woods and 50° beds for hardwoods. The bed angle is not significant to the choice of bevel angle in either case. Anything between 30° and 35° is quite acceptable. If you go much lower than 30° you encourage blade chatter; if you go much higher than 35° any wear dulls the blade much faster, but, more significantly, you could reduce the relief angle unacceptably, particularly on planes with a 45° bed.

BLADE-EDGE SHAPE

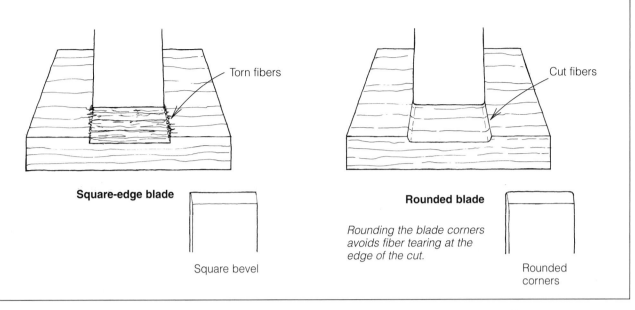

Square-edge blade

Torn fibers

Square bevel

Rounded blade

Cut fibers

Rounding the blade corners avoids fiber tearing at the edge of the cut.

Rounded corners

GRINDING A CROWN ON A BLADE

There are many ways to grind a crown on a blade. The jig shown here works with a dry grinder or belt sander. Using thin wood as a table extender, drill holes in it as required and use another piece of wood as a rotating arm. With the plane blade attached to the rotating arm with double-faced tape, you can select the amount of crown you want on a blade by picking a suitable point of rotation. About 7-in. radius is fine for a #4½ or #5½ plane blade. For fine adjustment, you can make the rotating arm adjustable in length.

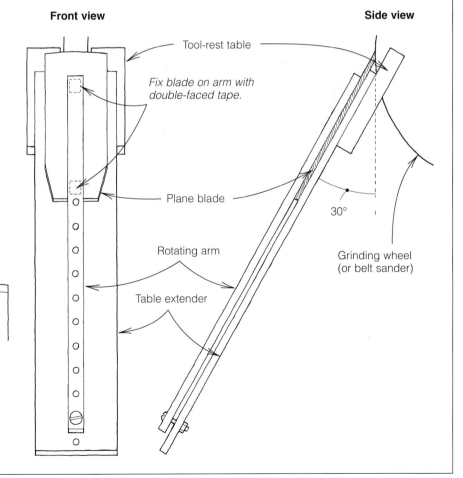

Front view

Tool-rest table

Fix blade on arm with double-faced tape.

Plane blade

Rotating arm

Table extender

Crowned blade

Side view

30°

Grinding wheel (or belt sander)

A scrub plane has a convex-shaped blade for removal of large amounts of stock in a relatively short time.

SCRUB PLANE

The scrub plane is the very roughest of the smoothing planes and is used for major stock removal. The blade comes with quite a sharply curved edge, which is fairly easy to maintain using exactly the same principle described in the sidebar on p. 81 (only in this instance a slightly modified jig would be necessary to hold the blade farther up). The grind radius can be as little as 1½ in.

JACK PLANES, JOINTER PLANES AND OTHERS (#5, #6, #7 AND #8)

Most woodworkers use these larger planes (jack, fore, jointer, trying and panel planes) only for working the edge of stock, in which case the blade can be ground and honed perfectly square. For use on surfaces wider than the plane, you would ease the corners of the blade as described under smoothing planes.

A GUIDE TO PLANE NAMES

Planes have many names, but a rough guide by length of plane is: 7 in. to 10 in.—smoothing plane; 12 in. to 18 in.—jack or fore plane; 20 in. and above—jointer or trying plane.

One exception to this structure is the type of plane made popular by Spiers and Norris in England (much like the plane shown second from bottom in the photo at right). These finely made planes, which invariably have steel bodies with wood infill, were used for work of high accuracy. Sized from 14 in. to 18 in., they are universally known as panel planes.

From top to bottom, a Bailey #30 jointer, a Stanley #7 jointer, a 16-in. craftsman-made panel plane and a Record #05 jack.

BLOCK PLANES

Whereas bench planes are generally used with the grain, the block plane was designed to work end grain. Today it is used for all types of cuts, but its name comes from its original use in dressing the top of butchers' blocks. As the various ways to shape the blade are discussed below, keep in mind that the recommendations are aimed at effective end-grain cutting.

Block planes provide an opportunity for some very innovative sharpening, but they are probably among the worst-made planes on the market today. For example, of the four block planes made by Record and Stanley (see the photo at right), only the Record #09½ has a lever cap that is long enough. Since block planes do not have cap irons, the lever cap has to do double duty whenever a cap iron would be desirable—usually only for face- or edge-grain cutting with a standard block plane; a cap iron is not needed when cutting end grain. Because these planes have only a narrow bed lip and a frog post for the blade to rest on, it is desirable that the lever cap extend at least to a point above the bed lip; otherwise, it will be pressing on an unsupported section of the blade.

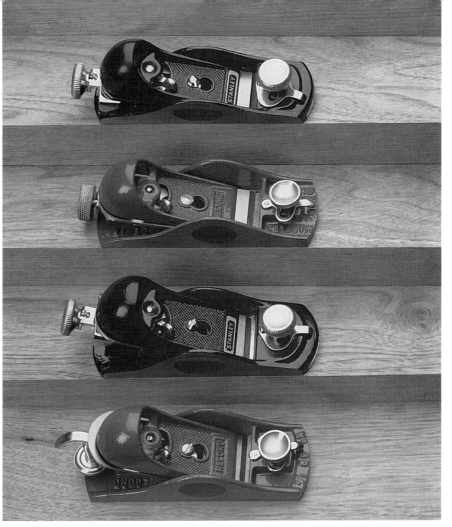

From top to bottom, the Stanley #60, the Record #060½ (both low-angle block planes), the Stanley #9½ and the Record #09½ (both standard block planes). Only the Record #09½ has a lever cap that is long enough, and then just barely. It would be better if the lever cap were ⅛ in. longer.

LOWERING THE BED ANGLE ON A BLOCK PLANE

If you have a short lever cap on your block plane, it will apply pressure behind the machined portion of the bed causing the end of the blade to be lifted away from the bed. To reduce blade chatter caused by this flaw, you have to lower the bed angle so that the blade rests on the bed at the mouth, not ¼ in. back of the mouth. To dress the bed, strip the plane (removing the adjustable nosepiece) and file the bed, letting the file pass through the open mouth and using the frog post as a guide since it is several degrees below the blade line on all modern block planes. (The low post is another flaw, but at least it works in your favor for this process.)

If you find it too difficult to get even seating of the tensioned blade along the entire bed, you can relieve just the back part of the bed so that the blade only touches at the mouth. That is still better than the condition you are correcting.

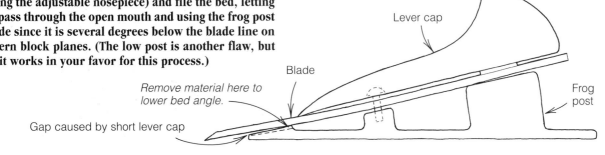

Lever cap

Blade

Remove material here to lower bed angle.

Gap caused by short lever cap

Frog post

The lever caps on both of the Stanley block planes are about ¼ in. short of what they should be, and the lever cap on the Record #060½ is nearly ½ in. short. To compensate for this, you should lower the bed angle by 1° or 2° to ensure that the pressure of the short lever cap does not cause the blade to arch away from the front of the bed (see the sidebar on p. 83). Assuming that you have done that and all the other necessary tune-up procedures, you can turn your attention to the blade.

BEVEL ANGLES

The standard block plane (#9½) has a bed angle of 20°. Since the blade is used bevel up, if we put a standard 25° bevel on the blade, we will end up with a cutting angle of 45°. This just happens to be the same cutting angle that we have for a smoothing plane, which has a bed angle of 45° but where the blade is used bevel down. So when you sharpen the blade of your standard block plane at 25°, you produce what is in essence a smaller smoothing plane.

But there is nothing to say that you can't put two bevels on a plane blade. You can easily grind and hone a 15° bevel on the blade and then put a 10° back bevel on the face of the blade (as shown in the top drawing at right). This would still leave you with a 25° included angle, but you would now have reduced your cutting angle from 45° to 35°. You are still left with a 10° relief angle, which is perfectly adequate for block-plane use.

Possibly more significant, you have sharpened the blade of your standard block plane in a manner that will give you a lower cutting angle than someone who sharpens a low-angle block plane in a standard fashion (12° bed angle plus 25° bevel, a total of 37°).

All of this dazzling footwork with bevel angles now raises the question, "Why do we bother with a low-angle block plane?" It is a good question. The answer is that lower bed angles not only let you use lower cutting angles but they also align the blade more closely with the direction of cut, thereby minimizing chatter. The lower you make the bed angle, the closer you approach the function of a chisel, which does not chatter.

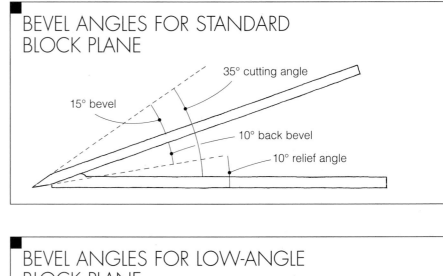

BEVEL ANGLES FOR STANDARD BLOCK PLANE

35° cutting angle
15° bevel
10° back bevel
10° relief angle

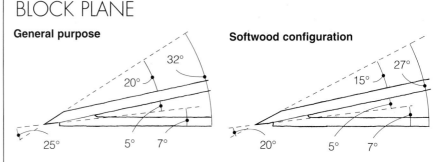

BEVEL ANGLES FOR LOW-ANGLE BLOCK PLANE

General purpose
32°
20°
25° 5° 7°

Softwood configuration
27°
15°
20° 5° 7°

In practice, whether or not you get chatter with a low-angle block plane depends almost entirely on the fit of the blade to the bed and how well you can tension your blade with the lever cap. A well-tuned standard block plane will chatter less on end grain than a low-angle plane with a blade just as sharp but that has not otherwise been tuned. In my view, once the blade is clamped in position properly with a lever cap of the right length, bed angles become a secondary consideration; cutting angles remain significant.

Given the curious state of block-plane production today, I would look first for a block plane that can be tensioned properly (e.g., a Record #09½), get an extra blade, and then have one

blade sharpened for regular block-plane use and the other blade sharpened for low-angle use.

LOW-ANGLE BLOCK PLANES

Having undermined the argument for having a low-angle block plane, let's take a look at them anyway. As explained in Chapter 2, you want the lowest possible cutting angle when you are working end grain. One aspect of cutting end grain is that the lighter the cut you make, the lower the relief angle required. This is fairly straightforward because the lighter cut causes less fiber distortion and therefore less springback.

So for fine trimming work on end grain (where you are not going to be taking heavy cuts), I would recommend that you put a 20° bevel on the blade and a 5° back bevel (see the drawing at left above). This will give you a 32° cutting angle. For working softwoods only, you can change this even more. You can put a 15° bevel on the blade and a 5° back bevel (see the drawing at right above). But if you do this and nadvertently use the plane on end-grain oak, you can expect to put some marvelous serrations in your blade.

It is difficult to be definitive about many of these bevel angles. Some people never skew a block plane in use; other people always skew it. If you normally use a block plane in a skewed position, you can get away with lower bevel angles. If you are always working clear pine, you can get away with very low bevel angles. Only you know which wood you will be working and how you will be working it. Experience will tell you what you can and cannot do. All I can do here is provide you with a rough road map.

In all of the block-plane drawings I have shown fairly long back bevels. This was done only to make the illustrations clearer. The back bevels should be very short, only enough to give you the edge strength that is required. In general, this means that a back bevel from 1/64 in. to 1/32 in. is ample. If you make the back bevels too long, they start to interfere with the fit of the blade in the plane.

By now you should also have realized that there is a strong argument for low-angle block planes. Not only can you get the total cutting angle as low as 27° (which is approaching the cutting angle of a chisel), but a block plane is far easier to use in a skewed position than is a chisel. If you then skew a block plane with a 27° cutting angle, you can drop the effective cutting angle further—to 20° at 45° of skew, and 14° at 60° of skew.

Whether or not you do any or all of the things suggested here is almost incidental to my purpose. What is particularly important is that you become comfortable with the principles involved so that you can tune your planes and shape their blades to suit your requirements and your practices.

Blades in planes like the Stanley #99 side rabbet (left) and the Stanley #140 block plane (right) are among the most difficult to sharpen accurately.

SPECIAL-PURPOSE PLANES

Although modern woodworkers are most familiar with the standard bench and block planes, earlier woodworkers had a great variety of special-purpose planes at their disposal. Many of these planes have been supplanted by electrical routers (and indeed some are no longer in production), but they all present some interesting sharpening dilemmas.

SKEW-TIPPED BLADES

The various skew-tipped blades, such as from the Stanley side-rabbet planes (#79, #98 or #99) and the #140 block plane, are sharpened in essentially the same manner as skew chisels (see p. 71).

The need to maintain an accurate skew angle is paramount in a plane such as the #140, because there is very little room to move the blade laterally on the bed in order to adjust for any errors in sharpening angle. The complicating factor with this plane is that the blade corner must be flush with the edge of the body to perform the rabbeting function properly.

The same is true of any of the Stanley side rabbets, but these are even more difficult to adjust because the bed angle is only about 7°. Add to this the fact that there is virtually no lateral adjustment possible because the blade runs in a machined slot and you have one of the toughest sharpening problems of any plane blade.

Since both of these styles have bevel-up blades, they are sharpened at the lowest angle consistent with the wood being worked. You will note from the photo above that the #99 side rabbet has the extra wrinkles of having the blade docked at two places on the corner as well.

To anyone who does not own a plane like these it is not immediately apparent why such planes should present problems. But low bed angles always present adjustment problems because the lower the bed angle, the greater the rotation of the blade on the bed to change depth of cut from one side of the blade to the other. If you combine this with the further limiting factor of having to have the very tip of the blade always flush with the side of the plane, you find that almost all maneuvering room has been eliminated.

Panel-raising planes Panel-raising planes usually have a double-ground edge. These should be treated essentially like two different blades, with each section sharpened separately and then the junction left crisp or slightly rounded as preferred. It is essential that you not change the length of either bevel to ensure that the blade continues to match the plane sole.

BULLNOSE AND SHOULDER PLANES

Bullnose planes, shoulder planes and standard rabbet planes have blades exactly the same width as the sole. They also usually have fairly low bed angles and limited lateral adjustment. This combination of factors makes it mandatory that these blades be sharpened perfectly square across the front.

Once again, a honing guide makes it much easier to keep these blades square. When you put such a blade in a honing guide and have it set at the correct angle (which involves most of the same considerations as block planes), you should take one or two strokes on the stone and then check whether or not your honing band is of equal width across the bevel. If it is not, you should adjust blade alignment and take another couple of strokes. By such a process, you get the blade perfectly square in the guide.

With a standard bench plane like a #4, you can be off-square by as much as several degrees and still compensate for it by lateral adjustment of the blade in the plane body. This is not the case with the blade of a shoulder plane. If such a blade gets seriously off-square, the best thing you can do is grind it square across the front and then restrike your bevel (see the drawing at left). In such a case, you now watch to be sure that the bevel being created is exactly parallel to the face of the blade. The easiest way to check this is by watching the line of light at the tip of the blade. What starts out as a wedge shape becomes a narrow rectangle if you hone properly and finally disappears as you come to a sharp edge.

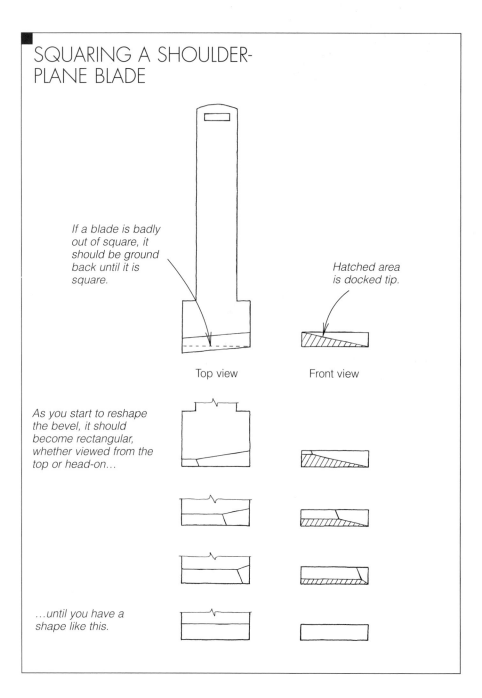

SQUARING A SHOULDER-PLANE BLADE

If a blade is badly out of square, it should be ground back until it is square.

Hatched area is docked tip.

Top view   Front view

As you start to reshape the bevel, it should become rectangular, whether viewed from the top or head-on...

...until you have a shape like this.

ROUTER PLANES

Router planes have largely been supplanted by electrical routers, but they are still used for some types of inletting and restoration work.

Router planes usually come with a square-tipped blade and sometimes with an additional spear-point blade. Both blades must be honed freehand. Router blades are set at a slight angle to the stem in order to give them the necessary relief angle. The blade should be lapped on the flat of the foot, and then the bevel is honed freehand. This is done most easily by letting the blade post overhang the edge of the stone, using one hand to move the blade back and forth and a finger of the other hand to hold the bevel in contact with the stone. Router-plane blades are actually quite forgiving and will tolerate minor variations in geometry without causing large problems in use.

A standard router plane with a spear-point cutter. The plane should also come with one or more square-tipped cutters.

MOLDING PLANES

Molding planes are little used today, both because of the change in the nature of house trim and the advent of routers and ready-made molding. If you have a molding plane, the blade should be sharpened the first time by honing the entire profile bevel with shaped stones and then lapping the face of the cutter. How you perform subsequent sharpenings depends on how long you want your cutter to last.

It can be a tricky business to hone the bevel of a molding cutter. It is far simpler just to lap the face of the blade when you wish to restore the edge. The difficulty with the latter approach is that you make the blades progressively thinner with each lapping. For most users, this thinning process is insignificant since the cutters will not be used that often. For someone dedicated to the use of molding planes on a frequent and long-term basis, honing the bevel each time rather than lapping the face will give longer life to the blade.

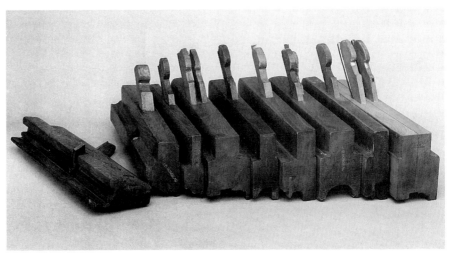

Molding planes like these filled the bottom of carpenters' tool chests before the invention of combination planes.

If you choose this route, you will find that you can hone many of the blades on a molding made by the blade. Just rub chromium-oxide honing compound on the molding and draw the blade along it. This technique works only for the blades with straight bevels. For blades such as ogees or ovolos, you will have to modify the molding slightly to make it a properly shaped hone because the blades are ground at an angle different from the one at which they cut. Therefore the hone will be a slightly different shape than the cut molding. Confusing? Trust me; it's a fact.

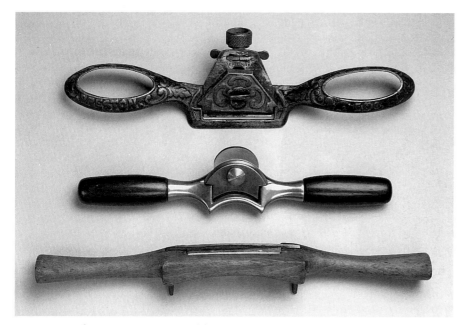

From top to bottom, an ornate, old Sargent spokeshave with a square blade, a modern concave spokeshave, and a traditional wooden model (shown upside-down to reveal the very low cutting angle of the blade).

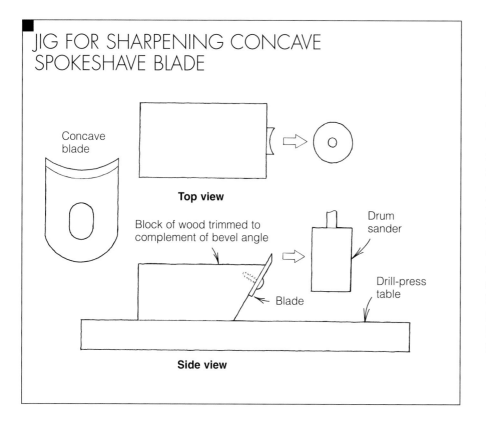

JIG FOR SHARPENING CONCAVE SPOKESHAVE BLADE

Concave blade

Top view

Block of wood trimmed to complement of bevel angle

Drum sander

Blade

Drill-press table

Side view

SPOKESHAVES

Square-ended spokeshave blades are sharpened exactly the same as plane blades. Special care should be given to lapping the face of the blade since these are often very poorly ground blades with a very rough surface finish.

Convex blades can be sharpened using the method described in the sidebar on p. 81. Concave blades can best be ground with a small drum sander (see the drawing below), and then honed with a stone or wooden dowel charged with honing compound. The U-shaped blade of the traditional wooden spokeshave is best done on a 1-in. belt sander with a fine sanding belt, followed by honing on a leather belt.

BLIND NAILER

There is no good reason to single out the blind-nailer blade for special attention, except that the proper sharpening of this blade is a good demonstration of applying the basic principles of sharpening.

A blind nailer is used to raise a shaving, leaving one end attached so that a nail can be driven in the trough and hidden by gluing the free end of the shaving back in place. I had been mildly intrigued by the Stanley blind nailer for years before I actually owned one. The first time I used it, however, I was very disappointed with the recommended ¼-in. chisel. Since the blind nailer had a bed angle of 15°, the chisel had to be used bevel up. This relatively high cutting angle created a shaving with frequent, very distinct breaks as well as tears along the edges. In fact, when such a shaving was glued back in place it was highly visible because of these two problems.

A blind nailer is a specialized small plane used to raise a small shaving of wood wherever a finishing nail needs to be driven. The end of the shaving is then glued back in place to conceal the nail. (Photo by Susan Kahn)

BLIND-NAILER BLADE SHAPE

Bottom of blind-nailer chisel

Docked bevel to give flat-bottomed shaving

Top of blind-nailer chisel

Before testing the blind nailer, the very limited blind nailing I had done had been under chips raised by a low-sweep carving gouge. The basic problem with the carving gouge was that you either had a chip that was too thin to cover a nail head adequately or too thick at the center for easy bending. After sharpening blades at a number of different bevel angles and a number of configurations I arrived at the current design, which is a double-beveled blade rounded on the back in a manner that makes part of the blade act like a chisel and part like a gouge. The key thing is that, like a gouge, it cuts the shaving on the bottom and the sides so that it can be reglued invisibly when carefully done; and, like a chisel, it gives a shaving of constant thickness for most of the blade width. The design is patented.

These blades seldom get dulled because it takes a huge amount of blind nailing to dull a blade. When it is dull, the easiest way to sharpen it is simply to hone the top bevel.

BLIND-NAILER ROADKILL

I was particularly delighted to be given a brand-new Stanley blind nailer by a New York friend a dozen years ago. After tinkering with it for awhile to develop the right blade, I decided to see if it would be economical to produce the tool again. I took it to a firm that specialized in small stampings and asked them if they could make it, and, if so, to quote a price. They wanted to use the Stanley as a model so I left it with them, cautioning them that it had sentimental as well as commercial value.

They made an excellent prototype and quoted a fair price for producing the necessary stamping. A production run was contracted for and everything was going swimmingly until I asked for the return of my Stanley blind nailer. It seems that the message about its value had been lost somewhere along the way. What I got back looked exactly like roadkill. My beautiful nailer had been unpinned and flattened so that the outline could be traced.

It makes absolutely no sense to get upset about a simple little tool, but I know that every tool collector out there will understand exactly how I felt when I saw the splayed carcass.

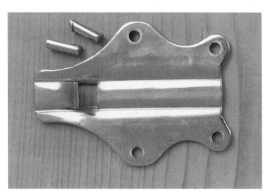

The blind nailer, unpinned and flattened.

CHAPTER 8
KNIVES

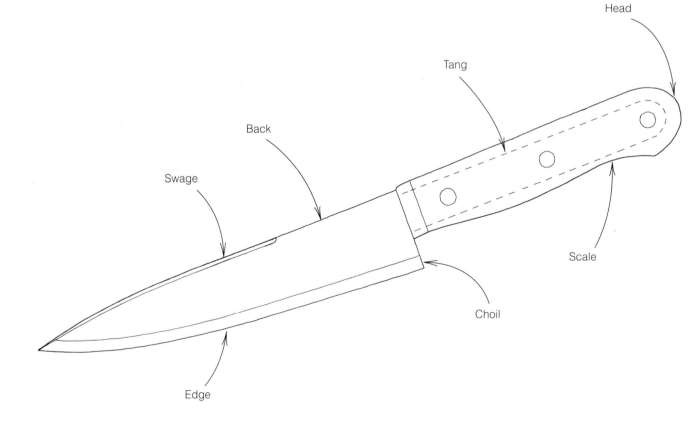

Head

Tang

Back

Swage

Scale

Choil

Edge

In woodworking, we are basically concerned only with knives that cut wood. But this is a fairly narrow view of the world. Over a lifetime, unless we just happen to be carvers, we will all probably spend more time using kitchen knives than woodworking knives. For this reason, I'm going to talk about kitchen knives first in this chapter.

Actually, there is a second reason. No non-woodworker is going to take a sharpening book seriously if it does not have basic instructions on sharpening kitchen knives. So this next section anticipates the question, "Are you telling me that you bought a book on sharpening and it doesn't even tell you how to sharpen a butcher knife decently?"

Finally, since edge-design considerations are so similar for kitchen knives, belt knives and woodworking knives, this digression into kitchen knives only reinforces the need to adjust edge shape to intended use.

KITCHEN KNIVES

Kitchen knives are very easy to sharpen, which is fortunate because most of them are left rattling around in drawers or abused in a variety of ways that dulls them very quickly. However, most kitchen-knife users seem to be satisfied with the condition of the knife as long as the cutting edge is keener than the back of the knife. The tolerance for dull knives is amazingly high in most kitchens.

The practical test of sharpness for a kitchen knife is whether or not it will slice soft vegetables, meat or bread. In all three uses, you do not want a knife with a classically sharp edge such as I have described for chisels and plane blades; you want a slightly serrated edge, a sort of combination between a knife and a saw.

Unlike wood, meat and soft vegetables have little rigidity to their structure. They are about 95% water held together with films and filaments of varying strengths. To cut them, you need an edge that will rend their fabric at very low applied pressure.

To sharpen a kitchen knife on a belt sander, hold the bevel against the belt in the unsupported area between the platen and the upper wheel. (Photo by Susan Kahn)

The skin of a tomato is sufficiently tough that it will maintain its integrity in the face of pressure from a smooth knife edge. Of course, you can only apply relatively light pressure, otherwise you tend to squash the entire tomato. You will find that a less finely finished edge, one that has many fine serrations in it from a medium-grit abrasive (400x to 1200x) will cut into the tomato much more easily because it is better designed to tear apart a film and sever fibers. Although the desirable amount of serration varies, you want a bit of tooth on any blade used for soft vegetables, meats and bread (see the sidebar at top on p. 92).

BEVEL ANGLES

Since these materials exert minimal forces on the cutting edge, you do not have to police your bevel angles very closely. You can sharpen most kitchen knives freehand and at a reasonably wide range of bevel angles, anywhere from 5° to nearly 20° (10° to 35° included angle) without being overly concerned about edge retention. There is a great deal of flexibility in all of this, and your guide should be an angle in this range that you can consistently reproduce.

There are some exceptions to the above statements. Any knife that will be used for chopping, particularly where bone may be present, should have an included angle (the combined bevel angles) of at least 30°. A cleaver should be at 50° or more to avoid edge nicking. The included angle should be proportional to the force that will be used or, put another way, to the resistance that will be encountered. For a kitchen knife used with hand pressure to divide frozen meat, 30° should be sufficient. For the same knife chopping up chicken or ribs, it should have a 50° or 60° included angle at the edge. In short, it should be sharpened like a cleaver because that is how you are using it.

USING A BELT SANDER

I do virtually all kitchen-knife sharpening on a 1-in. belt sander; a wheel grinder tends to undercut the bevel too much. For something like a meat cleaver, where you need a fairly straight edge or at least a fair curve, you should sharpen opposite the platen of the belt sander. But for all other knives I find it easiest to work in the unsupported area between the platen and the upper wheel (as shown in the photo above). You still have good control, and it naturally gives a

BREAD KNIVES

Bread knives should have a bit more tooth than other kitchen knives, because they must cut soft, spongy material. A touch on an 80x belt would be in order; or hone the knife with the coarsest stone you have, stroking directly across the edge. For those bread knives that have one bevel scalloped, it is adequate to hone only the non-scalloped side (at 5° or less).

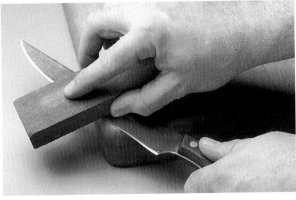

Stroke a coarse stone across the edge of a bread knife to achieve the necessary 'tooth.'

CHECKERING FILES

Back when hand sharpening was done commercially, one file used by the pros was a hand checkering file, also known as a corrugating file. Much like a checkering tool for wood, a checkering file cuts a series of regularly spaced grooves in an edge; in a sense, it degrades an edge rather than improves it. The file was used to dress the edge of hair scissors (if you have tried ordinary scissors on hair you'll know why), and it was used to give tooth to the edge of bread knives. The fine, regular serrations worked equally well in both uses.

Checkering files were traditionally used to groove the edge of a bread knife.

slightly rounded bevel for a strong edge (without blunting the overall shape too much). The basic concern is not getting the knife sharp, but getting it sharp without removing too much metal. Even a 240x belt will strip off metal at an alarming rate. Fortunately, you quickly get used to the action of the belt sander and will find that you can easily sharpen knives at the rate of about one a minute on the machine without excessive metal removal.

Unless you are sharpening at a very high included angle, you will almost inevitably get a wire edge no matter how careful you are. This should not be a matter of concern. When you are satisfied that all your knives are well sharpened except for the wire edge, just turn the belt inside out on the belt sander (putting the belt inside the platen to prevent damage) and remove the wire edge with an alternate trailing stroke on the cloth backing on the belt. Alternatively, you can remove the wire edge with a few deft strokes on a stone.

USING STONES

Stones are not quite as fast as a belt sander, but they are kinder to fine knives. Unless a knife needs major reshaping, a water stone in the 800x to 1200x range is fine. Such a stone will remove metal at a good rate and still leave just a nice amount of tooth in the edge.

I find the wooden-based water stones particularly suitable for knife sharpening. There is a 1000x stone in a ½-in. x 2½-in. x 7-in. size that is just right. It is easy to hold safely, is inexpensive and handles the full range of kitchen knives.

For slicing knives of all kinds, you can use quite low bevel angles for basic edge shape. Bevel angles of 5° (10° included angle) would be about right. Very seldom would the included angle be more than 20°. It is a simple matter to create bevels at 5° and restore them after dulling. Using the 1-in-60 rule (see the sidebar on p. 17), you would raise the back of a 1½-in. wide knife just ⅛ in. off the stone and take slicing cuts on the stone, first in one direction, then the other.

But you don't have to be particularly fussy about these angles. A slicing knife will work well with a 20° included angle, and if you find it easier to sharpen at that angle, do so. Just choose a motion that is comfortable to you and that you can repeat with reasonable certainty. If you imagine that you are trying to peel a layer off the stone with the knife, you should arrive at a fairly consistent sharpening action. If you want an inexpensive guide for knife sharpening, you can use a short section of a plastic spine clamp slipped onto the knife back (see the photo below). The spine clamps are available from stationery stores in several thicknesses, enough to accommodate the normal range of kitchen knives.

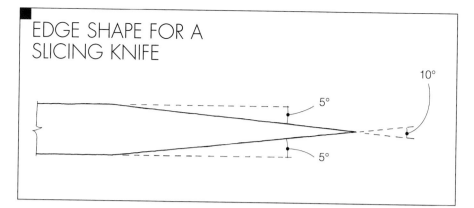

EDGE SHAPE FOR A SLICING KNIFE

10°

5°

5°

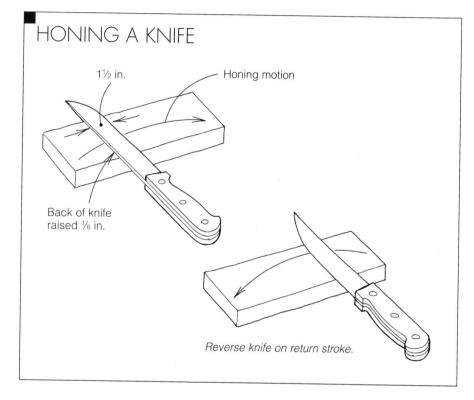

HONING A KNIFE

1½ in.

Honing motion

Back of knife raised ⅛ in.

Reverse knife on return stroke.

Slipping a plastic spine clamp onto the back of a knife will raise the blade just the right amount to hone the required bevel angle. (Photo by Susan Kahn)

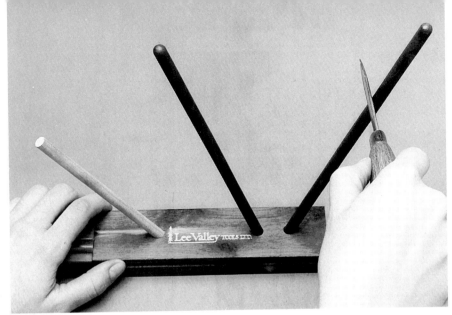

Ceramic honing rods can be used for touching up knives between sharpenings. (The rod at extreme left is for protection only.)

To use a knife steel, hold the steel vertically and take slicing cuts across it with the knife.

■ KNIFE-BLADE THICKENING

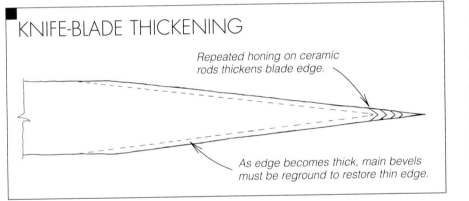

Repeated honing on ceramic rods thickens blade edge.

As edge becomes thick, main bevels must be reground to restore thin edge.

USING HONING RODS

Many people use ceramic honing rods for touching up knife blades between sharpenings. These honing rods are set at quite obtuse angles. The one shown in the photo at top left has rods set at 22½° to the vertical, which, if one follows the instructions for use, would give an included sharpening angle of 45°. This is a fairly blunt angle; while it would be suitable for something like a butcher knife, it would be too obtuse for a slicing knife.

However, it is not necessary to follow the instructions with these rods, which say to hold the knife vertically and draw it against one rod and then the other. Using the ever-handy 1-in-60

rule, you could hone at slightly more than 10° and still find that you were able to restore an edge fairly rapidly. Honing at 22½° as most instructions recommend would lead to fairly rapid thickening of the blade, as shown in the drawing above. This will cause no problems if you are prepared to restore ideal edge geometry on a belt sander regularly.

I prefer to use general-purpose sharpening equipment (stones, belts, micro-abrasive sheets) rather than specialized hones for knives.

USING KNIFE STEELS

A knife steel is a very hard steel rod (Rc 70+) that has a series of fine longitudinal serrations. When a knife is drawn against the rod, the blade touches only the tips of the serrations; the substantial point pressure actually deforms the steel in the blade, smoothing it and displacing it marginally. It is used to create an edge by reforming the steel adjacent to the edge.

The basic problem with knife steels is that they are of hugely varying quality, which is not always reflected in the price. Another problem is that most people use them incorrectly. There is not much you can do about the quality of the steel, other than take the advice of a reputable dealer. Regarding use, I strongly recommend that you adapt the stance shown in the photo above, where you hold the steel in position and draw the knife down and across the steel as if you were going to remove a shaving. The great chefs do freehand steeling of knives with a marvelous show of dexterity. If you are a great chef and have mastered this modified form of swordplay, I commend you. For the more faint of heart who would rather only slit their wrists intentionally, I recommend the illustrated process. It will give far more consistent results.

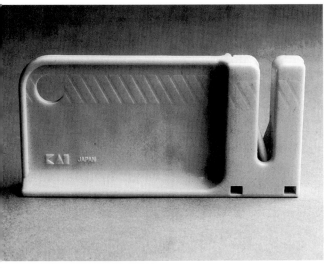

This compact sharpening device with crossed ceramic rods is suitable for Western knives, but not for Japanese laminated-steel blades.

Three pocket knives and, at bottom, a belt knife. The pocket knives are all of modern production, though the French knife in the middle is a style that has not changed in 200 years. (Photo by Susan Kahn)

One final point: Never use a knife steel on a laminated blade with a high-carbon core. It will chip the knife.

JAPANESE KITCHEN KNIVES

There are a number of laminated Japanese kitchen knives on the market today. Like Japanese chisels, these usually have high-carbon steel laminated to a piece of stainless steel or between two pieces of stainless steel. And like most Japanese tools, Japanese knives require a level of care and respect that most Westerners are unprepared to give to such an inanimate device.

Japanese knives will take a very fine edge and can cut paper-thin slices of meat or vegetables. One of the difficulties with them is that the high-carbon steel is very brittle and the knives should generally not be used for chopping of any kind. The edges chip too readily.

You should also be very careful when using honing rods of any kind with Japanese kitchen knives. The high-carbon steel is sufficiently brittle that it can be chipped on honing rods. In particular, you do not want to use one of the small devices with crossed honing rods shown in the photo at left above. The crossed rods are fine for Western knives, but if you draw a Japanese knife between sets of rods like these with any amount of pressure on the knife, you will virtually destroy the edge. It will have a series of small chips all the way along it caused by the wave action of the rods on the brittle steel core.

Some Japanese knives are of the single-bevel type with a flat or slight hollow on the opposite side. These are relatively easy to sharpen, since the basic bevel can be put on one side and the other side need only be given a couple of lapping strokes on the stone.

POCKET KNIVES AND BELT KNIVES

Having already included kitchen knives, there seemed to be no reason not to throw in pocket knives and belt knives as well. Although commonly used by woodworkers, these knives are seldom used for woodworking. Both can be sharpened on oil stones or water stones. The bevel angles chosen would be dictated by the intended use of the knife.

For example, if a belt knife is for general purpose use in camping, it should have quite a sturdy edge for making kindling, cutting rope, whittling tent pegs, and so on. The included angle of the two bevels should be at least 25° and preferably 30°. If the knife were to be used only for skinning and filleting, a 15° included angle would be ample. In both these cases, the sharpening process described for kitchen knives would be followed, but with the additional step of stropping the edge on a leather or wooden hone charged with chromium oxide. You do not need a toothed edge, so you can hone to maximum keenness.

The same general principles apply to pocket knives. The only difference is that if you have a pocket knife with two or more blades, you can sharpen the blades for different purposes.

As a matter of historical interest, traditionally pocket knives were sturdy utility knives with one or more blades pinned at one end of the haft. Pen-knives were much more refined, with very keen, hard steel blades (to shape pen nibs on goose quills) pinned at opposite ends of the haft. This distinction has now been lost, as evidenced by the photo at right above.

CHIP KNIVES

Chip knives are included here rather than in the chapter on carving tools only because their edge shape is more similar to knives than to the general line of carving tools. Of some ten different kinds of chip knives commonly available, about half are actually chisels rather than knives—relatively small chisels, but chisels nonetheless. The bevels on these can be treated exactly the same way you would treat the bevels on a chisel, leaving them straight and intersecting at whatever chosen angle you desire.

For the styles that are actually knives, the bevel almost inevitably requires a slight rounding in order to give the edge adequate strength and to allow you to change direction while cutting. In practice, all the chisel-like knives are used for stab cuts or straight lines. The rest are used for curvilinear work. Unless abused, these knives almost never need regrinding. All the work that is necessary can be done on a water stone, a bit of 600x silicon-carbide paper glued to a board, and a leather or wood strop with chromium-oxide (green) honing compound on it.

Any basic shaping can be done on 800x to 1200x water stones. This can be followed by stropping the edge either on a hard leather strop with green honing compound or a simple piece of softwood with the same compound on it. For convenience sake, it is useful to have a small piece of wood approximately 1 in. x 6 in. with 600x silicon-carbide paper on one side for thinning out the knife edge after repeated stroppings and a leather strop (charged with chromium oxide) on the other. While carving, it would be typical that the knife would be used for several minutes and then given very light stropping. After this has been repeated

Chip knives are available in a wide range of styles. The knives second and third from left are more popular for carving in the round than for chip carving. (Photo by Susan Kahn)

EMERGENCY HONING COMPOUND

Throughout this book I have recommended chromium-oxide honing compound. The most effective chromium-oxide compounds have an admixture of fine aluminum-oxide particles to speed abrasion, and the best ones are quite a dark green, showing a high ratio of chromium oxide to binders and fillers.

But if you need honing compound and specialized compound is not available, you can use chromium-oxide green oil-based artist's paint. It has a very high chromium-oxide content and can be painted onto any shaped hone you need. It cuts more slowly than the compound but still gives a mirror finish.

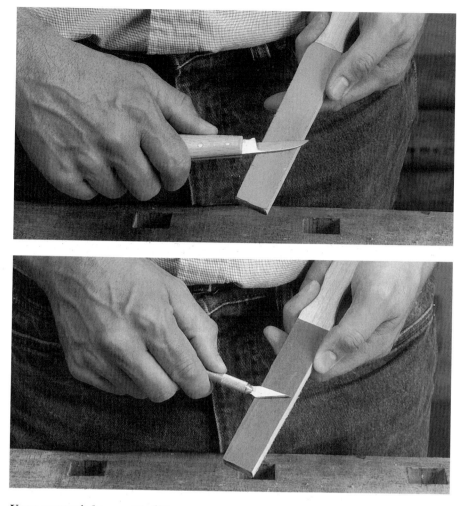

Use a carver's hone with 600x paper on one side (above) and a leather strop on the other (top) to maintain a sharp edge on chip knives and disposable-blade knives. (Photos by Susan Kahn)

The thick blade and steep bevel angles of a hacking knife give it the necessary strength for rough work.

a half-dozen times, you might then thin the edge with several trailing cuts on the 600x silicon carbide. Alternating between these two should keep the knife in perfect condition.

DISPOSABLE-BLADE KNIVES

Knives with disposable blades can be sharpened in exactly the same manner as chip knives. The blades may be disposable, but there is no reason that they should not be repeatedly honed to get maximum life from them. As with chip knives, regrinding is unnecessary, and all the maintenance of the blade edge can be done with 600x silicon carbide and a chromium-oxide strop.

HACKING KNIFE

A hacking knife is a substitute for the right tool. It is used in place of bolt cutters, side cutters, a cold chisel or even a small froe. It is always there to be sacrificed to save your good tools.

Because it is almost always used for dividing, edge shape is much more

important than keenness. It is an ideal candidate for sharpening on a belt sander since that will give you the profile shown in the drawing above. A rounded bevel with an included angle of 60° or more is suitable.

Two styles of marking knife: the top knife is beveled on one side of the blade only, the bottom knife is beveled on both sides and has an integral scratch awl.

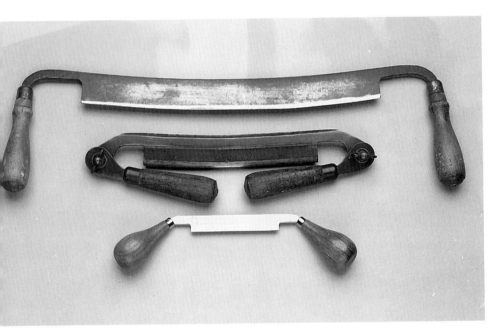

From top to bottom, a long drawknife for bark peeling, a classic carpenter's drawknife with folding handles to act as blade guards and a dainty carver's drawknife for fine work.

MARKING KNIVES

Used to scribe cut lines on stock, marking (or striking) knives are generally superior to pencils because they mark a narrower line and sever fibers at the same time, preventing splintering during the cutting process.

There are two basic types of marking knife: those beveled on both sides of the blade and those beveled on one side only (see the photo at top). The latter is the easiest to use with accuracy. Available as skews (not shown) or with V-points, the V-point style is the most versatile. It can be used left- or right-handed, and for striking a line away from you as well as toward you. The angle of the V should be about 120°, and the bevel angle about 25°.

Either style can be sharpened freehand on a stone (800x to 1200x). Some users prefer to adjust the skew angle so that the entire cutting edge is normally below the top of the try-square blade; others purposely dull a portion of the blade after honing so that it will not grate along the side of the try-square blade. For anyone using the brass try squares currently on the market, I strongly recommend the second technique to avoid accidentally dimensioning your try square.

FILLING KNIVES

Filling knives are used to place putty or filler and never need sharpening because they are not supposed to be sharp. On the other hand, you will find it worthwhile to buff a filling knife and

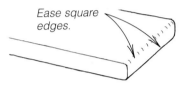

Ease square edges.

ease any square edges. This will prevent filler from curling up behind the knife as it is being pressed into a hole.

DRAWKNIVES

New drawknives usually require a fairly substantial amount of work to make them usable. As they come from the factory, drawknives usually have a bevel angle of 25° or 30°, which is far steeper than necessary and should be reduced to 20° as a first step in the sharpening process. Depending upon what you are going to do to the knife later, you may even want to start with a bevel angle as low as 15°.

Drawknives are designed to be used bevel up, but if the face of the knife is perfectly flat, only straight cuts can be made this way. Since a drawknife is more frequently used for general shaping than for straight cuts, it is often used bevel down so that you can not only cut into the wood but also change direction and cut out as well. There is an alternative to this. If you put a 15° basic bevel on a drawknife and dub from 2° to 5° off the face of the knife, you will find that it is much more maneuverable (see the drawing below). Only for a very sharp arc would it be necessary to turn the drawknife over and use it bevel down. Even then, you would have to round the primary bevel somewhat or you would still have difficulty making the cut.

So the basic bevel angle that you put on a drawknife is going to depend on the way you later intend to use it. If you bought it solely to remove bark from logs, you might want to hone it at whatever angle it had when you got it.

The standard drawknife can readily be sharpened on a belt sander or with a hand-held stone. I prefer to hone a drawknife by clamping the knife in position on the edge of a bench and then going to work on it with a water stone, stroking the edge at the angle I want. When using an 800x to 1200x stone, I would stroke into the edge, just as you might do with a file. When honing with a 4000x or 8000x stone, I

stroke from the back of the knife to the front, because it is too easy to misjudge the angle and put a gouge in the stone.

CARVER'S DRAWKNIFE

A modification of the standard drawknife, carver's drawknives usually have much shorter blades and often have the handles cocked at 45°, which gives them excellent control and makes them very comfortable to use. Also, unlike standard drawknives, these knives usually come with a lower bevel angle. Since they are used almost exclusively in woods with excellent consistency (i.e., woods that are knot-free), they can be sharpened at a 15° bevel angle and hold their edge well. Again, you may

wish to put a couple of degrees of back bevel on the blade. Often you will find that just holding a drawknife in position and stropping the edge on the unbeveled side will give you just about the right amount of back bevel. This is all a matter of personal taste, and you should adjust the process to what works best for you.

There are dozens of knife types that have not been covered in this chapter, but all can be sharpened with one or more of the methods outlined. Shape the blade for the action you want and the edge strength you need.

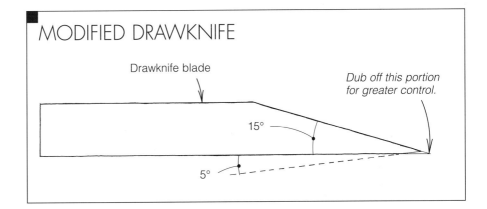

MODIFIED DRAWKNIFE

Drawknife blade

Dub off this portion for greater control.

15°

5°

BARK SPUDS

No tool demonstrates the importance of shape versus keenness as well as a bark spud, which is a specialized form of knife used to remove bark from logs (very necessary in log-house construction). Bark spuds usually have handles about 4 ft. long and are used longitudinally on the log. A good spud has a concave edge; it tends to keep the tool centered in use. But a spud is sharpened differently at different times of year.

When there is a choice, logs for lumber are cut in late winter when the wood is at minimum moisture content. On such

logs, the bark is intimately bonded to the tree. If you were to use such logs for building, you would need a spud with a decent edge on it to separate the bark from the wood. But if the log is cut when the sap is flowing and is peeled immediately, you want a dull edge on the spud. You want the tool to follow the cambium layer, which is fragile and "sappy" at that time. If the spud is too sharp, it will cut into the wood. You do not want it to cut; you want it to follow the line of least resistance and just separate the bark from the log.

A concave-edge bark spud. (Photo by Susan Kahn)

CHAPTER 9
CARVING TOOLS

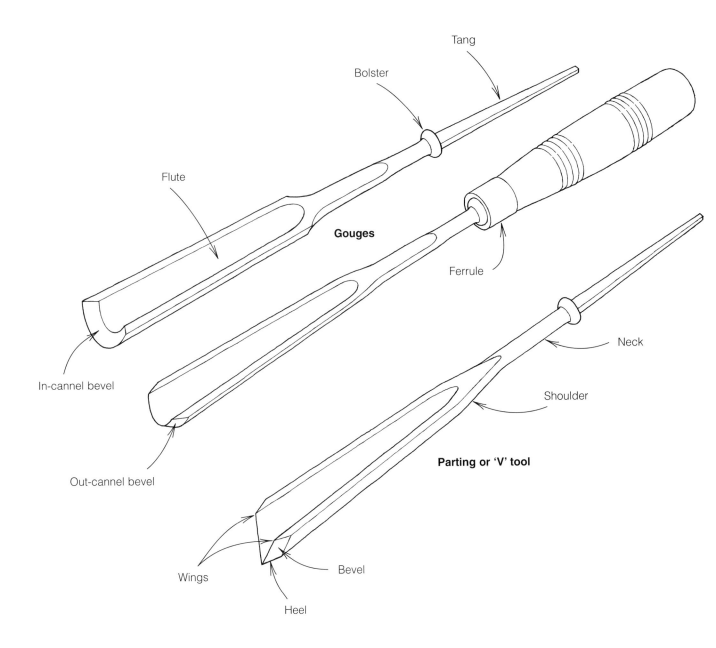

Tang

Bolster

Flute

Gouges

Ferrule

In-cannel bevel

Out-cannel bevel

Neck

Shoulder

Parting or 'V' tool

Wings

Bevel

Heel

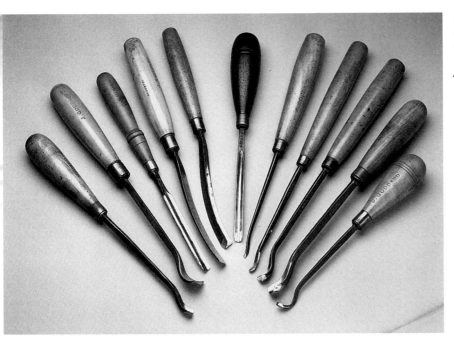

A selection of older carving tools, showing a variety of handle shapes. All but three of the tools were made in the famous Addis factory, the world's foremost maker of carving tools until it closed down a half century ago.

If you learn to sharpen carving tools well, you should be able to sharpen anything. Virtually every hand-tool shape considered in the rest of the book is included in the standard range of carving tools. The wide variety of shapes requires versatile grinding and honing systems. At the same time, the diversity often precludes the use of honing guides and demands the development of freehand sharpening skills in any would-be carver.

To complicate the carver's life, only a very few carving tools can be purchased in a ready-to-use state. Historically, carving tools were supplied with a basic grind only. In Britain, until recently, a sharp tool was considered to be a used tool. Since the supplier could not know how the tool was going to be used or on what woods, honing the tool would have required assumptions in both areas. There was a higher probability of being wrong than being right, so the tool was supplied with a basic grind only.

Today, some carving tools can be purchased in a ready-to-use state, which is a mixed blessing. On the positive side, it indicates to the buyer the degree of sharpness that can be attained, but on the negative side, it implies that the provided shape is the correct one.

As with all tools, edge shape has to be married to technique and the material to be worked; nowhere is this more important than with carving tools. Whether or not tools come from the store sharp or dull, you know that they will eventually become dull anyway, so good sharpening technique has to be developed by every carver. Fortunately, modern technology has provided a vast array of effective and flexible sharpening materials and systems, so the primary problem becomes one of determining what shape you want, not so much how to arrive at it.

GOUGES

The constant refrain of business consultants is to look at products from the customer's viewpoint to determine whether or not the products are appropriate. While this may sound a bit childlike, it is useful to do just that if you want to understand exactly why you should shape certain tools certain ways. You should look at them from the viewpoint of the wood about to be cut.

Consider the standard carving gouge that you might buy in an unsharpened state. You can almost be certain that this tool is incorrectly shaped, so whether or not it has a sharp edge is incidental.

CHOOSING A BEVEL ANGLE

One of the first things to be decided is a suitable bevel angle. For light cuts in cedar, pine or basswood, a 15° bevel angle would probably be adequate. For a bit heavier work you would beef this up to 20°, and for very hard woods you might want to make it 25°. If you are going to be using a mallet on the gouge you may want a 30° bevel or even 35° depending upon the nature of the steel in the tool. As usual, you want the lowest bevel angle consistent with edge retention, so let's assume an angle for general-purpose use of 25°.

Assuming that you have the gouge sharpened at a 25° bevel angle, you would find that it just begins to cut the wood at about a 30° angle of attack. There are times when you might want such a high angle of attack to clear surrounding work, but for most relief carving a lower angle of attack would give better control.

To consider this for a moment, think of using a carpenter's chisel to make a paring cut on wood. Using it bevel up, the applied force will be in line with the direction of cut. But if you are forced to make the cut with the bevel down (because of some adjacent obstruction), you know that this carries with it greater danger of a slip because you will be applying force at an angle (equal to the bevel angle plus a few degrees) to the direction of cut. You now not only have to overcome the resistance of the wood being cut, but you have also substantially increased friction between the chisel and the wood because of the additional downward force. And, as any physics teacher or your own experience in

winter driving might tell you, friction is at its greatest just before slipping occurs. These are the ideal conditions for an uncontrolled cut. So, we try to keep the shaft of the tool as closely aligned with the direction of cut as possible.

As you decrease the bevel angle on a gouge, you bring the shaft into closer alignment with the direction of cut. You also weaken the edge of the tool, but this is easily strengthened by putting some bevel on the inside of the gouge. This "in-cannel" bevel not only strengthens the edge by increasing the included angle, but it also makes it much easier to use. To understand this, you have to put yourself in the position of the wood. Consider a gouge that has been sharpened at a bevel angle of 25°: viewed head-on, it would look something like Drawing 1 on the facing page; but as the gouge is lifted up just past the 25° angle so that it can cut into the wood, it would look something like Drawing 2.

Notice that the gouge would be able to cut in this position only if it partially compresses the wood at the same time that it cuts, since, as presented, the gouge is wider than the cut it is going to make (the cutting edge is the smaller of the two semicircles). So to get any significant depth of cut, the gouge has to be tilted above 25° so that a reasonable portion of the gouge can enter the wood before wedging action takes place. This angle might be 30° or more (Drawing 3).

The problem with all of this is that only two points of the gouge have the correct relief angle behind the edge. Over the rest of the surface the relief angle is either too great, as would be the case at the very deepest point of cut, or too shallow, which would require compression of the wood for the gouge to penetrate.

Compare this situation to one where we have part of the bevel on the outside of the gouge and part of the bevel on the inside (see Drawing 4 on the facing page). Of course, now we have only to lift the gouge just above 15° in order to begin the cut because there is only 15° of outside bevel. It is interesting that at the cutting point (see Drawing 5), we see immediately that such a design would have much less side wedging than one where the bevel was entirely on the outside of the gouge. Lifted up to get the same amount of cut as in Drawing 3, we can see that the compromises are not as pronounced (see Drawing 6). There is still a section where the gouge is lifted past the ideal relief angle, and the cut will still be a compromise between some compression at the upper edges of the cut and some tearout at the very bottom of the cut, both combined with some control problems (though these would be substantially less than would be the case when all the bevel is on the outside of the gouge).

MECHANICAL ADVANTAGE

The repeated refrain of "the lowest bevel angle consistent with edge retention" has a special meaning in carving. Anyone who has carved knows that there is a constant threat of a sudden slip that can ruin a piece. For this reason, the carver wants to be able to cut using the least amount of pressure on the tool because this makes it the most controllable.

Well, the degree of sharpness is not the only thing that determines how much pressure must be applied. The carving tool is a wedge that is being driven into the wood. The shape of the wedge determines its mechanical advantage, and the mechanical advantage determines the force required for

penetration. Since mechanical advantage equals D/W (depth/width), as you lower the bevel angle on a carving tool, you decrease the force required to use it.

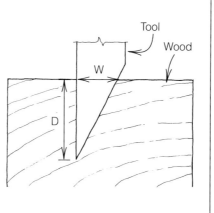

CARVING-GOUGE BEVELS

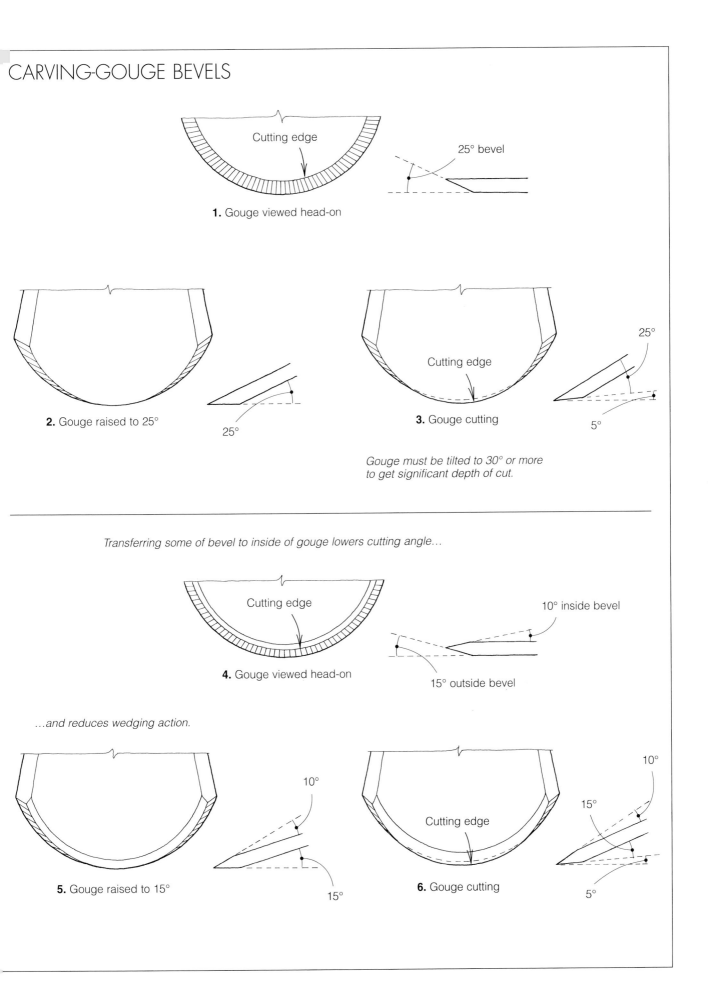

Cutting edge

25° bevel

1. Gouge viewed head-on

2. Gouge raised to 25°

25°

3. Gouge cutting

Cutting edge

25°

5°

Gouge must be tilted to 30° or more to get significant depth of cut.

Transferring some of bevel to inside of gouge lowers cutting angle...

Cutting edge

10° inside bevel

4. Gouge viewed head-on

15° outside bevel

...and reduces wedging action.

5. Gouge raised to 15°

10°

15°

6. Gouge cutting

Cutting edge

10°

15°

5°

IN-CANNEL AND
OUT-CANNEL GOUGES

As a general rule, carving gouges are out-cannel and patternmaker's gouges are in-cannel. Firmer gouges, which are heavier than carving gouges and shorter than patternmaker's gouges, can be either. The primary use for an in-cannel gouge is to make a straight groove of a known radius. This is important in patternmaking, where a shaft or similar machinery feature may have to fit into the groove of the casting made from the pattern. The same thing is true for millwrights who may have to make pillow blocks for shafts and would want in-cannel gouges for good control and a long straight cut.

The increased popularity of routers and the availability of low-cost large-diameter bits have virtually elimi-nated the demand for in-cannel gouges. They are so rarely used today that the term "gouge" is generally understood to mean an out-cannel gouge. In fact, to many people the term "cannel" is new to their vocabulary.

I bought the small in-cannel gouge being used in the photo below at some long-forgotten tool sale. It is very flexible and can be used just like a cranked-neck gouge. With just a breath of back bevel on it (in this case, back bevel means out-cannel) to compensate for the bend, it will cut dead true on any flat surface. It would be a fairly straightforward matter to make small gouges like this out of drill rod; only the tip would have to be shaped.

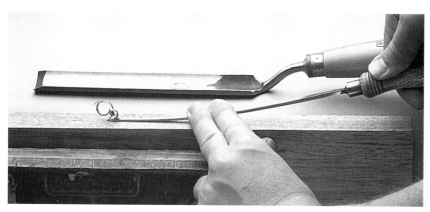

A slim, flexible in-cannel gouge can perform the same function as a cranked-neck gouge.

IN-CANNEL GOUGE

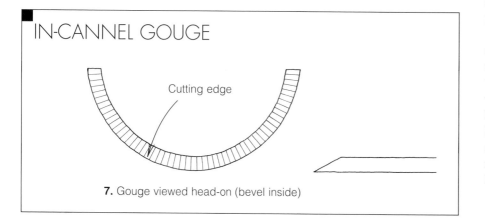

Cutting edge

7. Gouge viewed head-on (bevel inside)

If transferring part of the bevel to the inside is a good thing, why not transfer all the bevel to the inside? Well, if you do that you will have a gouge that can cut only straight grooves. Having no bevel on the outside, you could not change direction with it. This is called an in-cannel gouge, and, while it is much loved by patternmakers, it is virtually useless for carving since it can be used only on a flat surface where the cut is going to start at one edge and run some distance in a straight line at consistent depth of cut. In addition, since it would be used almost flush with the surface, it must either have a cranked neck or be very flexible, as shown in the photo at left.

Viewed head-on, it would look exactly the same as the gouge in Drawing 1 on p. 103, except now the larger-radius circle, not the smaller-radius circle, would be the cutting edge (see Drawing 7 below).

This shows that the need to be able to change direction while cutting can be maintained only by having a decent amount of the bevel on the outside of the gouge. But so far we have been a bit inflexible in the analysis. Why not change the amount of bevel transfer as we change position on the gouge? Taking our earlier example where we transfer 10° of the bevel to the inside so that we could get a 15° attack angle, we see that we could eliminate a lot of problems if we progressively trans-ferred bevel from the outside to the inside until it was totally in-cannel at the top. Viewed head-on the gouge would look something like Drawing 8 on the facing page. Raised to a 15° angle it would look something like Drawing 9.

This looks fine, but there are a couple of cautionary notes. First, the upper edges are quite weak with only 10° included angles. Second, the gouge would not look exactly like Drawing 9 because we have been playing fast and loose with geometry. In fact, if you had a gouge ground like one in Drawing 8, raised to 15° it would look more like Drawing 10.

TRANSITIONAL BEVEL

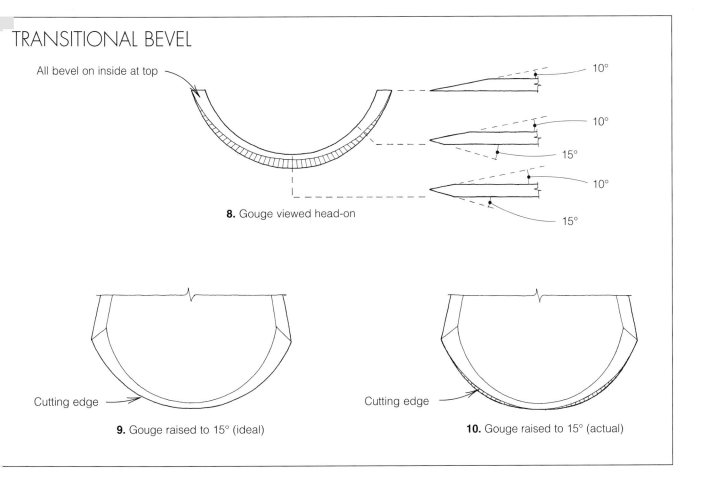

All bevel on inside at top

10°

10°

15°

10°

15°

8. Gouge viewed head-on

Cutting edge

9. Gouge raised to 15° (ideal)

Cutting edge

10. Gouge raised to 15° (actual)

There would still be some wedging action, because the cutting edge of the gouge would still be inside the overall profile presented to the wood. The only way to grind the gouge that would look exactly like Drawing 9 would be to have constantly changing bevel angles both inside and out. The outside bevel would start at 15° and be gradually reduced until it would reach 0° just as it disappeared. In the same manner, the inside bevel would start at 10° and continue to increase until it reached 25° at the top of the gouge. It is exactly this sort of transitional bevel both inside and outside that you should strive for when you sharpen carving gouges.

You do not have to follow the above examples slavishly when sharpening your carving gouges, but understanding the principles involved lets you understand what is happening when you are cutting wood. This prepares you for the day when you switch from carving basswood to carving cherry and wonder why your tools are suddenly not working the way you expect them to. You might find that you have been depending on wood compression to make a number of your best moves and that the much more unforgiving cherry will not let you make those moves. Just as you might have to increase the bevel angles to keep edges from crumbling, you might have to pay a lot more attention to relief angles so that you can retain some maneuverability in cherry.

At the other end of the scale, if you are always going to be carving soft-woods of consistent density, all of the bevel angles used in the examples are too great. You will get a much better finish if you lower them to something closer to 15° in total. The low bevel angles will give you a much smoother finish with less fiber pulling and crushing.

At the risk of being a bore, I would also say that if you have not understood all of the material in this chapter so far, you should re-read it. The principles explained are of critical importance to effective sharpening of carving gouges.

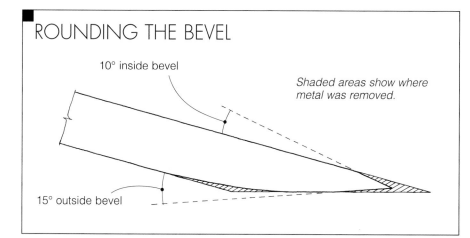

ROUNDING THE BEVEL

10° inside bevel

Shaded areas show where metal was removed.

15° outside bevel

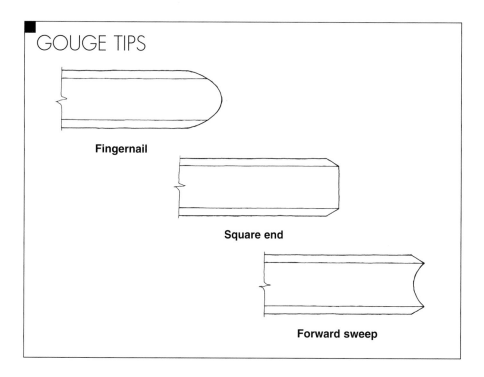

GOUGE TIPS

Fingernail

Square end

Forward sweep

and 10° inside bevel, you might want to shape the outside bevel as shown in the top drawing at left.

In this case, the outside bevel is more of a long, gradual curve than a flat bevel. You can be sure that this will work better than a flat bevel for most carving requirements. The question for personal technique becomes one of deciding the shape of curve you want. You will also notice in the example that the 10° interior bevel is much shorter than the 15° exterior bevel. This is something you would adjust to your own wood, tools and techniques. It is shown this way just to indicate that the bevels do not have to be of equal length, because any edge crumbling or rolling is going to take place only at the tip of the gouge unless you are making very heavy cuts or abusing the tool. Since it is far easier to grind bevels on the outside of gouges than on the inside, I prefer to keep the outside bevel long and the inside bevel short wherever possible.

GOUGE TIPS—FINGERNAIL, SQUARE END OR SWEPT FORWARD?

Most carvers like to have a slight fingernail on all their gouges because this is the easiest shape to hone. Others will have square-end gouges, and a few will have gouges with a slight forward sweep to the upper edges (see the bottom drawing at left).

Unless you have good reason to do otherwise, I recommend that you keep the ends of your gouges square. The shape is not so significant when you are cutting with the grain. But when you are cutting cross grain it makes sense to sever the ends of the fibers at the same time or slightly before dislodging the central part of the chip (see the photo on the facing page). You will see many sets of carving tools with fingernail ends on all of the gouges. Often this indicates only that the manufacturer found it easier to sharpen a gouge that way than to do it properly.

ROUNDING THE BEVEL

Unless you intend to use a gouge for long straight grooves of a constant depth, you are probably going to want some degree of roundness on the bevel. Otherwise, you will have difficulty changing your depth of cut in the wood. That should probably be rephrased; you will have no difficulty continuing to cut ever deeper if you have a flat bevel, but you will find it difficult to level out or to cut out of the wood. Both would require some prying with consequent damage to the wood, the chisel or both. Using the example above where we had 15° outside bevel

The clean cut on the left was made by a square-end gouge; there is no tear-out anywhere. The rougher cut on the right was made by a fingernail-end gouge.

DOT AND CROSS PATTERN

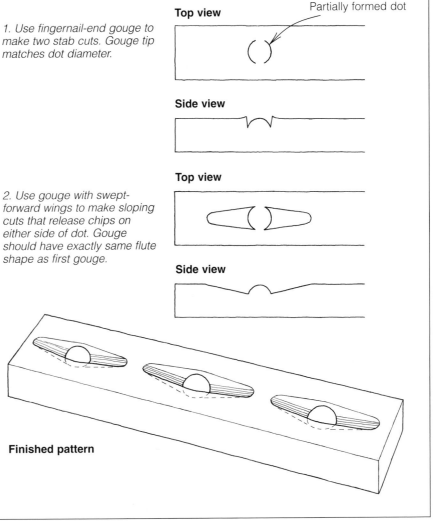

1. Use fingernail-end gouge to make two stab cuts. Gouge tip matches dot diameter.

Top view

Partially formed dot

Side view

2. Use gouge with swept-forward wings to make sloping cuts that release chips on either side of dot. Gouge should have exactly same flute shape as first gouge.

Top view

Side view

Finished pattern

There are times when you need a fingernail end, however. For example, if you were carving a dot and cross pattern (as shown in the drawing at right), ideally you would want two gouges of exactly the same size and curvature, one with slightly forward swept wings and the other with a fingernail end that exactly matches the sweep (curvature) of the gouge. This would allow you to make stab cuts that would almost exactly match the horizontal cuts. More important, it would prevent popping off any of the dots, which is what would happen if you were using a square-end gouge for the stab cuts. If you have ever tried this type of carving, you will know exactly the advantages described.

TRUING THE SWEEP

In cross section, most gouges are not true segments of circles. They are more often parabolic in shape. This may or may not cause you a problem when you are carving, but it will almost always cause you a problem when you are sharpening.

To deal with the carving aspect first, many carvers like to use a roll cut (see p. 14) when they are working cross grain or end grain. As they push the gouge through the wood, they rotate it. This has exactly the same effect as skewing a plane blade or chisel when cross-grain or end-grain cutting (see the discussion in Chapter 2). It changes the relationship of the forces acting on the wood and on the tool, generally providing a cleaner cut. However, to make an effective roll cut without bruising the wood, stressing the tool or tearing fibers, the part of the gouge in contact with the wood should be a

perfect semicircle. Tools with non-circular cross sections do not rotate well as they are cutting.

Fortunately, it is also easier to sharpen a tool with a semicircular cross section than it is with any other curved cross section. It is much easier to roll the tool to grind an even bevel when you are dealing with a regular shape. This happens to be one case where it is both easier and more effective to work on the inside of the tool than the outside. There are a variety of ways to true the sweep. If you have a cylindrical stone of the right diameter, you can true the inside of the gouge with that. Since the odds of this being the case are just

True the outside of a gouge on a belt sander, with the tool held at exactly 90° to the belt in the slack part between the platen and the upper wheel. (Photo by Susan Kahn)

When honing the outside bevel of the gouge on a leather belt, tilt the tool slightly downward so it will not dig into the belt as the belt is turning. (Photo by Susan Kahn)

slightly better than winning the lottery, the next best thing to do is to get a dowel that approximately matches the sweep, coat it with liquid sandpaper, or apply PSA-backed abrasive, chuck it up in a drill press or hand drill and grind the inside to shape. Alternatively, you can just wrap the dowel with abrasive sheet and do it all manually.

It is not necessary to dress the entire flute. It is desirable to grind as much of it as possible, but you have to true only the portion that will be coming into contact with the wood. Whatever you use for truing the sweep can also be used for any in-cannel beveling you may want to do.

After you have the inside true, if you grind the bevel on the gouge at a constant angle you will be able to see where the outside of the tool is out of round. The only reason you would want to true this, since it does not come in contact with the wood, is again to make grinding easier. If you were grinding a bevel on a gouge that is substantially thicker in some places than in others, it is more difficult to keep the edge even. The easiest way to trim up the outside is on a belt sander just above the platen (as shown in the top photo at left).

HONING A GOUGE

You probably thought that we were never going to get to this point, considering all the things that had to be done to the gouge already. For honing the outside bevel, my first choice would be a belt sander with a micro-finishing abrasive belt or a leather belt dressed with chromium-oxide honing compound. My next choice would be a hard felt wheel dressed with chromium oxide, and my last choice would be a manual method using either some combination of the above materials on a wooden backing or a fine Japanese slipstone.

On a belt sander, I prefer to hold the gouge nearly horizontal as I hone (as shown in the bottom photo at left). It is important that it be skewed slightly in the direction of travel of the belt. I prefer using a reversible motor on the belt sander, so that shaping can be done with the belt running from top to bottom and honing done with the belt running from bottom to top. It can all be done with the belt running only one way (from top to bottom, as shown in the photos at left), but it requires a few more contortions.

On a felt wheel, I would again use the same general grip, using a trailing cut on the side of the wheel or the face of the wheel depending upon light conditions. Generally, I use the side of the wheel for fine work because it allows better angular control (see the top left photo below). The face of the wheel is fine for heavy polishing or, if shaped, for honing as well, but you run a higher risk of dubbing an edge. Where shop lighting is directly overhead, it is easier to use the face of the wheel for everything (just another argument for good lighting at your grinding station).

For honing the inside of the gouge (and whether or not you put any bevel on the inside, you have to hone it to a mirror finish if you want a good cutting edge), I prefer a shaped felt wheel charged with chromium-oxide honing compound (bottom left photo below). But a very close second, and in some instances a first choice, is a piece of wood formed by the gouge itself for honing both the inside and the outside.

It is simple to cut the edge of a scrap of wood to shape for the inside of the gouge (top right photo below) and to

carve a groove in the face of the same scrap for honing the outside bevel (bottom right photo below). It is a highly effective sharpening device that can be made at virtually no cost. Dressed with chromium-oxide honing compound, the strop can be kept at hand when you are carving so that you can give a tool a quick touchup without having to leave your carving station.

When honing on a felt wheel, hold the bevel flat against the side of the wheel with a trailing stroke.

Hone the inside of a gouge on the rounded edge of a shaped felt wheel charged with chromium-oxide honing compound.

The flute and the outside bevel can also be honed with trailing strokes on a custom-made wooden strop charged with honing compound. (Photos by Susan Kahn)

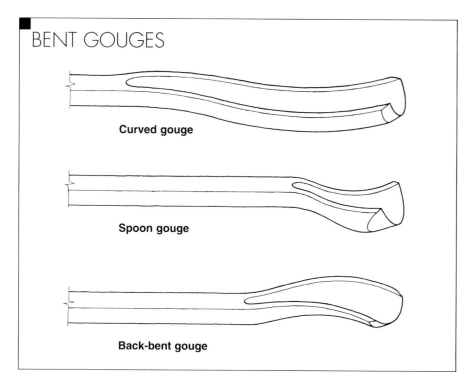

BENT GOUGES

Curved gouge

Spoon gouge

Back-bent gouge

The best method, one that will accommodate the curve of the gouge, is to shape a wooden disk of appropriate diameter to the correct shape and apply liquid sandpaper to it. Like the cone this could be used in a hand drill, clamped in a vise or in a drill press, either method leaving both hands free to manipulate the tool. The same basic shape will do for honing bent gouges, but in this case the wood should be charged with chromium-oxide honing compound only.

BACK-BENT GOUGES

Back-bent gouges present no unique problems that were not dealt with above. Today, only someone carving endless clusters of grapes would bother buying a back-bent gouge, since a small amount of inside bevel will let you use a regular gouge in place of the back bent.

VEINING TOOLS

Veiners are narrow, high-sweep gouges used for fine grooving. Again, the considerations for gouges in general apply to veining tools. The only difference is that veining tools are so small that it is often easier to deal with them purely manually rather than going near any power equipment. Making your own hones from wood and charging them with chromium-oxide honing compound is a godsend for veining tools. It lets you touch them up without risking geometric rearrangement, which is so easy on tools with such a small cross section.

PARTING TOOLS

For most carvers, these are truly the tools from hell. They are the most difficult carving tool of all to grind and hone and probably the easiest to damage in use. One of the primary problems with parting tools is that they are frequently badly made. They often do not have a crisp V-shaped bottom, and the wings of the tool are often not ground flat on the inside. It seems to me that the primary reason for these defects is sloppy manufacturing processes. Japanese parting tools tend

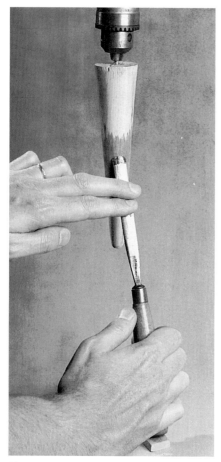

BENT GOUGES

Bent gouges, which are used on recessed surfaces, include curved gouges and spoon gouges. A curved gouge is used where there is a reasonable amount of maneuvering room, and a spoon gouge in very restricted spaces. Bent gouges are subject to all of the same considerations as straight gouges, although they do present some special difficulties when it comes to truing the sweep and honing the inside.

You can use the same general principles for truing the sweep on bent gouges as you do with straight gouges, but you must deal with a much shorter section of the tool because the tool is bent. A coating of liquid sandpaper or PSA-backed abrasive on a shopmade wooden cone is the easiest way to address the problem (see the photo at left). This will true only a short section of the gouge, but it can also be used for grinding the inside bevel of the tool.

To true the sweep using a drill-press-mounted cone, hold the gouge against the cone at a slight skew so that the cone gives a trailing stroke as it rotates.

o have good conformation even in the inexpensive sets. It is in the European tools that you will find the most problems.

You have two choices when you get a defective parting tool. You can return it to the vendor or you can correct it. Given the current state of world manufacturing, I would suggest that you keep the parting tool if it only needs a small amount of work to bring it into line. From personal experience, I can tell you that the vendors have a hard time finding perfect ones. The answer is not just to buy Japanese ones (unless you intend carving only soft-wood) because Japanese parting tools, like Japanese chisels, are usually laminated and can be quite tempera-mental in Western hardwoods.

Assuming that you have a tool with a defect like the one shown in the drawing at far right, the best way to restore it is with a diamond file. If you can find a 600x diamond file that is not itself defective, it does not take long to true the wing of a parting tool, although you will probably not get an ideally shaped V-bottom. To clean that up, I would recommend either a 75mm (3-in.) feather-edge file or a carefully fitted micro-finishing abrasive on a steel blank. Whatever you do, make sure you have the inside of the parting

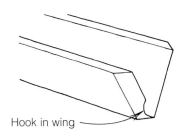

Hook in wing

tool dressed properly before you attempt to sharpen it. If you attempted to sharpen the defective parting tool shown in the drawing, you would find that the whole side would fall away in the area of the defect giving you a tool that looks something like the drawing above. The hook in the wing makes the tool impossible to use for anything but cutting parallel to the grain. In cross-grain cutting the fibers will be trapped in the hook and will tear out. The inside of a parting tool must be straight, so

that when you sharpen the wing it can be abraded evenly and in a line parallel to the inside of the wing.

SHAPING THE HEEL

The whole purpose of a parting tool is to take advantage of the play of light and shadow on the sides of the cut, with a very clear demarcation line where they meet. For best effect this junction must be kept sharp.

You can make the cut from a parting tool with a rounded V look crisp if you shape the heel carefully, and you can also make a cut from a parting tool with a sharp V look round if you shape the heel poorly. To give yourself the best mobility with a parting tool, you should use fairly short bevels and then relieve the tool for some distance back. You want a fairly short bevel so that you can

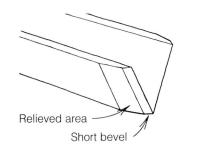

Relieved area

Short bevel

change direction quickly and still make a clean cut.

A parting tool always cuts a more obtuse angle than the angle of its wings. Taking a 60° parting tool as an example, it will cut a 60° V only at a 0° bevel angle. As soon as the tool is tilted, it cuts more than a 60° V. Depending upon the sweep of the wings, it could be cutting as much as a 90° V at a 45° lift angle. In fact, one of the early tricks you learn with a parting tool is to increase the attack angle when you are turning a tight curve, because it gives you a greater relief angle and greater maneuverability. In any event, you want to give yourself ample clearance so that the only mark left on the wood will be the crisp V made by the two intersecting cutting surfaces. However, if you have a parting tool that does not have a sharp V, you can simulate this by

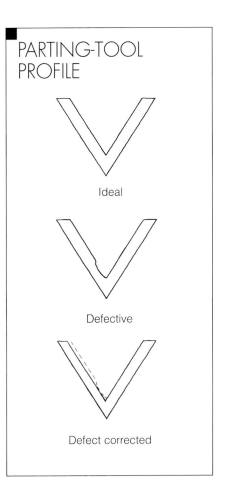

PARTING-TOOL PROFILE

Ideal

Defective

Defect corrected

shaping the heel into a sharp V so that in use the heel will press into the bottom of the cut and make it appear crisper than it really is. This is only a makeshift solution, and the bottom of the parting tool should be dressed out as soon as possible so that there is a crisp V there.

WING SWEEP

For a general-purpose parting tool, you want the wings to rise at 90° to the axis of the tool (see the drawing on p. 112). With the wings square, in use they will always be leading the heel of the tool. This is necessary so that the edges of the chip are severed before the bottom. If the wings were swept backward, the heel of the tool would have to be forced through the wood and, particularly dangerous, as the cut was ending the heel could be snapped off in an attempt to lever out of the cut. Wings that are square to the axis of the tool are actually swept forward in relation to the bevel so that the heel is not trapped as the tool comes out of the wood.

For long and deep cuts where there are no sharp curves, some carvers like to put a fair amount of forward sweep on the wings so that the chip releases more easily. This is more a matter of personal preference than necessity. It is also conceivable that you would want the wings on a parting tool swept back slightly. This would be the case if you were making stop cuts with the tool, cuts that butted some other feature.

As a final consideration, regardless of how you sweep the wings, you will find that reducing the bevel angle as you come up the wing will increase the maneuverability of the tool. The rationale is exactly the same as that given in the shaping of gouges. A reduced bevel angle reduces lateral wedging. In fact, there is no reason that the tool could not have some inside bevel, as recommended for gouges, to strengthen the upper wings.

The inhibiting factor in all of this shaping is that parting tools are so hard to sharpen well that you may want to stop when you have a keen edge and a workable shape, even if it is not ideal. You would not be alone if you did.

WING SWEEP

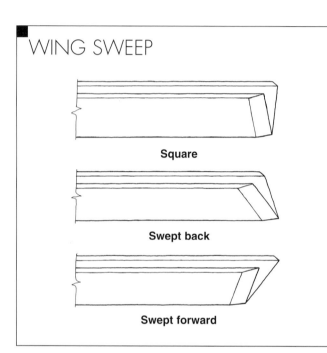

Square

Swept back

Swept forward

Sharpen the bevel of a parting tool over the platen on a belt sander, with the tool held more or less horizontal and the wing edge roughly parallel to the belt travel.

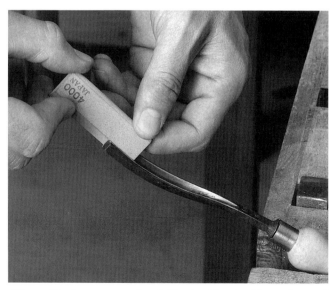

Alternatively, you can clamp the parting tool in a vise and use a slipstone on the inside.

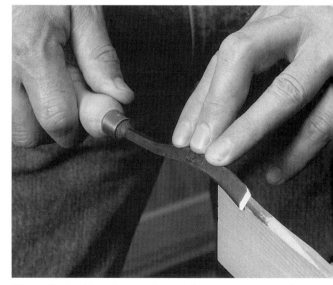

Hone the inside of a parting tool on a custom-made wooden form charged with honing compound. (Photos by Susan Kahn)

SHARPENING PARTING TOOLS

V-tools should be sharpened very carefully, and for this reason I would use a fairly fine belt (no coarser than 120x) on a belt sander. I would also hold the tool so that the wing edge is almost parallel to the direction of travel of the belt, as shown in the top photo on the facing page. This orientation makes it easiest to ensure an even grind along the entire edge. If you accidentally grind past the line of light at the heel, you must square up the wings and start over again. Otherwise, you will have a fiber trap at the heel that will constantly frustrate you in use.

A parting tool cannot be sharpened adequately on the face of a grinding wheel—it's much too finicky a job. If you don't have a belt sander or a horizontal wet wheel, I would recommend clamping the tool at a suitable angle and using a bench stone or slipstone to shape the edge (see the bottom left photo on the facing page). For honing, use a micro-finishing abrasive belt, a leather belt with chromium-oxide compound or custom-made wooden forms charged with chromium-oxide compound. As with gouges, a parting tool will shape its own hone (bottom right photo on facing page).

INSHAVES

Inshaves have a variety of uses, from dressing the inside of barrel staves to forming chair seats. Most inshaves sold in North America today come from a German manufacturer of drawknives. The stock blade is bent into shape, hardened, tempered and then ground only on the outside of the tool. This is probably the best example of the curious belief still held by some that a tool can be sharpened by working on only one of the two surfaces that make an edge.

An inshave is not an easy tool to use, and it must be very well sharpened to be effective. A new inshave of the type mentioned above needs a fair amount of work on the inside. This is best done with a sanding drum, as shown in the photo at left below. Whenever you are using a sanding drum for sharpening, use the largest-diameter drum that will fit in the curves of the tool. The smaller the drum, the more scalloped the edge you will create. Use a confident sweep of the drum on the tool (if it is being held in a flex shaft) or of the tool on the drum (if it is drill press mounted). Hesitation or indecision will leave you with a nasty little groove in one spot on the edge. When the lion's share of the work seems to be done, you can switch to using a gouge cone or a sandpaper-

covered wooden form to finish grinding the inside. Then use micro-finishing abrasives or chromium-oxide compound on a wooden form for final honing.

The outside bevel is very easily done on a belt sander or manually. For most uses, the outside bevel should be slightly rounded so that the tool can cut in a gentle arc, as is necessary when making chair seats, for example.

SCORPS

A scorp, commonly used for carving spoons, is a variation of an inshave and should be sharpened in the same manner; obviously the scale of equipment should be reduced to fit the size. Fortunately new scorps come with a far better finish than inshaves and frequently need only honing.

The outside of a scorp can be honed on a belt sander or by hand. I would avoid trying to do it on a felt wheel, because it is not an easy tool to control on a wheel. For the inside of the scorp, I recommend a wooden form, shaped as

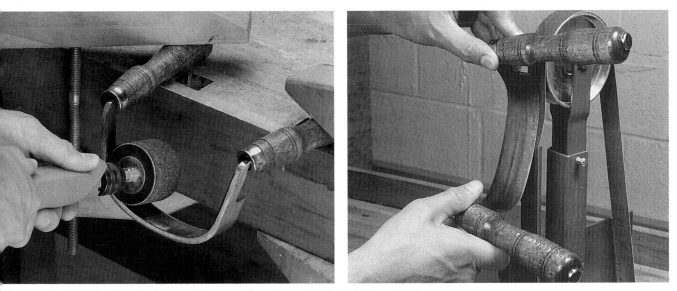

Sharpen the inside of an inshave with a sanding drum (left) and the outside bevel in the slack of the belt on a belt sander (right). (Photos by Susan Kahn)

shown in the photo below, charged with chromium-oxide compound and used much like a file, always stroking from the back to the edge.

For the outside of the scorp, a custom-shaped wooden form is fine, only in this case you should have three grooves—one for the center of the tool and one for each edge. Again, always stroke from back to edge. In this case, you would push the scorp through the formed troughs.

The included angle on the edge of both inshaves and scorps can be quite low, somewhere around 15°. Any damage that does occur to the edge in use is usually caused by a scraping or prying action on end grain, both of which are incorrect uses of the tool.

MICRO-SCORPS

These small tools bear about the same relationship to regular scorps as chip-carving knives do to butcher knives. A relatively recent innovation, micro-scorps are the ultimate miniaturization of the spoon gouge. They are un-questionably tricky tools to sharpen. You want to keep a semicircular edge all in one plane. Edge irregularity will cause fiber trapping and make the tool difficult to use.

To hone the inside of a micro-scorp, use a wooden dowel (a bamboo skewer also works well) charged with chromium-oxide compound. The dowel should be just slightly smaller in diameter than the hole of the scorp, and it should always be passed through in one direction only so that there is a trailing stroke on the edge. If you try to run it back and forth in the hole, you will cause edge dulling.

The easiest way to hone the outside of a micro-scorp is with a small wooden backed leather strop (see the photo at left on the facing page). It has just the right amount of forgiveness to prevent putting flats on the edge, and if you hone with a quartering stroke (diagonal to the edge) you will detect any problems before they become too great.

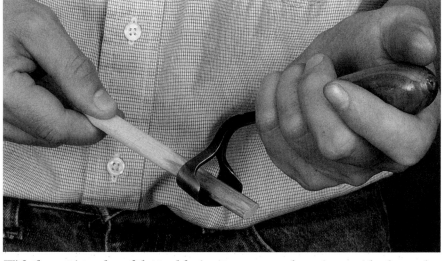

With the cutting edge of the tool facing away, use a chromium-oxide-charged wooden form to hone the inside of a scorp. Move the form much like a file, from the back inside of the scorp toward the edge. (Photo by Susan Kahn)

HONING WITH BAMBOO SKEWERS

Bamboo skewers are wonderful tools in the woodshop. They are ideal for putting glue in dowel holes. They can be pared flat on one end to make an epoxy mixing paddle that is also an excellent applicator. They are useful as small dowels. They are good spacers to keep glue squeeze-out off a bench. The list is endless.

They have a limited use in sharpening as hones for a few tools. Charged with chromium oxide, they make a strong hone for the inside of veiners, small parting tools and micro-scorps. They are just about the right size; if not, they can be pared to fit using the tool itself. In use, it is best to force the skewer into the micro-scorp from the back and pull it through as you might a needle. It works well.

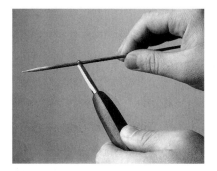

HOOK KNIVES

Hook knives serve similar purposes to scorps and inshaves in hollowing vessels and are sharpened in a similar way. Carver's hooks, which have a gently curved blade with a tight hook on the end, are best sharpened on a belt sander on the convex side and with an abrasive-covered wooden form on the inside. An appropriately sized wooden dowel can be used to hone the inside of a tight hook.

The larger hook knives of the Swedish style are honed similarly on the convex side but require slightly different treatment on the inside. Since these are double-edged knives, inside honing has to be done carefully, otherwise you might dull one edge as you are sharpening the other. A wooden dowel charged with green honing compound will still do the job, but I prefer to use one that is no more than three-quarters the diameter of the inside of the hook. You are honing through what is, in essence, a section of a cylinder. If your hone is the same size as the inside of the cylinder, you cannot tilt it at all to avoid scraping against the entry edge. If you use a smaller hone, you avoid this problem.

You invariably end up putting a small bevel on the inside of the tool, but this is no problem since the outside bevel can be reduced to compensate. When the knife is purchased, the outside bevel is usually a bit too steep anyway. Again, you are looking for an included angle in the range of 15°, 20° maximum for harder woods and heavy cuts. This is definitely one tool that you want to use at the lowest possible included angle in order to maximize your mechanical advantage.

KEEPING CARVING TOOLS SHARP

After doling out all this advice on how to sharpen carving tools, it seems worthwhile to offer some advice on how to avoid dulling them after you have them in the shape you want.

Carving tools do not dull quickly unless:
• they are being forced unnaturally, either through excessive mallet blows or because of prying action;
• they are being used carelessly or stored where they can rattle together;
• they are being used on dirty wood; or
• they are being used on wood of inconsistent texture. Pin knots in spruce cause faster edge deterioration than carving a hard, but consistently dense wood like ebony.

Half the secret of having sharp tools that stay sharp is in shaping the edges correctly; the other half is in not dulling them through ignorance and carelessness.

Use a leather strop to hone the outside of a micro-scorp, honing the edge with a quartering stroke. (Photo by Susan Kahn)

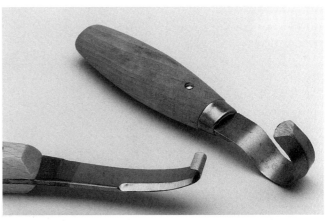

Hook knives include carver's hooks (left) and double-beveled Swedish-style knives (right). (Photo by Susan Kahn)

CHAPTER 10

TURNING TOOLS

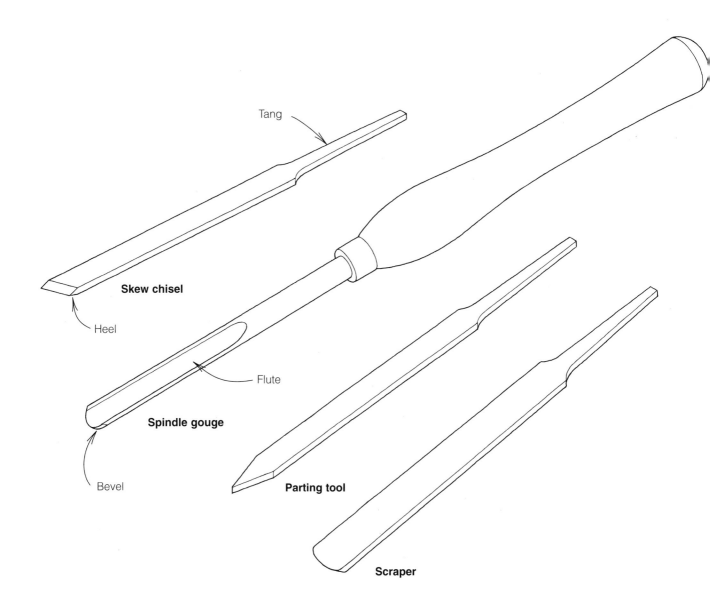

Tang

Skew chisel

Heel

Flute

Spindle gouge

Bevel

Parting tool

Scraper

Of all woodworkers, I feel particularly sorry for turners because they not only face conflicting advice on sharpening from the various authors in the field but also are unable to rely on the suitability of any of the grind angles on tools when they buy them. I have seen scrapers come from the factory with an 80° bevel angle, even though a 70° angle is advertised, and skews with a 90° included angle, triple the angle that most teachers would recommend.

After reading a number of books on turning over the years and having listened to a number of turning instructors, I have come to the conclusion that most good turners achieve their results by overwhelming their tools with tremendous innate skill. Unfortunately, many of these same turners who have developed specific techniques to overcome tool-shape inadequacies then go on to recommend these techniques to novice turners, when the novice should be learning good shaping and honing technique instead. In my view, this is the basic reason for the proliferation of techniques that we have seen in the last ten or fifteen years.

In this chapter, I am going to avoid the subject of turning technique entirely. Part of the reason is that good sharpening principles can be adapted to any technique. The other part of the reason is that I do not want to put myself in the same position as some of the turning authors who make very categorical statements about sharpening technique even when they have limited understanding of metallurgy or abrasives. Having drawn a line in the sand, I will try to stay on my side of it.

GRIND ANGLES/ BEVEL ANGLES

The same general theory developed in Chapter 2 applies to turning tools just as it does to chisels and plane blades, namely, "a cutting tool should be ground at the lowest possible bevel angle consistent with edge retention." The only difference is that turning tools are much more like power tools than hand tools and are subjected to more

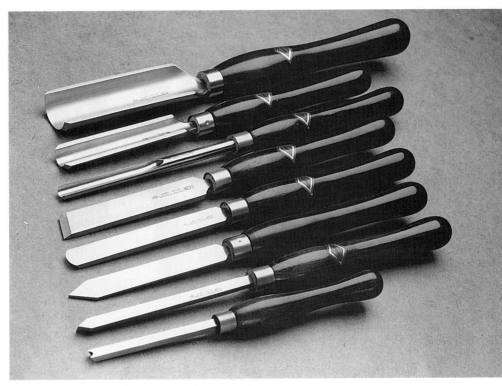

A typical selection of tools for spindle turning.

SETTING TOOL-REST ANGLES

Since you use only a small number of grinding angles for most shop tools, it is worth making a few angle templates to keep near your grinder or belt sander. Use at least ½-in. thick material and make the templates about 8 in. long and 3 in. deep. The angle you use to set your tool rest is 180° less the grind angle, but if you use parallel-sided stock for the template you will have both angles anyway. Mark the angles and give the template a coat of shellac to keep it stable.

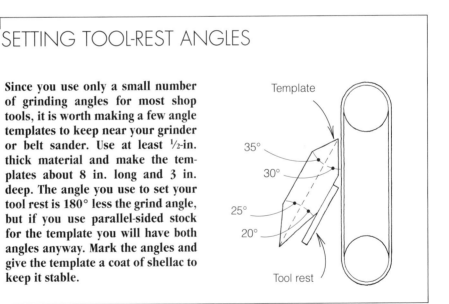

severe shocks than chisels or plane blades. This requires some increase in bevel angles in order to withstand the shocks, but the basic principle applies broadly in turning.

SCRAPERS

One of the continuing arguments in the turning community is whether or not scraping is an honorable activity. Some turners insist that virtually everything must be done with gouges and skews; they look down on turners who use scrapers to any extent. I believe that this state of affairs came about for two reasons. First, many of the scrapers used traditionally had virtually square edges and tended to pull the fibers out of the wood rather than cut them. Second, there is always a bit of snobbery involved in the competent use of a tricky tool like a skew, whereas virtually anyone can use a scraper acceptably.

Scrapers are far more predictable in use than skews or gouges. It is nearly impossible to get an inadvertent dig, or "catch," when using a scraper. So for all of those woodworkers for whom turning is a very occasional activity and who are just looking for a predictable result from their lathe, scrapers can be a godsend.

If you do a good job of sharpening a scraper, it is no longer a scraper, it is a cutter. Just as you can burnish a hook onto a well-prepared cabinet scraper to make a wonderful small plane, you can put the same sort of hook onto either a carbon-steel or high-speed-steel scraper that will give you clouds of continuous shavings. In fact, you can adjust the size and shape of the hook to make roughing scrapers as well as finishing scrapers.

SHARPENING SCRAPERS

Scrapers are very easy to grind, especially if you use a belt sander. Just set the tool rest at the bevel angle you want (usually between 70° and 80°), lay the scraper flat on the rest and grind freehand, as shown in the photo above.

There are four reasons I recommend using a belt sander. First, it is very easy to set angles accurately between two flat surfaces, and angular control is important here. Second, it is easier to control the grinding process on a belt sander, particularly with oddly shaped scrapers. There is much more maneuvering room than with a bench grinder where the motor is a limiting factor.

To grind a scraper on a belt sander, set the tool rest at the required angle (usually between 70° and 80°) and grind freehand.

The reason turning tools are more like power tools than hand tools is that they are used to work wood that is under power. In addition to the intermittent shocks experienced, there is generally greater stress and certainly greater heat in the cutting process. But, there are numerous similarities to hand tools; I would use the example of planing cylinders to make the point. It takes a substantial amount of skill to do a good job of planing a cylinder on a lathe using a skew chisel or even a flat chisel. Yet an ordinary bench plane can be applied to the rotating cylinder on the lathe, and you will find that it works very much like using a smoothing plane on wood. With the plane somewhat askew the cylinder, you will find that the wood passing by the plane is much like having the plane passing by the wood. Not, of course, that I recommend this technique because, as stated earlier, I intend to avoid technique and deal only with sharpening. As we look at different tools we will return to the subject of bevel angles repeatedly, but I wanted to emphasize at the beginning of this chapter that the same general theories apply to dimensioning wood in the turning process as they do in other aspects of woodworking.

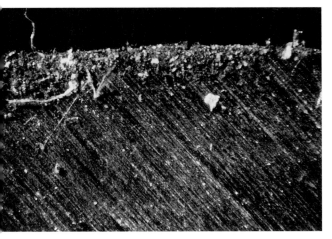

A magnified portion of the tip of a scraper as it comes from the grinder. Bits of broken abrasive particles are visible, as well as the edge burr and portions that are breaking away on the left and right of the photograph.

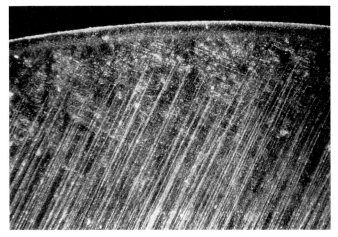

This is the same scraper after lapping and burnishing. The grind marks are substantially smaller on the scraper and disappear near the burnished edge. The keenness of the edge is apparent. (Photos courtesy Canadian Conservation Institute)

Third, you can change grit sizes in seconds as desired or required, and, fourth, you do not get a hollow grind with a belt sander. Since these scrapers are bevel-rubbing tools in use, a hollow grind is undesirable.

Most turners use scrapers just as they come from the grinding wheel or sander. Even with very fine grit belts or wheels, the scraper will have a burr on the top that creates a tiny cutting edge. As can be seen from the photo at left above, the burr does not vary a great deal in size since it tends to be cut off fairly soon after it is formed. The wire edge that has been released in such a manner is visible on the left-hand side of the photo.

But there is a far better way to get a cutting edge on a scraper that is sharper, stronger, more durable and of more predictable result. You grind the scraper as usual, then strip the burr off the top with a fine honing stone (a 6000x or 8000x water stone, a Black Hard Arkansas, etc.) or, my favorite, the 5-micron silicon-carbide 3M micro-finishing abrasive. It takes the burr off in no time and leaves a mirror finish on the top of the scraping tool. Then you burnish the hook that you want on the scraper.

HOW A BURR FORMS DURING GRINDING

At various times in woodworking literature you will see comments that the burr forms on the top of the scraper by a deposit process; hot chips of steel removed by the wheel are carried around a full rotation and deposited on the top of the scraper, sort of tack welded into position. This is not what happens.

The burr forms on the top of the scraper because a large number of the abrasive particles in a wheel at any one time have negative rake angles. Such particles tend to plow a groove in the steel without removing much material. When the particles first encounter the top edge of the scraper, they deform the steel at that point, raising a lip that is the burr that turners depend on for cutting.

Only a fairly small percentage of particles in a grinding wheel are actually cutting, taking out chips. Many are just scraping or plowing their way through. Scraping or plowing removes material but also generates a lot of heat by deforming the steel. For this reason, you always want a clean unglazed wheel with the maximum number of sharp particles exposed.

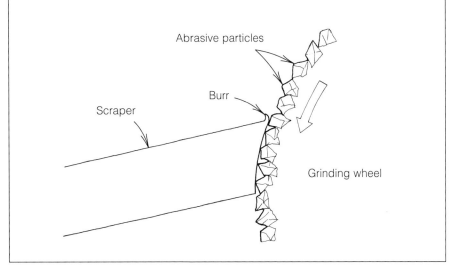

A commercial burnisher for high-speed-steel scrapers.

High-speed-steel scrapers are the toughest to burnish. To deal with these scrapers, I designed the burnisher shown in the photo at left. It is a carbide rod with a 10° conical tip set in an aluminum plate drilled for a lever pin. With the burnisher clamped in a vise, you can set the lever pin in one of several available holes (the one that best suits the scraper at hand) and use both hands plus your body mass to lean into the burnishing process. Even high-speed-steel scrapers are easy to burnish with this system. Scrapers ground at 75° and burnished at 80° with this device serve most turning needs, since the size of the hook can be controlled by burnishing pressure.

If you have never burnished a hook on a turning scraper before, you might be startled by the result. The burnished scraper is a potent cutting tool. If, for example, you have ground the scraper at 70° and burnished it at 80°, you will find that you have a roughing tool, capable of removing a steady stream of thick shavings, even from end grain. You will also find that the scraper tends to be drawn into the work. With a pronounced hook, you can even get digs!

To change from a roughing scraper to a finishing scraper, you just reduce the burnishing angle. This immediately gives you greater control, because you get a wider rubbing bevel. You will find that the process can be adjusted in either direction to accommodate a range of cutting actions. The operative word here is "cutting."

This is no longer a scraping tool; it is a cutting tool capable of giving a very fine finish. Using a light pass at a burnishing angle of 5° or less, you can create a fine hook that is easily controlled in use. You will find that such a scraper can make a substantial difference turning slim stock between centers. The hook draws the work to it, reducing whip by acting like a steady rest. You will find equally that you can get remarkable finishes on face-plate work with such a scraper. The finish

■ RPM AND CUTTING ACTION

You will find that the cutting action of any turning tool can be changed by altering the spindle speed. Once a blank has been roughed down to good balance, increasing the spindle speed will make most tools cut more predictably. Whether you notice it or not, you will invariably find that you are taking a lighter cut at the higher speed but removing wood at a faster rate. A tool such as a roughing gouge, which can readily dig at low speeds, becomes more controllable at higher speeds.

Nowhere do you notice this phenomenon more than with burnished scrapers. At sub-optimal speeds, they can catch; at ideal speeds, they will consistently take a beautiful, thin shaving.

So whenever you think that your tool's edge shape may be at fault, check the cutting action at higher and lower spindle speeds before resharpening.

Burnishing the tip Burnishing a turning scraper is not as easy as burnishing a cabinet scraper (see pp. 134-137). The turning scraper is much harder and is often an awkward shape. It can be burnished freehand, but I recommend that you wear gloves for the process since it is easy to slip and give yourself a nasty cut. As a bare minimum, clamp the scraper low in a vise (with wood-lined jaws) so that your hands are less likely to come in contact with an edge.

GRINDING WHEELS FOR TURNERS

Books on turning all offer sharpening advice, but only two of the ten in print as this is being written deal with the specific type of grinding wheel that should be used. Both recommend aluminum-oxide stones of medium hardness, 38A80H-8VBE in one case and 38A60J-8VBE in the other. The latter, although coarser than the former, is also harder, so the finished grind will be similar. A J-grade will last longer but grind hotter then an H-grade; it would be fine for high-speed steel but would require a light touch with a high-carbon steel.

For grinding high-speed steel, Jerry Glaser, a California tool designer and manufacturer, uses one of the new seeded-gel stones from Norton (see p. 39). The seeded-gel process bonds small particles together to form larger ones; these are then combined with standard aluminum-oxide particles in ratios up to 1:1. In use, the constructed particles tend to fracture rather than break away, creating a stone that gives a finer grind than the grit size would indicate. Glaser uses a 5SG60KVS, which indicates that 50% of the particles are seeded gel in a 60-grit wheel of K (medium) hardness with some sort of vitrified bond.

Norton recommends this seeded-gel stone for use only where sufficient grinding pressure will be used to ensure particle fracture; it is not for light cuts and is too hot for carbon steel. Used for grinding the basic shape on HSS tools, though, it is ideal.

Since HSS is reputed to have good red hardness, Glaser performed some basic tests to see how tool hardness might be affected by various heat levels (see the drawing below). As the results show, only the area that had been glowing red had serious softening; anything that had not been burned black retained the original hardness or close to it. This is quite different from high-carbon-steel alloys, where you can be certain that anything that turned blue during grinding has been unacceptably softened.

For anyone grinding both carbon-steel and HSS turning tools, I would still recommend a 38A80H-8VBE as the best all-round wheel.

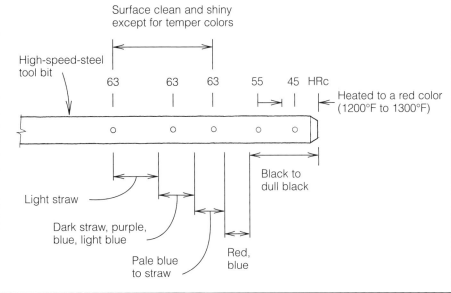

achieved and the degree of control that his system offers is truly remarkable. For example, you will find that you can tilt the scrapers to take shearing cuts. What else you do with them is a function of your technique and interest.

As with any other edge, the smoothness of the two surfaces intersecting to form the edge determines its keenness. Thus far I have mentioned honing only one of the two surfaces, the flat top of the scraper. I am reluctant to suggest honing the ground bevel, because even a slight angular difference can compromise the final hook. Another reason honing is less necessary in this instance is that a burnisher, used at an

angle so close to the primary bevel angle, tends to blend the grinding serrations into a smooth plane. It is a bit like a knife-sharpening steel in effect. And the final reason I would dodge honing the bevel is that if you sharpen scrapers on a belt sander as I recommend, you can use a fine belt to refine the grind without actually honing.

GOUGES

The three families of gouges used in turning (roughing, spindle and bowl) can all be ground on a bench grinder or a belt sander. With a bench grinder, you get a hollow bevel and with a belt sander, a flat bevel. Another consideration is that it is generally more expensive to grind with a belt sander, since belts cost more than stones for removing a given amount of steel. Finally, good gouge-grinding jigs exist for grinders but not for belt sanders. Taking all factors into account, I would recommend using a grinder with an 8-in. wheel, with a 6-in. wheel as an acceptable alternative. (See the sidebar above for more on grinding wheels.)

All gouges should have polished flutes. Sometimes it takes a fair amount of work initially to clean up the flute of a gouge. It can be done with successively finer abrasive paper on a wooden dowel (my preference), with slipstones or with a shaped felt wheel with chromium-oxide honing compound.

Whatever method is used, you want the flute of the gouge to be as smooth and straight as possible.

You may also want to hone the ground bevel. Many turners take their gouges directly from the grinder to their work without any kind of honing. That is a personal choice, but a honed edge will cut better, longer and cooler than an edge straight from a grinder. Obviously, it will also leave a smoother finish on the wood.

There are two reasons that most turners go directly from grinding to cutting. The first is that it saves time, and the second is that they do not want to risk creating a second bevel on the gouge, which would cause control problems. Both are legitimate concerns for a production turner, but there are ways around the two problems. The tremendous variety of bevel angles and tip shapes for gouges has precluded the development of sharpening jigs and fixtures that can meet all of the various demands, but the Glaser joystick (see p. 125) will solve most of the problems. It is particularly useful for complex grinds such as the side-ground gouge (discussed below), although it also guarantees a regular, single-bevel grind on other tools as well.

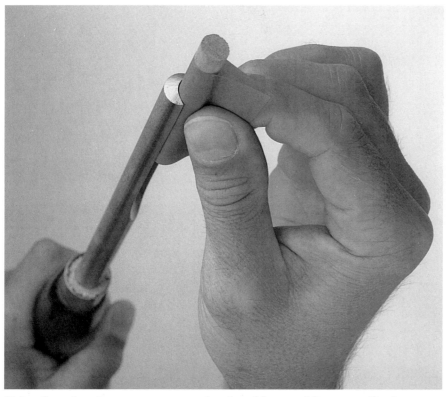

Using fine abrasive paper on a wooden dowel is one of the most effective ways to polish the flute of a gouge.

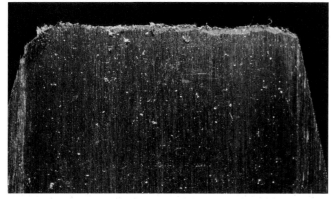

A gouge straight from the grinder has a burr that will cut, but it often has a weak hinge of metal (just visible on the right-hand portion) that will break off almost immediately in use.

A gouge that has been deburred and honed has a stronger and sharper cutting edge. (Photos courtesy Canadian Conservation Institute)

If you have a clean single-bevel grind, you should be able to hand-hone the tool without creating a second bevel. All you want to do is remove the serrations at the edge, not create a wide

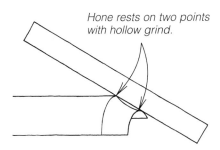

Hone rests on two points with hollow grind.

band of mirror finish. Also, if you have ground the tool on a wheel, you will have a hollow grind that makes honing substantially easier since you can rest the hone on two points as you work (see the drawing above).

ROUGHING GOUGES

Roughing gouges should be ground square across the front and have a bevel angle of about 45°. If you turn only softwood, such as clear pine, this bevel angle can be reduced to about 35°. If you turn only hardwood, you may want to increase the angle a bit. Roughing gouges take an incredible beating and need sturdy bevel angles to survive. As usual, you want the lowest bevel angle consistent with edge retention, but with this tool that angle is larger than you might ordinarily expect. As a rough parallel, you can imagine the forces that would be exerted on a carving gouge if you clamped the gouge upright in a vise and tried to carve a piece of wood by striking it against the gouge. This is approximately what happens with a roughing gouge when you use one to rough a square into a cylinder. A constant force is much easier on tools than an intermittent force, just ask any machinist.

WOODEN HONING FORM

For honing both the flutes and bevels of gouges, a wooden spindle can be turned that incorporates the necessary shapes. The wood is charged with chromium-oxide compound before use. The form shown in the photo below includes some shapes for carving tools as well as turning tools.

The form is most easily used on a drill press, with the tool honed on the trailing stroke. Chuck the form in the drill press with a stub in each end (I use lag bolts with the heads cut off). To provide an end bearing, the bottom stud should ride in a lubricated hole in a scrap of wood clamped to the drill-press table.

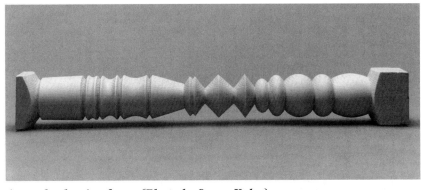

A wooden honing form. (Photo by Susan Kahn)

Roughing gouges, which are ground square across the tip, typically have a 45° bevel angle. These tools exemplify the design principle of form following function: The high wings clip fiber ends to prevent uncontrolled splintering as blanks are roughed down to size.

GRINDING JIG FOR GOUGES

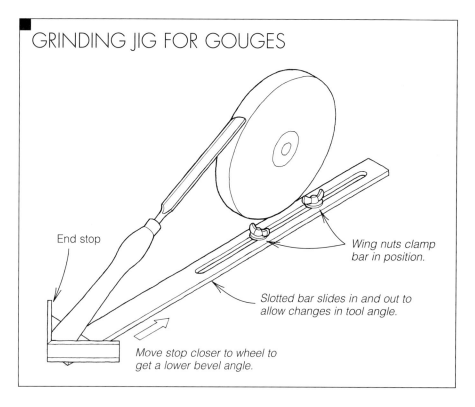

End stop

Wing nuts clamp
bar in position.

Slotted bar slides in and out to
allow changes in tool angle.

Move stop closer to wheel to
get a lower bevel angle.

MODIFIED SPINDLE GOUGE

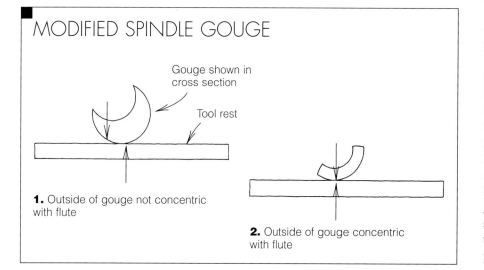

Gouge shown in
cross section

Tool rest

1. Outside of gouge not concentric
with flute

2. Outside of gouge concentric
with flute

For square-end gouges, such as
roughing gouges, a handle end stop to
control the bevel angle is a simple and
useful jig (see the drawing at top).
With the end stop controlling the bevel
angle, you need only rotate the gouge,
keeping it centered on the wheel.
(This jig can also be used to create a
fingernail end, if you dwell longer at
the limits of the rotation than at the
midpoint.)

SPINDLE GOUGES

Spindle gouges have a much easier life
of it than roughing gouges and can be
sharpened at 25°. As always, for very
hard woods this angle may have to be
increased a bit, and for very soft woods
it can be decreased. There are a couple
of things you can do to make your
spindle gouges easier to use. First, you
should ensure that the tip of the gouge

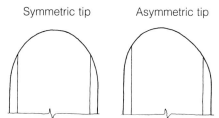

Symmetric tip   Asymmetric tip

is symmetrical when viewed from the
top (see the drawing above). A spindle
gouge is so often used like a skew that
it makes it much easier to use if the
fingernail tip is always centered. Novice
turners often find that they are having
difficulties with a spindle gouge
without realizing that the cause is just
bad shape.

As well as ensuring good tip design,
you can sometimes improve the functioning of a spindle gouge by adjusting
the cross-sectional profile. In his book
The Practice of Woodturning (The
Melaleuca Press, Australia, 1985), Mike
Darlow makes some very specific
recommendations. As one example,
he recommends that the outside of a
gouge should be concentric with the
arc of the flute, so that the reactive force
to cutting is in line with the gouge's
point of contact with the tool rest. This
eliminates the tendency of the gouge to
roll. In Drawing 1 at left, the reactive
force must be resisted by the turner or
the gouge will roll. But if the outside of
the same gouge was concentric with
the flute, the reactive force would be in
line with the point of contact with the
tool rest (as shown in Drawing 2), and
the gouge would not have a tendency
to roll.

GOUGES

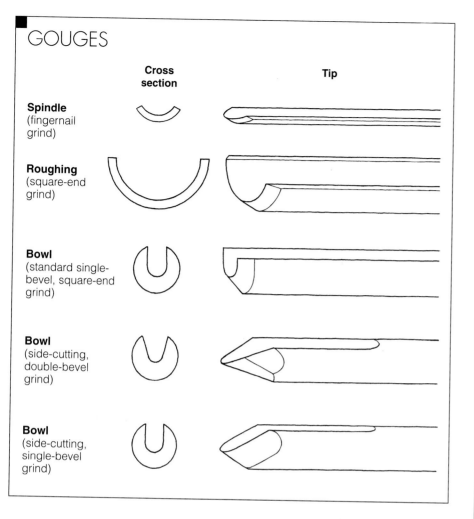

	Cross section	Tip
Spindle (fingernail grind)		
Roughing (square-end grind)		
Bowl (standard single-bevel, square-end grind)		
Bowl (side-cutting, double-bevel grind)		
Bowl (side-cutting, single-bevel grind)		

BOWL GOUGES

The angle at which you sharpen bowl gouges depends both on technique and on the nature of the work that you might be doing. Traditionally, bowl gouges were sharpened at a 40° bevel angle and square across the front, but this is one tool that is highly individualistic among turners. The drawing above shows a standard grind and two types of side-cutting gouges.

For a side-cutting gouge like the examples shown (the first use of which is usually credited to the American turner David Ellsworth or the Irish turner Liam O'Neill), it is almost mandatory to use a jig like the Glaser joystick to get a consistent grind. To attempt a grind like this freehand indicates a bravery verging on foolhardiness. It is extremely difficult to avoid creating multiple bevels as you attempt to get a cutting edge with a smoothly flowing line. One is usually sacrificed to attain the other.

There is another factor at play in a side-cutting gouge like this. To have any hope of a good grind, you have to have a smooth, straight flute. If the flute has been ground freehand or has been buffed too enthusiastically on a shaped leather or felt wheel, it will have a rippled surface, which will quickly

GLASER JOYSTICK

One of the most interesting sharpening aids to be developed in recent years is an adjustable joystick designed by Jerry Glaser, a California designer and manufacturer of turning tools. The joystick can be used to sharpen most turning tools (including radiused skews and spindle gouges), but it excels at putting a side-cutting fingernail grind on bowl gouges.

This exaggerated fingernail tip is very difficult to grind freehand. Glaser's device can be adjusted so that the user has to be concerned only about controlling grinding pressure and speed of lateral movement; the compound grind angles are controlled through the various angular and height adjustments in the joystick. Purists might call this de-skilling a process; realists will appreciate the control and repeatability such an aid provides.

The Glaser joystick in use on a test blank. (Photo by Susan Kahn)

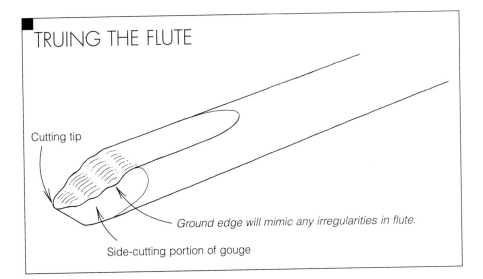

TRUING THE FLUTE

Cutting tip

Ground edge will mimic any irregularities in flute.

Side-cutting portion of gouge

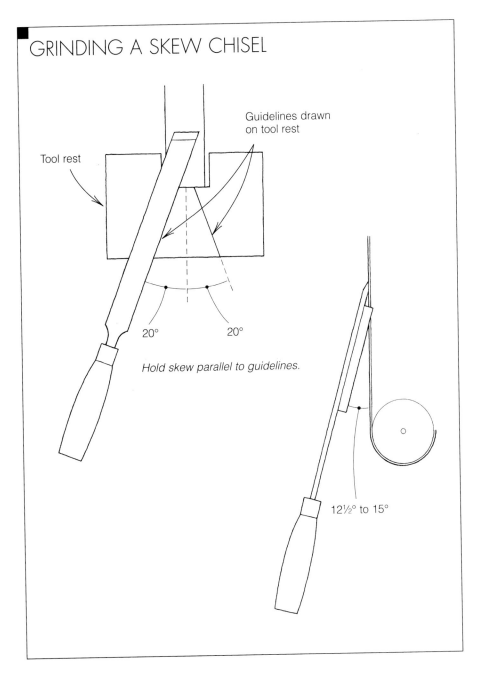

GRINDING A SKEW CHISEL

Tool rest

Guidelines drawn
on tool rest

20°   20°

Hold skew parallel to guidelines.

12½° to 15°

translate into a rippled edge on the side grind (see the top drawing at left). Before grinding, such a gouge would have to have the flute trued. In the home shop, this would best be done with PSA-backed abrasive on a suitably sized dowel or shaped wooden hone.

For a square-end gouge, the flute irregularities would be much less significant since the ground edge would be parallel to the wave crests and troughs. But even in this case the irregularities are seldom exactly parallel to the cutting edge. Inasmuch as they are not parallel, they will introduce edge irregularities unless they are dressed out.

CHISELS

Although many turners insist on using gouges straight from the grinding wheel, almost all turners believe in honing skew chisels. I read one British turning author who felt that it was a waste of time and preferred to drag the skew across the lathe stand in order to remove the burr, but this was an exception to the general practice.

STANDARD SKEWS

The standard skew chisel should be sharpened at about 70° of skew, with bevel angles from 12½° to 15° on each side. At 12½° you would get an included angle of 25°, which would be fine for softwoods. Higher bevel angles might be required for more difficult woods. Grinding a skew is quite straightforward on either a belt sander or a grinding wheel. The same sort of simple jig used for grinding chisels and plane blades will function perfectly well with a skew. Honing can be done with micro-abrasives, either freehand or on a belt sander. Honing can also be accomplished with a simple bench stone.

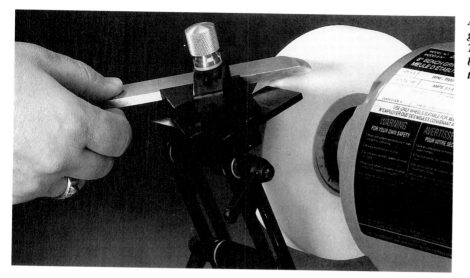

A skew-grinding jig allows you to grind a slight radius on a skew chisel. The radius of the grind is determined by the amount the skew projects from the jig.

RADIUSED SKEWS

A number of turners prefer radiused skews, particularly for turning beads, because they minimize the possibility of digs. You can buy a specially made jig for grinding radiused skews (see the photo above) or make one yourself. If you choose to make a jig, you need only drill a rotation hole in your tool rest and put a matching pin through a tool clamp.

SQUARE-END CHISELS

A standard firmer chisel is often used in place of a skew for planing cylinders or long tapers between centers. The chisel is used askew the turning but, of course, is beveled on only one side. The chisel for this purpose can be sharpened at 25° in exactly the same manner as you would sharpen a regular chisel.

PARTING TOOLS

There are many types of parting tools (the drawing at right shows most of the main types). Sharpening each of these is quite straightforward. The included angles vary from supplier to supplier (anywhere from 30° to 50°), but since they all function by tearing the fibers the angle is not critically important. However, there are a few things you can do to make parting tools function a bit better. These include easing the sharp arrises of the tool and burnishing the tip.

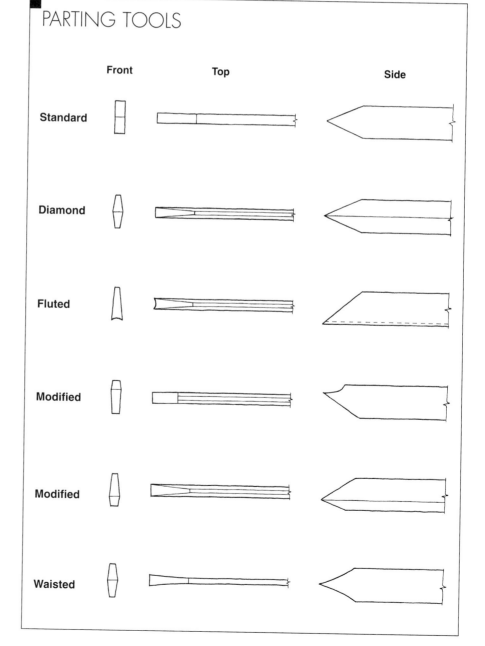

PARTING TOOLS

	Front	Top	Side
Standard			
Diamond			
Fluted			
Modified			
Modified			
Waisted			

EASING ARRISES

All of the samples shown in the drawing on p. 127 except two have tapered upper edges. Of the remaining two, the waisted tool does not require one. With the standard parting tool, it is best to

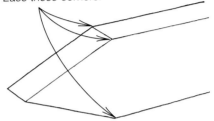

Ease these corners.

ease the sharp arrises of the tool. Otherwise, it can catch in a deep cut.

All except the fluted parting tool should have the very sharp bottom edges broken so that they do not continually scar the tool rest. In the case of the fluted parting tool, it is a good idea to put a plastic spine binder (trimmed to length) on the tool to keep it from chewing up the tool rest.

BURNISHING THE TIP

Although it does not reduce fiber tearing at the edges of the cut, burnishing a hook on the central portion of the parting tool tip reduces the friction and heat in the cutting process and lets the tool track better. It does not require much of a hook, and the hook should be modified to the central three-quarters to four-fifths of the parting tool. This can be readily done with the parting tool clamped in a vise. If you do not trust your technique, you can put two small wood scraps on either side of the parting tool tip to prevent the hook extending to the outside edge (as shown in the photo at left).

An easy setup for well-controlled burnishing of a parting-tool tip. It may appear that the parting tool is held too deeply in the wood scraps and that the burnisher will not be able to reach it. In fact, the burnisher being used has a teardrop cross-section and will touch all of the edge except the very corners, which is exactly what you want it to do.

BEADING TOOLS AND OTHERS

Square beading tools are sharpened like parting tools but without the optional burnishing. Shaped beading tools are honed only on the top; the profiles are not touched.

There are many fad shapes in turning that quickly gain in popularity and often as quickly fade. Ones such as ring tools and hooks can be sharpened in the same manner as carving tools of the same design. Others are usually just a variation of tools in the categories already covered in this chapter.

No area of woodworking has seen greater change in technique and tool design in recent years than wood-turning. Some tools that are now considered standard, such as roughing gouges, were barely available in the market twenty years ago. The same period has seen high-carbon steel replaced by high-speed steel in every-thing but introductory sets.

Fortunately, the new tools, techniques and alloys have been accompanied by advances in abrasives and grinding jigs. But turning tools remain one of the most complex areas of sharpening to master and merit a book, not just a chapter.

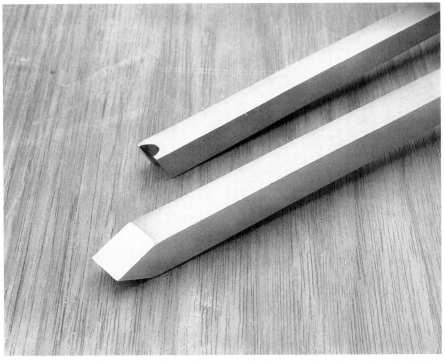

The beading tool at top is a shaped scraper; it is pressed against the spindle to form a bead. The traditional beading tool at bottom is used much like a skew to form a bead.

CHAPTER 11
SCRAPERS

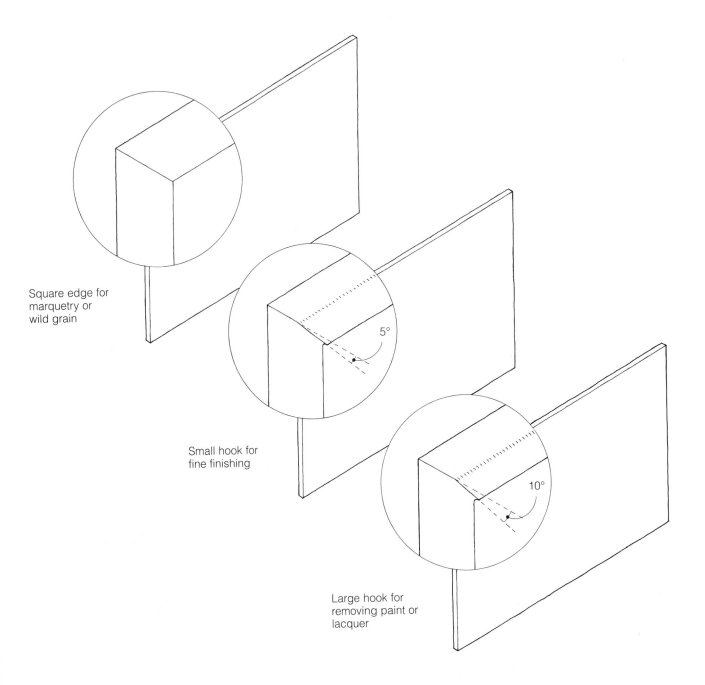

Square edge for
marquetry or
wild grain

5°

Small hook for
fine finishing

10°

Large hook for
removing paint or
lacquer

crapers, a type of hand plane, are the most useful tools in the woodworking shop. No hand tool gives you better control or is more versatile. Scrapers do not cause disasters by suddenly gouging out large pieces of wood and, in fact, are most often used to repair the damage caused by jointers and thickness planers, which are notoriously poor at dealing with varying grain. Scrapers are cheap and easy to sharpen, and they last practically forever. If I am beginning to sound like a revivalist preacher on this subject, it is because the wonders of cabinet scrapers were revealed to me much later in my life than I wish had been the case. I cannot imagine doing any woodworking without scrapers in some form being at hand.

CABINET SCRAPERS

Among the various scrapers available, rectangular cabinet scrapers are the most versatile and the least expensive. Although they can be made from old handsaws or steel similar in thickness and hardness, they are readily available from a variety of sources at moderate prices. Usually about 2 in. by 6 in., rectangular scrapers vary in thickness from 0.4mm (0.015 in.) to 1mm (0.042 in.). Until recent years, most of them were hardened to Rc38 to Rc42, the same hardness as most Western handsaws (not surprising, since they were frequently made from the same stock of steel). In more recent times, much harder scrapers have become available that are in the Rc48 to Rc52 range and will hold an edge longer than the softer scrapers.

JOINTING

Although some cabinet scrapers come with milled edges ready for burnishing (e.g., Sandvik and Veritas), most are just sheared from polished spring steel and have been deburred but do not have milled edges. The first thing that has to be done with such a scraper is to joint it to give it a smooth edge at 90° to the sides.

A well-sharpened cabinet scraper should make clean shavings, not dust. (Photo by Susan Kahn)

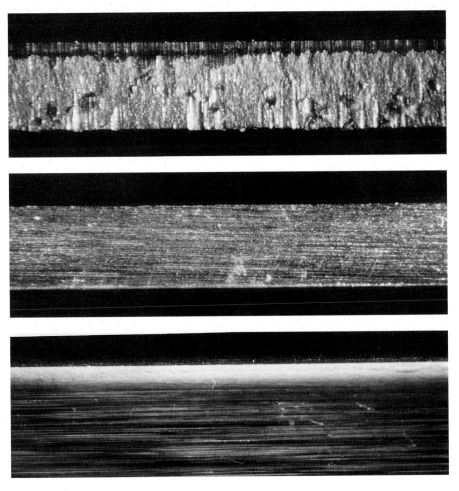

Three cabinet-scraper edges: at top, a sheared edge; in the middle, an edge after jointing with a file; at bottom, an edge (at greater magnification) showing the smoothing effect of stoning and burnishing. (Photos courtesy Canadian Conservation Institute)

The scraper should be clamped in a padded-jaw vise and jointed with a mill file. It takes at most a half-dozen strokes at moderate pressure, followed by a couple of strokes at light pressure for the finest possible finish. You can make a simple jointing jig by running a kerf the same width as the file in a block of wood (see the sidebar below), or you can buy one of several jointing jigs that are on the market. You can also joint the cabinet scraper using the file free-hand, but this can cause you problems in ensuing steps in the sharpening process if you do not get an edge that is dead flat or if you do not file exactly in line with the scraper.

Jointing a cabinet scraper creates a smooth edge at 90° to the sides.

JOINTING AIDS

There are many ways you can joint a scraper (or a handsaw) without using a commercial jointer. Some are detailed here, others you should be able to invent yourself. As with most things, if you know the principles, you can conceive a solution. In jointing, the principles are: (a) keep the edge flat, (b) keep the edge square.

Option A. Make a jointer from a piece of wood. Make the kerf a press fit for your file, or put two wood screws in it to clamp the file. Clip the sharp ends off the screws so that they have bearing flats.

Option B. If you are so impoverished that you can't afford a mill file, drill a hole that is a drive fit for a triangular file and run a saw cut up to it. Add screws if it would make you feel more secure or if the hole is oversize. Be sure the flat of the file is at 90° to the kerf sides.

Option C. If the first two methods are too complex, just use two scraps of wood. Hold them to the file with finger pressure (thumbs on top of the file). Clamp the scraper between two pieces of hardwood in your vise and file the scraper until it is flush with the wood. (Note that I would not use this system with a handsaw, because it is too easy to slip.)

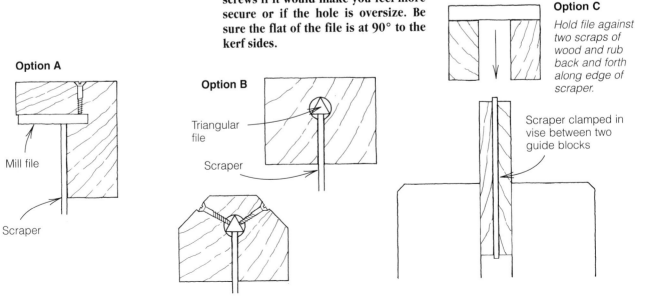

Jointing the cabinet scraper will eliminate the ragged edge caused in the shearing process and replace it with a series of very fine serrations, which will be exactly parallel to the edge if you have used a jointing jig (see the top photo below). If you have done your filing freehand, these serrations will not be parallel to the edge and could result in an uneven interface with the scraper side (see the bottom photo below).

If you have done a good job of jointing the cabinet scraper, you should have a good usable edge that requires no further work for some purposes. For example, if you are removing a layer of crazed varnish in a restoration project or a bit of glue seepage in marquetry, the square edge will do the job nicely without removing much wood (see the drawing on p. 130). But for most purposes, you'll have to go on to burnish the scraper, or better yet, to stone first and then burnish.

Whether or not you decide to stone the scraper depends upon what you intend to do with it and how fussy you are. You can go directly to the burnishing process (see pp. 134-137) if you have filed carefully, or if you are only using the scraper for something like paint removal where the edge will get torn quickly anyway. Stoning is not mandatory, but I strongly recommend that you try it at least once so that you can compare scrapers prepared both ways.

STONING

Just as you want two perfectly smooth surfaces to create a good edge on a chisel, you need the same thing for the best possible edge on a cabinet scraper. It is for this reason that you stone the edge of the scraper. If you have done a good job of filing, you can move directly to a relatively fine stone, something like a 1200x water stone.

For ease of control and to avoid damage to your stones, I recommend that you always stone your scrapers on the side of the stone. This is easily done in a couple of ways. You can set the stone on your bench with a scrap of wood next to it and, holding the stone with one hand, run the scraper back and forth against the edge of the stone using the wood as support (see the photo below). This keeps the scraper at a true 90° to the face of the stone.

Using a scrap of wood to support and align the scraper, stone the edge on the side of a stone.

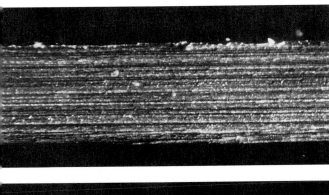

Two magnified scraper edges, one jointed straight (top), the other jointed at an angle (above). After burnishing, the scraper jointed at an angle will have small hooks in the edge wherever the filing grooves intersect it. (Photos courtesy Canadian Conservation Institute)

Another method is to set the stone on edge projecting over the side of your bench and use the face of the bench to maintain a 90° angle as you stone the edge.

If you have used a jointer that holds the file perfectly flat in the jointing process, you will find that it does not take long to stone the edge of the scraper. For a fine edge, you should move on to a 6000x or an 8000x stone and repeat the process. Since these stones usually have wooden bases (see the photo at right on p. 133), the first method is recommended as the easiest to maintain a square edge.

Be careful that you stone a scraper only once on any one spot on the stone, since you will develop a groove in the stone that can round the edge of the scraper. As with any stone, you should be sure that the surface you are using is flat before you begin to use it. You can use a stone a number of times on the side before you have to true the side of the stone, since you have only to vary the thickness of the backing block to adjust the height of the scraper to an unused portion on the stone.

With some scrapers that have not been well polished originally, you will also want to dress both faces of the scraper on a fine stone. (You would also do this to remove any burr raised in the general stoning process.) If you do all of these stoning steps carefully, you should have a very crisp edge on the scraper that can be used as is for fine work such as marquetry or you can then proceed to the next step, burnishing a hook on the scraper.

BURNISHING

The purpose of burnishing a cabinet scraper is to deform the steel to create an edge that has an included angle of something less than the 90° that you started with. To do this, you need a burnisher that is appreciably harder than the cabinet scraper you are burnishing. This would be at least Rc60 in steel, or it could be a finely ground carbide rod in the Rc80 range. You also want a burnisher that is smooth so that it is not abrading the scraper at any time; you want the burnisher to mold the steel to shape, not remove any steel

Some woodworkers recommend using the shank of a screwdriver, the back of a chisel, or even a valve stem to burnish cabinet scrapers. While you may find a screwdriver shank that is hard enough to burnish your cabinet scraper, this is normally only the case if the shank is chrome-plated or nickel-plated. The plating is hard but it is also very thin. As soon as you break through the plating you can cause major damage to the edge of your cabinet scraper. The back of a chisel is the wrong shape, is not smooth enough and is almost never hard enough to be an effective burnisher. Automotive valve stems have nicely formed shanks, but they too are not sufficiently hard, particularly for the modern hard scrapers.

If you want to avoid buying a burnisher, one of the very few things you can use with any confidence is a file that you have very carefully ground to remove the teeth and then completely polished to a smooth finish. In this process, you have to be certain that you don't draw the temper of the file; otherwise, you may soften it below an acceptable level.

There are four basic shapes of burnishers on the market: triangular, round, oval and teardrop (see the sidebar at left). The teardrop-shape cross section is actually a combination of the other three. Historically, the triangular burnisher was used on rectangular cabinet scrapers, and the round and oval burnishers on curved scrapers. The teardrop shape can be used on either.

BURNISHER SHAPES

Although a curve is supposed to touch a line at a point, that is not the case with burnishers. As soon as pressure is applied to a burnisher, it begins to sink into the scraper. Just how far it sinks depends on the applied pressure, the radius of the burnisher at the point of tangency and the hardness of the scraper.

You can roll a hook with light pressure and a small-radius burnisher or use a larger-radius burnisher with more pressure. No burnisher should have any corners; all curves should blend into each other or, in the case of the triangular burnisher, with the plain sides. The round burnisher is the least versatile of the four shapes; the teardrop burnisher is the most versatile because it offers a range of radii.

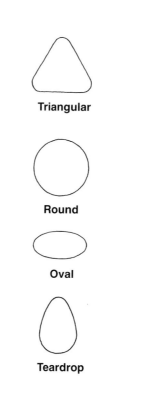

Triangular

Round

Oval

Teardrop

There is a reason for the various shapes. Using the teardrop shape as an example (since it incorporates the others), you would use the largest radius portion for the smoothing strokes on a cabinet scraper and the middle radius portion for burnishing a hook. On very thin cabinet scrapers, which tend to bend when you are burnishing them, you would use the smallest radius so that you would get maximum point pressure without causing the scraper to bend away from the burnisher. In general, you want to use the largest radius that will do the job effectively since it will cause the fewest ripples in the hook. You will quickly learn that by adjusting the pressure you put on the burnisher, you can change the action of it and get exactly the sort of hook you are looking for.

Having chosen your burnisher you are ready to burnish a hook on the cabinet scraper. Before you touch the burnisher to the scraper, you should put some form of lubricant on the scraper. You can use oil (which means you will have to wipe it clean after use), candle wax or whatever machine-top wax you have at hand.

I prefer to rub the tip of my finger along the side of my nose or behind my ear and then rub it along the scraper edge. There is just enough natural oil in either spot to provide the lubrication you need for this process. The great advantage of using this natural lubricant is that it is nearby, there is sufficient supply for almost any amount of burnishing and it will not contaminate your scraper with something that may later end up on your workpiece. If you do not put some lubricant on the cabinet scraper, you will find that the burnishing process generates enough heat to risk damage to either the cabinet scraper or the burnisher. It is a very simple trick, but one that I recommend you always use.

BURNISHER TECHNIQUE

We all have little idiosyncrasies in technique that are important to us but may have greater imagined than real effect on a process. Two of mine are the way I hold a burnisher and the way I always try to travel slightly across an edge as I burnish.

I always hold the unhandled end of a burnisher with the tips of two fingers and a thumb, rather than using a very firm grip. This reduces the amount of pressure that I can apply. If I don't do this, I find myself rolling on hooks that look like tidal waves.

Another habit, which I believe has merit, is to travel just slightly across an edge as you move the burnisher along it. Not only does this feel right, but it avoids overheating the burnisher at one spot with the danger of drawing the temper and then grooving it. It also prevents even minor traveling the opposite way, which seems intuitively wrong to me.

Holding the tip of the burnisher loosely reduces the amount of pressure you can apply and results in a smaller hook. (Photo by Susan Kahn)

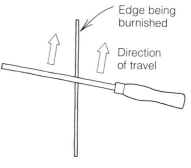

Always let the burnisher travel slightly across the edge as you burnish.

With an unstoned scraper, you should first take one or two strokes using moderate pressure with the burnisher parallel to the scraper edge. This tends to burnish down any serrations left from jointing (which would have caused friction in use later) and will begin to swell the edge of the cabinet scraper. With soft cabinet scrapers (those in the Rc38 to Rc42 range), you may find that this gives you just the right amount of hook, since it is next to impossible to keep your burnisher exactly parallel to the edge without laying on a few degrees of hook accidentally. You'll be able to feel any hook on the scraper by plucking the edge of the scraper with your fingernail. If you have never used a

cabinet scraper before, you should now try the scraper on a piece of hardwood before any further burnishing to see what sort of effect you get.

For any substantial wood removal, you are probably going to need more of a hook than you will get with the burnisher parallel to the edge of the scraper. You will probably want to put at least 2° of hook on the scraper and possibly as much as 15°. The amount of hook is highly subjective. I prefer a relatively low angle, almost never greater than 5°. Perfectly competent

SETTING A BURNISHING ANGLE

If you are uncomfortable doing freehand burnishing of a cabinet scraper, there is a very simple jig you can use to control angles. Clamp the scraper in a vise (always with wooden or padded jaws) next to a 1½-in. wide piece of wood. If you let the cabinet scraper project ⅛ in. above the 1½-in. piece of wood and then let your burnisher blade rest both on the cabinet scraper

and on the piece of wood, you will have a 5° burnishing angle. For a 10° angle (see the drawing below), have the burnisher project ¼ in. above the block of wood; for a 15° angle, let it project ⅜ in., and so on. This is an application of the 1-in-60 rule discussed on p. 17.

It's well worth trying this technique at least once so that you get a good idea of

what the different angles look like from your normal working stance. Whether or not you use the guide all the time depends on your technique. Some people have great hand-eye coordination and can get nearly perfect repeatability when freehand burnishing. Most people cannot.

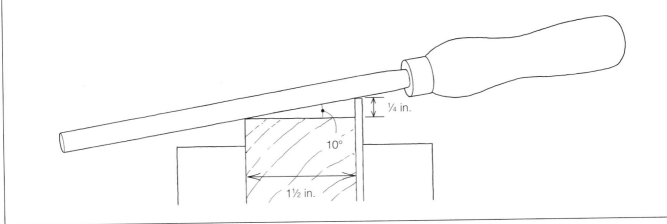

A variable burnisher makes it possible to burnish cabinet scrapers accurately and consistently at angles from 0° to 15°.

cabinetmakers I know prefer to put a much larger amount of hook on a scraper, often going up to 15°. The difficulty I have with such a large angle is that the scraper must be tilted so far forward in use that it makes it far easier to burn your knuckles.

Setting the angle of the burnisher is difficult to do by eye, and I would suggest you use the angle-setting system described in the sidebar at the top of the page. Alternatively, you can use a jigged burnisher like the Veritas variable burnisher, which has a carbide rod that can be dialed to any burnishing angle from 0° to 15° (see the photo above). Incidentally, you never have to

worry about overheating the carbide rod. It can take it. But you should still put a dab of lubricant on the scraper edge; although friction will not hurt the carbide, it can cause a tear in the scraper hook.

SCRAPER RELIEF ANGLES

The rolled edge on a scraper works much like a plane but with some significant differences. First, it has a higher cutting angle than most planes. Second, the depth of cut is controlled by the size of the hook and the relief angle. A large hook will let the scraper take a thicker shaving, but the depth of cut can be reduced by tilting the scraper back a bit. The reduced relief angle will reduce the depth of cut.

If you have vigorously burnished your scraper to the point that it will cut only if you lean it forward until your knuckles are scraping the wood, don't despair. Instead of filing the hook off and starting again, take a couple of jointing passes on the scraper. You can often change the relief angle enough that the scraper will work properly. The hook might be a bit weak but it beats starting from scratch again.

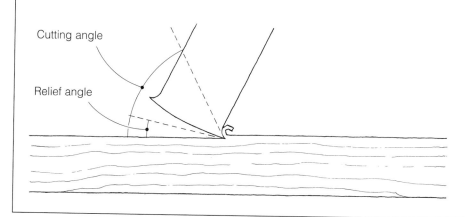

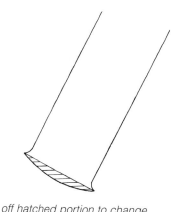

File off hatched portion to change relief angle.

Regardless of the final hook you intend to put on, I recommend that you put it on with as few passes as possible. The number of passes you need depends upon the hardness of your scraper, the pressure you are applying to the burnisher and the shape of that portion of the burnisher that is touching the cabinet scraper. You can arrive at the best combination by experimentation. This is not a process that can be readily detailed for everyone. Whenever possible, I lay on the hook in a single pass, which can be done easily with softer scrapers, though the hard scrapers usually require several passes.

If you have followed the steps reasonably carefully, you should be able to bow the scraper in your hand and take long, virtually transparent shavings from a piece of hardwood. If you only get dust, you have done something wrong. A well-sharpened cabinet scraper is one of the finest planes there is. It automatically controls the depth of shaving it will take, and you should be able to work very

difficult grain with it far more readily than you can with any one of your bench planes.

RESHARPENING SCRAPERS

Two cabinetmakers I know say that an edge can be "picked up" once or twice by running a sharp point along it before you have to resharpen the scraper. Both of these cabinetmakers use a jeweler's burnisher for this process. I am not sure why some jeweler's burnishers have a sharp point on them and others don't, but it is only those curved burnishers with a sharp point that can be used for this process. I have found the whole business of picking up a hook to be very tricky and cannot recommend it. Neither am I pig-headed enough to say that it does not work. What I have found is that it is fairly easy to tear the hook with the burnisher point.

Assuming that your scraper edge is dulled and that you have "picked it up" as many times as practical, you now have to resharpen starting at the first step, which is jointing. When you resharpen, you should remove all of the former hook. This may take a dozen passes with a mill file, but you should be sure that all of the old hook is gone before you start once again.

This process is not as ominous as it sounds, since rectangular cabinet scrapers have four perfectly usable edges and you won't have to resharpen them that frequently if you look after them. First, you do not have to put the same degree of hook on all four edges of the cabinet scraper. You can put different angles and sizes of hooks on each of the four corners and mark them accordingly. To avoid having to resharpen more often than necessary, either keep your cabinet scraper in a vinyl sleeve when it is not being used or keep edge protectors on it. Much like files, more cabinet scrapers are rendered useless when they are not being used than when they are. Just like a file, if it is allowed to rattle around in areas where it will come in contact with other pieces of metal, the cabinet scraper will quickly be dulled. Unless sharpening is your main aim in life, you should keep the edges protected.

SOME PROBLEMS WITH SCRAPERS

Although cabinet scrapers are incredibly useful tools, they can cause problems as well as solve them. As you are busily cleaning up a bit of torn grain caused by your planer, you will sometimes find that you have put a dished area in the wood that will be very noticeable once you have applied a finish. You should take longer strokes to minimize this dishing effect.

Another problem you may encounter is a washboard effect—a series of ripples in the wood you are working. Skewing the cabinet scraper as you work, first one way and then the other, will avoid creating washboard. It will usually give you a better shaving as well, for the reasons covered in Chapter 2. When you skew the cabinet scraper it has the same effect as using a bench plane with a longer sole; you are effectively lengthening the sole of the cabinet scraper as you skew it.

Since washboard is caused by the way the scraper is forming shavings or chips, you can also reduce washboard by tilting your cabinet scraper farther forward, essentially increasing the cutting angle so that you get a different type of chip formation. Although this reduces the washboard effect, it also gives a slightly fuzzier finish.

CURVED SCRAPERS

Curved scrapers are used for bowls, some types of fielded panels, turnings—in fact, anywhere that a curved form is necessary or will serve better than a rectangle. There are many shapes on the market; the two most common are shown in the photo at left.

The convex edges are most readily ground in the slack part of a belt sander. If a 280-grit belt (or finer) is used, no stoning is necessary. The concave edges can be ground on a suitably sized sanding drum. With both edges, some sort of fence or rest should be used to maintain a true 90° face on the scraper. If you have neither a belt sander nor sanding drums, you can stone the edges freehand.

Clamping and burnishing considerations for curved scrapers are the same as for rectangular scrapers.

CABINET SCRAPERS AND SOFTWOOD

The very high cutting angles of cabinet scrapers make them unsuitable for softwoods. If you are very careful when you stone and burnish a cabinet scraper, you can get a hook that will almost work on softwoods like pine and butternut, but it never quite makes it. There is a tendency to crush the fibers rather than cut them.

The crushed fibers catch on the edge of the scraper and will then strip out of your work, leaving long gouges.

By the very nature of the way they are used, cabinet scrapers apply substantial pressure on wood. Even if you did not tear softwoods, you would compress them with a cabinet scraper. Good as they are, even cabinet scrapers have their limitations.

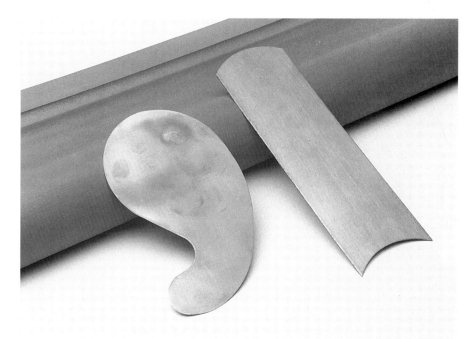

Curved scrapers can handle a wide range of scraping jobs. The scraper with convex/concave ends is suitable for bowl work or for scraping spindles. The comma-shaped scraper is used almost exclusively for fluting and bowl interiors. (Photo by Susan Kahn)

SCRAPER PLANES

Hand-held scrapers tend not only to follow contours but also often emphasize them when used with bad technique. Scraper planes were developed to minimize this effect. A scraper plane is really just a cabinet scraper held in a steel body that makes the process more controllable in some aspects. You won't get the dishing effect mentioned earlier; with a plane the surface will be much more regular. The other great advantage of scraper planes is that you can work a piece of stock vigorously without tiring or burning your thumbs.

Scraper planes are not just jigged cabinet scrapers, however; their blades are designed differently. The blades are usually beveled and require a different burnishing technique than hand-held scrapers.

The bevel angle on scraper-plane blades is usually 45°, although some come with a factory grind of 30°. You might get a marginally cleaner cut in some woods with the lower bevel angle, but you also have a weaker hook and will experience more blade vibration. The 15° difference in bevel angle does not seem to make a great deal of difference when you come to burnishing a hook. Because of the bevel on the blade, a hook can be rolled on very easily. As shown in the drawing below, the burnishing angle should be about 15°. If you go as far as 20°, you get too much scraping and not enough cutting. The higher angle also increases blade chatter. If you go too far the other way (for example, as low as 5°), you risk curling the hook into a semicircle so that it will not cut at all.

If you use very light pressure when you are burnishing, you can get reasonably good cutting action over a fairly wide range of burnishing angles, but I find the tool works best with a fairly pronounced hook put on at 15°.

SCRAPER PLANES

The two types of scraper planes most commonly used today are similar to the Stanley #12 and the Stanley #80, both discontinued by Stanley in 1947, though replicas are now made by others. The Stanley #81 style, with its rosewood sole and nickel-plated body (discontinued in 1941), has not been replicated as far as I know.

The Stanley #12 had the great advantage of having a blade-angle adjustment built in. With this scraper, you can be fairly cavalier about your burnishing angle and adjust the blade angle to compensate. With the Stanley #80 and its cousins, there are no second chances. You have to get the angle right the first time.

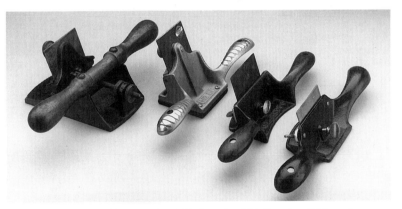

From left to right, the Stanley #12, Stanley #81, Stanley #80 and Stanley #80 replica.

BURNISHING A SCRAPER-PLANE BLADE

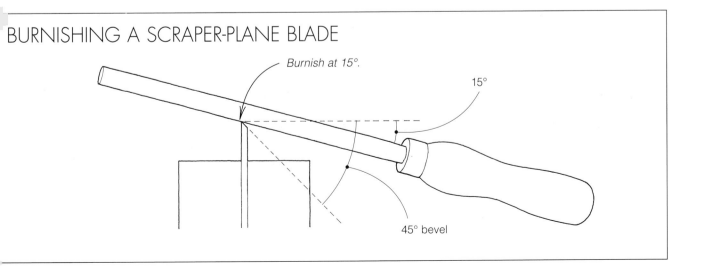

Burnish at 15°.

15°

45° bevel

Just like hand-held cabinet scrapers, scraper-plane blades should be face-lapped to take out grinding marks, and the bevel should be honed with as much care as possible. These blades are too wide to fit most honing guides, so they usually must be sharpened freehand. It makes everything much simpler if you have a jointer with a 45° setting as well as the 90° setting for hand-held scrapers. Well jointed, the blades can be honed quickly freehand, or you can hold them next to a guide beveled at 45°, as shown in the photo below.

To hone a scraper-plane blade, clamp the blade against a 45° block and pass the stone across the bevel. The tape wrapped around the stone prevents abrasion of the block.

The craftsman-made scratch stock at left was made to form the cap molding shown. The commercial beading tool at right has interchangeable blades for beading, reeding and fluting. (Photo by Susan Kahn)

SCRATCH STOCKS

Blades for scratch stocks (also called beading tools) are scrapers. You can bevel the edge or you can leave it square. Both edges work well in hardwoods and are more forgiving in softwoods than regular cabinet scrapers. Since blades for scratch stock are frequently craftsman-made, you should concentrate on getting the profile you want, hone that profile and then turn your attention to the faces of the blade. I say faces specifically because I believe that a square-edge scratch stock is more versatile than a beveled-edge blade since it allows you to cut in either direction. You can always be cutting with the grain.

With the profile finished, it is a simple matter to lap the faces of the blade as required to get a smooth finish and create a sharp edge. The coarseness of stone you start with will be dictated by the nature of the stock that you chose for your blade. Highly polished stock will need little work; coarsely ground stock will need quite a bit. In any event, once you have a crisp edge on the blade you will find that you can use it for quite a long time before it needs to be resharpened.

This is one scraper blade that you lap only, not burnish. In general, you should avoid touching the profile after it has been initially formed and honed; you need only lap the blade to resharpen it. Lapping the blade will make it marginally thinner each time you sharpen, but it is easier than trying to maintain an accurate profile through repeated honings of the profile itself. Besides, the blade is usually made for a specific project and will not see that much use.

PAINT SCRAPERS

Most paints are very abrasive because of the pigments in them, and as a result they are very hard on a sharp edge. The person who coined the term "working edge" must have been thinking of paint scrapers. I always take "working edge" to mean an edge that is not particularly sharp but is functional. That seems appropriate for a paint scraper.

For resharpenable-blade scrapers (including disposable-blade scrapers), I recommend sharpening on a 1-in. belt sander with a 120x belt. You get a remarkably good edge, and you get it quickly.

For people doing a lot of serious paint scraping, there are very inexpensive carbide paint scrapers on the market that are far more durable than steel ones. The blades are reversible and inexpensive. If you must scrape paint, you might as well treat yourself to one of these scrapers as compensation for having to do such a miserable job.

RESTORATION SCRAPERS

Anyone who has had to remove several layers of old finish in any restoration project knows the nightmare of trying to get even a thoroughly softened finish out of nooks and crannies. The easiest way to do it, particularly if you are dealing with a fair amount of reeding and fluting, is to make scrapers to fit the profile of the moldings.

An excellent raw material for making these scrapers is commercial steel strapping. It comes in a variety of widths, but the ½-in. steel strapping seems to be about the handiest. Strapping is spring steel of relatively low Rockwell hardness, which is quite easy to file and grind. The narrow bands are particularly useful for getting into difficult areas. The profiles you need can be made very quickly using files, a belt sander and sanding drums.

As with blades for scratch stocks, it is easiest to leave the edge square so that you can work with the grain at all times. You can even shape a piece to clean up a bit of router burn on new work. A square-end piece of strapping can be used to winkle glue out of corners, and you will also find that you can burnish a hook on strapping to make a small, flexible cabinet scraper. As you may have noticed, all this has very little to do with sharpening, but it's such a useful idea that I could not resist including it. Besides, the strapping can be had free-of-charge almost anywhere that goods on pallets are being handled.

Refinishing scrapers made of steel strapping are handy for removing finish from moldings. (Photo by Susan Kahn)

REFINISHING SCRAPERS

When stripping off an old finish, you can scratch a patina if you use a metal scraper. Often you want to maintain the patina and therefore need scrapers that will not mark the surface in any way. Scrapers made from a close-grained hardwood (boxwood is best) do an excellent job and will not damage the piece being worked on. It is also a simple matter to make small wooden scrapers to fit specific moldings. You can get very crisp edges on such scrapers that will do an excellent job of removing a softened finish.

Hardwood refinishing scrapers. (Photo by Susan Kahn)

CHAPTER 12
HANDSAWS

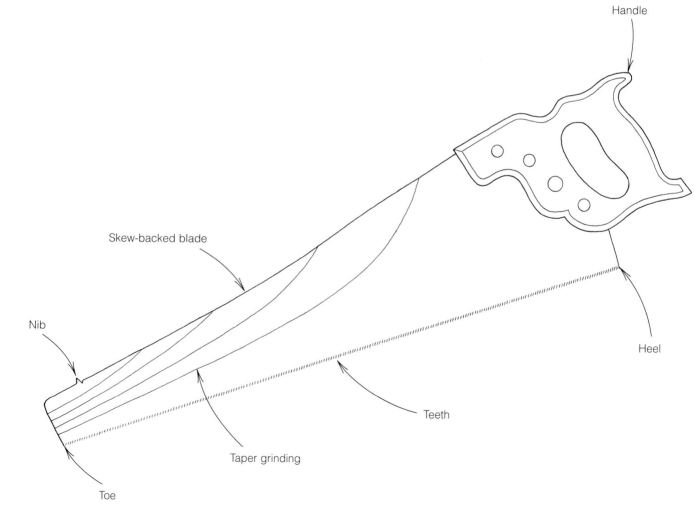

Handle

Skew-backed blade

Nib

Heel

Teeth

Taper grinding

Toe

SAW TEETH

Teeth are alternately set about halfway down.

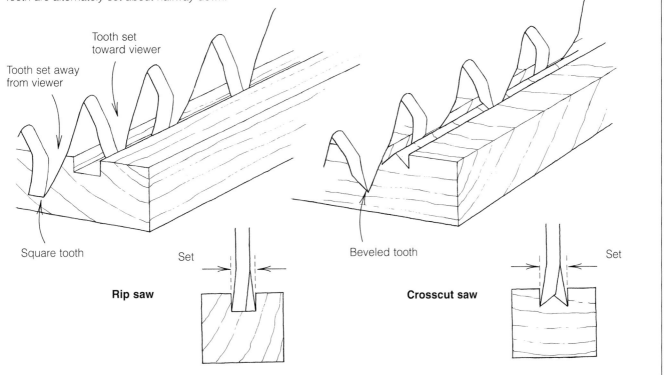

Tooth set toward viewer

Tooth set away from viewer

Square tooth

Beveled tooth

Set

Set

Rip saw

Crosscut saw

Although most people use powered saws today, a good understanding of handsaws is basic to understanding power saws because power tools are really just hand tools operating at speed.

There is another reason to pay particular attention to sharpening handsaws: It is nearly impossible to find a sharpening service today that will sharpen your handsaws as well as you can do it yourself the very first time you try. If you value your saws or even if you just want them to operate efficiently, it is worth spending some time learning how to sharpen them.

HOW SAWS WORK

A saw is just a number of tiny chisels arranged in a linear pattern designed to cut small chips of wood and carry them out of the kerf. The tips of the small chisels, called teeth on a saw, are shaped according to whether the saw will be cutting with the grain or across the grain, in dry wood or in green wood, in softwood or in hardwood, and so on. In every instance, you want the saw to work as efficiently as possible, with the greatest cutting speed and the least effort.

The two simplest cases to consider are the standard rip saw and the standard crosscut saw. As the drawing above shows, a rip saw has square teeth because it is designed to cut with the grain. A crosscut saw has beveled teeth because it cuts across the grain and must sever fibers, not just divide them. Obviously, a lot of sawing is done somewhere between these two orientations, and this will be dealt with in more detail later. For the moment, a

good rule of thumb is that you normally use a crosscut saw if you are cutting across the grain at any angle. Only when you are cutting parallel to the grain do you use a rip saw.

For a saw to work effectively, a few other conditions have to be met:

Adequate set The kerf that the saw makes in wood must be wider than the thickness of the blade to prevent the saw from binding. To attain this wider kerf, the teeth are bent, or "set," slightly outward. How much set the teeth are given depends on the saw type and the wood to be cut. On a fine-toothed backsaw for use with dry hardwood, 0.005 in. would be adequate; for a two-man crosscut saw in green wood, 0.020 in. would be more appropriate. There is much more fiber springback in green wood than in dry.

Jointed teeth Teeth performing the same function should be at the same height in order to do the same amount of work. Uneven heights create inefficiency and uneven wear. Regular jointing keeps teeth even.

Adequate gullets The space between teeth has to be large enough to carry the accumulation of chips created by the sawing process until the chips can be dumped outside the kerf. The total space is determined by the distance between teeth and the depth of the gullets.

Effective rake The leading edge of the tooth must be formed at the most efficient angle for creating the chip.

GENERAL SHARPENING PROCEDURES

To ensure that saws meet these various requirements, the sharpening process involves the following steps: jointing, shaping, setting and pointing. Although not all steps are necessary each time, they are always performed in the same sequence. For example, if a saw requires only setting and pointing it should be done in that sequence, not in reverse.

JOINTING

A saw should be jointed every time that it is filed. I can hear the rustle of rising eyebrows out there, but keeping even tooth height is so basic to good saw operation that it should be constantly maintained. This is not a big deal. If a saw needs sharpening, it obviously has dull teeth. Passing a jointer over the teeth is not going to dull them much more, but it will ensure that they are all the same height. Besides that, any time you joint a saw you should only joint it until you just touch the shortest tooth. Any jointing past that point is a waste of saw and a waste of sharpening time. Often, a single pass with the jointer is all that is needed.

To maintain even tooth height, a saw should be jointed every time it is sharpened. This backsaw shows the uneven tooth pattern that can result if a saw is not jointed.

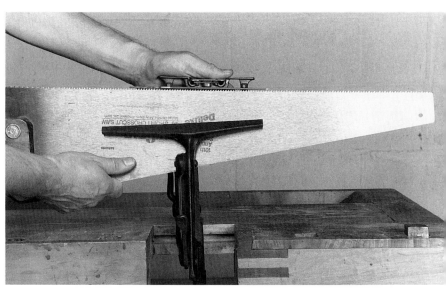

Joint a saw by passing a mill file over the teeth. A jointer holds the file at 90° to the blade. (Photo by Susan Kahn)

Jointing a saw is much like jointing a cabinet scraper. If you turn to the sidebar on p. 132, you'll find a variety of suggestions for making jointers. Alternatively, you can buy one from any specialty tool dealer; you can also find excellent saw jointers in flea markets, garage sales and antique shops. A few styles are shown in the photo at right. The really exotic ones will not only do flat jointing but have an integral screw that can be used to flex a file to match the crown (or circle) of a saw. Such a jointer might also include a raker gauge and setting gauge, as well as the facility to mount a file for side-dressing a saw. I have never been able to resist buying just one more jointer; the result of my decades of weakness is that I had no trouble at all trotting out the selection shown in the photo.

SHAPING

If you perform all the other sharpening functions well, you should never have to worry about shaping teeth. However, if you have been slovenly (or if you want to restore or convert a saw), you will have to address the question of tooth shaping.

After jointing, you may be faced with a tooth pattern that looks something like that shown in the drawing below. This pattern is evidence of bad previous sharpening technique, and

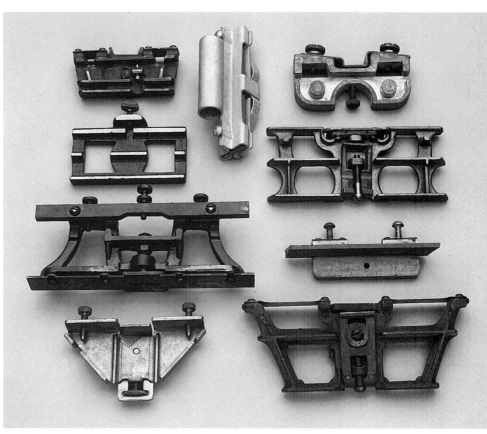

A selection of saw jointers. Each one will clamp a file, but some have integral screws that allow you to bow the file and some have raker gauges.

Bad tooth pattern requires reshaping of teeth.

The only thing you can do with a blade like this is to shape the teeth properly before you go any further in the sharpening process. To shape the teeth, file directly across the blade. Only after you have all the teeth properly shaped should you go on to bevel them. Experienced saw filers can do both at once, but I suggest that you try the two-step method first.

For crosscut saws that are going to be used both in hardwood and softwood, the rake angle of the teeth is negative, varying from 15° for quite an aggressive cut to 30°, which is the standard peg-tooth pattern (see the drawing at right). The 30° angle will give a smoother cut than a 15° rake but will also sacrifice some speed and sawdust-clearing ability. When we look at two-man crosscut saws and Swede saws later in this chapter, we will deal almost exclusively with the higher negative rake angles because these saws have raker teeth that handle the bulk of sawdust clearing.

Rip saws usually have 0° of rake, though they are sometimes given a bit of negative rake for better control in difficult grain conditions.

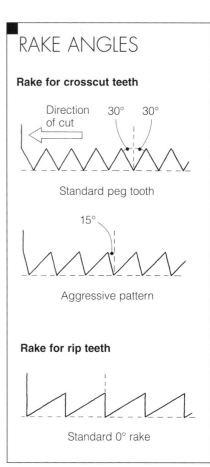

RAKE ANGLES

Rake for crosscut teeth

Direction of cut   30°   30°

Standard peg tooth

15°

Aggressive pattern

Rake for rip teeth

Standard 0° rake

Use a rake-angle guide held horizontally to maintain the correct tooth rake angle. The guide is a small, flat block, drilled to accept the file tip, that press-fits onto the end of the file. (Note that for better illustration the filing stance shown here is more open than usual.)

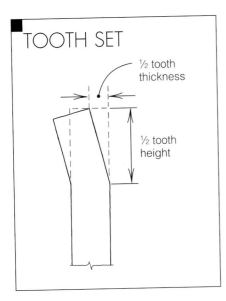

TOOTH SET

½ tooth thickness

½ tooth height

Dealing with a messy tooth pattern of the type shown in the drawing on p. 145 is a bit tricky. The best thing to do is mark a new gullet-bottom line and cut all the gullets down to a common base line. To establish greater control of the process you should make a rake-angle guide to slide onto the tip of your file, as shown in the photo above. You will quickly find in filing saws that it is very handy to have handles on both ends of the file. You are always controlling at least two angles when you are filing (the rake angle and the 90° angle to the blade), and most people can use all the help they can get. As you are reshaping the teeth you need only keep the guide horizontal to ensure that you are putting the correct rake angle on the front of every tooth. Using the guide and a scribed base line, you should be able to recreate a regular tooth pattern.

As you are filing, you will find that one face of the file will cut more aggressively than the other. You can compensate for this with hand pressure, equalizing the amount of bite

when desirable. This is one of the few times that you will do all the filing from one side of the saw. The only thing you are worried about in shaping is getting the correct rake angle and depth of gullet, and this can all be done from one side where you have marked the base line for the gullets.

After you have completed shaping the teeth, it is a good idea to pass the jointer over the saw again. You do this for two reasons: first, because you've probably not done a perfect job of shaping, so a light jointing would be useful anyway; and second, because you need tiny flats on the tips of the teeth in order to guide you later in the sharpening process.

SETTING

Most saws have too much set for cabinetmakers. They are set for general-purpose use in both hardwoods and softwoods at all sorts of moisture contents. If you are going to be using a saw only for dry wood, it requires less set, and if you are going to be using it only for dry hardwood, you require less yet. In general, a saw cuts the straightest with the least amount of set. Excessive set allows the blade to flop about in the kerf, changing cutting angles as it does so.

A couple of other points worth noting are that you should never reverse the direction of set of a tooth; it weakens the tooth unacceptably and could even break it. Also, set only the top half of a tooth. The depth gauge on your saw-setting tool should regulate this quite easily. An amount of set equal to half the thickness of the tooth should be ample. This will give a kerf that is double the thickness of the saw blade, which is more than enough in anything but the wettest and softest of woods.

There are numerous tools for setting saw teeth, but the most practical one is the commercial pistol-grip sawset. The sawset should have a dial anvil that is adjustable for the number of teeth per inch and for the setting height on the tooth. When you are buying such a sawset, try to find an old one that has a range from 4 to 16 tpi. Most, if not all, on the market today have a range from only 4 to 12 tpi. If you have one of the latter sawsets, you can cheat your way up past 12 tpi by reducing the amount of tooth that you set. A given set angle applied to the top quarter of a tooth will result in half the amount of offset that would be the case if it were applied to the top half of the tooth. With this knowledge filed away, you should be able to adapt your sawset to your needs even if it is a 4 to 12 tpi model.

To set the teeth, clamp the saw in a vise and set every other tooth. Squeezing the handles of the sawset together drives a beveled punch against an anvil, bending the teeth outward. When half of the teeth have been set, reverse the saw in the vise and set the balance of the teeth. Try to use the same amount of pressure for setting each tooth and ensure that the sawset is resting squarely on the teeth each time.

POINTING THE TEETH

Normally called "sharpening" (even though the word should refer to the whole shaping process not just one step), pointing the teeth is the step in the process where you establish the cutting bevels and eliminate the flats from the jointing process, all without changing the tooth outline. Filing of a Western saw is always performed after the teeth are set; with Japanese saws, the teeth are sometimes set first.

Of particular importance in this process is to use a vise that clamps the saw firmly. There are various

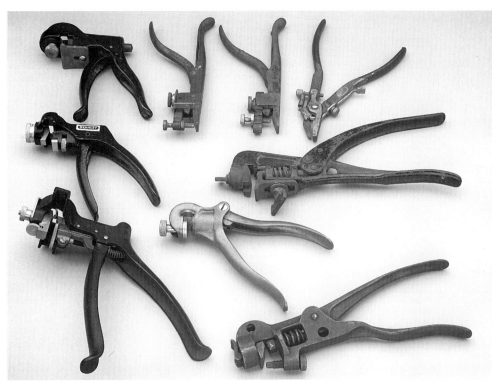

Like jointers, sawsets were (and still are) available in a wide range of styles, from the pistol-grip models at left to the plier styles at right.

With the saw clamped in a vise, use a sawset to bend the top half of the teeth alternately to the left and right.

CLAMPING A SAW

All saw filing except jointing requires a vise that will clamp the saw as close as possible to the teeth (to minimize vibration) and not get in the way in any of the filing processes. The best saw vises are the old ones that clamp to a table top and are jointed for tilting (see the photo on the facing page). These vises are slim at the top and ground slightly hollow so that clamping pressure is equalized across their width.

You can readily make a wooden clamp that drops into a bench vise or mechanic's vise to serve the same purpose. Since the hinges are not mortised, the jaws will tilt inward slightly on any saw being held. This should compensate for any bowing of the clamp as pressure is applied to it by the vise. If your woodworking vise does not have a jaw that is slightly canted in at the top (as it should be), you may have to apply a few layers of tape just below the riding ledge on one side to ensure that sufficient clamping pressure is transferred to the jaw end of the clamp.

commercial vises available, or you can make a simple wooden one as shown in the sidebar at left.

As a minor complication in the filing process, you should use files that are specific to the number of teeth per inch in the saw, as detailed below:

7-in. regular	5 to 5½ tpi
7-in. extra slim	8 tpi
6-in. extra slim	10 tpi
6-in. double extra slim	12 tpi
4-in. extra slim	15 tpi
4-in. double extra slim	22 tpi

This advice may seem somewhat odd since these are all triangular files, all have 60° face intersections and all will fit between the teeth of any of the saws listed. But there is a logic to it all. As the files reduce in size, the cut becomes finer. In addition, the flats on the files are equal to slightly more than double the face length of the teeth for which they are specified. In essence, this gives you three complete files in one. This gradation system balances the wear on the file, because you are never using more than half of the adjoining flats at any one time (see the drawing below). If, on the other hand, you were to use a 6-in. extra slim to file a 5-point saw, the file would be useless once two of the flats were dulled.

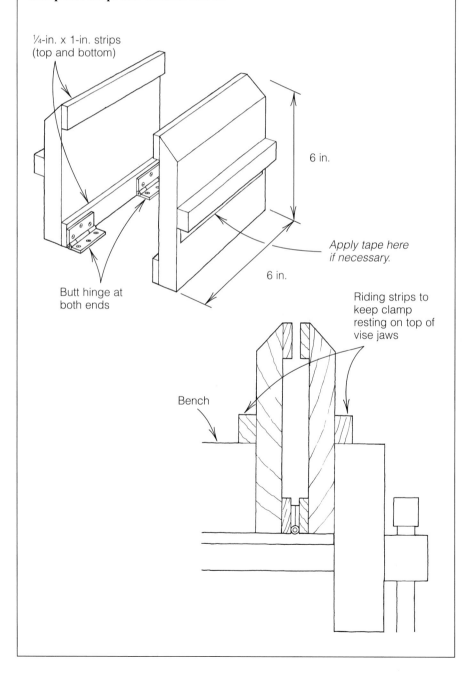

¼-in. x 1-in. strips (top and bottom)

6 in.

Apply tape here if necessary.

6 in.

Butt hinge at both ends

Riding strips to keep clamp resting on top of vise jaws

Bench

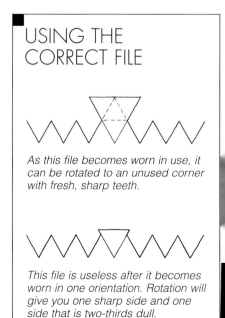

USING THE CORRECT FILE

As this file becomes worn in use, it can be rotated to an unused corner with fresh, sharp teeth.

This file is useless after it becomes worn in one orientation. Rotation will give you one sharp side and one side that is two-thirds dull.

Obviously, you do not have to hew religiously to the table on the facing page, but you would certainly find it difficult to sharpen a dovetail saw with a 7-in. regular saw file. The cut would be too coarse, and you would have a hard time seeing what you were doing.

A variety of other files are used for sharpening saws (e.g., web-saw files, great American crosscut files), but triangular files are all you need for rip and crosscut handsaws.

CROSSCUT SAWS

Crosscut saws are the most commonly used style of saw and will therefore be the ones most frequently sharpened. Regardless of the size of saw or the number of teeth per inch, the procedure is the same, although some of the equipment might change.

JOINTING

The only variation from the standard jointing process is if you have a saw with a bit of crown in it (such as breasted handsaws, flooring saws and many log saws). You have three choices in jointing such a saw.

If you have a jointing jig with an integral screw to set file camber, set the camber to a point just less than the crown of the saw. Some jointers have outrigger shoes to accommodate saws with camber. If you have such a jointer, you can use it, or you can make outrigger shoes to retrofit an existing jointer. The easiest approach, and an eminently practical one, is to run the jointer over the teeth in a nice, even sweep; you will find that you can maintain the crown quite adequately in the process.

As always, joint only until you have touched the shortest tooth.

One way to joint a saw with a crowned blade is to use a jointer that has a screw to set file camber. (Photo by Susan Kahn)

TOOTH BEVEL ANGLES

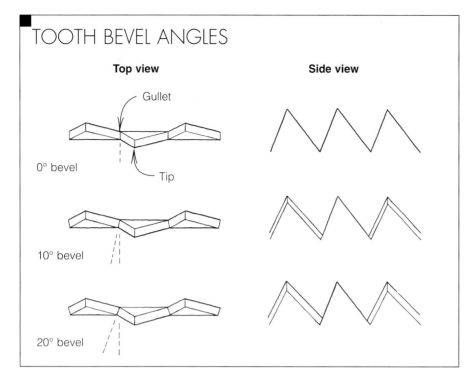

Top view   **Side view**

Gullet

Tip

0° bevel

10° bevel

20° bevel

GULLET ANGLES AND FILES

For Western saws, gullet angles are always stated as 60° because triangular saws (with equal face widths) are standard. For accuracy, it should be noted that the gullet angle is only 60° for saws with no tooth bevel (i.e., rip saws). As bevel is introduced, the gullet angle increases. For example, at 45° of bevel the gullet angle is about 81° (see the drawing at right).

This increase becomes quite significant when you get to higher bevel angles, for example, what you might need on a Swede-saw blade. If you intend to maintain a 60° gullet angle, it is only possible to use a triangular saw file if you also drop the file handle the same number of degrees as the bevel angle. With 10° of bevel, drop the handle 10° below horizontal; with 30° of bevel, drop the handle 30°, and so on.

In practical terms, this is not worth the effort. It is better to set your rake angle and bevel angle and then file at whatever angle to the horizontal you

find comfortable. You will not have 60° gullet angles, but it is doubtful that the variation from 60° will materially affect the performance of your saw. In fact, as you use higher bevel angles the tips of the teeth have a more fragile configuration. If the included angle at the tip increases (as it would if the file is not tilted enough to compensate), it tends to strengthen the tip.

Top view

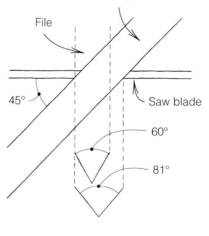

File

File

45°

Saw blade

60°

81°

SHAPING AND SETTING THE TEETH

Very seldom is reshaping necessary in the full process dealt with earlier, but it is useful each time you sharpen a saw to check the general tooth pattern to see if any irregularity is creeping in. A bit of adept filing can often correct the problem in time to avoid a full-blown reshaping session. If you joint the saw regularly, you will maintain tooth shape effortlessly.

Set the teeth as explained on p. 147, making sure that you have the dial anvil set for the correct number of teeth per inch and that you use equal pressure on each tooth.

POINTING THE TEETH

To point the teeth, put the saw in the vise with the teeth no more than ¼ in. above the vise jaws. Choose the amount of bevel (or "fleam") that you want for the teeth. This is usually around 10° but could be as much as 45, depending upon exactly what you are going to use the saw for.

At 10° you really just have a modified rip saw, whereas at 45° you will have a crosscut saw that goes through wood like butter but will require frequent sharpening. It will also work best cutting directly cross grain and will diminish in effectiveness in angle cuts as it approaches the parallel grain (or rip) configuration. As a general rule, you will find that anything between 10° and 20° will give you a general-purpose crosscut. Above that, it becomes a faster-cutting saw but one that is more intolerant of variable grain alignment.

With your file aligned with a bevel guide, drop the handle the same number of degrees as the amount of bevel you are using (see the sidebar at left). This means that you will be filing up toward the tips of the teeth. Not only does this tilt maintain the 60° gullet angle, but it also substantially reduces vibration. If you did not file upwards in this way, you would find that no matter how careful you were the saw would vibrate annoyingly just as it tends to do when filing rip teeth.

Remember that you are sharpening two faces at once (the back of one tooth and the face of another) and that you want to remove only about half of the flat on the tip of any tooth (the other half will be removed when you file from the other side). File confidently with a smooth, firm stroke. You will very quickly develop the pattern and find after a while that you do not need the bevel guide—you will be too busy checking tops of teeth to pay any attention to it anyway.

Tremendously helpful in all of this is the correct light. Natural light is best, and you should have your vise set up facing a window, not a point source of light. If you sit at the right height, flats on the tip of the teeth will shine like beacons and you will have no difficulty gauging your progress (see the bottom photo at right).

Once you have filed half of the teeth, reverse the saw and do the other half.

DRESSING THE BLADE

Filing a saw leaves a burr on the teeth. This wire edge is usually left on, but it can be removed if you wish. Before you even think of deburring the blade, try a test cut. If you have been a bit light with your set, you may want every scrap of burr on the teeth for kerf clearance.

Another reason to take a test cut first is to see if the saw has any tendency to run in the cut. If this is the first time you have ever sharpened a saw, there is an excellent chance that you filed off a bit too much when you reversed the saw in the vise. You not only filed until the flats disappeared but you took an extra little poke just to be sure. Having all the teeth set one way just a bit shorter than all the teeth set the other way is virtually guaranteed to cause the saw to fade to the side with the longer teeth.

If this is the case with your saw, take a fairly fine stone (1200x or finer) and dress the saw teeth on the side to which the blade is running. Dressing removes the burr on the teeth and will also remove a bit of the set.

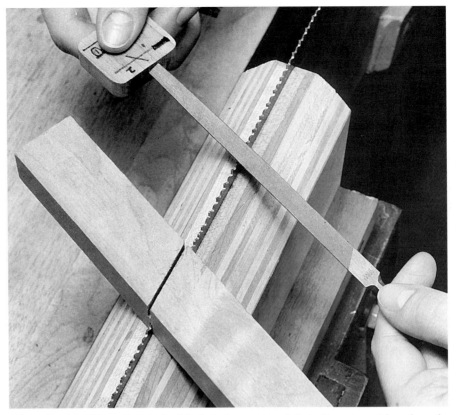

A bevel guide slipped over the blade helps you maintain the correct bevel angle when filing crosscut saws.

Light reflected from the jointed teeth serves as a visual reference when pointing tooth tips.

Take another test cut. If the saw now runs true, be grateful that you got out of trouble so easily. If it now runs to the other side, take a light dressing off the opposite side of the teeth. If this is done carefully, you should not have to go past dressing one side only. At worst, you should go only as far as a light dressing on the second side. If it still runs, rejoint, reset if necessary and take greater care in filing.

RIP SAWS

Rip saws are jointed and set in the same manner as crosscut saws, but the teeth are pointed differently. Rip teeth usually have 0° of rake and are filed straight across the saw. Keep the file horizontal and at 90° to the blade (see the drawing below). The saw should be clamped low in the vise with no more distance between the bottom of the gullet and the top edge of the vise than you need for filing room.

It is easy to get vibration when you file straight across the saw, and you will end up putting an edge on your own teeth as well as the saw's teeth. It is just marginally more pleasant than fingernails on a blackboard.

Theoretically, you could file all the teeth from one side of the saw, but it is a good idea to file every other one,

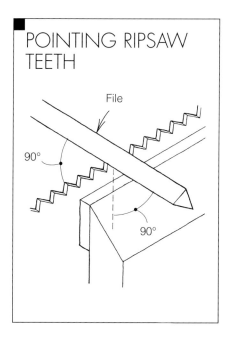

POINTING RIPSAW TEETH

File

90°

90°

reverse the saw in the vise and then file the balance. This puts an even amount of burr on both sides of the saw and also compensates for any bias that you have in the system. You might be dropping the file handle 5°, or you might be filing at 85° instead of 90°. In either case, if you make the same errors on both sides of the saw they will tend to balance out.

For ripping very dense wood with wild grain, you may want to put some bevel, or fleam, on the tooth of your rip saw (about 10° should do). Not only does a little bit of fleam help with wild grain, but it allows a rip saw to work better in a cut that is slightly diagonal to the grain.

TROUBLESHOOTING A RIP SAW

If you find that your rip saw is hard to use—you have a hard time starting the cut, for example—you may want to modify the tooth pattern. As well as putting a bit of fleam on the tooth to handle difficult grain, you may also want to put up to 10° of negative rake on the tooth as well. In essence, what you are doing is converting the rip saw into a combination rip and crosscut saw. There is nothing particularly wrong in this. It will make the saw a little slower in the ripping process but more controllable in difficult woods or in bias cuts. You do what you have to do to make it work for you.

FINE-TOOTHED SAWS

Filing and pointing saws with very fine teeth can present some problems. Since most pistol-grip sawsets will not accommodate saws with more than 16 teeth per inch, you either have to use an alternative setting technique or cheat in the manner mentioned on p. 147, where you use the sawset at the 16 tpi setting but set a smaller portion of tooth.

An alternative is to clamp the saw to a piece of hardwood and set the teeth with a pin punch and a small hammer. This is not as difficult as it sounds, and the minor variations in set can be corrected with side dressing after the teeth have been pointed.

For pointing very fine teeth (as on a gent's saw), you may find that a 4-in. double-extra slim saw file is still too large and it may be necessary to use either a feather-edge file or a very fine (#3 or #4 cut) triangular needle file. For extremely fine saws (such as blitz saws and slotting saws), you might have to use a magnifying glass and the teeth should be filed square across the blade. Filed alternately, you will find that the amount of burr left from filing gives the blade adequate set, which is a good thing because it is nearly impossible to do a competent job of setting teeth finer than 25 tpi with normal shop equipment.

DOVETAIL SAWS

If you use a saw only for dovetail work, you will find that rip-sharpened teeth with 10° of negative rake, 10° of bevel and minimum set will work very well. I recommend this bias toward the rip pattern, because you will undoubtedly have other saws for crosscutting but this might be your only choice for dovetailing; you want to be sure that it works as well as possible in this use even if that limits its use elsewhere. And since dovetailing is essentially ripping, the saw should be sharpened accordingly.

Many years ago I asked a Scottish cabinetmaker if he would tell me exactly how he went about sharpening his dovetail saw. He laughed and said that he had never had the nerve to try. He had been using it for some fifteen years for cutting dovetails, and at his current rate of production he felt he would never have to sharpen it and he certainly had no intention of doing so. He said that it took him long enough to adapt himself to its idiosyncrasies and that he had no intention of introducing new ones. I have thought of his comments many times since and have found other cabinetmakers who did not have the nerve to touch their dovetail saws. I leave it to you to determine where the line is between bravery and stupidity in this field.

VENEER SAWS

The two most common types of veneer saws are the French style, which has a curved blade with the teeth raked toward the center from either side, and the standard, rest-of-the-world style, which has peg teeth cut to chisel tips. Regardless of which type you own, you will probably never have to file either one because you need to cut a huge amount of veneer to wear the teeth down to the point that they need filing.

If you should ever need to file a veneer saw, file it straight across like a rip saw. You are not really sharpening the teeth when you file the saw but redefining them. You sharpen the teeth by stoning the bevels. With the French-style, the teeth are beveled on one side only. Stone the flat and the bevel with the finest, hardest stone you have. With the rest-of-the-world style, stone both bevels with a trailing stroke.

TWO-MAN CROSSCUT SAWS

Two-man crosscut saws are little used today, although they were a vital part of the logging industry well into this century. There are two reasons to include them in this book. First, a good understanding of two-man crosscuts gives us a better understanding of Japanese saws (see pp. 158-161), which are very popular today. Second, there is a renewed interest in logging-arts competitions in North America, and competitors desperately search for detailed sharpening information in the hopes that they can knock a couple of seconds off their best log-buck time.

Although two-man crosscuts come in two basic styles, felling and bucking, only the bucking saw will be dealt with here. The sharpening considerations for a felling saw are almost exactly the same, since the only real difference is that a felling saw is much thinner and more flexible, reflecting the

Two styles of veneer saws: at left, a French veneer saw; at right, a standard veneer saw. (Photo by Susan Kahn)

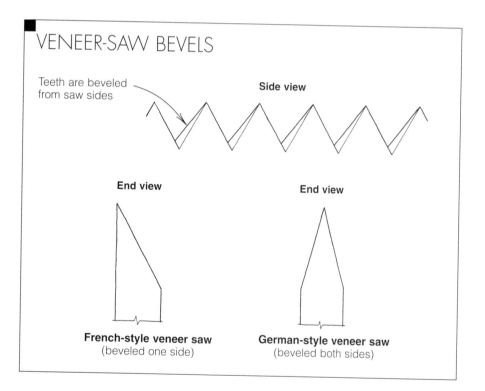

VENEER-SAW BEVELS

Teeth are beveled from saw sides

Side view

End view
French-style veneer saw
(beveled one side)

End view
German-style veneer saw
(beveled both sides)

THE ONE-MAN SAW

There were numerous inventions in the 1800s aimed at easing the lot of the sawyer who either had to or wanted to work alone. One device that left little imprint in the sawdust of time was Giles' Drag Sawing Machine (shown at right). It is hard to conceive of a device more difficult to move around in the bush.

But the one enduring tip for the feller was to use a "rubberman." Most felling saws were too thin and flexible to be used by one man. They could not be pushed through the cut; they had to be pulled. A shop tip of the 1800s was to use a strong rubber band on one end of the saw to draw the saw back and to keep the end from flopping in the dirt. This assist was called a rubberman.

Giles' Drag Sawing Machine.

CROSSCUT-SAW TOOTH PATTERNS

Lance tooth

Lance-perforated tooth

Champion tooth

requirements of its specific use and the fact that it was almost invariably a two-man saw.

The bucking saw, on the other hand, is used as a two-man saw in competition today but was made stiffer and heavier than the felling saw so that it could be used by a single sawyer. The rigidity was needed for the push stroke in one-man use, and the weight was needed to increase the speed of cut.

Further simplifying things, the only tooth pattern that will be considered here is the lance-perforated tooth (see the drawing at left). The considerations are nearly the same as those for the champion tooth, the other popular style. The lance-tooth pattern is also popular, but it is exactly the same as the lance perforated except that the cutters are less rigid and less predictable.

CLEANING THE SAW

The sharpening sequence for a two-man crosscut is quite straightforward. Begin by removing any pitch from the saw with saw-blade cleaner, and any rust by stoning the entire saw. The stoning serves two purposes. It will remove any rust that has accumulated and reveal any kinks or bumps in the blade. Without going into great detail, it is usually better to have the kinks removed by an experienced saw doctor than attempt it yourself.

JOINTING THE SAW

The saw should be jointed exactly the same way as a handsaw. Since most two-man crosscuts are crescent-shaped, either a jointer with outriders should be used or one of the cast-iron pointers that has the curvature adjustment screw (see the photo on p. 149).

RAKER SHAPING

Raker teeth in a crosscut saw remove fibers from the center of the kerf that have already been clipped at the ends by the cutting teeth. The trick is to set the rakers at a height that will remove all of the central ridge of wood but not tear any fibers. A crosscut saw that works well will yield clean, curly shavings. When the rakers are too long, the fibers will be torn along the edge and the shavings are said to have whiskers (see the bottom drawing at right). Obviously, this would increase cutting resistance.

Because the cutting teeth compress fibers as well as sever them, there is some fiber springback after the cutting tooth passes, much like the springback that is experienced behind a plane blade (see pp. 16-17). To set the raker height properly the amount of springback has to be calculated. This is not particularly simple since the springback varies between wood types, is very dependent on moisture content and is affected by the shape of the cutter, the weight of the saw and the technique of the user.

Optimum raker height can vary from as little as 0.005 in. short of the cutters for a light saw in dry hardwood to as much as 0.035 in. short for a heavy saw in green softwood. For competitions

JOINTED CROSSCUT TEETH

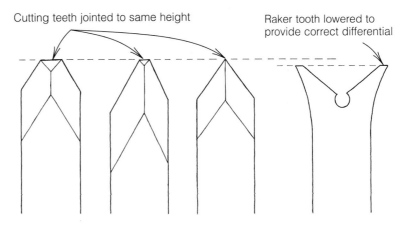

Cutting teeth jointed to same height

Raker tooth lowered to provide correct differential

With the teeth jointed, the next step is to point the teeth and file the relief angles on the rakers. In the example shown here, the middle tooth of the three cutters should be filed only on the right-hand side in order to restore shape. This is one exception to always filing away half of the jointing flat from each side.

CROSSCUT-SAW SHAVINGS

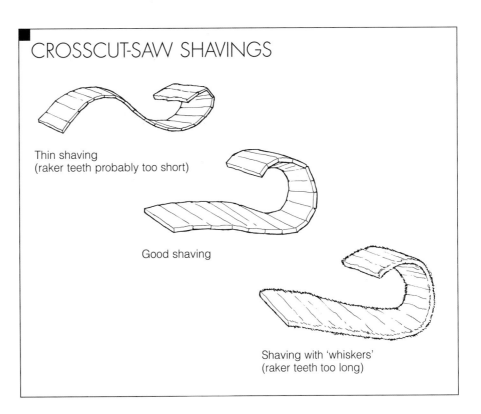

Thin shaving
(raker teeth probably too short)

Good shaving

Shaving with 'whiskers'
(raker teeth too long)

MAKING A RAKER GAUGE

A simple raker gauge can be made from channel stock or material bent in a brake. It can be filed in steps or in one continuous slope for calibration.

Another method is to use a simple L-shaped piece of angle drilled and tapped for a large diameter ($\frac{1}{4}$ in.$\pm$) $\frac{1}{4}$-20 or M-8 bolt. The bolt is used as a simple micrometer. For example, one full turn of a $\frac{1}{4}$-20 bolt is 0.050 in. If you want rakers that are 0.025 in. below the cutters, you first set the bolt flush with the inside top of the angle and then advance it one half turn. You would then file rakers until they would just clear the bolt tip.

Gauge made from channel stock

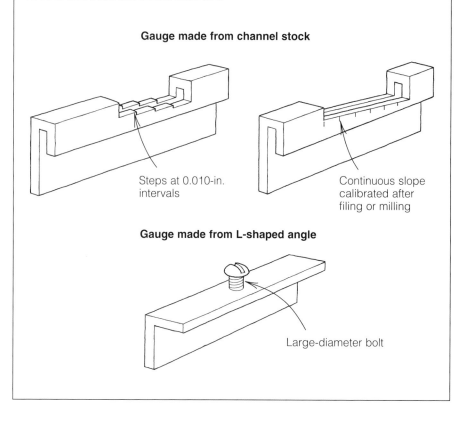

Steps at 0.010-in. intervals

Continuous slope calibrated after filing or milling

Gauge made from L-shaped angle

Large-diameter bolt

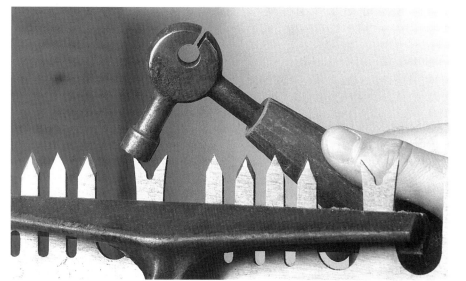

Use a swaging hammer to set the rakers below the height of the cutting teeth. (Photo by Susan Kahn)

where the material being bucked is a turned bolt, raker height will have to be about 0.015 in. below cutter tips. Rakers should not be set there initially; they should be set higher and dressed back by experiment just until they produce no whiskers. One of the many secrets to fast sawing is to have the rakers remove the maximum amount of wood but not tear any fibers. This reduces the friction of the cutting teeth and creates the most efficient combination of tooth action possible.

There are many ways to measure raker height in a two-man crosscut. The various jointers mentioned on p. 145 often have raker gauges. If it is not possible to find one of those, it is a simple matter to make a raker gauge, as shown in the sidebar at left.

Rakers can be filed to height, or they can be swaged. If a swaging hammer cannot be found, a 16-oz. riveting hammer or Warrington hammer will do the job. The tip of the raker should be struck as shown in the photo at left and checked against the pin of the raker gauge.

SETTING THE TEETH

There is a fair amount of discussion among logging-arts competitors about whether setting or filing should come first. The argument for filing first is that you get a better shape if you are filing an unset tooth. In fact, a tooth always has some set in it so it makes very little difference whether it is filed first or set first. What does make a great deal of difference is whether you end up with a short tooth. For that reason I would set the teeth, give them a preliminary dressing and then file them.

It is very important in competition sawing that the setting be highly regular. For this reason, if the teeth are set and then given an initial dressing, the dressing will remove a portion of the flat spot and guarantee that the filed tooth will not accidentally be dressed short later. If the procedure is reversed, side dressing could cause some teeth to be shorter than others.

Crosscut teeth can be spring set, though it is difficult to maintain a regular setting. (Photo by Susan Kahn)

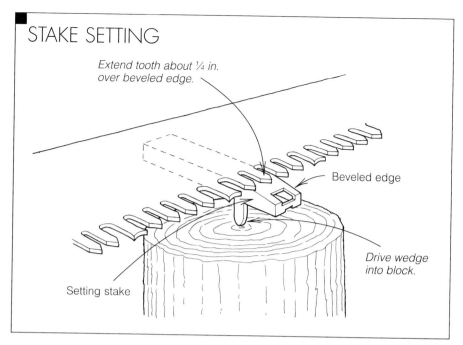

STAKE SETTING

Extend tooth about ¼ in. over beveled edge.

Beveled edge

Setting stake

Drive wedge into block.

Teeth can be spring set with a wrest, or hammer set. Spring setting (see the photo above) is too much of an uncontrolled process to give good results. The most common method is to use a setting stake, letting the tooth extend about ¼ in. over the beveled portion (see the drawing at right) and striking it with a hammer. The same hammer used for swaging is quite acceptable. For narrow teeth (which is exactly what you have with a lance-tooth pattern), an 8-oz. hammer may be necessary to avoid interference with adjoining teeth. An 8-oz. Warrington hammer is suitable.

There is one difficulty with this process; it means that there is a lot of saw handling as the teeth are set and then checked. Every tooth should be checked with a spider gauge (see the sidebar at right) and must be lifted off the setting stake each time, which is somewhat cumbersome. The alternative is to use a hand anvil, which requires more skill. The final choice is usually determined by what is available.

If the saw has consistent steel in it, you should be able to come very close to the right amount of set after you set the first two or three teeth. For an overset tooth, draw it back from the

MAKING A SPIDER GAUGE

A spider gauge is used to check the set in saw teeth. A gauge can be made in minutes with four screws and a scrap of wood. To set a spider gauge for use, put a feeler gauge under one tip and adjust the screw at the other tip.

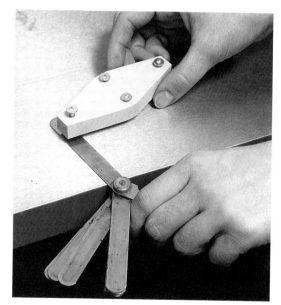

Setting a spider gauge.

CUTTING LOGS SOFT SIDE UP

To ensure logs of exactly the same diameter for logging-arts competitions, it is a common practice to have a plywood factory or a veneer mill peel a log to the exact diameter. Often this is done as much as a week before the competition, and the peeled logs are left in the open air at the competition site.

When these logs are lashed up in the frame for the bucking competition, it is important that they be soft side up; otherwise, the tips can be broken off the cutters that have been so carefully shaped and honed. A log lying in the sun for even a couple of days can develop an extremely hard shell on the top half of the log. In a well-run competition, this shell is placed at the bottom when the log is lashed up. But since the log has to be constantly relashed, competitors should be aware that they might be sandbagged by a log that is hard side up.

beveled portion and give it a tap to straighten it partially, and then carefully reset the tooth with several light blows, checking each time with the spider gauge.

POINTING THE TEETH

For competition sawing you want "hungry" teeth, that is, teeth with low bevel angles that come to a finely honed point at the tip that will slice into the wood. The secret is to get the teeth as thin as possible so that they slice deeply into the wood yet with enough strength to stand up to the aggressive pace of competition sawing.

The V-tip should be somewhere between 35° and 45°; the bevel should be 30°. It is possible (but risky) to

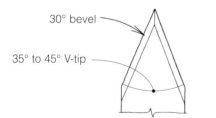

30° bevel

35° to 45° V-tip

reduce both of these angles. (Note that in this case bevel is being used differently than earlier in the book, where 30° of bevel was 60° off a square edge; in saw filing, 30° of bevel is 30° off a square edge.)

The teeth are easiest to see if the saw has been clamped in a vise that is tilted toward the light. The filing is best done in an enclosed area facing good light. The teeth should be filed until there is just the tiniest flat left at the tip; the flat will be removed when you hone the bevels with a stone.

After filing, the final strokes on the teeth are done with a fine stone. A hard Arkansas knife file is best for this purpose, although a small water stone can be used if handled carefully. In general, water stones are a bit soft for this type of work and the swarf too readily obscures the edge. The back of the tooth should be deburred before stoning is complete so that the finest possible tip is made on the tooth.

CAUTIONARY NOTE

If you are going to be at all serious about competitive sawing, you should have two saws, one for practice and one for competition. It takes several hours to do a first-class job of sharpening a competition saw, and it usually needs to be done at home not at the competition site. A second saw lets you practice your timing to get it down pat at any time without risking any last-minute damage to your competition saw.

SWEDE SAWS AND BUCK SAWS

Where I grew up, a saw with a wooden frame and a turn-buckle tensioner (with a 32-in. or 36-in. blade) was called a buck saw. A saw with a tubular-steel frame, a lever tensioner and a standard 42-in. blade was known as a Swede saw. Nobody took buck saws seriously with their funny little peg-tooth blades, and everybody used Swede saws with the standard four-cutters-and-a-raker pattern. Properly sharpened and tensioned, Swede saws cut quickly with very little effort. With reasonable set in the teeth, it was possible to make cuts that would not even have been attempted with a two-man crosscut because it would have bound in the kerf for sure. The slim Swede-saw blade was next to impossible to trap in a cut. It was the standard cordwood saw.

Buck saws are sharpened exactly like crosscut handsaws, and Swede saws are sharpened like two-man crosscuts.

JAPANESE SAWS

With some minor exceptions, I do not recommend that you attempt to sharpen Japanese saws. Almost without exception, the teeth have been formed and sharpened with diamond wheels, and it is not possible to get as fine a finish using a file. Even if you could create as fine a finish, it is unreasonable to expect that you could develop reasonable competency without sacrificing several saws.

The geometry of Japanese saws is far more complex than that of Western saws. It is rare to find a Japanese saw where two bevels extend from gullet to tip to form a point. There is usually a third bevel and sometimes a fourth bevel incorporated in the tooth. It is not reasonable to expect that you could perfectly recreate this geometry by freehand filing.

Cutting dovetails is probably a good parallel. I doubt that you did a decent job the first time you cut dovetails or even the second time. Yet with dovetails you are dealing with a fairly simple shape in a size that is readily

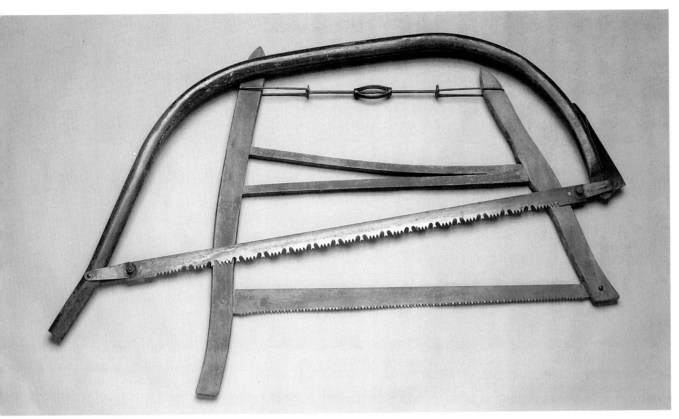

A Swede saw with a typical four-cutters-and-a-raker blade and a buck saw with a peg-tooth blade. Buck saws look nicer hung on a wall; that's where they should stay.

seen, and the shaping is done with tools that are quite controllable. If you contrast that with using a feather-edge file on flexible steel under a magnifying glass with the prospect of the tiniest slip seriously damaging an adjoining tooth, I think you will agree that your time might be better spent practicing your dovetailing.

There is some cause for hope in all of this. Virtually every type of Japanese saw is now available in a disposable-blade model. The blades are very durable and generally represent very good value for the money. And there are some Japanese saws that you can resharpen or at least touch up several times without having to apprentice to a temple builder for five years.

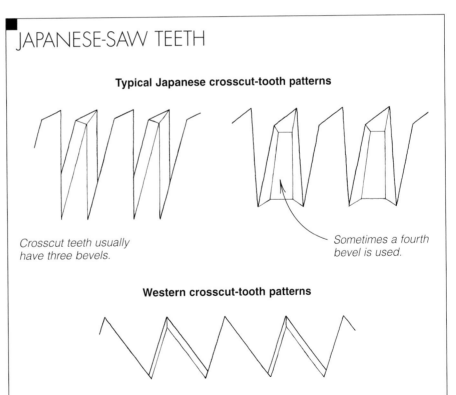

JAPANESE-SAW TEETH

Typical Japanese crosscut-tooth patterns

Crosscut teeth usually have three bevels.

Sometimes a fourth bevel is used.

Western crosscut-tooth patterns

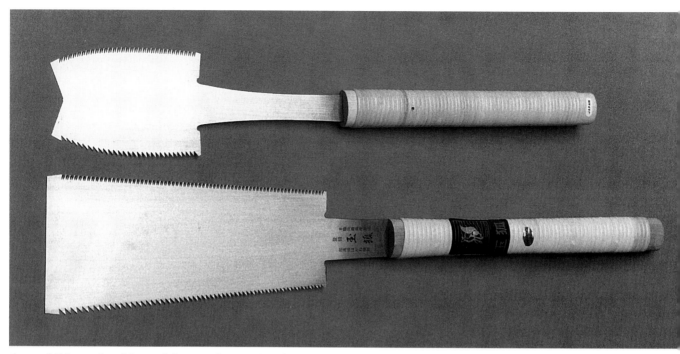

An azebiki saw (top) is used for cuts in restricted areas; it is particularly appreciated by boatbuilders. A ryoba (bottom) is the standard carpenter's saw in Japan. Both saws have rip teeth on one edge, crosscut teeth on the other. (Photo by Susan Kahn)

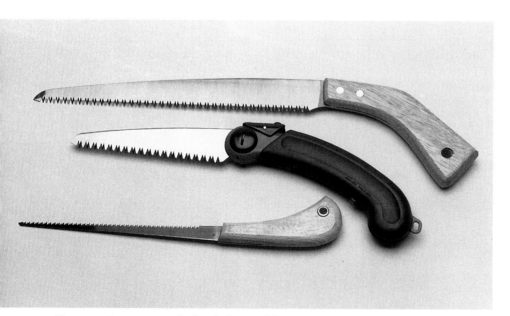

Two pruning saws and a keyhole saw. The saw at top, which has set teeth, is typical of Japanese pruning saws (though made in Taiwan). The middle saw, which has a tapered blade, is a top-of-the-line folding pruning saw made in Japan. The keyhole saw at bottom is just as effective in plasterboard as in wood. (Photo by Susan Kahn)

RIP SAWS

Several Japanese saws (ryoba, azebiki, etc.) have rip teeth fashioned in much the same manner as the rip teeth in Western saws, though the geometry is quite different and the blades are quite a bit thinner. These saws should be clamped close to the gullet and sharpened with a feather-edge file, a 4-in. file for larger teeth, and a 3-in. file for the balance. Otherwise, use the same sharpening sequence as you would for a Western saw.

KEYHOLE SAWS

Japanese keyhole saws usually have no set; they do not require any because the

Cross section of keyhole saw with tapered blade

blade is radically tapered from tooth to back. These saws can be sharpened much like Western crosscuts—all you have to do is maintain the original geometry.

PRUNING SAWS

With their large teeth, Japanese pruning saws are relatively easy to touch up. They come in two patterns: a fairly standard pattern with set teeth, and a rigid blade pattern that has no set (the blade is tapered from tooth to back). Both usually have secondary bevels at the tips of the teeth to make a stronger tip.

To sharpen one of these saws, it is usually not necessary to touch either of the primary bevels; you need to file only the secondary bevel to redefine the tip of the tooth. Despite the complex geometry, if you clamp a Japanese pruning saw in a saw vise between you and the light and tilt the vise until the light reflects directly into your eyes from the secondary bevels when you are in your filing stance, you will be able to file these bevels quite handily with a 3-in. feather-edge file. You will quickly become accustomed to the filing angle because you have the light reflection to guide you.

I am seldom able to file a Japanese saw without having the file slither off at least one tip and grate down the side of an adjoining tooth. For this reason, I prefer a safe-edge file. I also prefer to hold the file in one hand while I put my other thumb on top of the file and a fingertip behind the blade. This dampens the vibration of the blade and it also provides a brake for the file. I find that the file does not go astray nearly so often if I hold my finger behind the tooth. With a safe-edge file, even if you do slip off the tooth tip you cause minimal damage.

There is one final benefit to touching up these saws by filing only the secondary bevel. You will find that you can maintain even tooth height by keeping the secondary bevels the same size. When you file a bevel it becomes slightly larger with each stroke. The size difference is sufficient that you can use this as a guide to maintain tooth height without having to resort to jointing. Since the teeth are very hard, particularly in the rigid-blade pruning saws, I always find it a very unnerving process to joint the saw. The file dances all over the place unless you swap your normal bastard-cut mill file for a #2-cut

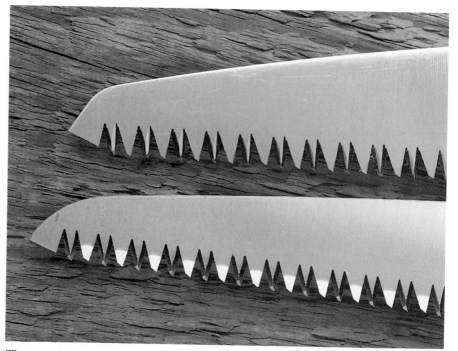

The pruning saw at top has a tapered blade to prevent binding; the saw at bottom has set teeth.

Swiss pattern. Even then it is an uncomfortable feeling to joint a hard-tooth saw. I have touched up the disposable blades of pruning saws three or four times without a discernible difference in tooth height developing.

Incidentally, if you have never used a Japanese pruning saw you should treat yourself to one. They are a joy to use. Many years ago, I tried to convince Western saw makers to buy Japanese sharpening machinery so they could make similar saws, or at least saws that were as sharp and had accurately formed teeth. This plea was always greeted with a bemused promise to "look into it." They never did. It is doubtful now that many of them will be able to make up for lost time. Several Taiwanese firms are soaking up a large part of the market with very well made saws, sharpened on Japanese equipment but sold at a fraction of the price of Japanese saws. Even Stanley now offers a Japanese-tooth-pattern saw made in Asia.

CHAPTER 13
AXES, HATCHETS AND ADZES

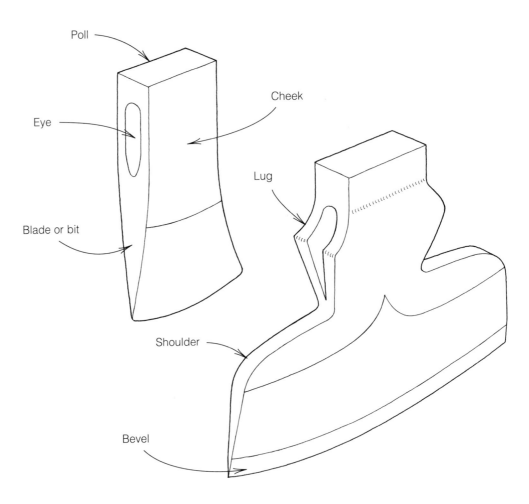

Poll

Cheek

Eye

Lug

Blade or bit

Shoulder

Bevel

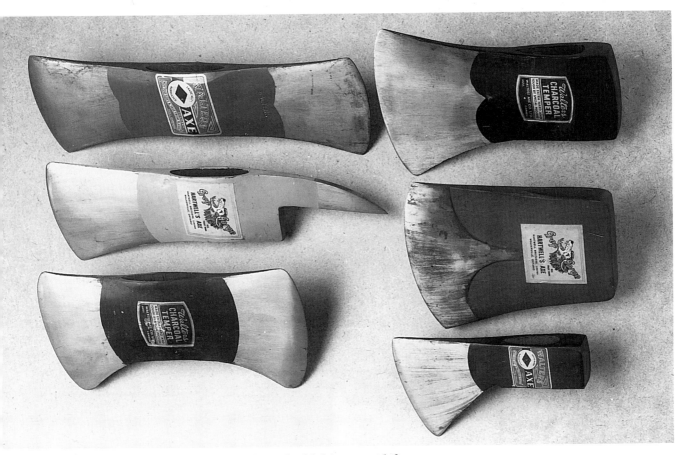

A selection of felling and notching axes. The three double-bit axes at left are (from top to bottom) felling, rafting and swamping styles. The three single-bit axes are (top to bottom) general purpose, full-wedge notching and carpenter's tomahawk pattern.

This book is devoted to the shaping and honing of the wide variety of wedges that we use as cutting tools. If edge tools were separated into the categories of basic and advanced wedges, axes, hatchets and adzes would be considered basic wedges. This is the only category of woodworking hand tool where applied force and direction of cut are both determined before the tool touches the wood. The effectiveness of the wedge is controlled solely by its mass and shape and the skill with which it is flung at the wood.

There are two basic types of ax: those with a centered cutting edge (the most common kind), and those where the blade has a single bevel and the cutting edge is not on the central axis of the head (side axes).

Of the centered-edge type, there are three basic shapes—one for felling or general shaping, one for splitting and, most ubiquitous of all, the utility ax. Describing how to sharpen a utility ax is a bit like describing how to sharpen a handsaw for both crosscutting and ripping; it is hardly worth the effort. The tool becomes such a mass of compromises that it performs no single function well. All that can be said of a utility ax is that you have two choices: either you continue to sharpen it the way it came from the factory, concentrating on a keen edge and ignoring edge geometry, or you can bias the shape to suit the work most frequently demanded of the tool (that is, rework the basic shape as required). Actually, there is a third choice. Get rid of the utility ax and buy what you really need.

FELLING AND NOTCHING AXES

Felling and notching axes are the ballerinas of the ax world, graceful, delicately shaped and a joy in performance. A well-shaped felling ax can drop a 4-in. diameter tree with two strokes. It will notch a tree for felling in seconds, or shape timber more rapidly than a power tool. To use a good felling ax on green wood is to experience the origins of the Paul Bunyan stories.

AX ABUSE

The ax face in the block of wood is mute evidence of abuse. The user tried to split a block of wood with a felling ax. When the ax became seized in the wood, he first hammered on the poll to drive it deeper, hoping to split the wood and free the ax. When he saw that the ax cheeks were beginning to distort, he switched to hitting the ax on the side to free it. The ax head snapped at the point of most stress, next to the wood.

If you are ever faced with a similar problem, saw partway through the block just below the face; this will allow the wood to open and free the ax. Better yet, if you use tools for their intended purpose, you can avoid such problems.

mortise chisel. The difference is that the direct cross-grain cut is usually made first when mortising but last when deepening a notch with an ax. The forces on the ax edge are still uneven but less so than in the case of the mortise chisel.

The other case where extraordinary forces are applied to a felling ax is in trimming dead branches, where there is deadwood encased by the branch collar. Just as pin knots are the enemy of the smooth plane, dead branches are the enemy of the ax.

If you watch experienced woodcutters limb trees, they will use the back of the ax head to knock off dead branches. In cold weather, they will also use the same technique with small live branches, as long as the wood is frozen so that the branches will snap off readily just at the branch collar. Partly this is done for general efficiency, but also to avoid cutting into dead branches, which have the same effect on an ax blade as pin knots have on a plane. The concentration of resisting forces on a small section of blade can cause the section to curl or crumble.

If after shaping an ax head you find the edge too weak in use, just increase

A felling ax is designed for maximum penetration and minimum wedging action. It excels at severing fibers and should never be used to split wood. It is not just that it splits wood poorly, but it can become lodged so solidly in the end grain that it might have to be cut out. Any attempt at levering it out using the handle would only break it.

For working dry wood, either milled timbers or deadwood, the edge should have an included angle of about 20° to 25°, 10° to 12° per side. For green wood, this can be reduced to an included angle of 15° to 20°. These angles may seem low compared with something like a mortise chisel, which performs basically the same function, but the forces experienced by an ax blade are normally more balanced.

A chisel has the bending forces applied primarily to the beveled side. With an ax, the forces are applied more evenly to both sides of the blade; the head tends to follow the path of least resistance as it penetrates the wood.

There are exceptions to this general rule. In notching a tree for felling, an ax is used somewhat like a mortise chisel.

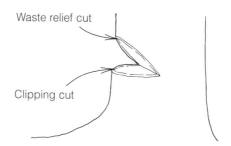

Waste is relieved from the upper part of the cut and then clipped off at the bottom with a horizontal cut (see the drawing above). The horizontal cut most closely imitates the action of a

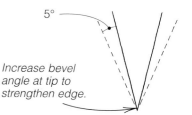

Increase bevel angle at tip to strengthen edge.

the bevel angle a few degrees (no more than 5°), for the last $\frac{1}{16}$ in. or so, as you would with a chisel (see the drawing above). This will strengthen the edge without materially affecting performance. The ax will not penetrate quite as deeply with each swing, but it will work consistently without the need for constant maintenance.

DOUBLE-BIT AXES

Double-bit axes (shown in the photo on p. 163) are seldom seen today, but they were in common use a century ago. In fact, they were more commonly used as felling axes in North America than were the single-bit style.

There were three main reasons that double-bit axes were preferred. First, they have better balance than single-bit axes; the center of gravity of the head is at the middle of the eye. With a single-bit ax, there is usually more mass forward of the eye. Second, double-bit axes have two edges; if one is dulled accidentally, it is not necessary to stop and sharpen that edge immediately. And, third, the two edges were often used for different purposes and accordingly were often shaped differently.

A double-bit ax has quite a different feel from a single bit. The handle is straight and usually more oval in cross section. The perfect balance makes it easier to aim accurately and generally lets you do more precise work. To be efficient in using any ax you should be able to strike the same point repeatedly. This is particularly true in large-diameter work where a cut may have to be extended some distance around a log. Unless it is extended in a single plane, a lot of effort is expended in tearing fibers rather than severing them.

For the modern user, probably the most important feature of the double-bit ax, next to the wonderful balance, is the ability to shape two edges differently, one for felling and one for limbing. The edge for limbing would have a higher included angle than the edge for felling. To avoid confusion, it is useful to have a handy visual indicator that tells you which edge is which. Initially, the label on the ax head can be used as a guide, but if that has been removed either intentionally or with wear, put a dot of paint on the head or the handle as a guide.

THE DESTRUCTION OF A BEAUTIFUL AX

When I was growing up in northern Saskatchewan in the 1940s, the main source of cash for my parents was wood. We cut our own firewood for cooking and heating, and we cut endless hundreds of cords of spruce (usually 8 ft. long) for pulp mills as well as 4-ft. lengths of poplar to be split and dried before selling as firewood. It was all done with hand axes and Swede saws.

My father looked after his tools well; they were always well cared for and sharp. They had to be since they represented a substantial investment. It took over a day's woodcutting income to buy an ax in 1945.

I remember as yesterday when my father bought a new felling ax for my uncle, who lived with us. It had the slimmest blade of any ax I'd ever seen. Two inches back from the edge that ax would have been no more than ¼ in. thick, and the face must have been a full 6 in. wide. I was jealous because I always had to use some hand-me-down ax with a handle frayed from limbing overstrikes and bound with a makeshift guard of stovepipe wire wrapped around the first 2 in. back of the head. It was suited to my skill if not my aspirations.

My father was never very thrilled about the way my uncle looked after his ax; in retrospect, I suspect that he coveted that ax because it was unquestionably the best in our diverse collection.

We always had to travel somewhere to cut wood. Anything larger than 6 in. in diameter had long since been cut on our homestead, so we would cut wood on crown land or the section of land owned by the Hudson's Bay Company, both several miles away. We would set out in the morning with a team of horses and a bare-bunked sleigh, the axes slung in their holders on the back side of the bunks (the front sides plowed snow!) and the Swede saws hanging from a bunk post.

Saskatchewan winters were always cold; there was no hint of global warming in the '40s. By the time we got to the bush, we were often half-frozen and the tools might be at a cool -40°F. My father knew the danger of using an ax at that temperature, so he would tuck his under his backside on the sack of straw that he used as a cushion and insulator when driving and warm the ax for the last ten or fifteen minutes of the trip. My uncle never warmed his ax before using it, and my father would grumble about this carelessness but, being a gentle man, never forced the issue.

One particularly cold morning (memory makes it even colder than it was and the bush even farther away from home), my uncle unslung his ax from the sleigh bunk, walked over to a poplar, cleared snow from a spot on the ground for solid footing and prepared to notch the tree. With the first swing, he took the entire face out of his ax. I can still remember the huge crescent-shaped piece of steel stuck in the tree. I can also remember how angry I was because I had never had the chance to use that beautiful ax and now it was no more.

I have bought many axes since that incident and, just as the weather used to be colder then, I am equally certain that axes used to be more beautiful than they are today.

Using an 8-in. mill file, file the ax away from the edge.

FILING AN AX HEAD

An 8-in. mill bastard file is ideal for shaping most ax heads. The steel in the head is usually no harder than Rc55 and can be filed readily. A mill file will remove stock quickly and controllably. With a bit of practice, it is easy to maintain angles, particularly when you use the height of the file above the ax eye as an indicator of angle. It is also safest to file an ax from the eye side of the edge, although almost every woodsman I have known files directly toward the edge with cavalier abandon.

To get a consistently shaped wedge, it will probably be necessary to remove more material from the center portion of the head than at the tips of the face (see the drawing below). Among older axes you will often find a substantial

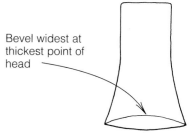

Bevel widest at thickest point of head

swelling toward the center of the head, feathering off both fore and aft. When you file such an ax you will get a much wider bevel in the center of the head than at either tip. One log builder I know files his felling ax by resting the tip of the file at the center of the ax head near the poll and then using a draw-filing technique in a semicircular motion to shape the face. It seems to work well for him, although I find it to be an uncomfortable motion and prefer striking a basic bevel angle at the center of the face and extending it in each direction.

There is a tendency to file a steeper bevel angle at the center of the face than at either tip. Partly this is dictated by the above-mentioned swelling at the center and partly by the tendency to file the lowest bevel angle where it is easiest to file the lowest bevel angle. There is no great harm in doing this unless the included bevel angle near the edge becomes too small and weakens the edge. More usual is that the bevel angle is too great at the center of the ax, causing too much wedging action in use and reducing penetration.

HONING THE EDGE

Honing the edge of an ax is similar to honing a drawknife or any other tool that requires freehand stoning. For reasons of tradition, this is still one tool that I prefer to hone with an oil stone. Unquestionably a large part of this is the memory of my father honing axes. He used a bit of 3-In-One or neat's-foot oil, whichever was handiest, and an easy rotary motion with the stone. This echnique leaves a surface finish a bit like the geometric pattern that you find on the inside of an old pocketwatch case. After honing with the oil stone, I finish off in a highly untraditional manner—a chromium-oxide-charged felt wheel on a power grinder. It would have made my father shake his head, I'm sure.

There is no reason that all of this could not be done with water stones in sequence, or with just one water stone in the 1000x range and a rigid strop charged with chromium oxide. You could also hone the edge with several grits of belt on a belt sander.

MAINTAINING THE EDGE ON AN AX

As well as shaping the face properly and using an ax only for its intended purpose, the next best thing you can do is keep it in a sheath to avoid accidental dulling. In the same vein, be aware that there is often a lot of grit embedded in the bark near the base of a tree. In books on early logging practices, you will see photographs where the bark has been removed in a ring around the tree where the saw cut will be made. This was done to remove the grit-impregnated bark so it would not dull the saw blade. You can do the same in the area where you intend to notch the tree with your felling ax, but since you would normally have to use an ax to remove the bark this all gets very fussy. With some trees it is very easy to strip the bark from a safe cut a foot or more up the tree, with others not so easy. The degree of fussiness you bring to your woodworking activities I leave to you.

SPLITTING MAULS AND SPLITTING AXES

The two basic types of splitting instruments are splitting mauls and splitting axes. A splitting maul is a cross between a post maul and an ax; it has a maul eye, oval-shaped and much smaller than an ax eye. Like a splitting ax it has very thick cheeks so that the head can be reversed and the tool used as a maul to drive splitting wedges. Some people believe that the thick cheeks on these tools are designed so that a lodged head can be driven through the block with a post maul. All I can say to these people is that I hope they enjoy replacing handles, because there is no easier way to ruin handles on either of these tools than by driving them through wood with another sledge. The vibrations caused in the undamped handle will soon cause it to split between the annular rings.

SPLITTING MAULS

It is virtually impossible to lodge a splitting maul in sound wood. The face is formed by two intersecting arcs, which result in minimal surface contact as it splits the piece of wood. The two pieces of the block are tangent to the maul head so there is only a very narrow band of contact on either side of the head (see the drawing at right).

Anyone who has split a great deal of wood by hand will recognize the advantage of this shape. The only time it is difficult to remove a splitting maul from a block of wood after an unsuccessful blow is if there is a punk section in the block. Wood that has just begun to rot will deform readily and virtually mold itself around the head of the maul. Otherwise, you will seldom have any difficulty removing a splitting maul for a second strike.

There is not much to say about sharpening a splitting maul. Remove any major flat spots from the edge and give the head a shot of wax, Dri-Cote or other lubricant to reduce friction. Unless you are very careful, you will shortly have another flat spot on the edge anyway so there is no use spending a great deal of time dressing it.

Splitting tools available today are seldom ideally shaped. The splitting maul at left comes closest to an ideal shape but is heavier than most people can comfortably use. The splitting ax at right is easier to use but could benefit from fuller cheeks.

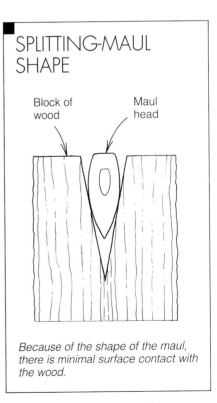

SPLITTING-MAUL SHAPE

Block of wood   Maul head

Because of the shape of the maul, there is minimal surface contact with the wood.

SPLITTING-AX SHAPE

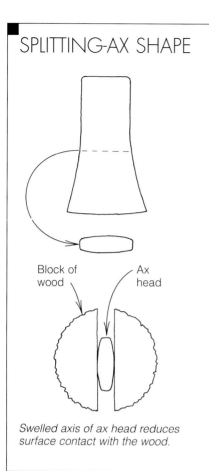

Block of wood

Ax head

Swelled axis of ax head reduces surface contact with the wood.

SPLITTING AXES

A splitting ax is shaped differently from a splitting maul; it is much closer to a utility ax in shape, although usually much heavier. A well-shaped splitting ax will also be swelled substantially along the vertical axis of the head (see the drawing at left). Once again the principle is to reduce surface contact with the two halves of the block being split, only this time the line of tangency is at 90° to that of the splitting maul. That is not quite true since a well-shaped splitting maul strives for point contact rather than line contact, and it would be swelled along both the horizontal axis and the vertical axis.

The swelling at the center makes it possible to lever a splitting ax out of a block of wood after an unsuccessful strike. If it cannot be levered out, the ax should have sufficient eye strength that it can be driven through but, as mentioned above, this risks breaking the handle. If you must drive it through,

strike the head dead-center with a one-handed blow while the other hand is on the handle dampening vibrations.

Like the maul, the splitting ax is basically a blunt instrument for primitive work. Maintain the bevels so that there are no flat spots on the edge and forget any fancy honing. In use, the cutting edge comes in contact with wood only as the head first enters the block; otherwise, the splitting crack runs well ahead of the edge. Your time is better spent concentrating on reducing friction along the sides of the head rather than worrying about the keenness of the edge.

MAINTAINING THE EDGE

The main concern you have with a splitting tool is to keep it from striking the ground and becoming dulled on pebbles or stones. To prevent this, and to make the whole splitting process a lot easier, find a good-sized block of unsplit wood, bed it solidly in the ground and use it as a splitting base. Many people do not appreciate the importance of getting the block on a solid base. The base is important since you do not want the inertia of the descending head to be absorbed in deformation of any material other than the block you are trying to split. Using a splitting base that is sitting on springy turf will waste a lot of your effort.

WEDGING AN AX HANDLE

A loose handle in an ax can be tightened easily with hardwood wedges. If the handle can be removed completely, do so, and make saw cuts where you intend to wedge. If the handle cannot be removed easily, use a chisel to open the wood where you want to wedge. In general, the wedges should be driven parallel to the minor axis of the eye. This best resists the usual compressive forces exerted on the handle when it is "levered" out of a cut, and, equally important, it avoids the danger of distorting the eye.

If some spreading across the minor axis is required, make the wedge cuts at a 45° angle to each axis. Avoid wedging parallel to the major axis. A wedge is a powerful device; it can damage the eye permanently if misapplied.

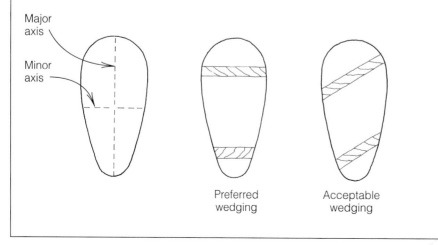

Major axis

Minor axis

Preferred wedging

Acceptable wedging

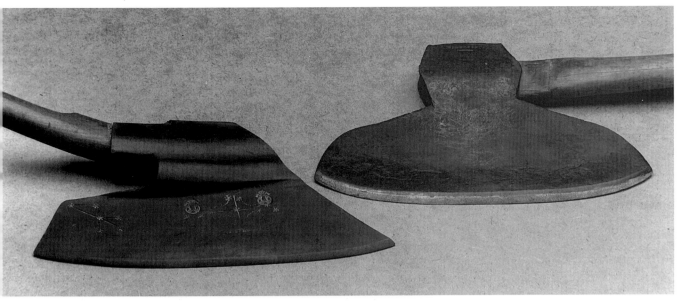

The European bearded ax (left) and the Canada-pattern broad ax (right) are the two most common styles of broad axes.

SIDE AXES

A side ax is any ax that has a bevel on one side of the blade only. The two most common types are broad axes and bench axes. In general, they differ only in size. The broad ax is intended for two-handed use, the bench ax for one-handed use.

BROAD AXES

Of the various styles of broad axes, the two most common today are the Canada-pattern broad ax (the style most used in North America) and the bearded ax, a European style.

Both types are used for squaring timbers, but the European ax is not nearly as heavy, weighing about 6 lb., and is more suited to the European style of building construction. The North American ax was used for heavier work, in working the generally larger pines for log houses and hardwoods for railroad ties. Some Canada-pattern axes weigh as much as 12 lb. They also usually have a cambered face, whereas the European axes are normally flat. Both styles have offset handles to avoid knuckle-barking.

The North American style can be used to make cross-grain cuts; the European style always has to be used askew the grain to avoid the tips digging in. As a final difference, the European axes have thinner blades and usually lower bevel angles, reflecting the more delicate nature of their use. The North American axes needed beefier edges to slash through the knots in hardwood.

Because of the tremendous variability in the steel of these old axes, it is a good idea to start out with a bevel of about 30° and work your way either up or down in bevel angle according to your intended use and the quality of the steel in the ax head.

SHARPENING A BROAD AX

As with any single-bevel tool, you should focus your attention first on the back side of the blade. It should be flat, smooth and free of defects. The latter point is particularly important if you have bought an old broad ax (see the photo at right). Almost without exception, these have been left to rust in a shed, barn or damp basement. You have to remove the rust and then eliminate any pitting on the back of the blade. Since you want to keep the back

This classic old Canada pattern broad ax (made by Lyman Perkins, Hull, Quebec, sometime prior to 1834) shows rust pitting and a typical scarf weld.

EARLY AX MANUFACTURING

Like early chisels and plane blades, the major parts of ax heads were made from mild steel or iron with forge-welded, higher-carbon-steel bits. There were three basic methods for attaching the steel bit to an iron ax head: the overcoat method, the insert method and the scarf joint.

All began the same, with a flat piece of iron that had the two halves of the eye partially formed in it and a bit of end treatment. The iron was then formed over a removable mandrel before forging the two halves together. The steel bit was welded to the iron, and finally the edge was formed.

With broad axes, the iron body was feathered to an edge and then the steel bit was scarfed onto the blade. Oddly enough, some of the scarf joints were the reverse of the one illustrated below. This meant that you would run into the iron faster with repeated sharpening.

All this is not just of historic interest; it has application for today's tool buyer. Anyone who wants a cambered Canada-pattern broad ax has to buy an antique. The smart buyer will ensure that there is still enough of the steel bit left to give reasonable service.

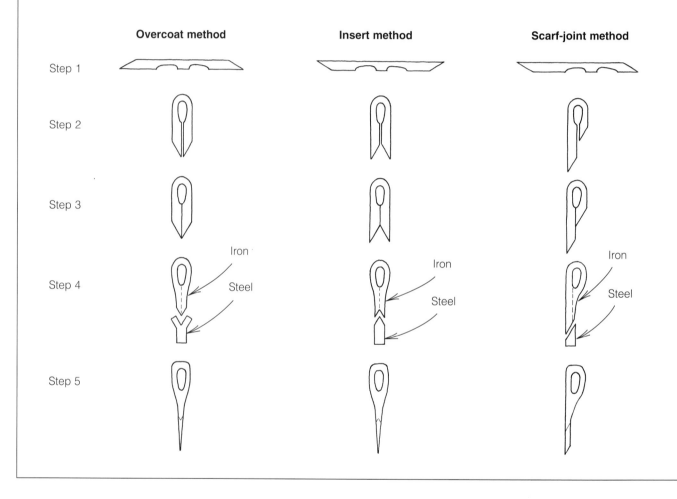

of the blade as regular as possible, the fastest way to dress the back of the blade is on a 3-in. (or larger) belt sander mounted upside-down in a vise. Using a sequence of belts from coarse to fine, strip the back of the blade until you have a defect-free surface and a smooth plane. For the final touches, a medium-grit water stone (800x to 1200x) works well.

Depending upon your individual technique and the nature of the work you will be doing, you may want to put just a touch of back bevel on the blade. This may seem like heresy to some of you, but it can make a difficult tool much easier to use for the novice. The inertial mass of a vigorously swung

broad ax exerts a tremendous amount of force on the blade edge. Because the force is all from the beveled side, any deflection of the blade will cause it to bite into the wood more deeply than intended. It is far easier to prevent damaged work by using an ax that has a slight tendency to cut away from the line than it is with an ax that tends to cut toward the finish line and possibly past it.

There is no easy rule of thumb for putting back bevel on a broad-ax blade. For knot-free pine, buffing the back of the edge will usually give you enough back bevel to make the ax highly controllable. The amount of bevel is almost invisible to the naked eye. For heavier work in hardwoods, you may want to stone a visible bevel on the back of the blade. Until you have some experience with back bevels, approach them the same way you would a porcupine. You can cause damage if you become too aggressive. Avoid long shallow back bevels unless you are absolutely certain that is what you want. It takes a long time to dress away an unwanted bevel, even with a belt sander. It may even be necessary to

take an extra 1/16 in. or 1/8 in. off the main bevel in order to restore a blade that has been the object of overexuberance.

Other than the above considerations, a broad ax can be sharpened with the same equipment used for a felling ax. The steel is usually fairly soft in a broad ax and will file readily. The edge can be refined with stones and strops as necessary.

HATCHETS

Hatchets are miniature axes. They come in center-bevel and side-bevel (or broad hatchet) styles. They are little used in most types of woodworking today, although they remain as handy as ever for one-handed shaping. The sharpening considerations for hatchets are exactly the same as for axes.

Kindling hatchets should be shaped like splitting axes; camping hatchets like felling axes; and broad hatchets like broad axes. The same equipment is used to shape and hone them.

The shingling hatchet (see the drawing on p. 172) is one special case worth mentioning. Although originally designed for use with wooden shingles and lath, it is more commonly used today with asphalt shingles. Instead of being used in the classic manner to split and shape shingles, it is used much in the manner of a cutting knife. The back corner of the blade is used to cut or deeply score an asphalt shingle so that a portion can be removed; the poll is used to drive roofing nails.

It is difficult to keep the handle tight in a traditional hatchet (center) because the eye is short. Any levering on the handle causes fiber compression, which quickly loosens the head. For axes subject to lateral leverage, the cheeks can be extended fore and/or aft to form lugs that create the effect of a deeper eye. The two hand-forged hatchets at left and right have this feature.

MODIFIED SHINGLING HATCHET

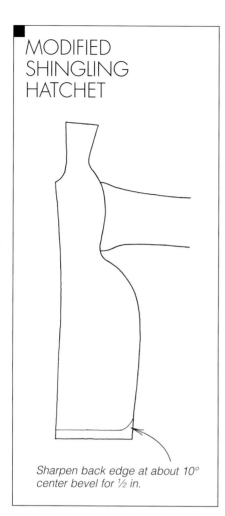

Sharpen back edge at about 10° center bevel for ½ in.

For anyone using it in this manner, it is worthwhile paying particular attention to the back corner of the blade to keep it sharp and as friction-free as possible. To improve the cutting action, the bevel can be reduced to about a 10° included angle for the last ½ in. of the blade; the back edge should be center-beveled at about 10° for ½ in. as well (see the drawing at left).

After the corner has been shaped, honing is still worthwhile, not because the sharp corner will last longer than a few hours in use but because the smooth surface (particularly when coated with a dry lubricant) will reduce friction in the cut. In short, it should be adapted to its new use.

ADZES

Adzes are one step up the evolutionary ladder from axes. Traditionally, they were used to refine many of the rough shapes created by axes. As an example, old timber-frame houses will often have exposed joists that show very fine adz work. The builder would use a broad ax to square the beam and an adz to dress it. Although use of either tool took skill, there is an inherent danger in using a foot adz to square a beam that separated the user from others in the trade, much like the difference between a trim carpenter and a framing carpenter today.

A foot adz is so called not to differentiate it from a hand adz but to reflect the nature of its use. The carpenter would make cuts directly under one foot, using the foot pressure on the shaving as a check-stop. There are many apocryphal stories about carpenters betting workmates that they could separate the sole of their boot from the upper without cutting a thread of their sock. Whether or not these stories have any factual basis, there is no question about the developed skill of some users.

STRAIGHT ADZES

A straight foot adz compares most directly with a broad ax. It is sometimes used parallel to the grain of the wood or askew the grain, but most commonly cross grain to achieve a reasonably flat, regular surface.

A selection of straight adzes: from left to right, a pin poll adz (railway style); a half-head adz, or sledge poll; a standard adz (whole head or flat head); and a half-head variation.

Like a broad ax, an adz sometimes has a slightly cambered face so that the corners do not catch and cause the head to twist. Some crown is put on the edge for the same reason (see the drawing at right). It tends to keep the blade moving in a straight line. The amount of camber is usually dictated by the tool, although you can vary it slightly, but the amount of crown is your choice. For cutting with the grain, you need little or no crown; for cutting cross grain, you want as much as is necessary to control splintering. Almost all users put a slight crown on an adz edge, except for a lipped adz, which is used with a straight edge.

Like most single-bevel tools, the unbeveled side of the adz is often ignored. It should not be. The back of the adz should be linished, or stoned, until it is a smooth plane. A 120x belt sander or disc sander will do the brute work; use 240x to refine it, and then stone it or use a power buff to finish.

The basic bevel angle should be 25° to 30°, depending on whether you intend to use the adz for roughing or finishing and whether or not you like back bevel on the tool. Like most single-bevel impact tools (broad axes, carpenter's hatchets, etc.), an adz can benefit from some back bevel. It allows the tool to cut a shallow scallop rather than a straight plane. For roughing, I recommend a 25° bevel for softwood and 30° for dry hardwood, if you intend to have no back bevel. If you want back bevel on the blade, these angles can be dropped by as many degrees of back bevel you intend to use. For example, with 5° of back bevel you could drop the primary bevel to 20° for softwood and 25° for hardwood. For work where you would be making shallow cuts to achieve a fine finish, the bevel angle could be dropped another 5°.

The back bevel should be very shallow and slightly rounded. Use a stone to set the bevel, resting the stone on a $\frac{1}{16}$-in. thick piece of material about 2 in. back of the edge (see the sidebar on the 1-in-60 rule on p. 17). This will give you a 2° back bevel. Then strop the bevel to refine the surface. The stropping will tend to round the bevel a bit. It is usually enough.

As always, your desired result combined with your technique of use will determine the degree of back bevel you want. Start with a very shallow angle (about 2°) and make the bevel short. You can always take more off, but you can't put it back on.

These are starting points only. The nature of the work you intend to do and the nature of the steel in your adz could dictate a stronger edge. Starting with a fairly low basic bevel as we have here, it is easy to beef it up with a steeper micro-bevel if needed.

With a new adz, or one new to you, simply hone the edge in the shape you found it. Then test the tool and your technique. If it cuts well and you are happy with the action, there is no need to tinker with it. If you find it digging in uncontrollably, then adjust the bevel.

LIPPED ADZES

A lipped, or shipwright's, adz (see the photo on p. 174) presents special sharpening problems. It is designed specifically for cross-grain work. The turned-up lips clip off splinters that the main edge has raised.

Like other adzes, lipped adzes were once made by a number of manufacturers in several variations of width, eye angle, and so on. To my knowledge, there is only one factory in Europe that makes lipped adzes today, and they do not make them well. The adzes are drop-forged but are not smithed afterward. Smithing is a hand process whereby a tool is refined in some way on an anvil. For example, paring gouges need smithing to straighten them after they are forged. So do lipped adzes.

In the adz-forging process, the head is formed in steps; the last step is to turn the lips. But there is some springback, which causes the adz face to arch upward next to the lips. The thicker

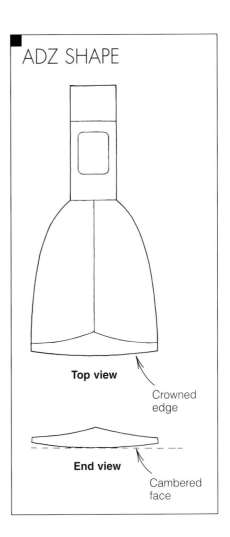

ADZ SHAPE

Top view

Crowned edge

End view

Cambered face

If this lipped adz does not have the recurve removed from the center, it will always be difficult to use because the corners will catch first, twisting the adz.

On a lipped adz, use a sanding drum matched to the inside radius to sharpen the bevel in the lip area. (Photo by Susan Kahn)

central portion of the blade resists the pressure, and the result is a bit like the recurved shape of a hunting or target bow. (The photo at left shows the recurve.)

To make such an adz usable, you first have to rework the back. This can best be done with a belt sander or a sanding disc with a coarse belt (start at 80x). As you approach flatness (or a fair curve, whichever you want), change to finer grits as necessary, ending at 240x with a light touch. Only after this major reworking can you turn your attention to detailed shaping of the edge.

In all probability, you'll be faced with a nasty, ragged-looking edge after you have reworked the back of the adz. In particular, you will probably have fairly deep indents in the areas of the lips. The entire edge should be ground back until it's straight; then you can re-establish the bevel.

A lipped adz is particularly tricky to sharpen in the area of the lip. The brute work can be done with a flex shaft and a sanding drum of a radius just smaller than the radius at the corner of the lip. Use a light touch to prevent overheating and when the line of light becomes uncomfortably narrow, switch to slipstones or cylindrical hones.

Whether or not you choose to put some back bevel on the main part of the edge, you do not want any on the lips themselves. There should be no back bevel from the top of the lips to the point at which they become tangent to the flat part of the face. Any back bevel in this area would cause the adz to wedge laterally in the cut. Since this adz is designed for trenching cuts, you do not want it to be wider at any point than the trench that it is cutting.

ADZ-HEAD DESIGN

There are two immutable features of an adz that should be considered before purchasing. The first is head curvature. The curvature you want depends on your height, since you want the head curvature to match the arc that the head makes when you are swinging the adz.

This curvature is closely allied to the second thing that you cannot change about an adz, the angle of the eye to the blade. Most adzes do not have heads of constant curvature. They usually have a shallow curve in the forward part of the head and then either a progressively tighter curve or a break point where the shallow curve intersects with a sharper curve. The minimum arc through which the adz can be swung is determined by the shallower of the two curves. The center of this arc is called the true rotation point (see the drawing at right).

If you want to use a fairly full swing with a lipped adz, you will want a rotation point at least 25 in. from the edge. Fortunately, most lipped adzes are designed that way. Most foot adzes, on the other hand, are designed with tighter curvatures so that at least one forearm can be braced against the front of a thigh to control the cutting action. It would be very difficult to take anything near a full swing with such an adz. It has to be used with a short, choppy swing.

The true rotation point varies from adz to adz but is important to its use. If this point is too close to the head you will have to choke up on the handle to get a controlled cut. You would also find it hard to get a shallow, relatively flat cut without using unusual technique. At the other end of the scale, if the rotation point is too far from the head, substantial back bevel could be necessary to bring the rotation point closer to the head.

While some of this discussion may seem peripheral to sharpening, it is not. The purpose of the tool and the technique of the user are key to shaping the edge for effective use. If a tool cannot be shaped to fit the user's style and to meet the user's purposes, there is little point in putting a keen edge on it.

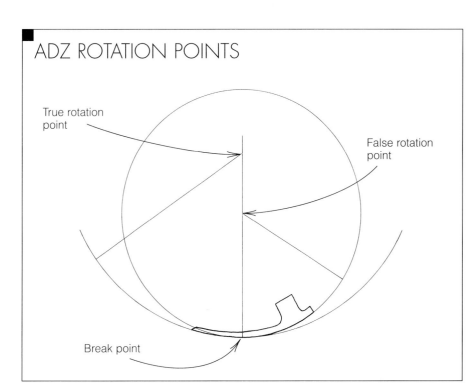

ADZ ROTATION POINTS

True rotation point

False rotation point

Break point

CHAPTER 14
POWER-SAW BLADES

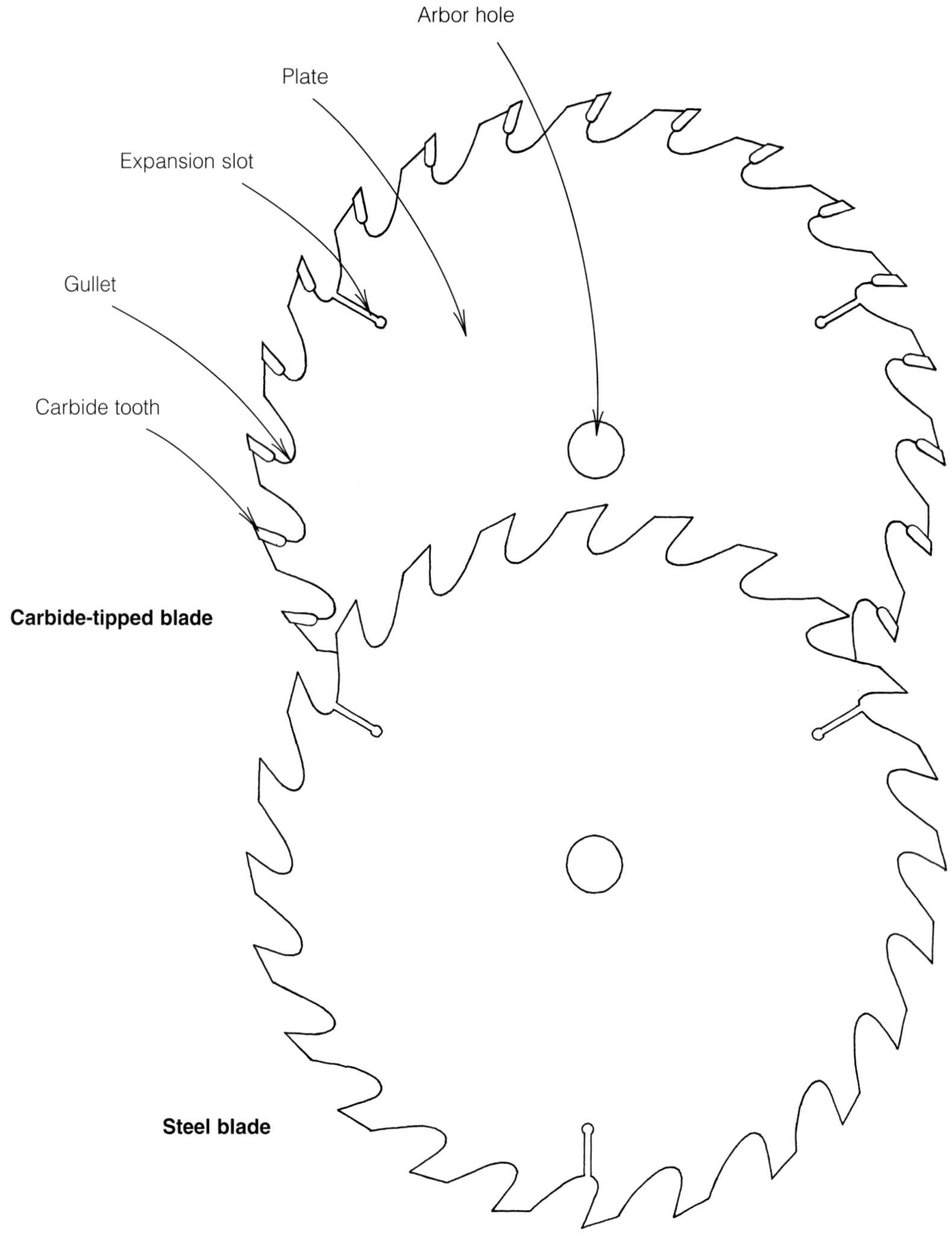

Arbor hole

Plate

Expansion slot

Gullet

Carbide tooth

Carbide-tipped blade

Steel blade

Although very few craftsmen sharpen their own circular-saw or bandsaw blades today, some understanding of saw sharpening and tooth shape is necessary to understand how a saw functions. Whether or not you ever intend to sharpen your own saw blades, an understanding of the principles will help you identify and solve problems with them, as well as guide you in blade selection.

Very few all-steel blades are used today; tungsten-carbide-tipped blades have taken over the market. For this reason, some of the information in this chapter will have limited application for many readers. It will be useful for instrument makers and model makers, who still use small-diameter all-steel blades. At the other end of the scale, it is equally applicable to the blades still used in cordwood saws and some small mills.

FACTORS IN BLADE PERFORMANCE

A circular-saw blade is basically a plate with chisels fashioned in the rim. Saw teeth cut like miniature chisels, and the forces on them are similar. There are several complicating factors with circular saws, however. Unlike a chisel, where your primary concern is a single keen edge at a suitable bevel angle, sharpness of a circular-saw blade is only one of several factors that affect the cutting action.

BLADE STIFFNESS

A blade that runs true is necessary for a clean cut. Assuming a perfectly functioning drive mechanism, there are still a number of factors related to blade stiffness alone that contribute to true running. These include the thickness and tensioning of the plate, and the speed of rotation.

Plate thickness A thick plate is usually stiffer than a thin plate. Unfortunately, it also makes a wider kerf and wastes more material. The trade-off becomes one of waste versus minimum required thickness. While you can usually afford some additional thickness in a cutoff-saw blade (because most material needs to be docked anyway), a thick rip-saw blade wastes an amazing amount of material. Just how thin you can make a rip blade depends to a great extent on the consistency and thickness of the material to be worked. Inconsistent material such as knotty pine causes more problems than a consistently hard material like birch. A saw blade naturally tends to dodge a hard spot in the wood, particularly when the knot is encountered tangentially. Cutting straight through the center of a knot causes fewer problems than clipping the edge off one.

Stiffening washers, also called blade stabilizers or blade flanges, are useful on any blade but particularly on thinner ripping blades. You should always use the largest size of stiffening washer that is feasible given the depth of material you want to cut; washers should be at least one-third the diameter of the blade. Good stiffening washers contact the blade only in a narrow band at the edge of the washer. The centers of the washers should be relieved so that pressure is focused at the perimeter band. Washers substantially improve the performance of thin blades by forcing the blade to cut in a straight line instead of dodging hard spots.

Plate tensioning All-steel saw blades must have properly tensioned plates, otherwise they will run untrue as soon as the rim begins to heat from cutting action. As the rim heats, it expands and if the plate cannot accommodate the expansion, the rim will adopt a snake-like shape. A well-tensioned plate will be slightly loose in the center. On blades over 18 in. in diameter this looseness can be visible; the portion between the arbor hole and the rim will bow away from a straightedge just slightly. As the rim heats, the loose portion will firm up with rim expansion. The blade will then run true at its normal operating temperature.

Because it is very difficult to tension small-diameter saw blades adequately by any automated process, manufacturers cut expansion slots in the rim of the blade. In some cheap blades there are no slots. In others the slots terminate in round holes to avoid stress risers that would cause blade cracking. Unfortunately, blades with holes in them tend to be exceptionally noisy because the holes act like whistles when the blade is running at speed. Some manufacturers have attempted to solve this problem by putting soft copper slugs in the holes to reduce the noise. This is only a satisfactory solution when the holes are slightly countersunk on each side first so that the slug can be riveted into position. Otherwise slugs can shift, causing rubbing on the end of the slug and throwing the blade off. Some blade manufacturers have now gone to a type of laser-cut expansion slot much like an inverted question mark that avoids stress risers and still allows the blade to run relatively quietly. Better blades have expansion slots.

Speed of rotation High rotation speeds tend to make a blade run cooler because of the increased cooling action of air on the teeth. This, in turn, reduces expansion at the rim. Blades sometimes have recommended operating speeds but almost always have maximum rotation speed limits. Contrary to what you might think, speeds beyond the rated limit make a blade looser, not tighter, causing dangerous flutter with reduced quality of cut and substantial risk of blade damage. You should never run a blade beyond the stated limit.

TOOTH HEIGHT

If the teeth of a saw blade are not all exactly the same height in relation to the center, not only will some teeth be doing more work than others but the uneven force will cause spindle stress, resulting in minute lateral displacement of the teeth. This will cause a slightly serrated finish on the wood as well as increased wear on the drive train.

GULLET SIZE

Most steel-tooth saws can be sharpened a number of times before you have to be concerned about the size of the gullets. Nonetheless, it is necessary to have gullets of a sufficient size to carry away the chips cut by the tooth. Undersized gullets will cause sawdust packing, which will quickly cause a

number of other distortion problems. Gullets are usually dressed out with a suitably shaped file.

FINISH DRAG

Any part of the tooth or saw blade that touches the wood during cutting should be as smooth as possible. Numerous research projects have shown that a rough finish substantially increases rate of wear as well as increasing heat through friction. Sharpened teeth should be finished as finely as possible even to the point of stoning them if required. The saw blade should be kept free of any gum or glue buildup and should be lightly waxed or sprayed regularly with a low-friction coating.

DRIVE MECHANISM

The best-maintained blade cannot cut well if the drive mechanism is worn or untrue. Spindle bearings have to be maintained; untrue spindles should be corrected or replaced, and worn saw collars should be refaced as necessary. Problems with the drive mechanism are more frequently the source of poor performance than bad saw blades.

STEEL CIRCULAR-SAW BLADES

Steel circular-saw blades require essentially the same treatment as handsaw blades (see Chapter 12): jointing, gumming, setting the teeth, filing the teeth and side dressing. Sharpening technique differs somewhat for rip blades and crosscut blades.

SHARPENING RIP BLADES

Circular rip blades, like the hand rip saw, have chisel-tipped teeth designed for cutting with the grain. The first step in sharpening a rip blade is to joint the teeth.

BASIC EQUIPMENT FOR SHARPENING

A typical bench setup for sharpening steel circular-saw blades includes:

1. A saw-blade vise, either commercial or shopmade.

2. Tools for spring setting the teeth: either a pistol-grip sawset for relatively thin, small-diameter blades of 4 tpi or more, or a commercial or shopmade stake-and-anvil for setting larger, heavier-gauge teeth. Swaged teeth will require a swaging tool and hammer.

3. Files for sharpening: these might include feather-edge files, triangular or square-section files, round-edge flat mill files or round files; and a stone for jointing.

4. A set gauge, raker gauge and gullet compass (all of which can be shopmade) to control tooth-shape tolerances.

5. For frequent blade sharpening or reconditioning, a grinder or other powered arbor, plus a diamond-point dresser to shape your own abrasive grinding wheels for saw-blade gumming.

Jointing Jointing accomplishes three things: it removes the rounded shoulders on tooth tips caused by prolonged cutting; it levels the teeth in preparation for the filing of crisp, new tips; and it ensures that the blade is round.

To prepare for jointing, rip partway through a hardwood board, clamp the board in position and adjust the blade height until the teeth are just proud of the board, as shown in the photo at right. Unplug the saw and rotate the blade by hand, bringing one tooth to apogee. Using the horizontal top surfaces of the board as a guide, file or stone the tip of the tooth to create a very small, new flat. Then rotate the blade to move on to the next tooth.

Gumming Gumming is the process of enlarging tooth gullets to maintain chip-carrying capacity. Gumming is not usually required until a blade has been sharpened several times.

The shape of the gullet contour also establishes the rake angle of the tooth. In the case of a rip blade, "half pitch" describes the geometry where the lead edge of a tooth, extended toward the center portion of the blade, falls halfway between the center hole and the perimeter (see the drawing at right). Well-rounded gullet lines are needed to clear chips and to prevent cracks from forming. Gullets must be uniform to ensure balance as well as even distribution of heat and stress. To establish a new line for gullet bottoms, scribe a circle with a pair of trammel points or a compass.

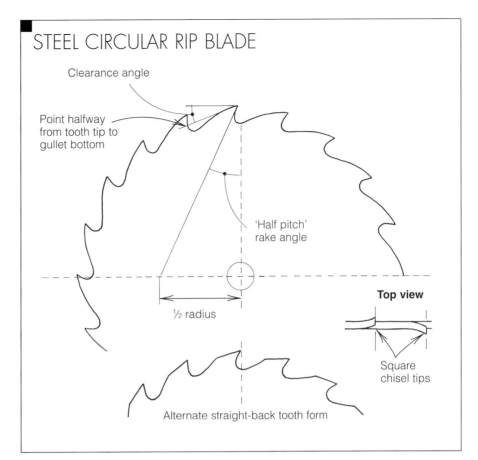

STEEL CIRCULAR RIP BLADE

Clearance angle

Point halfway from tooth tip to gullet bottom

'Half pitch' rake angle

½ radius

Top view

Square chisel tips

Alternate straight-back tooth form

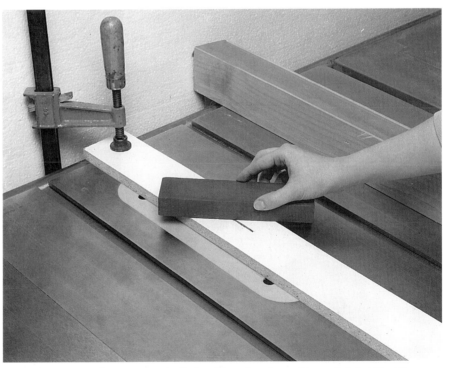

With the saw teeth just proud of a kerf in a hardwood board, joint the tips with a stone.

Gum rip-tooth gullets to half pitch with an 8-in. or 10-in. round file (second-cut), deepening and shaping the gullet lines by eye down to the new line. The blade should be held in a saw vise (as shown in the photo at top left below). Take the same number of file strokes per gullet to ensure balanced metal removal.

A power-driven abrasive gumming wheel will also do the job, potentially faster and more uniformly. Use a diamond-point dresser to shape an abrasive wheel to the proper profile. Then mount the wheel on a table saw, radial-arm saw, bench grinder, mandrel or electric drill and make a jig to control the angle of attack and ensure square-edged gullets as you move from tooth to tooth (see the photo at top right below). Power gumming should be done very slowly to prevent heat buildup.

Gum rip-tooth gullets to half pitch with a round file.

Power gumming can be done with a thin, round-edge abrasive wheel mounted on a radial-arm saw. Note the clamp and indexing pin to register successive teeth.

A saw wrest is a traditional saw-setting tool used on large, thick blades.

File across the backs of the rip teeth, sliding the file up toward the tips.

Setting the teeth The alternate bending over of tooth tips called "set" creates the kerf clearance that prevents binding and the dangers of stock kickback. The set must be even to reduce strain, chatter, vibration and the tendency of the blade to lead to one side during the cut. The amount of set should be no more than half the thickness of the tooth, and can be less when dry hardwood is being cut.

In the past, for large, relatively thick blades, a wrench-like notch tool called a saw wrest was used to bend teeth over, with the amount of tooth set judged by an experienced eye (see the photo at bottom left on the facing page). More common, however, and much easier to control is a commercial stake-and-anvil with a spring-loaded punch or hammer.

To measure the amount of set, make a four-bolt side-set gauge called a spider, which can be read or preset with the help of a feeler gauge on a flat surface (see the photo on p. 157). It's advisable to duplicate the amount of set noted when the blade was new, though cutting thin, dry hardwood will permit considerably less set than that required for thick, wet softwoods. To keep the amount of necessary bending force to a minimum and to avoid setting up strains that might endanger the gullet bottoms, don't set more than one-third of the way down the tooth set. Set alternate teeth in one direction; then turn the blade over and set the remaining teeth in the other direction. Never reverse the set of a tooth.

Swaging In production ripping operations, especially where green lumber is sawn in quantity, teeth on larger-diameter blades are sometimes swaged rather than set. This is a technique whereby the steel tip of each tooth is spread so its extra width at the flared point is given clearance on both sides, allowing fast ripping and high feed rates, but a rough cut. This is done with swaging anvils, eccentric swaging machines or simple upset swagers.

After swaging, the tooth sides must be taper-dressed with a file to create tip-to-body clearance, and to even the set in preparation for the final filing of the tips.

Filing the teeth Rip teeth need square chisel tips for proper cutting. After gumming and setting, mount the blade in a saw vise. File straight across the backs of the teeth, sliding the file upward toward the point during each stroke to create the curved back slope of the tooth, as shown in the photo at bottom right on the facing page. Depending on the size of the teeth, use a triangular taper file or a flat mill file (bastard cut). To maintain an adequate clearance angle and ensure that the backs of the teeth don't end up higher than the points, keep in mind a line from the tip of the tooth back to a point halfway between the bottom of the gullet and top of the next tooth. Maintain the original factory clearance angle, which should be in the range of 12° to 20° near the tooth tip.

File alternate teeth (*with* the set to avoid chatter), knocking off the burr with a scrap of wood to see more clearly the results of filing. Then turn the blade around and complete the remaining teeth. File the backs of the teeth until the flats resulting from previous jointing have just disappeared. Note that on some rip blades, the back of each tooth is a straight line that finally dips into a gullet contour (see the drawing on p. 179). Maintain this straight back during filing. Don't file the leading edges of the teeth. Commercial file guides are available to regulate the filing stroke, but they are not really

necessary if you're prepared to do a little practicing to minimize the arm's natural tendency to arc during the freehand filing stroke.

Side dressing To even the set and remove burrs, do a very light side honing with a flat stone on the side of the blade after sharpening. A more accurate dressing can be accomplished by laying the blade flat on an abrasive disc or on a supported sheet of silicon-carbide sandpaper or fine emery cloth, then slowly turning the blade backward for one revolution.

SHARPENING CROSSCUT BLADES
The crosscut-blade category includes plywood- and veneer-cutting blades, as well as blades designed for some cutoff saws and smooth trimmer saws. Unlike rip-saw blades, crosscut blades tend to be fine-toothed with alternately beveled tips to sever the fibers during the cut. Teeth may be spring-set on a flat-blade body, or without set when the blade is hollow-ground. Because of the sheer number of cutters to sharpen on these blades, and the fact that equally smooth cuts can often be made with a more versatile combination planer blade, steel crosscut blades are playing a dwindling role in woodworking shops. They tend to be reserved for small-scale work in thin materials, typically by musical-instrument makers and model makers.

Jointing Joint only enough to create small flats on all teeth, using the method described for rip blades.

Gumming In the smaller diameters of crosscut blades, gullet-shaping (gumming) occurs as part of the final filing step, described below. On larger-diameter blades with rounded gullet bottoms, use a round file for gumming, in a manner similar to that described for rip blades.

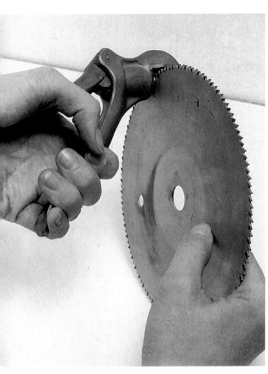

Set teeth on a steel plywood blade with a pistol-grip sawset.

Setting the teeth Blades with relatively coarse teeth (more than ¼ in. point to point) will require the use of a stake-and-anvil for setting. Finer teeth (below ¼ in. pitch) on thinner, smaller-diameter blades can be set with a heavy-duty pistol-grip sawset, as shown in the photo at left.

Filing the teeth To file the teeth, first clamp the blade in a saw vise. In general, try to maintain the original factory bevel angles and tooth profiles when filing crosscut saw teeth. As with cross-cut handsaws (see Chapter 12), the teeth must be beveled on the face opposite the set. Orient the file handle to conform to the factory gullet shape and bevel angles, then file alternate teeth. Reverse the blade and file the remaining teeth until the jointing flats disappear.

On large, coarse-toothed crosscut blades, where the teeth are more than ⅜ in. from point to point and the gullets are rounded, use an 8-in. or 10-in. mill bastard file with two rounded safe edges. Tooth pitches below ⅜ in. will

require a thinner section flat file, an 8-in. cant saw file or a tapered triangular file, depending on tooth configuration and gullet shape.

To cut through the cross-banded layers, plywood blades must function as combination rip/crosscut blades. As such, their fine teeth will have relativel small tooth bevel angles (around 10°) and can be sharpened with triangular files, handled according to the same technique as for crosscut handsaws, where the file dresses the face and bac bevel angles of adjacent teeth at the same time.

Rake angles Rake angles of crosscut teeth vary considerably with different styles and applications. Some coarse cutoff saws have V-teeth ("peg" teeth) with equal 30° back and negative rake angles (see the drawing below), while others have a milder 10° negative rake angle. One common style incorporate what are called "center pitch" teeth,

RAKE ANGLES FOR STEEL CIRCULAR CROSSCUT BLADES

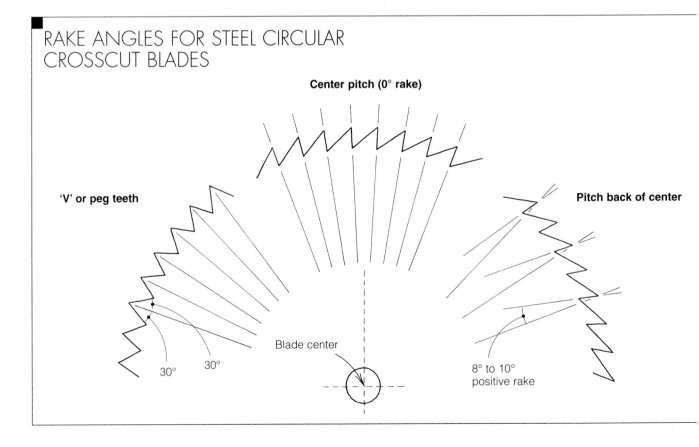

where the rake angle is zero. All these teeth have 60° gullet angles and can be sharpened with triangular files. However, blades whose teeth have a *positive* hook angle (e.g., 10° back from center pitch), such as are found on some smooth trimmer saws, have gullet angles less than 60° and won't accommodate triangular files. Instead, they require either a feather-edge file or grinding against a narrow, profiled abrasive wheel.

SHARPENING COMBINATION BLADES

There are a number of different styles of steel combination rip/crosscut blades (see the drawing below), each with its own sharpening requirements. Fortunately, all the teeth are either rip or crosscut teeth and would be sharpened accordingly.

SHARPENING DADO-BLADE SETS

Steel dado-blade sets consist of two outside cutting blades and a set of inner chipper blades (see the drawing on p. 184). The outside blades have repeating groups of cutters separated by a deep-gullet raker; the inner chippers, usually with blade-body thicknesses of ¼ in., ⅛ in. and 1/16 in., have two diametrically opposed raker teeth. The two outer blades, in combination with one or more chippers plus suitable shims, allow accurate dado and groove cutting of any width from about ¼ in. to 1 in.

Though the pair of outer steel dado blades superficially resemble combination planer blades, they differ in that the groups of cutting teeth are all set one way and filed alike. Rakers and inside chipping teeth are filed straight across, 1/64 in. lower than the cutters. The rakers on the two outside blades are left unset, while the chippers have swaged chisel points.

The first step in the sharpening sequence is to joint all the teeth of the outside blades, as well as the inner

chippers, to the same height. (This step may not be necessary for a minor touchup.) Next, gum the raker gullets on the outside blades to about one-third pitch.

If necessary, set the outer-blade cutter teeth (sometimes called the spur sections) in groups, all on one side, left or right, in an alternating pattern. Use a pistol-grip sawset or, on thicker, larger-diameter blades, a stake-and-anvil.

After setting, file the outside cutter groups with either a triangular file or a mill file held at a low angle, to achieve about a 20° face bevel angle, while maintaining the factory rake angle. Note that some dado sets use a different geometry, with outer blades having chisel-pointed spur sections ground straight across rather than beveled edges.

File the backs of the outer-blade rakers and the inner chipper teeth straight across until the flats produced by jointing disappear. Then add one or two strokes to bring all rakers and

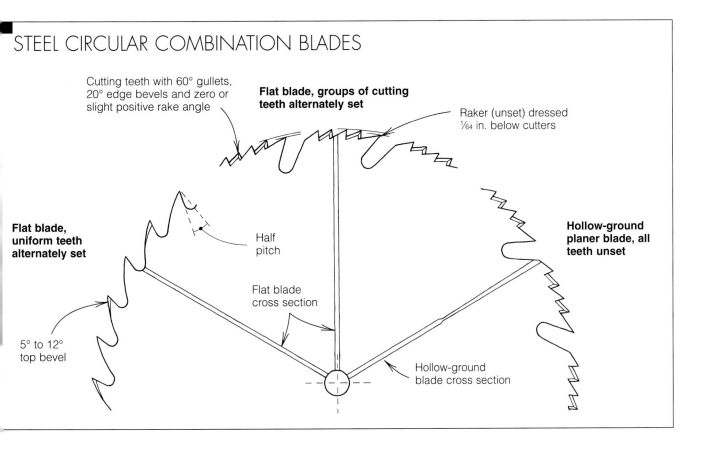

STEEL CIRCULAR COMBINATION BLADES

Cutting teeth with 60° gullets, 20° edge bevels and zero or slight positive rake angle

Flat blade, groups of cutting teeth alternately set

Raker (unset) dressed 1/64 in. below cutters

Flat blade, uniform teeth alternately set

Half pitch

Flat blade cross section

5° to 12° top bevel

Hollow-ground planer blade, all teeth unset

Hollow-ground blade cross section

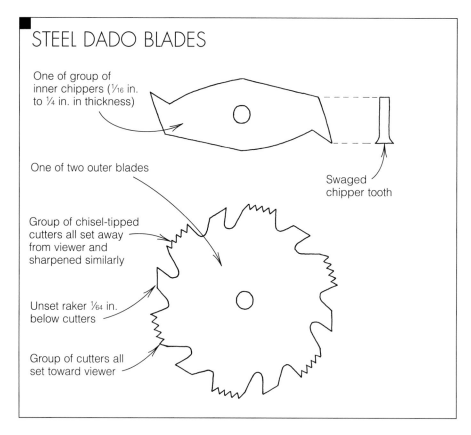

STEEL DADO BLADES

One of group of inner chippers (1/16 in. to 1/4 in. in thickness)

Swaged chipper tooth

One of two outer blades

Group of chisel-tipped cutters all set away from viewer and sharpened similarly

Unset raker 1/64 in. below cutters

Group of cutters all set toward viewer

chippers down 1/64 in. below the level of the cutters. Use a shopmade raker gauge (see p. 156) to check this distance.

When setting up dado blades for use on the saw, be sure to stagger the chipper blades in relation to one another, and to nest the chipper teeth in the gullet spaces of the two outside blades, so that all blade bodies rest flat against each other. When the inner chippers have lost too much swage to refiling, send the complete set out for professional reconditioning. Some things are better left to the professional.

The wobble dado The wobble, or quick-set, dado is a single blade with an adjustable body core that can be turned and locked to cut a given width of dado, which is characterized by a somewhat concave floor. These blades come in the various tooth patterns described above. If you have not yet bought a dado set, do yourself a favor and buy a stacking model. They put less stress on your machine than wobble dadoes and are capable of much greater accuracy.

CARBIDE-TIPPED CIRCULAR-SAW BLADES

In recent decades tungsten-carbide-tipped circular-saw blades have generally replaced steel blades in both commercial and home woodworking shops. Though expensive, they cut smoothly, stay sharp much longer and can stand up to hard abrasive materials such as particleboard, medium-density fiberboard (MDF) and woods with silica content.

Tungsten carbide is a manmade alloy made through a sintering process, whereby tungsten, carbon and other ingredients are mixed, heated and fused together under pressure. The resulting compound is almost diamond-hard and can work at high temperatures, but it is too brittle to be shaped into very thin or finely tapered sections for working wood. The sections must be fairly blocky to survive shock.

High-quality carbide-tipped circular-saw blades have a number of features in common. Teeth are made from the appropriate grade of carbide, for the best balance between shock resistance and wear resistance. They have precisely machined blade bodies, balanced and tensioned for smooth, safe operation, and are rated for the rpm at which they'll be used. Good blades have adequate expansion slots and teeth of generous thickness, brazed into plate pockets (see the top drawing on the facing page). The brazing will be gap-free and non-porous.

Low-quality carbide blades have untensioned plates, the carbide teeth are not in pockets but are just brazed to the flat face of the tooth, and the brazing is often porous, causing a weak bond between plate and tooth. They can have a host of other problems as well, but lack of pockets and poor brazing are the immediate indicators.

A wide variety of carbide blade types are available for specific applications, including basic rip, crosscut and combination cut, as well as blades designed for plastics, particleboards and laminates. The various blade types are available in a range of diameters and numbers of teeth per blade.

The geometry of carbide teeth is generally more complex than that of steel blades. The effects achieved by setting and swaging in steel teeth are achieved through grinding with carbide teeth. Not only is it possible to have a variety of tooth patterns on the same blade, but the teeth often have both top and side clearance angles to improve cutting action while reducing friction in the kerf. In addition, huge strides have been made in the formulation of carbides. At one time, you had only to be concerned with the grade of carbide suitable to your purpose. The grades ranged from C1, which is the most shock resistant but the least wear resistant, to C4, which is the least shock resistant but has maximum wear resistance. Today you also have to take into consideration micro-grain carbides, which, like finely grained steel, hold an edge better because of the very fine grain structure that can be sharpened to a more perfect edge. More about that later.

TOOTH PATTERNS

Some of the basic tooth patterns for carbide blades are shown in the bottom drawing at right. They include:

Flat top These teeth have chisel-like tips particularly suited to ripping. They give a square-bottomed kerf. Although very effective in ripping solid woods, flat-top teeth tend to be dulled easily by abrasive materials such as MDF and particleboard.

Alternate top bevel (ATB) Alternately beveled, these teeth are effective in shearing fibers and reducing tearout, giving a smooth cross-grain cut even in stringy materials. They are a standard choice for cutoff work.

Combination This is a multi-purpose blade suited for the user who wants a single blade for both ripping and crosscutting. The usual design features five closely grouped teeth with a deep gullet between groupings. The first tooth in the group is a raker tooth followed by four alternate-topped bevel teeth. Although a compromise design, combination teeth give an acceptable finish in crosscutting and are still quite efficient in ripping. This is the blade to have if you can afford only one.

Triple-chip grind (TCG) Specifically designed for dense abrasive materials such as MDF, particleboard and plastic laminates, these blades have a unique cutting action. The triple-beveled chippers knock out a central groove, and the ensuing flat-top raker dresses it out to full width. This not only minimizes the shock on an individual tooth but also substantially reduces blast-out in laminates.

Hollow-ground teeth This is another design that strives to reduce blast-out in laminates. Teeth that are ground hollow on the face encourage material to collapse toward the center of the kerf. Teeth alternately clear the center of the cut then the edges. This design is particularly effective in reducing chipping of double-faced melamines, but it is not a style that can be sharpened by all sharpening services.

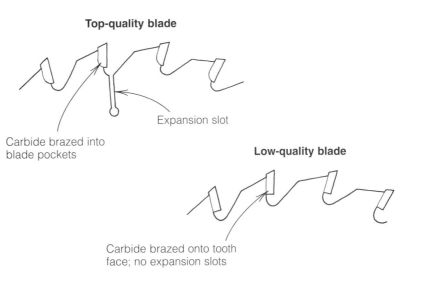

CARBIDE-TIPPED CIRCULAR BLADES

Top-quality blade

Expansion slot

Carbide brazed into blade pockets

Low-quality blade

Carbide brazed onto tooth face; no expansion slots

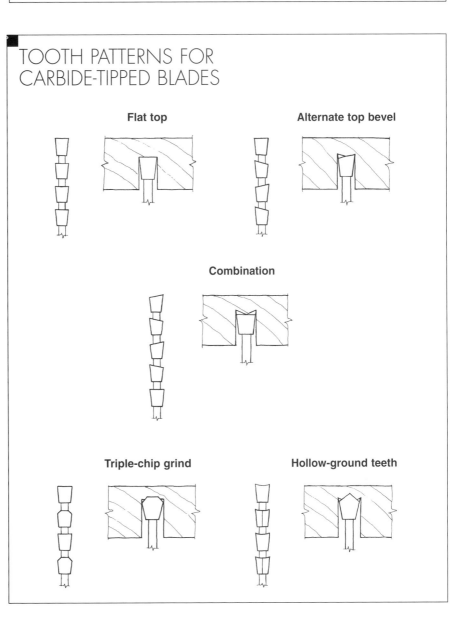

TOOTH PATTERNS FOR CARBIDE-TIPPED BLADES

Flat top

Alternate top bevel

Combination

Triple-chip grind

Hollow-ground teeth

SHARPENING CARBIDE SAW BLADES

In general, you should not attempt to sharpen your own carbide saw blades. The hardness of carbide requires that you do it with a diamond hone. If you use a hone coarser than 600x, you risk fracturing the carbide. Regardless of the care you take, you also risk all the other problems of inadvertently changing clearance or bevel angles, causing uneven tooth height, and so on.

If you absolutely must touch up a blade to finish a project, do the absolute minimum of work and do it carefully. You will change tooth height and affect tooth geometry the least if you work only on the face of the tooth (except for hollow-ground teeth). Use a good quality 600x (or finer) diamond hone.

Even with a 600x hone you will leave a much rougher surface than is achieved with a 600x power wheel. A power wheel tends to leave a fine finish if it is set to remove a given amount and then traverses the tooth. The set amount will be removed in the initial stage of the traverse, and the balance of the wheel will refine the surface, just removing the high spots.

You will protect your investment best if you send or take the blade to a reputable sharpening service. The service should use 600x diamond wheels with flood coolant. Dry grinding can cause cracking from heat buildup. The coefficient of expansion of carbide is much less than steel; the differential can be deadly if heat is not minimized.

Most services use 400x for facing the tooth and 600x for topping. This should be the minimum; 600x for both is better. Some teeth are now sharpened with an 800x wheel, but that fine a grit is uncommon.

Unless a tooth is chipped, in which case it may have to be replaced, sharpening should remove no more than 0.005 in. from the tooth face and 0.010 in. from the top. A good service will remove the minimum amount of carbide, sometimes as little as 0.003 in.

AN OUNCE OF PREVENTION...

Good sharpening technique goes hand in hand with tool care that minimizes dulling in the first place. There are many things you can do to avoid dulling your saw blades.

1. Choose the appropriate blade for the material and for the type of cut being made.

2. Don't run a blade beyond its rated rpm, and use an appropriate feed speed that keeps the blade cutting without bogging down.

3. Try to use a setup that keeps at least three teeth in contact with the stock.

4. Examine blades routinely for sharpness, cracks, runout, warp, imbalance and rust. Don't store blades in direct sunlight that can heat and distort the body. Use a light coat of oil, wax or water-displacement chemical to keep invisible rust from nibbling away at the teeth.

5. Don't touch the teeth unless it is necessary. Many people have acidic perspiration that causes rust almost instantaneously. With carbide teeth, perspiration can etch the teeth.

6. Some blades come from the factory coated with lacquer to prevent rust. Strip off this coating, taking particular care in the area of the arbor hole and support flanges to ensure smooth seating and to reduce the chance of blade flutter. Accumulated gum and pitch can cause binding, kickback, friction and heat. To remove sticky resins, soak your blades in kerosene or use a commercial gum and pitch remover. Don't scrape off accumulations with an edged tool, however, since the scratch marks will attract more residues.

7. Keep the table-saw top aligned with the plane of the blade.

8. Check that support flanges are clean and flat, and that they are at least one-third the diameter of the blade in use.

9. Don't overtighten the arbor nut.

10. Ensure that the rip fence is aligned and that the throat-insert plate is flat and flush with the table top.

11. Don't try to bore out the arbor hole on your circular blade since this can adversely affect tensioning and concentricity.

12. Never let the teeth touch steel. If you lay the blade down, lay it on wood. Be very careful when changing blades.

13. Never let a carbide blade overheat. The cobalt in the carbide can virtually evaporate. At temperatures as low as 300°C (572°F) chemical reaction, particularly when cutting MDF, can cause the cobalt to sublimate.

14. Always use a steady, controlled feed rate for work. Blades usually last longer in production shops with power feeders than at the hands of hobbyists, who often feed work at alarming rates and then puzzle over bad cuts.

Variable feed rates cause two problems. First, a fast feed rate can cause shocks that will fracture the teeth. Second, because a saw blade is just like a gyroscope, reaction is at 90° to applied force. An uneven feed rate causes the blade to waver laterally as it reacts to the force differences.

from the face and 0.005 in. from the top. If there are no chipped teeth, such light removal can often fully restore a blade.

SOME FINER POINTS OF CARBIDE SAWS

Carbide teeth are brazed onto saw blades by various methods, the two most common being either freehand with an oxyacetylene torch, or in a more controlled manner with induction heating coils. The traditional brazing material was silver solder in wire form, which wicked into the joint by capillary action. One problem with both methods is that the metal plate expands much more than the carbide during the brazing process. This can cause microscopic cracking of the carbide even when a high-silver-content solder is used.

Tri-met brazing More recently, some manufacturers have begun using a tri-metal sandwich between the pocket and the tooth. This is a silver-copper-silver sandwich 0.012 in. or 0.015 in. thick that prevents the fracturing by providing some flexibility; it also provides a cushion to absorb shock. The technology originated in the manufacture of shaper bits and larger router bits, where the problems are magnified.

Micro-grain carbides Just as with steel, the finer you can make the grain in tungsten carbide the better the edge you get and the finer the finish you can put on it. The micro-grain carbides are all in the C4 category, which means that they have good wear characteristics but are subject to shock fractures. In some ways the toughness is increased as particle size is reduced, because it provides a greater number of inner-connective bonds. In general, as the cobalt content is reduced in micro-grain carbides, the hardness and wear characteristics are improved. Some have as little as 4% cobalt and in the sub-micron range as little as 3%.

One of the difficulties here is to know just what a micro-grain carbide is. The measure used is 1 micron, but it is used differently in different parts of the industry. Some carbide manufacturers say that it is micro-grain carbide if the majority of particles are less than 1 micron in size. Others say that it can be called micro-grain if 20% of the particles are less than 1 micron, and still others say that all the particles have to be 1 micron or less. In fact, some manufacturers offer coarse, medium and fine micro-grain carbides but tend to be a bit vague about the particle size. If you want to unnerve your blade supplier, you might want to ask the size of the micro-grain carbide in their saw teeth. Most suppliers cannot answer the question. As an aside, these teeth must be sharpened with at least a 600x diamond wheel, otherwise much of the edge effect of the finer structure will be lost.

BANDSAW BLADES

At one time, bandsaw blades were routinely resharpened, but their relative cost has dropped to the point where it is more economical to replace them than send them out for resharpening. In addition, bandsaw blades almost universally have flame-hardened tips, and while it is possible to resharpen several times it is not possible to set the teeth without breakage. Each time the blade is sharpened you lose a bit more set.

If you should want to sharpen your own bandsaw blades, there is really only one practical approach—using an appropriately sized diamond burr in a flex shaft or a small Dremel-type hand grinder.

In general, you want to retain the original tooth geometry of the blade. This is most easily done if you remove the blade from the bandsaw and clamp it in a vise, as you would a handsaw. Selecting a diamond burr of the right diameter, you will find that you can sharpen each tooth quite quickly with very little experience.

CARBIDE AND CHEMICALS

Most woodworkers are familiar with the non-wood constituents of chipboard and particleboard. These materials are notorious for high levels of grit and the occasional piece of metal. Only affluent woodworkers would use their best saw blades on them. But most woodworkers are unaware of other problems lurking in these reconstituted materials, such as the chemical composition of glues and binders.

Medium-density fiberboard (MDF) is a popular woodworking material today. It is equally popular with sharpening services, since blades can be dulled at an alarming rate when working MDF. One of the unanticipated problems in working MDF is that there are occasional resin globules encapsulated in the material. These are particularly hard and can cause a substantial shock to a carbide tooth. Combined with this is the high density of the material, which causes heat buildup through friction, and, finally, the nature of the binders themselves, which can cause chemical interaction with tungsten carbide, even with high-speed steel.

A substantial amount of research has been done in this area of hot corrosion, and three phenomena have been studied in detail—high-temperature oxidation, high-temperature halogenation and high-temperature sulfidation. These chemical effects outstrip the normal wear effect of cutting the material. The extent of these problems is leading the industry into the development of new carbides and has already been instrumental in the introduction of ceramic router bits.

CHAINSAW TEETH

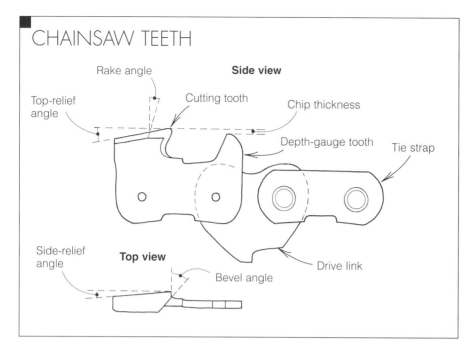

Side view

Rake angle

Top-relief angle

Cutting tooth

Chip thickness

Depth-gauge tooth

Tie strap

Side-relief angle

Top view

Bevel angle

Drive link

FILE ANGLE FOR SHARPENING CUTTERS

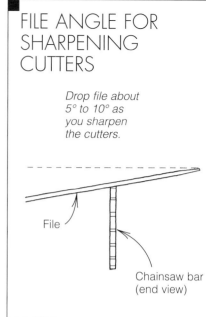

Drop file about 5° to 10° as you sharpen the cutters.

File

Chainsaw bar (end view)

Set up for sharpening a saw chain by clamping the chainsaw bar in a mechanic's vise, with the chain tightened until you can just rotate it with a stick by hand. (Photo by Susan Kahn)

CHAINSAWS

I have always found it curious that people who will quite cheerfully sharpen their own chisels and plane blades will take their saw chains to a commercial sharpening service. In my opinion, it's easier to do a competent job sharpening saw chains than sharpening plane blades.

Your chain specifications (rake angle, bevel angle, gauge-tooth height, pitch, etc.) will all be specified in the operator's manual. The manual will also tell you what diameter round file you should use for sharpening.

There are several hand-held electric chain sharpeners on the market, as well as several filing jigs. All come with instructions for use. Here, I will cover only the basic method using an unjigged file by hand.

SHARPENING A SAW CHAIN

Begin by clamping the center of the bar of the chainsaw in a mechanic's vise, as shown in the photo at left. Tighten the chain until you can just rotate it using a stick of wood on the chain with one hand on each end.

Using the round file recommended in your operator's manual, take as many strokes as necessary to sharpen a cutting tooth, maintaining the original rake (or "hook") angle and bevel angle (typically 30° and 35°, respectively). The file should be held with the handle just slightly dropped (5° to 10°) as you do this (see the drawing at right above). Repeat for two or three more teeth, advance the chain and then repeat the operation until you have sharpened all the teeth that can be sharpened from one side. Reverse the chainsaw in the vise and do the other half of the teeth.

Once every two or three sharpenings, you may also have to file the depth-gauge teeth. The indications that these need attention are reduced rate of cut and fine, not chunky, sawdust. For this job, you'll need to slip a depth-gauge tool over the chain to check the setting. You can either buy a gauge specific to your saw, or make one as

escribed in the sidebar on p. 156,
sing the gauge-height information in
e operator's manual.

Be careful not to overfile gauge
eth or the chain will grab and cut
oughly. It's better to leave them a bit
o high than too low. Also, always
estore the curved profile after shorten-

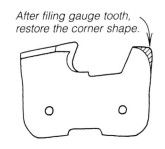

*After filing gauge tooth,
restore the corner shape.*

ng the teeth; otherwise, they will grab
the cut causing chain chatter.

estoring damaged teeth Unless you
ave hit a stone, one or two file strokes
ould be enough to sharpen each
oth. You have to be fairly ham-
anded to change the tooth geometry
gnificantly with one or two strokes.
owever, if you have dulled the chain
y hitting a stone, you may have to take
half-dozen strokes or more to remove
l tooth rounding (see the top drawing
right).

For this many strokes, more care
ill have to be taken to maintain the
riginal tooth geometry. It is fairly easy
maintain the bevel, though if you
annot do so by eye you can make
ourself a bevel guide (see p. 151). The
al trick is to maintain the rake angle.
he natural tendency is to press down
n the file rather than drawing it lateral-
into the tooth; the result of downward
ressure is that you increase the rake
ngle by undercutting the tooth. An
ncrease in rake angle (like a short
auge tooth) causes the chain to grab
nd run rough in the cut.

To prevent this problem, position
ourself almost directly over the chain
nd note how much of the file is
overed by the link tooth and how
uch is exposed before you start filing
see the bottom drawing at right). As
ou file, keep the same amount
xposed and you will not change the
ake angle.

RIPPING CHAIN

The vast majority of chainsaws are
used in crosscut work only. To do a
competent job of ripping, they require
a different chain sharpened quite
differently. The most common need for
ripping with a chainsaw is in chainsaw
lumbermaking. A crosscut chain can be
modified for efficient ripping by
converting it to 0° bevel and 50° rake,
but it is better to buy chain designed
specifically for ripping. Ripping chain is
generally available at specialty chainsaw dealers, who can also provide the
necessary filing specifications.

SOME CHAINSAW DOS AND DON'TS

Because of the relief angle built into the
top of a cutting tooth, each time you
sharpen it you lower the cutting edge.
The secret to keeping teeth all the same
height is to keep them the same length.
Every few touchups on a chain you
should measure the length of the teeth
and, exactly as you would do if you
were jointing a handsaw, file them all to
the length of the shortest tooth. This
will automatically make them all the
same height.

The allowable depth of cut of an
individual tooth can be greater in
softwood than in hardwood, and
greater in green wood than in dry. If
you intend to use your chainsaw for
general-purpose work, you should file
the gauge teeth to accommodate the
hardest, driest material that you will be
cutting. This will slow you down a bit in
green wood or softwood, but you will
have a far safer tool with substantially
reduced risk of kickback.

Throughout this book, I have
generally avoided repeating the phrase
that you shouldn't run with sharp
objects in your hand because it is self-
evident. But a chainsaw is potentially
the most dangerous tool you can use.
You should not even think about
starting up a chainsaw unless you are
wearing safety pants or chaps. You
should also have a hard hat, hearing
protectors and other safety equipment
suitable to the work you are doing.

You add a substantial margin of
safety to the operation of your saw if
the chain is properly sharpened.

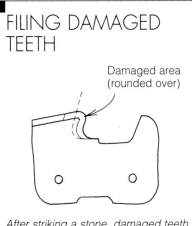

FILING DAMAGED TEETH

Damaged area
(rounded over)

*After striking a stone, damaged teeth
must be filed back to eliminate any
rounding.*

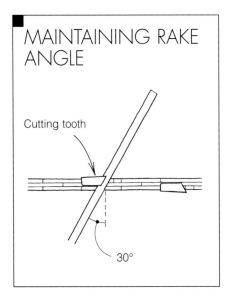

MAINTAINING RAKE ANGLE

Cutting tooth

30°

Learning how to sharpen your own
chain is a bit like learning how to pack
your own parachute—it's your health
that's going to be involved in the use of
this tool, and you should rely on
yourself to protect it.

CHAPTER 15
DRILL BITS

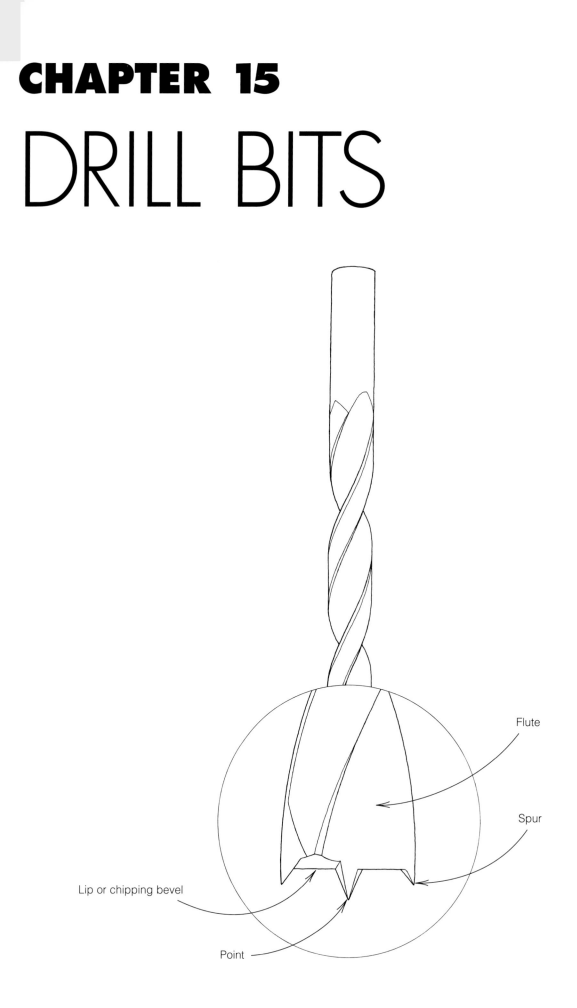

Flute

Spur

Lip or chipping bevel

Point

Of all the cutting tools that wood-workers use, drill bits have more demanded of them and less attention paid to them than any others. We expect them to drill end grain and cross grain equally well and are immediately suspicious of them, not ourselves, when we find that holes we drill are untrue or oversize. But the ultimate insult to drill bits is that we do not bother sharpening them as long as increasing amounts of pressure will still cause them to cut.

We do the most damage to our bits when we underfeed and overspeed. All drill bits, from inexpensive carbon-steel bits to top-of-the-line carbide-tipped bits, will last longer and hold their edge better if they are not overheated. Almost without exception, wood-workers run their bits at excessive rpm for the feed rate that they are using.

If you think about the way you use a brace and a bit, you will realize that you never produce such thick chips when you are using an electric hand drill or a drill press. This is because you are almost invariably underfeeding for a given rpm. You should either increase the feed rate or cut back on the rpm. Otherwise, you stand a good chance of overheating the bit from a lot of unnecessary friction. Anybody who owns Forstner bits will know exactly what I mean. If Forstner bits are not used at low speeds and maximum feeds, the chances of generating enough friction to burn a rim are very high. Yet properly used, Forstner bits cut the cleanest, most accurate holes of any bit in the shop. There is an incentive to act intelligently.

GENERAL SHARPENING CONSIDERATIONS

Unlike chisels, planes, turning tools and many other cutting tools that you buy today, drill bits are usually ready to use when they are new. Also, unlike the other tools just mentioned, it is usually wise to honor the manufacturer's geometry. In other words, you should maintain the same cutting angles, the same clearance angles and the same rake angles that the manufacturer used originally. You will be considered no less of a craftsman for not introducing your own idiosyncrasies to these particular tools.

Honoring the geometry of the bit also means that you should leave the center of the bit where you find it. The two fastest ways to ruin a drill bit are to grind the tip off-center and to tinker with the circumferential surface. Either can change the effective cutting diameter of the bit and render it useless for anything other than drilling approximately sized holes.

One last cautionary note is that you should always do the least amount of sharpening possible. This is one place where more is not better. You will find it sufficiently challenging to maintain bit geometry using a minimalist approach. If you approach the problem determined to regrind, rehone and restore every visible surface, you will be dead in the water before you know it. In many ways, it is fortunate that most woodworkers ignore their drill bits since undue attention brings with it substantial potential for damage.

DRILL-BIT METALLURGY

In no category of tools do we find a broader range of metals than in woodworking bits. Bits range from the simple carbon tool steel of an auger bit through complex alloys, various varieties of high-speed steel, surface treatments like nitriding, inserted tips of various types, to bits that are solid tungsten carbide from shank to tip. Just as this wide range of materials has a wide range of edge-holding abilities, heat tolerances and purchase prices, each requires different sharpening materials and tactics.

In general, the ease of sharpening is inversely proportional to the complexity of metallurgy. You can easily touch up a steel auger bit with an auger-bit file, whereas your entire sharpening arsenal will probably be useless to you when you are facing a badly chipped carbide bit. Just as you should not feel inadequate for neither wanting to nor knowing how to reorganize the geometry of your drill bits, you should recognize that some things are best left to specialized services. Excessive sharpening zeal can cause you as much trouble as do-it-yourself surgery.

TWIST BITS

Everybody owns a set of twist bits. They are used for drilling wood, metal, plastic, plasterboard, virtually anything that needs to be perforated around the house. Twist bits are sharpened differently for different materials. For example, a much more acute point angle is used for wood than for metal. Since this book is all about sharpening woodworking tools and twist bits are far from being the best choice for woodworking, I think that it makes more sense to deal with the general-purpose style, still a very necessary set of bits in any shop.

The vast majority of twist bits are ground in the standard configuration shown to the left in the photo on p. 192—that is, 118° point angle and 30° of rake. These are perfectly fine bits and will give good service. A variation that I prefer for general-purpose use is the split-tip style shown at right in the photo. These bits have the same rake angle with a somewhat more oblique point angle (140°), but the primary difference is that this style has greater chip-carrying capacity because of the parabolic flute design; it also tends to drill a tighter tolerance hole because of the wider edge margin. These bits seem to work equally well in metal; in fact, the split-tip point virtually eliminates skating. A center dimple is usually not needed to start a hole.

STANDARD TWIST-BIT GEOMETRY

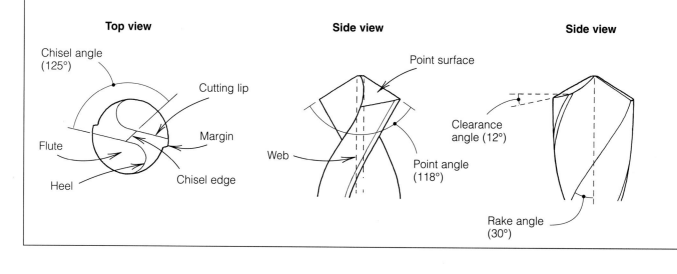

Top view

Chisel angle (125°)

Cutting lip

Flute

Margin

Heel

Chisel edge

Side view

Point surface

Web

Point angle (118°)

Side view

Clearance angle (12°)

Rake angle (30°)

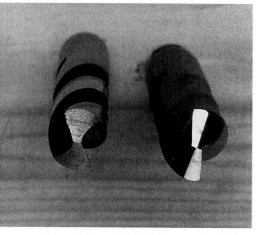

Two styles of twist bits: standard tip (left) and split tip (right). The split-tip bit has less tendency to skate on entry. (Photo by Susan Kahn)

Rather than spending a great deal of time describing shopmade jigs and devices that give indifferent results with twist bits, or telling you how to go about the freehand grinding of twist bits (which is a direct road to hell!), I would make two strong recommendations. First, buy only American-made high-speed-steel twist bits. They are still the best of any made in the world and will stay sharp for an incredible length of time if not abused. Second, buy a twist-drill sharpening jig and follow the instructions. For bits up to ⅜ in., I prefer the curious little hop-along model made by Eclipse in England, but the bench-mount models for use with a grinding wheel are also serviceable (see the top photo on the facing page). There are also a number of electric-drill-powered models that do a reasonable job.

If you absolutely must do freehand sharpening of a twist bit, deal only with the flute side of the bevel using small abrasive rods or a conical bit in a powered hand unit (see the photo at bottom left on the facing page). You will probably change the rake angle a bit, but this will cause fewer problems than you will undoubtedly create by freehanding your way around the bevel.

TAPER-POINT TWIST BITS

Taper-point twist bits are a very specialized version of twist bits adapted for drilling tapered holes for wood-working screws. They are normally used in combination with countersink/counterbore units to drill holes for screws so that the head will be flush with the surface of the wood or, in the case of counterboring, below the surface of the wood so that the hole can be plugged.

These bits rarely need sharpening. They are high-speed steel (if you have bought American ones) and will drill thousands of holes before showing any discernible wear. Only boatbuilders are likely to use taper-point twist bits enough to need to sharpen them (and even then the bits are more likely to break than become dull).

If you should find that you need to sharpen a taper-point twist bit, whether it be the tip or the edge of the margin, I recommend that you use a thin, round-edge slipstone in the flute (see the photo at bottom right on the facing page). This will properly hone the margins and restore the tip to service-able condition. You might be able to use a sharpening jig for the tip, but the taper usually eliminates this alternative.

Sharpening jigs for twist bits include a drill-powered sharpener (left), a 'hop-along' model that supports the bit as it is rolled over a sheet of sandpaper (middle) and a bench-mounted guide for use with a grinding wheel (right). (Photo by Susan Kahn)

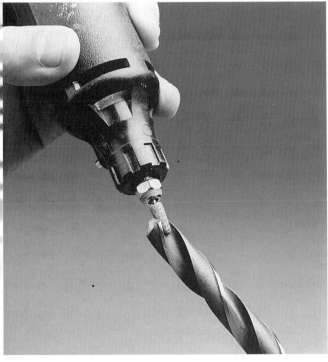

To sharpen a twist bit freehand, use a conical power stone and work only on the flute side of the bevel.

Taper-point twist bits can be honed with a thin, round-edge slipstone.

SPADE BITS

These inexpensive flat bits are ideal for rough work where you need approximately sized holes. Spade bits do not enter wood very cleanly, and the holes that they drill are often slightly oval. They have a strong tendency to wander in end grain. Most are designed with a zero rake angle, although some manufacturers have incorporated a groove in the face of the bit immediately above the bevel that does give the bit a positive rake angle. Most flat bits have a clearance angle of about 10°. On some bits, the cutting lips are at 90° to the axis of the tool; on others, they are canted slightly to ensure scoring of the circumference of the hole before chipping action starts.

Spade bits can be sharpened freehand with an auger-bit file, or you can make a simple jig for sharpening them, as shown below. The problem with freehand sharpening is that you run the risk of getting the cutting lips at slightly different heights, causing one to do more work than the other. This will tend to make the holes even more oval than they might ordinarily be.

The point of the spade bit is normally sharpened by lapping the flats on either side (see the top photo below). Sharpening it this way you do not run the risk of sharpening the point off-center. On bits with a V-groove running back from the point, the V-groove can be touched up on the inside with either a square or triangular stone file (see the bottom photo below).

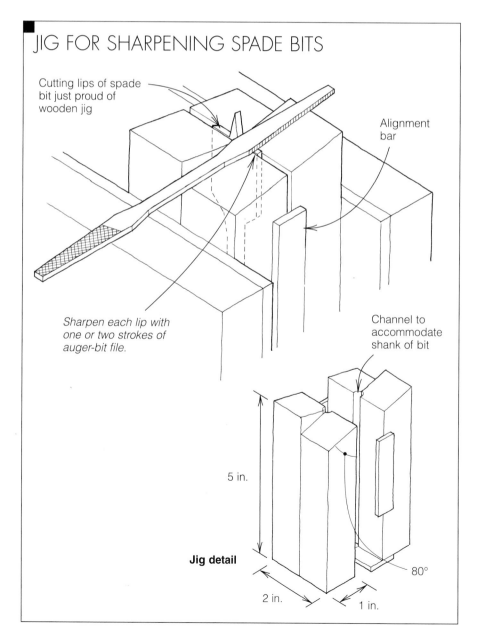

JIG FOR SHARPENING SPADE BITS

Cutting lips of spade bit just proud of wooden jig

Alignment bar

Sharpen each lip with one or two strokes of auger-bit file.

Channel to accommodate shank of bit

5 in.

Jig detail

2 in.

1 in.

80°

Sharpen the point of a spade bit by lapping the flats on either side.

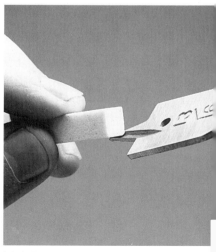

Touch up the inside of a V-groove on a spade bit with a stone file.

AUGER BITS

Auger bits used to come in a bewildering array of styles, with great variety in type of shank, tooth pattern, lips, spurs and lead screws. The one common feature was the auger flutes to carry away chips.

As with all other bits, the original geometry of the bit must be respected in the sharpening process. In fact, it was to maintain this geometry that the auger-bit file was developed, so that some surfaces could be abraded while adjoining ones could be preserved.

LEAD SCREW

Unless the bit has been abused, the lead screw will never require work. If it has been damaged, the grooves can be chased using a feather-edge file or a suitable Swiss pattern file (see the bottom photo below). This should be done lightly. It is relatively easy to do with a bit intended for use in softwood, which has a coarse lead screw, but is a much trickier process on an auger bit intended for hardwood, which has a fine lead screw. In either case, though, the screw should be kept in good condition, since it is the screw that pulls the bit into the wood.

If a screw is beyond repair, or if you want to convert an auger bit to machine use, the screw point can be converted to a brad point. In making the conversion, be sure that the tip of the brad point extends past the spur(s) of the auger bit if it has any. When used in a drill press or driven by a power hand drill, auger bits should be used at very low rpm.

The auger bit at far left, a single-twist 'barefoot' (or bullnose) style, is prized for end-grain boring since it has no tendency to grain-follow. The center bit is for rough work; the sharp wing partially compensates for the lack of a spur. The double-twist auger at right would cut the smoothest hole and has the greatest chip capacity.

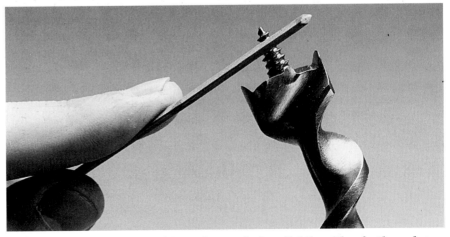

The lead screw on an auger bit can be touched up lightly with a feather-edge file.

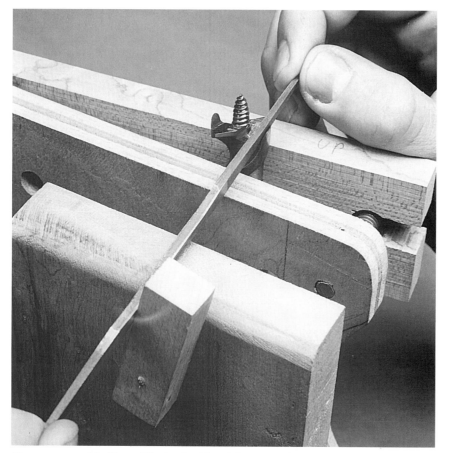

Use an auger-bit file to file the inside of the spurs (making sure the safe edge of the file is against the lip).

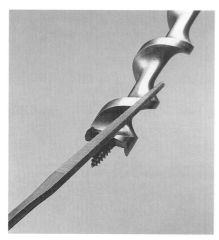

File the cutting lip of an auger bit with an upward stroke through the throat of the bit.

Use a slipstone to sharpen the inside lip of a shell auger.

SPURS

Only file the inside of the spurs, not the periphery. Using an auger-bit file, the safe edge of the file can be against the lip with the cut edge against the spur (as shown in the photo at left). If stoning is sufficient, a thin piece of plastic or similar material will protect the lip while the spur is being stoned. Never take off any more than is absolutely necessary, since an auger bit without spurs is limited in use.

CUTTING LIPS

The cutting lip of the auger bit is filed with an upward stroke through the throat of the bit at the original bevel angle (see the photo at bottom left). Be careful to maintain the chipping bevels at the same height so that they do the same amount of work. As with the outlining spurs, the cutting lips can be stoned as long as the lips are protected.

SHELL AUGER

I don't know how this tool came to be named a shell auger since it is not an auger at all. It is a shell bit and is normally sharpened on the inside of the lip in large sizes, although it can also be sharpened on the outside since the geometry is fairly straightforward to maintain.

BRAD-POINT BITS

Also referred to as brad-point spur bits or brad-point drills, these bits have generally replaced auger bits in wood-working. (This went hand-in-hand with power hand drills replacing braces.)

As shown in the top photo on the facing page, there are three basic types of brad point. The bits at far left and far right are examples of the single-lip, single-flute style, a very direct imitation of classic auger-bit design. This style is still available but uncommon.

The two most common styles are the utility brad point and the double-lipped brad point (usually just called "lipped brad point"). The utility brad point is an inexpensive model, whose entire tip geometry (lips, spurs, brad) is created by two passes of a 90° milling cutter through the tip at an angle of 20° to the

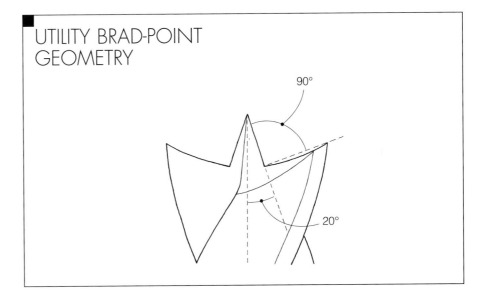

Brad-point bits developed hand in hand with portable drills. Initially, they mimicked auger bits (far left and far right), but now they are almost all made in one of the two center styles (lipped brad point, center left, and utility brad point, center right).

axis of the bit. Essentially the outer limits of the chipping bevels become the outlining spurs.

Lipped brad points have a more complex tip grind. As shown in the photo above (second bit from left), an actual outlining spur is ground on the tip, which gives a somewhat slimmer brad point. In use, the lipped brad point almost invariably enters the wood more cleanly than the utility model, but a slight hesitation on entry will give a clean hole with either one. A more basic problem with economy models is that they are usually made offshore; just as the best twist bits are made in the United States, lipped brad points are ground from twist bits and the best lipped brad points are still made in the United States. This is not rampant nationalism (I'm Canadian, after all), just the simple truth. (There are some bits, including Forstner-style bits and sawtooth bits, where the best bits, in my view, are not made in the United States. Given the rapid transfer of technology in all fields, it will be only a very short time until good brad points start flowing in as well.)

There is a variation of the double-lipped brad point that has lips shaped a bit differently from the model just mentioned. This type of lip is not highest at the leading edge but has a parabolic tip. Bits of this type give very clean entry but are prone to overheating, since there is much more friction on this type of lip as it presses its way into the wood. Not much different in style, there are now also

UTILITY BRAD-POINT GEOMETRY

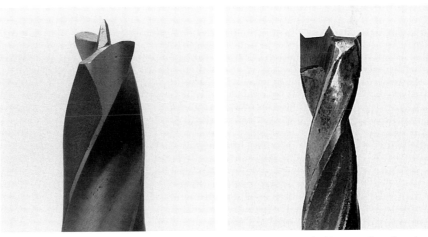

Variations of standard brad-point bits include the parabolic-spur brad point (left) and the carbide-tipped brad point (right). (Photos by Susan Kahn)

carbide-tipped brad points on the market. These tend to have somewhat finer lips and are very durable.

SHARPENING BRAD-POINT BITS

The easiest of all brad points to sharpen is the utility brad point, which can be filed with an auger-bit file along the chipping bevels, or honed in the flute as shown in the photo at left. These are usually carbon-steel bits, and by the time they have become dull they have usually been overheated once or twice so they are quite easy to file. They can be filed a number of times before the center brad becomes both too wide and too long for the bit to function properly. When the bit gets to this condition, rather than tinker with the center brad you should treat yourself to a new bit.

But if you must tinker, first file a small flat on the point and then sharpen it as you would the tooth of a saw, filing from one side until half of the flat is removed and then filing from the other just until the rest is removed. This will leave a narrow chisel tip that can be used as is, or you can file half of the chisel away from one side and half from the other to recreate a point.

Use a small, round stone in the flute to hone a utility brad-point bit.

Sharpening is not quite as straight-forward for lipped brad points as it is for the utility brads. It is difficult to come up with sharpening gear that is both fine enough and small enough to hone the flats of the chipping bevels and the flutes. I prefer to use a conical power stone or abrasive rods if the bit is very dull, but otherwise use a wooden dowel, slightly undersized to the flute, well charged with chromium-oxide honing compound. The bit can be drawn along such a dowel held in a vise with a trailing stroke; the dowel will polish the inside of the flute and restore the lip to razor-sharp condition.

The basic geometry of the bit is maintained almost in total. Over time, you will decrease the rake angle slightly, but only by a negligible amount. Don't worry if in either grinding or honing the inside of the flute you happen to put a mark in the trailing edge of the margin farther up the bit. This will not affect the action of the bit one iota. If you have created any roughness, smooth it but otherwise don't be concerned about it. As always, it is better not to tinker with the brad point itself unless you absolutely have to.

Lastly, in sharpening the carbide-tipped brad points (should you ever have to) it is best to use a very fine diamond abrasive. The 9-micron size of 3M abrasive seems to do a good job.

FORSTNER BITS

Forstner bits are a joy to use, but they carry with them the seeds of their own destruction. Since the rim on a well-ground Forstner is about 0.005 in. higher than the chipping bevels, it scores the circumference of the hole before the chipping bevels begin to remove wood. Therein lies the problem. It is easy to generate a lot of rim heat as these bits are used. Even when they are used properly, it is very difficult to avoid overheating in hard, resinous woods. It is mandatory that Forstner bits be used judiciously and be kept free of resin. They should be cleaned frequently and have a dry lubricant applied to them.

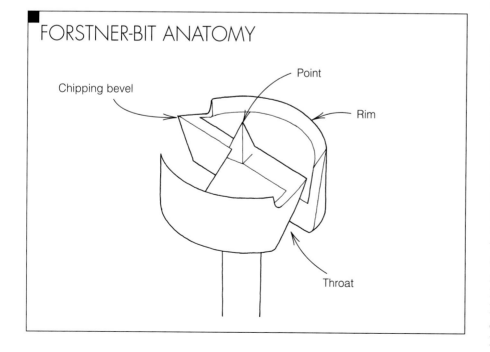

FORSTNER-BIT ANATOMY

Chipping bevel

Point

Rim

Throat

SHARPENING FORSTNER BITS

Forstner bits are not particularly difficult to sharpen. The inside of the rim can be sharpened with a small, round honing stone, and the chipping bevels can be dressed with a fine file or stone directly through the throat. The periphery of the bit should never be touched, and the back of the chipping bevels should be touched only when they need to be dressed down below the rim. When working on chipping bevels, it is easiest to do a major portion of the relief with a small power hone brought in from the end (see the drawing below), and then complete the job with a fine needle file or diamond file. For repairing major damage, see the discussion under sawtooth machine bits.

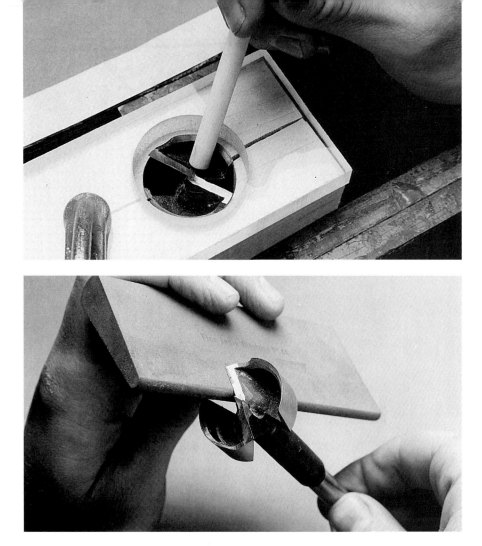

Use a round honing stone, with the aid of a jig that keeps the stone at the correct angle, to sharpen the inside rim of a Forstner bit (top). A slipstone can be used to touch up the chipping bevels (above).

SHARPENING FORSTNER-BIT BEVELS

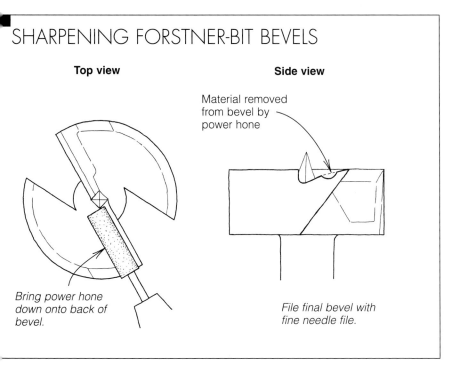

Top view

Bring power hone down onto back of bevel.

Side view

Material removed from bevel by power hone

File final bevel with fine needle file.

SAWTOOTH MACHINE BITS

The classic sawtooth bit (also called a multi-spur bit) has one or two chipping bevels and a ring of outlining spurs patterned after rip-saw teeth—usually flat-topped teeth at zero rake angle. Because they cut with a sawing rather than slicing action, sawtooth bits tend to heat less than Forstner bits. At the same time, they do not enter as cleanly because the unbeveled teeth cause some cross-grain splintering.

Partly to resolve the entry problem and partly for economy of manufacturing, manufacturers began producing multi-spur bits by modifying standard Forstner patterns. There are at least three different patterns of this new style of bit (see the drawing at left), and all have slicing tips on the spurs rather than narrow chipping bevels like the classic sawtooth. As a result, they require some of the sharpening techniques of Forstner bits with adjustments according to tooth variation.

SHARPENING SAWTOOTH BITS

In general, I would recommend that you sharpen all styles the same as a classic sawtooth. Over time, this means that the spurs will develop narrow chipping bevels like the classic sawtooth. You can restore the original slicing tip if you wish, but it is an incredibly fiddly business and I recommend that you use good drilling technique (i.e., a slight hesitation on entry) to compensate for the changed geometry.

The main chipping bevel(s) on a sawtooth can be sharpened the same as on a Forstner bit. For sharpening the teeth, a triangular file is best (see the photo at left below); a feather-edge file can be used where a triangular file will not fit. It is usually sufficient to address the leading face of the tooth only. The file should be held level, with one edge aimed directly at the center brad.

If major work has to be done on a sawtooth bit, the entire face of the bit has to be jointed first. The photo at right below shows a sawtooth mounted in a drill press being jointed on a sharpening stone sitting on the drill-press table. The center brad must be

SAWTOOTH BITS

Classic sawtooth pattern

Modified Forstner patterns

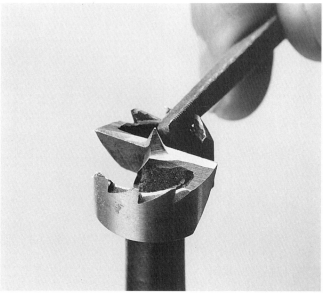

Sharpen the teeth of a sawtooth bit with a triangular file.

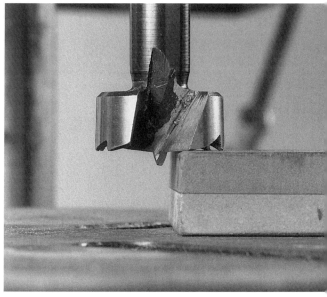

With the sawtooth bit mounted in a drill press, joint the face of a the bit on a bench stone. (Photo by Susan Kahn)

kept clear of the stone and only the balance of the bit jointed just until the shortest tooth is touched. The top left photo at right shows the newly jointed bit with fairly substantial flats on some teeth but lesser flats on others; the shortest tooth has just been touched by the stone. The stone has also touched the chipping bevel, partly eliminating the relief angle.

To restore the bit, first the rim teeth have to be front filed until flats on the top just disappear. Since the center brad has been damaged on the bit shown in the photos, it needs some attention. Fortunately, it can be filed flat across and still function. It will not be reduced in height by very much, and, rather than risk destroying the centricity of the brad by filing the edges, it is simplest to create some sharp edges by filing it straight across the top. The brad will still penetrate quite well, and it will not have lost its centricity.

Finally, the relief angles have to be restored to the chipping bevels, and the chipping bevels have to be brought to a level 0.005 in. below the teeth. Rather than try to get the entire chipping bevel 0.005 in. below the teeth, it is best to file the chipping bevels at a slight angle, upward toward the center. It will not matter if the center of the chipping bevels are at the same height as the teeth as long as they slope off to a point approximately 0.005 in. below the teeth at the perimeter.

A handy device for gauging your progress in all of this is a small piece of hardwood with a good flat surface that has a hole drilled in it to accommodate the center brad. File the chipping bevels at about a 10° angle until you can just slide a piece of good-bond typing paper under the end of the chipping bevel when the teeth are flush against the face of the hardwood jig (see the photo at top right). If you are going to err on one side, be conservative.

WOOD BITS

These bits do not have a distinctive name on the market. Called different things in different countries, wood bits originated as installation bits for

A sawtooth bit that has been jointed to make all teeth the same height.

The chipping bevels of a sawtooth bit should be filed slightly lower than the perimeter teeth. Gauge the height by setting the bit on a piece of hardwood and sliding a piece of typing paper under the bevel.

Although this wood bit does not have the versatility of a Forstner bit, it is much more practical for production work. (Photos by Susan Kahn)

European hardware and are now available in a full range of sizes. They are also available in a full range of materials from high-carbon steel through high-speed steel to bits with carbide inserts. As with all bits of this type, the periphery is not touched. The outlining spurs are honed on the inside flats with an abrasive suitable to their metallurgy, and the chipping bevels are honed through the throat the same as one would do with a Forstner bit or a sawtooth bit.

HOLE CUTTERS

Sawtooth hole cutters usually have an adjustable twist bit that acts as a pilot for the ring of rip-sharpened sawteeth. The rim teeth are sharpened just as you would sharpen a rip saw. They are usually sufficiently fine teeth that a double extra-slim saw file can be used. For harder, high-speed-steel versions, either a triangular honing file or a triangular diamond file would be used. Do not try to set the teeth in these saws.

EXPANSION BITS AND ADJUSTABLE HOLE CUTTERS

There are a host of expansion bits on the market. In every case, they are some variation of an auger bit, a wood bit, a sawtooth bit or a Forstner bit. You can check under each of these to see how to sharpen the various components. For adjustable hole cutters, it is usually just a case of filing the cutter bevel and lapping the face of the cutter.

Sharpen the teeth of a sawtooth hole cutter with a triangular file, just as you would sharpen a ripsaw.

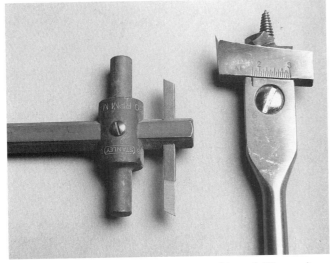

The adjustable hole cutter at left (used in a drill press) and the expandable auger bit at right are typical of bits that adjust to cut a range of hole diameters.

Lapping the face of a cutter for an adjustable hole cutter.

PLUG CUTTERS

Plug cutters require quite a different sharpening philosophy from virtually all other bits, because the concern with these cutters is not the periphery of the bit but the central core. Since plug cutters are used for cutting plugs of a predetermined size, it is not the outside diameter of the hole they make that is of concern but the inside diameter of the hole, where the plug is formed. There are two basic types of plug cutters: fluted cutters and barrel-type cutters.

FLUTED PLUG CUTTERS

There are three subdivisions of fluted plug cutters: the two-flute cutter, the four-flute cutter and the four-flute Snug-Plug cutter. The first two make cylindrical plugs, the third makes a plug that is one-quarter cylindrical and three-quarters tapered, like a cork. All are sharpened the same way. The tips of the teeth can either be filed or stoned; be sure to maintain the relief angle as you do it. You can increase the relief angle without materially affecting the function, but decreasing it even slightly could cause bevel rubbing.

To form the best point on the individual teeth, it is also a good idea to hone the flat leading edge of the tooth (as shown in the photo at right). With the tapered plug cutters this is mandatory, because the teeth cut the major diameter of the plug and the minor diameter is formed by the scraping action of the upper part of the teeth. This action creates the smoothest plug of this type but does require that the leading edge of the tooth be maintained; there must be a crisp intersection with the inside of the tooth for good scraping action.

Fortunately, there is not much danger that you will be tempted to tinker with the inside of the plug cutter since it is awkward to get in there. There are times, however, when it may be necessary to do some deburring on the inside, particularly if the plug cutter has been dropped. If any of the teeth tips are bent over, they are invariably bent toward the center of the plug cutter and, if they are not dressed back

The two basic types of plug cutters are fluted cutters and barrel-type cutters. Shown from left to right are a two-flute cutter, a four-flute Snug-Plug cutter and a barrel-type plug cutter. (Photo by Susan Kahn)

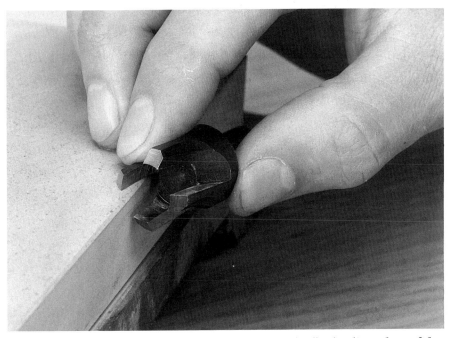

With the cutter pinched up against the stone, hone the flat leading edges of the teeth of a tapered plug cutter. (Photo by Susan Kahn)

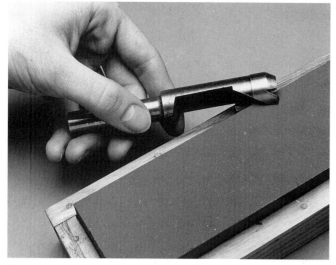

To sharpen the chipping bevel of a barrel-type plug cutter, hone the face on a stone.

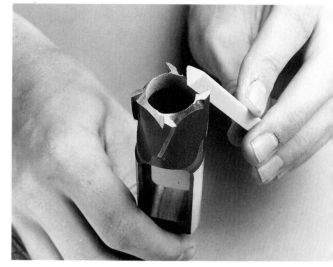

On barrel-type cutters that have four chipping bevels, use a triangular stone to hone the bevels.

A tenon cutter. (Photo courtesy W.L. Fuller, Inc.)

to the original interior diameter, the cutter will always cut undersized plugs. Fortunately, it is quite easy to dress them back using a round honing stone and a bit of care.

BARREL-TYPE PLUG CUTTERS

There are several makers of barrel-type plug cutters, but the cutters have common geometry. These are almost like Forstner bits turned inside out. They have a raised lip that scores the outside perimeter of the plug and a chipping bevel that removes wood from outside the scored circle.

Barrel cutters are not bits that you want to damage because they are not much fun to sharpen. Sharpening the chipping bevel is very straightforward since you need only hone the face (as shown in the photo at top left). There is no easy way to hone the rim of the cutter. You cannot touch the interior since that would change the diameter, so you are limited to honing the outside bevel of the rim with a small hand-held stone or a bench stone. Fortunately, this very seldom has to be done. Some barrel-type plug cutters have four chippers; these have to be honed with a triangular stone, as shown in the photo at top right.

TENON CUTTER

A tenon cutter is just a specialized type of plug cutter. The basic difference is that the tips of the teeth are shaped so that they form a clean shoulder on the tenon. Otherwise, it is sharpened exactly the same as a plug cutter—the leading edges of the teeth are lapped, and the tops of the teeth are honed, maintaining the original relief angle.

A drill-press mortising attachment.

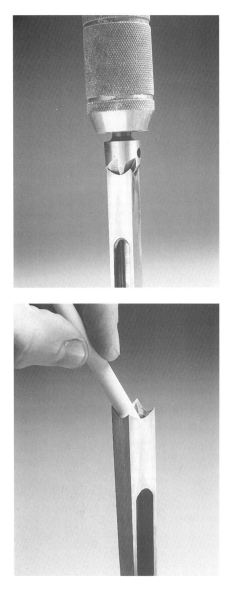

The hollow chisel of a drill-press mortising attachment is sharpened with a countersink-like device (top) and then honed with a round stone (above).

DRILL-PRESS MORTISING ATTACHMENT

The drill-press mortising attachment is a combination of a hollow square-mortise chisel and an auger bit. The auger bit is sharpened in the same manner as any auger bit, but the hollow square mortise chisel presents a shape problem. To overcome this problem, the chisel manufacturers have designed a special countersink-like sharpening device with either solid or inter-changeable pilots to fit the inside diameter of the various hollow chisels. The cutting lips of this bit dress the inside bevels of the mortise chisel. To complete the sharpening of the chisel, you should then hone the interior.

If you find that the chisel requires excessive pressure to penetrate, you can dress each of the inside corners with a very fine cut round or oval file. With the chisel clamped in a vise you should stroke toward the inside and remove only enough to reduce the wedging action of the inside corners. To remove any remaining burrs, it may be necessary to lap the four outside faces of the hollow chisel. This is readily done on a bench stone.

CHAPTER 16
PERIPHERAL MILLING CUTTERS

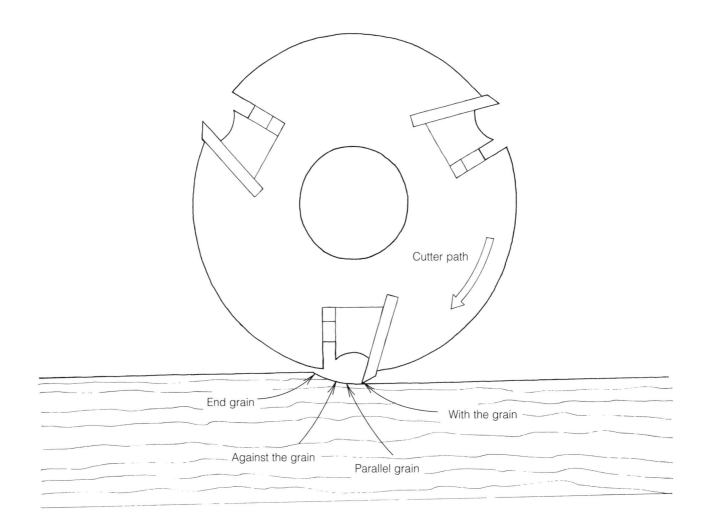

Cutter path

End grain

With the grain

Against the grain

Parallel grain

Peripheral milling is the phrase used to describe the cutting action of knives attached to a rotary cutterhead. This could be at low speed (e.g., a cutterhead used in a drill press) but usually refers to the high-speed, high-torque machines such as routers, jointers and shapers. With all of these machines, the cutting action is a series of overlapping arcs taking evenly spaced bites out of the wood.

Because these machines work at very high speed and the cutting edges have to deal with all grain configurations (see the drawing on the facing page) as well as withstand substantial shock, all edges are formed to cut at very low rake angles and have relatively high included angles.

It is beyond the scope of this book to deal with all of the considerations that go into deciding the appropriate rake and relief angle for these cutters, since they vary by cutterhead diameter among many other things. Thus, it is assumed here that all edges will be resharpened honoring the original blade geometry.

JOINTER AND PLANER KNIVES

Most woodworkers have the nagging feeling that they should be sharpening their own jointer and planer knives rather than buying extra sets and having their knives sharpened commercially. However, unless you are doing a huge amount of milling or are living in a remote area, sharpening your own knives really does not make sense. The time consumed is usually out of all proportion to the money saved, and the end result is usually of lower quality than that you could expect from even a run-of-the-mill sharpening service. This is truly one area where equipment overwhelms technique by a substantial margin. If you do not have an excellent system for holding a blade straight and rigid, you will be in trouble from the opening gun.

KEEPING KNIVES SHARP

There are a couple of ways to minimize the amount of sharpening you have to do with jointer and planer knives. First, you can keep your lumber clean so that it does not have grit on the surface. Second, if you have to deal with dirty lumber, make all the roughing cuts with one set of blades and then either resharpen or change to a new set of blades for final dimensioning. Otherwise, you will often find that one set of blades will last for only half the job because of the very rapid deterioration from grit on the lumber. Although the second set of blades may complete the job for you, you will find that you have two sets of dull blades when you are finished. If you make all of the roughing cuts with one set of blades, they will certainly be dull, but the replacement set should still be perfectly usable after the rest of the dimensioning passes.

It is worth stressing that the cause of blade dulling in a small shop almost invariably is not the abrasive effect of the wood itself on the blades; it is the damage caused by the dirt on the surface of the wood.

While I am sure that none of you do it, absolutely one of the most abrasive things you can put through your equipment is lumber with old paint on it. It does not matter how clean it looks or how free of nails the lumber is, paint will dull your knives in minutes. Many paints have metallic oxides in them that are very abrasive. (As mentioned on p. 96, the artist's color chromium-oxide green makes a good honing medium.)

But all of this is begging the question. There are some of you out there determined to sharpen your own knives regardless of the economics. Fortunately, there is one thing that most people can do that will probably save both time and money: touch up the blades while they are still in the machine.

SHARPENING KNIVES "IN SITU"

Blades that are not removed from a machine do not have to be put back. This is an obvious but important fact. With the exception of the Tersa quick-change cutterhead, systems for fixing and adjusting blades in jointers and planers have changed little in the last fifty years. For most machines, changing a blade is an aggravating process and one to be avoided if possible. Thus, any time you can bring blades back to usable condition without removing them from the machine you should do so.

One system that can be used is shown in the top photo on p. 208. This system operates on the same principle as the manual honing system, except that a trim router and a cup wheel with the appropriate rpm rating are used. This is not a system for the faint-of-heart, and I do not recommend it. It is possible to grind jointer knives well with this system, but it requires very close control of the depth of cut and it is easy to burn a blade through minor inadvertence.

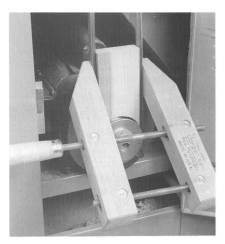

This sharpening system for jointer knives uses a trim router and a cup wheel.

On jointers with feed belts, lock the cutterhead in position by clamping the belt.

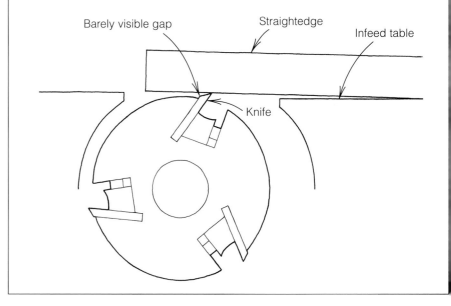

SETUP FOR BLADE HONING

Barely visible gap

Straightedge

Infeed table

Knife

Some large thickness planers are designed with built-in tracks to accommodate a cross-feed electric grinding head to grind the knife bevels. If you have such a planer, read no further. If not, however, you can mimic this activity in a low-tech way by taking advantage of high-tech abrasives to achieve a similar result.

First, unplug your machine. Then adjust the infeed table until you can lay a straightedge on it that will also rest on the knife bevel, which should be just shy of parallel to the infeed table and slightly above it (see the drawing above). Parallel to the infeed table would be fine, but this is not easy to judge by eye so I recommend erring on the side of increasing the bevel angle slightly. Since this reduces the relief angle, you have to be careful. But this is a touch-up process, and the original relief can be fully restored the next time the blades are sharpened commercially.

With the blade bevel as close as possible to parallel to the infeed table, lock the cutterhead in position. Depending on the make of your machine, this could be done by clamping the feed belt as shown in the bottom photo at left.

Now comes the fiddly part. Since you are going to hone the blade with a standard bench stone (and you do not want to abrade the infeed table), you need to wrap tape around the stone in two places. The infeed table should be lower than the knife edge by the thickness of the tape you are going to use plus a couple of thousands of an inch.

This is really not that complex. Put the tape on the stone and rest the stone on the knife so that the stone is supported by the knife and the tape at the other end of the stone. Now slowly raise the infeed table until the other strip of tape just touches the table (see the drawing on the facing page). Before you start honing, you should make a wedge gauge (see the sidebar on p. 210) and mark it so that you can set the other knives in exactly the same position when the time comes. The distance to measure is the distance between the infeed table and the knife edge. When the head is rotated to the next knife, you want to maintain this distance exactly.

In the honing process, you do not want the honing stone going directly across the knife; otherwise, you risk either loading the stone in that one spot or wearing a groove in it. To avoid this,

HONING A BLADE

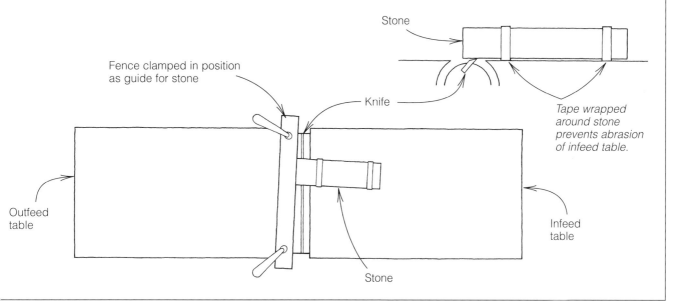

Fence clamped in position
as guide for stone

Knife

Stone

Tape wrapped
around stone
prevents abrasion
of infeed table.

Outfeed
table

Infeed
table

Stone

lamp a fence askew the infeed table an
ppropriate distance away from the
nife, as shown in the drawing above.
hen hone the knife. If, when you have
nished honing, the knife is not yet
harp, remove one layer of tape from
ach band on the stone and continue
oning. If that does not do the job,
ne knives did not need a touchup in
ne first place—they needed to be re-
round. In any event, you will quickly
earn how many layers of tape to put
n. Tape is amazingly consistent in
nickness, which makes this a very
ccurate method. You do have to
emember to finish each blade with
ne same number of layers of tape on
ne stone. This keeps all blades the
ame height.

If you have honed with a fairly
oarse stone (600x or coarser), you
hould refine the edge with a finer grit
efore rotating the cutterhead to the
ext blade. To do this, put tape only on
ne end of the finishing stone away
rom the guide fence; make sure that
ne tape is in the same position on the
nishing stone (relative to the fence)
hat it was on the coarse stone. If you
se one less layer of tape, you will
ave made a tiny angular change at the

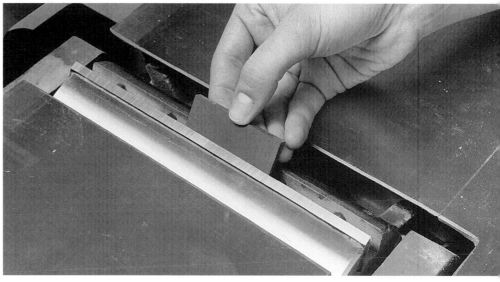

Use a small stone to deburr the face of the knife after honing.

blade. With the finishing stone (1200x
to 6000x) resting on the tape at on end
and the blade at the other, take a half-
dozen passes over the blade and you
will have honed a small micro-bevel.

After you have honed all the blades,
it is a simple matter to remove any burr
from the face of the blade with a small
stone if necessary. Just slide the stone
along the blade, ensuring that it is
perfectly flush with the face (see the
photo above).

Commercial honing devices can be used to hone the bevel and deburr the knife edge. (Photo by Susan Kahn)

ACCURACY OF A WEDGE GAUGE

There are dozens of situations in the shop where you want to measure the size of a gap and it is either impossible to use a dial caliper or you do not have one. You can make incredibly accurate gauges from hardwood or scrap aluminum by a very simple process.

Cut a gently tapered piece of material, mark it off with thicknesses and then put graduation marks between them. If, for example, you use a wedge that has a rise of 1 unit for every 25 units of length, you have effectively enlarged your measurement scale by a factor of 25. It is the principle of the dial caliper in linear form. By magnifying the scale, you can take readings to an accuracy that would be impossible to take in any other way. You may need to borrow a micrometer or caliper to establish the major thickness accurately, but from there you can interpolate the rest. The system is just as effective with a V-gauge as it is with a wedge gauge.

Using the example of the wedge between the cutterhead and the infeed table, you do not care what the distance is as long as you can replicate it accurately. A wedge gauge best lets you do that because it is more accurate than any other means you can devise.

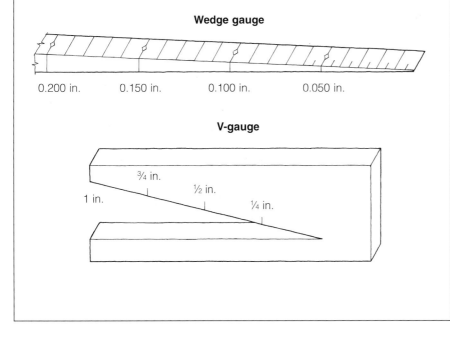

Wedge gauge

0.200 in.   0.150 in.   0.100 in.   0.050 in.

V-gauge

¾ in.
½ in.
1 in.
¼ in.

There are small honing devices on the market that can be used to hone the bevel and to deburr the knife edge (see the photo above). Most of these have pitifully coarse abrasives in them; they do not create a very fine edge and tend to weaken the knife edge because of the grooves that they score in the bevel. I suspect that these hones would work much better with a tiny strip of the 3M diamond micro-finishing abrasive (9-micron size) stuck to a block of aluminum in place of the honing stone. The diamond would cut quickly but still leave a very fine finish. This could be followed up with an even finer micro-finishing abrasive on another face of the block.

SHARPENING KNIVES REMOVED FROM THE MACHINE

Once you have removed the knives from the machine, you have several choices. My first choice is to send the knives out to a good professional sharpening service. Unless you have a high production shop where the knives of several machines have to be sharpened, it is hard to justify the investment in a system that will do a good job with jointer or planer knives. Whatever system you use, you want to ensure that all knives in a set are eated the same, so that their dimensions are the same and they weigh the same amount. The latter point is often ignored and can lead to an unbalanced cutterhead. Another reason to keep the dimensions the same is to provide some automation to the sharpening process.

A good shop grinder for jointer knives could be of the style shown in the photo at right, or it could be one of the various wet-wheel horizontal grinders on the market that have special jointer-knife honing jigs. The advantage of the latter unit is that other tools can be ground and honed on it as well.

There are various designs of jointer-blade sharpeners that you can make, but they all require a substantial investment of time and effort to get second-class results. If you cannot justify the cost of a good manufactured system, your best bet is to develop good technique for honing blades but leave the regrinding to the specialists.

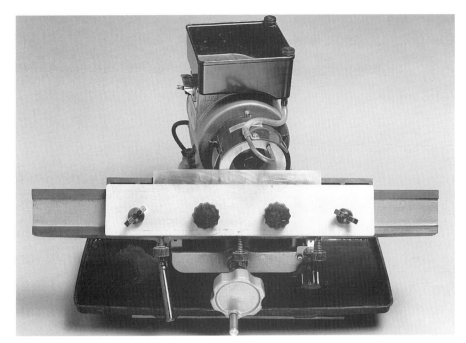

A typical shop grinder for jointer knives.

ROUTER BITS

A few bits used in a router, such as spiral bits and burr-cut bits, must be sent out for professional precision grinding; this will remove the least amount of metal while still maintaining bit geometry and overall balance.

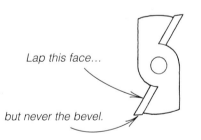

Lap this face...

...but never the bevel.

But the vast majority of router bits used today are double-flute bits with carbide inserts. With some minor exceptions (e.g., very small bits), these bits can have the flat face of the carbide insert lapped on a diamond hone to restore the edge. Under no circumstances should you attempt freehand grinding of router-bit profiles, and only with single-flute bits should you ever consider honing the bevel.

DON'T TOUCH THAT BEVEL!

You will often see a photo in tool catalogs something like the one shown below extolling the virtues of some particular honing device for router bits. A photo like this is misleading. First, it indicates that you can readily do freehand honing of the bevels on a straight bit. This is not the case. Second, it implies that there is nothing wrong with honing the bevel on a router bit; this is equally misleading. It is important that router-bit cutting edges be equidistant from the axis of the cutter. If not, one edge will be doing more work than the other, but, more important, it will no longer be balanced if more is taken off one cutting edge than the other.

You can also cause imbalance in a router bit by lapping one face more than the other. Whenever you are honing a router bit, you should take approximately the same number of strokes on each face to avoid introducing any imbalance in the bit.

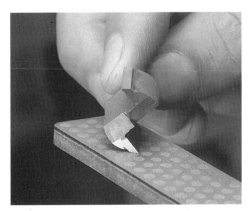

NEVER hone the bevel of a double-flute router bit! (Photo by Susan Kahn)

If you have a bit that cannot be restored by lapping the face, it should be sent out to a professional sharpening service or it should be replaced. In today's world, it is often less expensive to replace the bit than it is to have a nick ground out of it.

SHARPENING CARBIDE ROUTER BITS

For standard bits, the face of the carbide can be lapped on a diamond stone, but you will need a diamond file for honing the new style of chip-limitation router bit that has a slot next to the carbide insert rather than an open 90° quadrant. Just slide the bit back and forth on the file using light to moderate pressure and a touch of very light oil, such as WD-40. Heavy pressure puts deep score marks in the carbide and can dislodge diamond crystals from the file.

Craftsmen frequently feel that they should get the same degree of finish using a 400x diamond hone as the manufacturer did when originally grinding the router bit with a 400x diamond wheel. This is an unrealistic expectation, since a wheel taking a specific depth of cut will cut to the predetermined depth on entry and then essentially knock the peaks off all the ridges as the cutting wheel is withdrawn. In a more sophisticated form this is called cutting to "spark out." This means that you pass the wheel over the work at a predetermined height (or run the work past the wheel) until no more abrasion is taking place (i.e., there are no more sparks).

When honing by hand, the router bit and the diamond hone are not in any fixed relationship. The diamond hone will continue to cut as long as it is pressed against the router bit or, conversely, the router bit is pressed against it. The process by which the tops are knocked off the ridges never occurs, so the finish is always rougher than it would be with a power system using the same grit size.

In view of this, if you want a finish on your router bit that is as fine as the factory one, you are going to have to use finer-grit diamond than the manufacturer did to achieve it. Most router bits have had the insert face lapped with a 400x diamond wheel. A few use a 600x wheel, and at least one uses an 800x wheel. You can achieve about the same surface finish as a 600x wheel using a 1200x diamond stone. Just as you would do if you were sharpening anything else, you may want to start lapping the router bit on a 400x or 600x diamond and finish on a 1200x to save time. This depends on the amount of sharpening that has to be done to restore the edge.

As you reduce diamond particle size, also reduce honing pressure. The very fine diamond particles can be dislodged more readily than the larger ones. The basic reason is that the nickel plating must be thinner to avoid masking the cutting action.

HIGH-SPEED-STEEL ROUTER BITS

Steel router bits are almost a thing of the past, which is unfortunate since much higher rake angles are possible with steel bits than with carbide bits. Because of the higher rake angle, they do a much cleaner job on end-grain

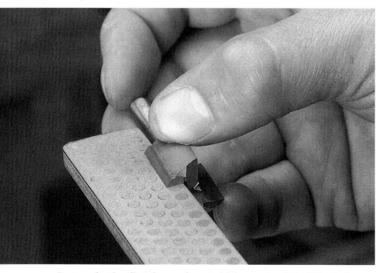

Lap only the flat face of a carbide router bit. (Photo by Susan Kahn)

Chip-limitation router bits (left) have a narrower gap between the carbide insert and the body than do standard bits (right) and require a diamond file for honing. (Photo by Susan Kahn)

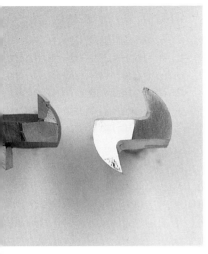

The rake angle of the cutting edge can be higher with a high-speed-steel router bit (right) than with a carbide bit (left) without prejudicing the strength of the edge. (Photo by Susan Kahn)

softwoods; they cause far less fiber pulling. Although the higher rake angle could cause problems in highly variable grain, it gives a smoother finish working with the grain and on end grain.

High-speed-steel router bits can be sharpened in exactly the same way as carbide-insert bits, but you have a greater choice of abrasives—it is not necessary to use diamond stones.

OTHER PERIPHERAL MILLING CUTTERS

Each year several more designs of milling cutters come on the market, usually to fade away within a few seasons. But three basic styles that have been with us for decades are shaper blades, molding-head cutters and mortising bits.

The sheer size of shaper blades often makes it impractical to consider lapping the face with a diamond hone. It can be done, but it is a time-consuming process. It is generally more practical to have shaper blades custom-ground on a profile grinder.

Simple molding-head cutters, on the other hand, can be touched up fairly readily. Just remove the knives from the head and lap them with finger pressure on a suitable stone, as shown in the photo at top right.

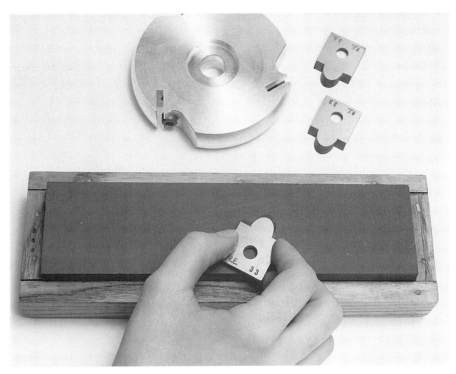

Molding-head cutters can be lapped on a stone.

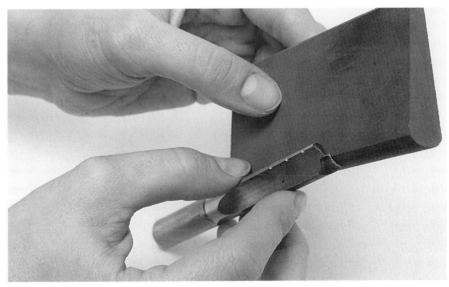

Use a slipstone to hone a chair mortising bit.

Mortising bits come in a variety of styles but have similar shapes to router bits. A chair mortising bit can be honed with an appropriately shaped shop stone (see the photo above), and a miller bit can be done on the edge of a diamond lap the same as one would hone a router bit.

CHAPTER 17
OTHER SHOP TOOLS

In many parts of this book as much time has been spent on shaping and conditioning tools as on putting a keen edge on them. Nowhere will this be the case more than in this chapter. Here we will be dealing with fettling tools more than sharpening them. "Fettle" is a fine old English word that means to trim, clean or adjust something to put it in good condition. Or, as it would have been said a century ago in North America, to put it in fine fettle.

An ideal example is a standard pair of tweezers. Most tweezers that you buy are made to look like tweezers but almost never act like tweezers. They have clubbish, malformed tips that are barely capable of gripping a matchstick let alone the fine splinter of wood that has just been driven under your fingernail. Such tweezers require fettling, not sharpening. We do not want them to cut, we just want them to work properly. So it is with many of the other tools discussed in this chapter. Some will require sharpening, but many others will require only pointing, serrating or shaping in some way to perform their task better.

TWEEZERS

Having introduced the subject of tweezers, besides wondering what they are doing in a book of woodworking tools, you might also be wondering just how tweezers should best be shaped to perform their tasks.

Most tweezers look like they should work but often will not. If you were to try to grip something with the tweezers shown in the top drawing below, you would find that the tips do not meet well originally and become progressively worse as pressure is applied. In addition, the surface is far too rough to provide a good grip. It actually has the potential to crush and sever a sliver where the excessively large ridges meet rather than clamping it properly for removal.

To shape the tips properly you have to grind back the serrated faces to make them more or less flat but with many fine cross serrations. The coarse work can be done on a belt sander. To finish off you have only to fold a piece of sandpaper and run the tweezers back and forth on either side with a firm grip, as shown in the photo at left below. This will abrade the inside of the tips so that they are approximately parallel under firm grip and will therefore always touch first at the extreme limit of the tip, just where you want the first contact to be made.

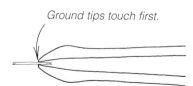

Tweezers do not meet at tips.

Coarse serrations can easily break or sever sliver.

Bad tips

Ground tips touch first.

Good tips

Once the serrated faces of the tweezers have been ground back, finish off by passing the tweezers back and forth over a piece of sandpaper. (Photos by Susan Kahn)

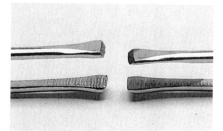

Tweezer tips, before and after interior shaping.

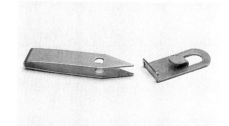

These tweezers, the best design in the author's opinion, have tips ground to a fine point with a light cross-score on the inside to grip slivers. (The device on the right is a tip guard.)

MAKING AN ECCENTRIC TRAMMEL POINT

Cheap trammel points have symmetrical pins, and all length adjustment must be made by tapping and sliding the clamp heads. More expensive trammel sets have one eccentric point so that fine adjustments can be made by rotating the eccentric point.

It is quite simple to make an eccentric pin if you are making yourself a set of trammel points. All you have to do is chuck a pin between two jaws of your hand drill and adjust the pin tip until it just crosses the centerline axis of the drill, as shown in the drawing below. Now go to your belt sander and sharpen the rod just as if it were a regular conically tipped tool. You will find it very easy to make the eccentric pin you want.

Concentric and eccentric trammel points. (Photo by Susan Kahn)

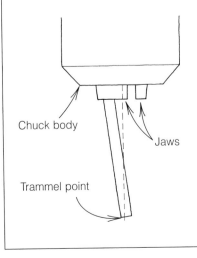

Chuck body

Jaws

Trammel point

To sharpen a concentric trammel point, chuck the tool in a drill press and hol *a stone against the point as it turns. (Photo by Susan Kahn)*

TRAMMEL POINTS, CENTER PUNCHES, AWLS

The secret to sharpening any conical-tipped tool is to have the tool rotating while you are sharpening it. For tools that have no handle, like a trammel point or a center punch, the easiest way to sharpen the tool is to chuck the blade directly in a drill press and use a bench stone to shape the tip as the tool is rotating, as shown in the photo above. You can use the same technique for tools that have easy-to-remove handles (often the case with scratch awls and garnish awls).

Alternatively, you can chuck the tool directly in a hand drill and sharpen it on a wheel or belt sander. If the handle cannot be removed, the tool can be rotated by hand against a belt sander.

AWLS WITH BEVELED TIPS

The traditional brad awl has a double-beveled tip with the bevels meeting at the axis of the awl. Pressed into wood with the wedge at 90° to the grain and rotated back and forth slightly, the tip tends to sever fibers and minimizes splitting. An awl like this can be sharpened in a variety of ways, but the simplest is probably on a bench stone The geometry is not particularly critic

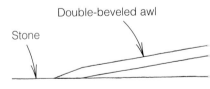

Double-beveled awl

Stone

although wood penetration is better with shallower bevel angles.

A less common but very effective tool, particularly for working in hardwood, is the square awl. You twist the awl as you push it in and it drills a hol Once a square awl has been ground, needs lapping of the four faces on a bench stone only occasionally. For th

To convert a round awl into a square awl, use a square piece of wood on the awl as a visual guide while you grind. (Photo by Susan Kahn)

process, it is not difficult to keep the awl properly oriented by feel alone. Because the awl drills by scraping the sides of the hole, it should be lapped whenever the facet intersections have become at all rounded.

If you want to make a square awl from a round awl, it is most readily done by pushing the round awl through a thin square piece of wood and using the edges of the wood as a visual or physical guide while you grind. Using the wood square as a visual template, you have a far better chance of getting a square cross-section than if you tried to gauge everything by reference only to the tiny flats on the tool.

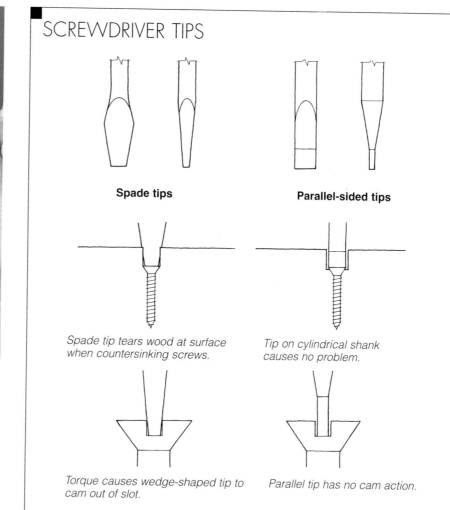

SCREWDRIVER TIPS

Spade tips

Parallel-sided tips

Spade tip tears wood at surface when countersinking screws.

Tip on cylindrical shank causes no problem.

Torque causes wedge-shaped tip to cam out of slot.

Parallel tip has no cam action.

SCREWDRIVERS

Restoring screwdriver tips is not strictly sharpening, but you can have more effective tips if you apply a bit of sharpening cunning to them.

Probably fewer than 1% of the readers of this book have ever tried regrinding any screwdriver other than a slotted one. I suspect that fewer than one in ten of you have even done that. I am always amazed at the number of screwdrivers in people's shops (including my own) that are virtually useless but are kept around "just in case." I have no intention of trying to reform the world on this issue, but it is not beyond the wit of man to repair a screwdriver tip. Slot screwdrivers are particularly easy to repair; in fact, you can usually make them better than new. Other tip shapes present more problems.

SLOT SCREWDRIVERS

Not only are slot screwdrivers the easiest to reshape, but they are also usually the ones most in need of it, even when new and unused. Just like chisels, slot screwdrivers do not come out of the package ready for use: the tips are invariably wrongly shaped for woodworking. They are wedge-shaped in both axes, when what you need is a tip of constant diameter with the flats parallel for a distance at least as great as the depth of slot of any screw they are to be used on.

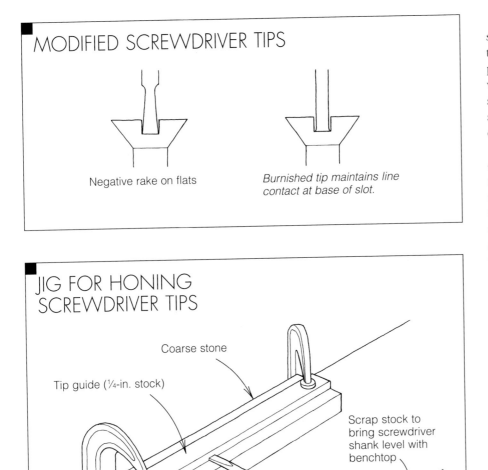

MODIFIED SCREWDRIVER TIPS

Negative rake on flats

Burnished tip maintains line contact at base of slot.

JIG FOR HONING SCREWDRIVER TIPS

Coarse stone

Tip guide (¼-in. stock)

Scrap stock to bring screwdriver shank level with benchtop

A cylindrical shank will follow the screw without damage. The same is true when driving a screw next to some protruding detail; a cylindrical shank will not mark an adjoining surface as a spade tip can. In the other axis, a wedge shape encourages the screwdriver to cam out of the slot. Parallel sides do not.

If you want to be particularly cunning, there are two ways you can redesign the tip to improve the grip even more. One is to put a slight negative rake on the flats (see the top drawing at left). The rake has to be very slight since the modification weakens the tip. However, it ensures that the line of contact is always at the bottom of the slot.

But the easiest and most effective method is to form the tip with parallel sides and then burnish the end. It takes a fair amount of pressure (use a triangular burnisher or the small-radius edge of a tear-drop burnisher), but you need only a slight swelling to achieve your purpose. You now have a tip that will tolerate minor misalignment and still maintain line contact at the base of the slot.

This design is particularly effective with brass screws. The burnished edge cuts into the brass at the bottom of the slot, virtually locking the tip in position as long as there is torque on it. Incidentally, if you find the tip too hard to burnish, you can clamp the screwdriver in a vise and roll the hooks on the tip by tapping the tip with a hammer.

Whatever you do to the tip of a new screwdriver will probably improve its shape, but you should be careful not to overheat the tip and soften it. Reshaping can be done on a coarse bench stone with minor jigging (see the drawing at left), or with a file if the tip is soft enough. The minor serrations from the bench stone improve tip grip by resisting cam-out. Do not polish them off. In fact, this is what is called a cross-ground tip in tool catalogs.

For woodworking use, it is important that no part of the screwdriver be wider than the tip. The best example of the need for a parallel-sided tip is when you want to countersink screws for plugging. A spade-shaped tip can score the sides of the counterbore, making it impossible to do a decent job of plugging because of the damage done to the walls of the countersunk hole (see the drawing on p. 217).

SQUARE-RECESS SCREWDRIVERS

Unlike slot screwdrivers, square-recess (or Robertson) screwdrivers usually come with properly shaped tips. If well hardened originally, they seldom deform in use because they seldom slip. Square-recess power bits, on the other hand, can be more readily damaged in use (just like all power bits).

The power bits are made to be disposable, but not so the screwdrivers. To restore their shape, they have to be docked at the tip and the flats extended at the original angles and cross-sectional dimensions. Since the tips are usually milled originally, the flats will be tangential to the arc left by the milling head. This may require you to remove a fair bit of metal the first time you reshape the tip.

With care, this shaping can all be done on a grinding wheel; alternatively, you can use a diamond file. The tips are usually too hard for a steel file. To guide your eye when filing, clamp the screwdriver between two pieces of wood with the flat to be filed parallel to and just proud of the wood (see the drawing at right).

RESTORING SQUARE-RECESS SCREWDRIVER TIPS

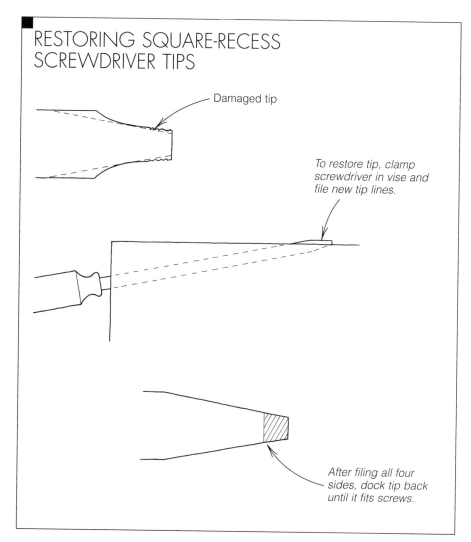

Damaged tip

To restore tip, clamp screwdriver in vise and file new tip lines.

After filing all four sides, dock tip back until it fits screws.

WOODEN VISE JAWS

Whenever you have to use temporary wooden jaws in a vise and the jaws have to be even (as when reshaping a screwdriver tip), there are at least three easy ways to do it.

Option A. Put double-faced tape on the outside of the wooden jaws, line them up with the vise jaws and close the vise. You can then open and close the vise at will, and the jaws will stay tacked in position.

Option B. Kerf a piece of wood just slightly narrower than the item you want to hold. Press the item into the kerf and put the whole thing in the vise.

Option C. For very wide items, tack thin stock on a base that is the same width as the item you want to hold.

Any of these methods is easier than trying to hold two jaws with something positioned between them as you try to close the vise.

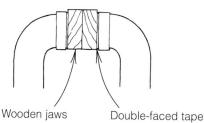

Wooden jaws   Double-faced tape

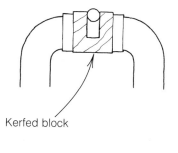

Kerfed block

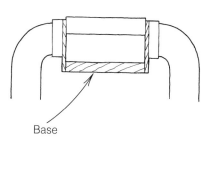

Base

PHILLIPS SCREWDRIVERS

Restoring a Phillips screwdriver tip is just a matter of restoring the original geometry. Well, not quite. The first thing you find as you apply a square file to the tip grooves is that the manufacturer did not create the grooves this way, because you find the file cutting only at opposite ends of the groove. The groove was originally formed by a radius-tipped die or cutter. This means that you have to do a bit of filing before you get to the area that needs restoration. No matter, the grooves are easy to file.

If you are questioning why anyone would file the grooves first rather than the four flats, the primary reason is that you want as much reference face as possible on the groove sides to orient the file, particularly because the file touches initially only at the groove ends. Once the grooves are evenly filed, you can address the flats. File the flats back to the width required (i.e., the original width). Finally, dock the end of the screwdriver so the driver will seat properly in screws.

Filing a Phillips tip is all a bit awkward the first time, but you quickly get the hang of it and find that you can restore tips to a condition at least as good as the original and often better. To make filing as easy as possible, clamp the screwdriver in a vise with the grooves approximately horizontal.

OTHER SCREWDRIVER STYLES

There are several other types of screws on the market, but the shaping principles for their drivers are the same as those already described, only the shapes differ.

To reshape a damaged Phillips screwdriver tip (top), first file the grooves, then the flats (middle) and finish by docking the tip (bottom).

MARKING AND CUTTING GAUGES

Marking and cutting gauges are frequently used for the same purposes. Only occasionally does a woodworker use a cutting gauge for cutting something to depth; more commonly it is used for some purpose like marking tenon shoulders, where it is prized for the crisp shoulders it makes.

In Western tradition, a cutting gauge had a knife beveled on one side as a cutter, and a marking gauge had a conical pin as a marker. In Japan (possibly in other countries) knives were used in all woodworking gauges. The question of which style to use is nearly irrelevant since there is a huge amount of evidence in used gauges to show that most Western marking-gauge owners spent a great deal of time trying to make their gauges cut better by filing the pins to double-beveled points that looked suspiciously like knives.

For those of you unfamiliar with cutting gauges, they are always used with the knife bevel to the waste side of the marked cut. In this manner, it is possible to eliminate the width of the cutter as a consideration in marking a line. It also severs the fibers so that any tearout from a saw will be on the waste side of the cut.

SHARPENING CUTTERS

The knife in a cutting gauge should be sharpened as you would any knife beveled on one side. Remove the cutter from the gauge, grind and hone the knife bevel, then lap the other side.

If you have a Japanese marking/ cutting gauge and use extensive central heating during the winter, you will find that the knife will probably be seized in the gauge stem. Japanese manufacturers often make these gauges from wood with 10% or more moisture content; as this dries down in winter, the knife gets locked in place.

It is a good idea to open the knife slot a bit, cut a wedge mortise and fashion a small wedge to hold the knife just the way Western cutting gauges are designed. Otherwise you might snap

From left to right, a slide-mechanism mortise/marking gauge, a screw-mechanism mortise gauge and a simple Japanese marking/cutting gauge. (Photo by Susan Kahn)

The knives in Japanese marking/cutting gauges can be difficult to remove for sharpening. The knife shown here snapped when removal was attempted.

the knife trying to remove it, as has happened to the knife in the gauge shown in the photo at top right.

SHARPENING PINS

With many marking gauges, it is not possible to remove the pins for sharpening. Since removal and replacement would tend to loosen them anyway, sharpening the pins in place is common.

There are at least three schools of thought on sharpening marking-gauge pins. The first, to maintain the conical point, is the least-followed practice. The second is to file both sides of the pin to bring it to a sharp point. The last is to file the side next to the gauge head vertically and put all the bevel on the side away from the gauge head. I call this "knife envy"; it is an attempt to convert a marking gauge into a cutting gauge.

One problem with sharpening pins in place is that there's a danger of filing grooves in the gauge stem at the same time as you shape the pins (see the photo at right). However, there are several ways to avoid this problem. You can: use an auger-bit file that has safe edges; use a feather-edge file, after grinding (and buffing) the apex to make it safe; use a square-edged file with tape covering the edge; modify

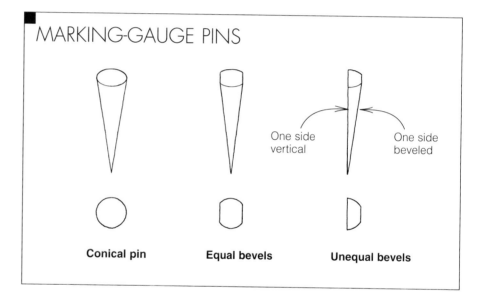

MARKING-GAUGE PINS

One side vertical — One side beveled

Conical pin   **Equal bevels**   **Unequal bevels**

a cheap needle file for the purpose; or make a safe-edge file with PSA-backed abrasive.

Once a pin becomes too short and it is not possible either to drive it out farther or remove it, just file it close to flush, tap it back into the stem out of the way, drill a hole next to it and put in a new pin. Only with a graduated-stem gauge does it matter exactly where the pin is on the stem.

The stem of this old marking gauge has been scored by repeated filing of the marking pin.

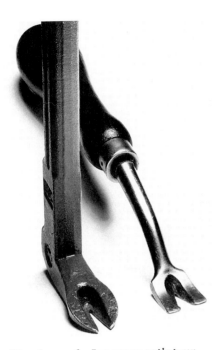

The claws of a Japanese cat's paw (left) are quite different from those of a traditional Western tack lifter (right). The relief grinding in the nail slot, the pointed tips and the rounded bottom differentiate them.

Hammer claws should be ground to smooth strong wedges, as shown on the hammer at front. The tips of the claws on the back hammer are much steeper than necessary. (Photos by Susan Kahn)

CLAW TOOLS

Hammers, renovator's bars, cat's paws and tack lifters are all likely to need some redefining of their claw tips at some time. In each case, the shape of the claws should be related to the force that will be applied to them.

For example, the claws on most tack lifters are much thicker than necessary for removing tacks and small brads. If the claws are not thinned at the tips and brought to a finer wedge shape, they will always be more destructive in use than is necessary. With a fine tip, they can be slipped under a tack head without gouging large chunks out of the wood.

CAT'S PAWS

A Japanese cat's paw shows how a tool can be effectively designed to be pressed under a nail head with minimal disturbance of surrounding wood. Whereas a Western tool might have flat chisel-tipped claws, a Japanese cat's paw has claws that are pointed on the tips as well as being relief-ground away from the nail slot. It is far easier to force such claws under nail heads. The design manages to give precision in use with substantial strength. That is what you should aim for when you sharpen any claw tool.

HAMMERS

Since hammer claws are as often used for prying as they are for nail removal, they should not be ground to mimic cat's paws. They have a dual purpose, and both purposes should be served. In the photo above, one set of claws has been ground to smooth strong wedges; the other has been docked abruptly, weakening the very tip and making the first ¼ in. or so a much steeper wedge than necessary.

RENOVATOR'S BARS

The prying tips of bars should be ground to suit their purpose. Two well-designed tips are shown in the top photo on the facing page. The large tip is on a Swedish renovator's bar, so called because it is as useful in construction as it is in demolition. The tip is designed to be driven into very narrow cracks to wedge apart fastened structural members with minimal damage to either. The other tip (on a Japanese renovator's cat's paw) has the same objective, but for smaller-scale work like room trim or cabinetry.

Both tools are designed in relation to their length as well as to their purpose. They are as thin as they can be given the width of their tips and their

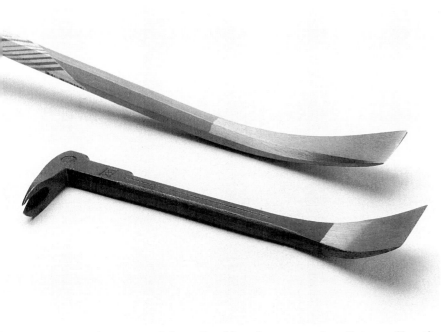

The prying tips of renovator's bars (back) and renovator's cat's paws (front) should be ground as thin as possible. (Photo by Susan Kahn)

ength. Whenever you regrind a tool like this you should keep the length of the tool in mind, because someone will eventually use all of the leverage afforded and the tool has to be able to withstand the force.

There is one particularly difficult grinding problem with claw tools. This is the set of claws that has a "hole" worn in them; all but the largest nails escape their grip. The only thing that can be

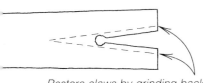

Restore claws by grinding back to dotted lines.

done in this case is to lengthen the claws, moving the nail slot farther back in the head as shown in the drawing above. Although time-consuming, this can be done with grinding burrs and/or discs. There are now inexpensive and aggressive diamond burrs and discs on the market that are ideal for this sort of job.

NAIL SETS

Nail sets have a conical or spherical depression in the tip; they depend on a sharp lip for their grip on a nail head. There are two styles: the standard tip and the European tip (see the drawing at right).

The standard tip is stronger than the European tip but will not follow as cleanly when you want to countersink nails. With either style, once you flatten the lip, the set will not grip a nail head securely. On a larger nail set, you can recreate the tip with a ball-tip or flame-tip diamond or carbide burr (see the photo at right). On a very small nail set where you might not be able to do that, I would recommend that you first try to make a crater with a center punch and then do some judicious peripheral grinding. You will need some magnification if you attempt this.

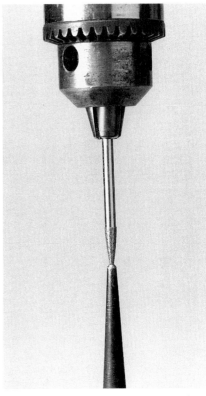

Use a flame-tip burr to recreate the tip of a flattened nail set. (Photo by Susan Kahn)

A very easy fix, although not quite as good as the ones described, is to grind the nail set flat on the tip and then drive it against a double-cut file. This will create several points on the tip of the

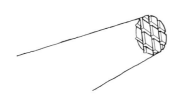

set (see the drawing above) that will grip a nail head.

But the best thing you can do, as usual, is to look after your nail sets in the first place. Nail sets are hard. Nail heads are soft. If you avoid using your nail sets as pin punches, they will probably never dull unless you happen to be a finish carpenter and use them every day.

PLIERS

About the most you can do for a pair of pliers is to sharpen the teeth when they get dull. A triangular diamond file works well. The jaws would normally be case-hardened and be too hard for a steel file.

If the pliers have side cutters, they can usually be sharpened once before the rest of the jaws interfere with complete closure. It is generally best to sharpen the outside bevel only, respecting the original geometry and ensuring that the cutting edges remain straight and meet evenly. Altogether, this is a daunting task and there are no handy jigs to take the skill out of it.

END CUTTERS, NAIL PULLERS

End cutters and nail pullers look so similar that it is tempting to use them in the same way. I did and took a huge chunk off the corner of one jaw of my favorite end cutters as I was trying to wrench a reluctant spike from its moorings. In general, end cutters are harder than nail pullers and have a slimmer jaw profile. They are designed to cut (not to have substantial lateral pressure applied as I did) and can therefore afford a lower included angle on each jaw than can nail pullers.

Pliers' side cutters can usually be sharpened once or twice before the serrated jaws meet.

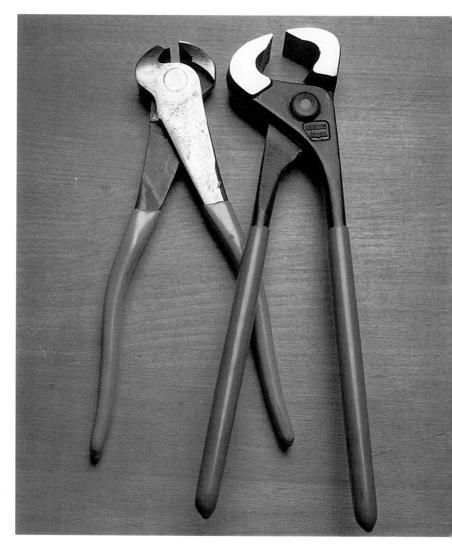

A nail puller (the longer-handled tool at right) can be used as an end cutter, although it is not as efficient because it is hinged well back from the jaw edges. However, an end cutter (at left) cannot be used as a nail puller because the jaws are too brittle (note the corner off one jaw).

Either tool can have the jaws restored by judicious work on a belt sander (a 1-in. belt sander lets you work around the jaw limitations quite

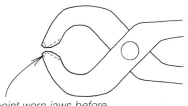

…oint worn jaws before …ing bevels.

…asily) or by filing. In either case, the …riginal jaw geometry should be …aintained and, to ensure that the jaws …ontinue to meet evenly, they should …e jointed before the bevels are filed.

It is fairly easy to joint the jaws and …en adjust the flats so that they meet …venly. Only then should you file the …evels to recreate an edge. With the flat … guide you, it is straightforward to file … bevel correctly; just keep the flat of …ven width as you file. And, finally, do …ot file the bevel to the point that the …ointing flat disappears entirely; leave a … arrow line of light the complete …ength. There are two reasons for this. …irst, you want the jaw edges not only … be parallel to each other, but to meet, …ot bypass. So, when you file the …econd jaw, you may find that a bit …nore must be filed off one edge or the …ther of the first jaw so that the two can …neet properly. Second, you should …eave a very slight flat on each jaw …nyway to maintain edge strength.

…CISSORS …ND SHEARS

…op-quality scissors and shears should …e sharpened professionally; sewing …enters frequently provide the service. …ut for the under $10 variety, the kind …nost of us have in our shops, there is …o reason not to have a go at them. …ith a bit of care, you can do a perfect-…y serviceable job.

Scissors are most easily sharpened …n a belt sander. With the table set at …hatever bevel angle was originally on …he scissors and the scissors open,

grind one side, then the other, always with the belt running into the edge. Usually a single pass on a 120x belt will do it. After grinding, very carefully deburr the edge by taking a light pass on a fine stone (1000x or finer) with the flat of the blade.

Scissors usually dull as a result of the blades abrading each other; the material being cut is usually the lesser cause. As the blades pass each other they wear off a tiny amount each time.

Grind blades back to dotted lines.

In the drawing above, the blades would have to be ground back to the dotted line to be restored.

In general, you can regrind scissors at the found bevel angle, but this should not be less than 45° for utility use. For cutting very thin materials, a narrow flat on the edge is sometimes used.

PUNCHES

It is just possible that one in a thousand readers might be faced with the task of sharpening a veneer punch some day. More probable is that you will need to sharpen a leather punch or a punch-style washer cutter. Sharpening any style of punch is a challenge, but with care anything is possible.

The most difficult aspect of sharpening a punch is keeping the cutting edge in one plane. It has to be flat to work properly. The first thing to do is joint the punch edge on a bench stone—800x to 1200x is fine. Joint it only until you can see a line of light all the way around the punch. Then, starting at the thickest part of the edge, work your way around the edge with a slipstone or a small bench stone, sharpening it the same way you would with a gouge until there is a barely discernible or no line of light left.

Using a hard leather strop or a wooden strop charged with chromium oxide, carefully finish the edge. If you accidentally go too far in one spot, lightly rejoint the punch and start again.

Although not possible with a veneer punch because of its irregular shape, a circular punch can be honed and stropped on a belt sander if you are confident of your technique. But since

Punches like the two above are used for cutting leather, cork or any soft, nonmetallic material. The punch head on the left has a cam-lock mechanism; the one on the right threads into the holder. (Photo by Susan Kahn)

To sharpen a rotary cutter, mount the cutter on a mandrel in a drill press and hold a stone against the bevel while the cutter is turning. Use a steady rest to support the stone at the correct angle. (Photo by Susan Kahn)

Miter trimmers are used only for trimming stock, usually taking off less than $1/8$ in. per pass.

MITER-TRIMMER BLADES

Fortunately, miter-trimmer blades do not need frequent sharpening. Since they are large, awkward tools and have to be exceptionally keen to work well, that is a good thing. As with jointer and planer blades, if a good sharpening service is available, these blades are as well left to professionals. They can use a traversing jig for grinding, something you cannot readily duplicate.

If the blades need only honing and are not nicked, this is something that you can readily do. The blades are thick enough and long enough that the bevel provides quite a large reference surface for a sharpening stone. It is time-consuming, but the entire bevel can be honed. You should start with an 800x water stone for good speed of cut and do 90% of the work with that stone, finishing off with a 6000x or an 8000x stone.

A shopmade honing jig that works well is a piece of wood sliced at the bevel angle of the trimmer blade (see the drawing on the facing page). Screw the blade to the block with small-shank screws and washers (to give yourself lots of adjustment room) and clamp the block in a vise. With the blade projecting just above the block and a wrap of tape on the far side of the stone to prevent abrasion of the wood, you can control the honing process. You may increase the bevel angle by a few minutes, but not enough to be concerned about. You can fine-tune everything by adding or removing layers of tape on the stone.

it is so easy to overshoot the mark with power equipment, I recommend hand honing.

ROTARY CUTTERS

Rotary cutters have long been popular for cutting fabric but have only recently infiltrated the woodworking shop for veneer cutting. Most rotary cutters have disposable cutter wheels, but these can also be resharpened.

The secret is to mount the cutter on a mandrel in a drill press, or in an electric hand drill clamped in a vise, and sharpen the cutter while it is turning. For a very dull cutter, use a medium-grit stone (e.g. 800x) followed by a 4000x or 8000x stone.

In both instances you should use a steady rest of some kind that lets you hone at the original bevel angle of the cutter, as shown in the photo at top. Be particularly careful in this process since the rotating cutter can give you a serious cut.

It is a simple matter to make a mandrel from a piece of dowel and use a screw to hold the cutter in position. The neck size of the screw should be the same as the center hole of the cutter.

When you have finished honing the bevel you will probably have created some burr on the edge, however minor. Of paramount importance in removing this burr is that the face of the blade be kept dead flat. Even minor buffing on the inboard face can cause the blade to veer off-line, unless it is done very carefully. The best system is to put a sheet of 0.5 micron chromium-oxide lapping film on a piece of flat hardwood plywood. With the blade flat on the sheet, draw it across with a trailing stroke; that will refine the edge sufficiently. Any more than that could introduce error in the cut.

CORNERING TOOLS

The easiest way to sharpen a cornering tool is not to touch the convex side at all. The geometry is fairly involved, and it is simpler if the convex side be left alone once it has been properly honed once.

A 1-in. diameter sanding drum is ideal for the concave side of a cornering tool. All you have to do is press the cornering tool against the rotating sanding drum to grind the inside. If a fair amount of work has to be done, start with a coarse sleeve and then move to a fine sleeve for finishing.

To put a very fine edge on the cornering tool, finish off with a 1-in. dowel and green honing compound. One end of the dowel can be turned down so that it can be chucked in a drill press, or the dowel can be mounted between centers on a lathe to speed everything up. Alternatively, it can be used just as one uses a slipstone.

At various times, cornering tools that are incorrectly ground come on the market; usually the bevels of the two cutting edges are in the same plane. This fault can be corrected with time and effort, but it is wiser to return the tool to the vendor. Although you often have to accept tools that need honing, you should never have to accept tools that have manufacturing defects.

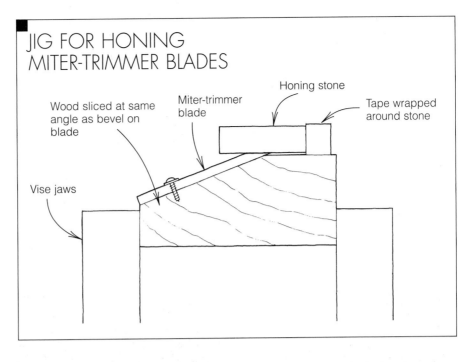

JIG FOR HONING MITER-TRIMMER BLADES

Wood sliced at same angle as bevel on blade

Miter-trimmer blade

Honing stone

Tape wrapped around stone

Vise jaws

Sharpen a cornering tool by pressing the inside curve against a rotating 1-in. sanding drum. (Photo by Susan Kahn)

AFTERWORD

There is no question that I have failed to cover some tools in this book. As I was reading the final draft, I realized that I had missed nicker spurs, those miserable little cloverleaves screwed to the sides of combination planes. I could launch into an explanation of sharpening a nicker spur, but, after 227 pages, I would hope that you could gaily seize the wretched thing, deftly shape the bevel, lap the face and be plowing a clean groove seconds later.

All this should be possible because you should now know that sharpening is mostly common sense augmented by a few basic principles, some standard abrasives and a few cunning jigs. Be assured that your sharpening skill will increase with confidence. Also be assured that once you have used really sharp tools, you will be happy with nothing less; both your tools and your craftsmanship will benefit from your new knowledge and confidence. And remember, even if you apply your new knowledge only to kitchen knives, you can still be a neighborhood hero.

APPENDIX 1
CHIP CLASSIFICATION

Dr. Norman C. Franz, now retired and living in Vancouver, was a Professor in the Dept. of Wood Technology at the University of Michigan for many years. Although he contributed a great deal to the literature of wood machining over the years, his 1956 doctoral thesis is of particular significance to tool users since it established a framework for chip (or shaving) classification that made it possible to understand many aspects of wood cutting and wood-cutting tools that had been poorly explained in the literature until then.

It was never Dr. Franz's intent to light the way for hand-tool users. He was trying to analyze what happened during rotary power cutting but found the complications of setting up adequate test equipment so great that he chose to use orthogonal cutting (cutting in a straight line) instead to develop his analysis. If you have a rotary cutting device of infinite diameter, you have straight-line cutting anyway. Dr. Franz used rake angles, relief angles, and so on, that are common primarily to power tools not to hand tools, but the results he

obtained are still applicable to hand tools in many ways. It is unfortunate that his work was not given greater publicity before now, because it so clearly explains many of the effects we see when using tools like bench planes and chisels.

It is not possible to do justice to a 150-page thesis in these few pages, but, with Dr. Franz's assistance, I have extracted those parts that would be of greatest interest to non-industrial tool users.

Dr. Franz used this modified milling machine for most of his test cuts. It allowed him to control depth of cut at the same time as he measured forces and photographed the action with the movie camera mounted opposite the cutter. All of the photographs that show chip formation on the following pages were taken on this equipment.

CHIP FORMATION

Throughout this analysis, wherever you read the word "chip" you can substitute "shaving," if that makes you feel more comfortable. For definitional reasons, Franz used "chip" to describe removed wood whether or not it was in the continuous form of a shaving or in smaller particles that laymen might call chips. He classified chips in three basic types.

TYPE I

This is the type of chip that is formed when the wood splits ahead of the cutting edge, then rides up along the front of the cutting tool until the bending force breaks the chip. It is the type of chip that is typical of bench planes with bed angles of 50° or 55°. Such a chip gives a very smooth surface when cutting with the grain (or exactly parallel to the grain, as shown in the top photo at right), but it gives a very rough surface when cutting against the grain (as shown in the middle photo), because the chip repeatedly breaks below the intended cutline.

Top: A Type I chip produces a very smooth surface when cutting parallel to the grain.

Middle: When cutting against the grain, the same chip produces a very rough surface.

Bottom: The rough surface produced by Type I chips when cutting against the grain.

TYPE II

With this type of chip, the wood fails in a plane (extending from the cutting edge to the work surface) that roughly bisects the angle between the rake face and the direction of travel. This is the type of chip that you could expect from a scraping plane or other tools with a low rake angle (see the top photo at left).

At times, Type I and Type II chips occur in combination with each other, as shown in the middle photo. When cutting with the grain or parallel to it, the resulting finish is excellent, as shown in the bottom photo.

However, when both chip types occur cutting against the grain, the resulting surface would be more similar to that shown in the bottom photo on the facing page.

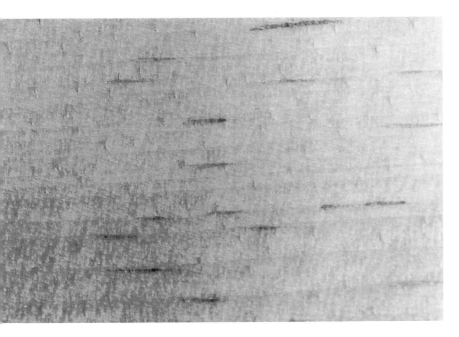

Top: A Type II chip.

Middle: Type I and Type II chips occurring in combination in parallel-grain cutting.

Bottom: The smooth surface produced by Type I and Type II chips occurring in combination when cutting parallel to the grain.

TYPE III

This type of chip occurs when conditions produce compression and shearing failures in the wood ahead of the cutting tool. As with the Type I chip, this is a cyclical, not a continuous, process. The Type III chip is associated with very small or negative rake angles where the ruptured wood does not freely escape up the front of the advancing tool (see the top photo at right).

In some instances, a built-up edge of compacted material develops at the edge, creating a false edge with a positive rake angle that momentarily produces a Type I chip before the process begins again (see the middle photo). Because the surface generated with the Type III chip is determined by wood failures ahead of the tool, these failures can extend below the intended cutting line and the damage remains prominent in the finished work, producing what is commonly described as fuzzy grain (see the bottom photo). The false edge that develops with a Type III chip is encouraged by negative rake angles, a high coefficient of friction between the chip and the tool face, and tool dullness; the rounded edge of a dulled tool has the effect of creating a greater negative rake angle because of the rounding.

Top: A Type III chip showing a built-up edge.

Middle: A built-up edge that exhibits a large positive rake angle about to create a Type I chip.

Bottom: Fuzzy grain resulting from Type III chips.

THE WORK OF DR. WILLIAM MCKENZIE

Because Dr. Franz's intent was to analyze rotary cutting, none of his experiments used very high rake angles (low cutting angles), thin shavings or the very sharp edges that we associate with low-angle hand planes or paring tools that most woodworkers look to for a very fine finish. In fact, this shortcoming was brought home to him by an Australian, Dr. William McKenzie, who pointed out that there was actually a Type 0 chip that could be created by a very sharp blade with a very low cutting angle cutting with (or exactly parallel to) the grain. The chip created was a continuous shaving of the type we associate with low-angle planes.

Dr. McKenzie had been schooled well. He studied with Dr. Franz at the University of Michigan from 1958 to 1960, when he presented his own doctoral thesis on a subject that directly paralleled Dr. Franz's and had in fact been inspired by Franz's earlier work.

Using much the same equipment that Franz had used, McKenzie analyzed the factors at play when cutting end grain.

In classifying the types of chips created when cutting end grain, McKenzie found two basic types, each with a variant. Because McKenzie, like Franz, was attempting to simulate machining conditions (in this case, sawing), he used relatively high cutting angles (low rake angles) and work-sharp edges. So, once again, the effect of very low cutting angles that one might find when using a low-angle block plane or a paring chisel with a keen edge was not encompassed by the study. Rather than dealing with chip type, McKenzie dealt with the nature of the failure of the wood, so it is the failures that are classified by type rather than the chips.

TYPE I FAILURE

McKenzie found that the distinguishing feature of a Type I failure is that splits occur parallel to the grain below the cutting plane. In Type I(a) failures, as shown in the top photo at left, such splits are short and regular, leaving comparatively high surface quality. In Type I(b) failures (bottom photo), several short splits occur between fairly regularly spaced longer splits that leave a substantially poorer quality of surface.

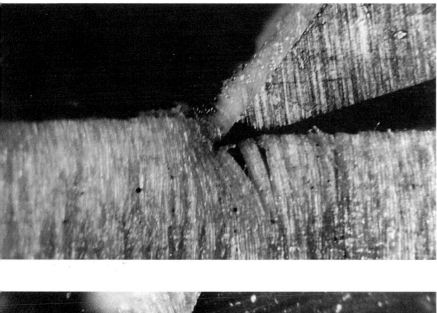

Top: Type I(a) failure in saturated eastern white pine; 40° rake angle; 0.010 in. chip thickness; 30x magnification.

Bottom: Type I(b) failure in eastern white pine at 5% moisture content; 30° rake angle; 0.030 in. chip thickness; 30x magnification.

TYPE II FAILURE

The distinguishing feature of a Type II failure is that the wood fails at some distance below the cutting plane but parallel to it. In a Type II(a) failure (top photo at right), the failure is intermittent, but in a Type II(b) failure (middle photo), it is continuous.

In this testing, McKenzie found that moisture content had a great effect. The bottom photo shows the quite different effect of the cutting action on end-grain maple at 5% moisture content and 14% moisture content.

In all of the above material, careful note should be taken of the rake angles of the cutting tools and the fact that the cutting edges were not as sharp as those that would normally be used on hand tools today. They are probably still reflective of the general keenness of power tools. In spite of such differences, there is a wealth of information to be drawn from this research that could inform further research.

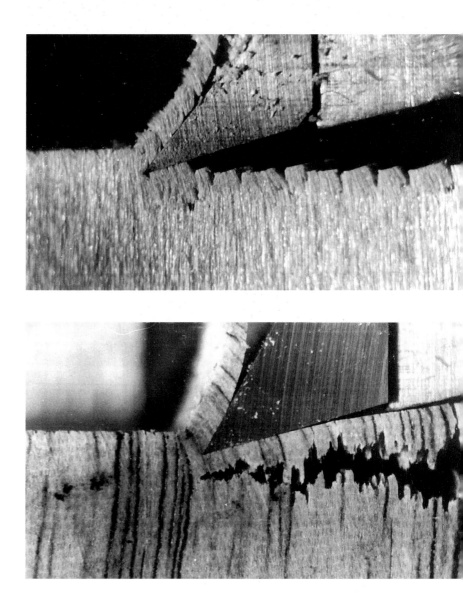

Top: Type II(a) failure in yellow poplar at 5% moisture content; 40° rake angle; 0.030 in. chip thickness; 10x magnification.

Middle: Type II(b) failure in common persimmon at 5% moisture content; 40° rake angle; 0.030 in. chip thickness; 10x magnification.

Bottom: The effect of moisture content on the rupture pattern in cutting sugar maple: back sample, 5% moisture content; front sample, 14% moisture content.

APPENDIX 2
INTERNATIONAL GRIT STANDARDS

Of the various grit-grading systems in use today, three dominate. The most familiar to North Americans is the U.S. standard used for grading loose grit, sandpaper and stones. The P-grade (or FEPA) system used in much of Europe is very close to the U.S. standard in grits below 240x but varies widely above that. The same is true of the Japanese standard (JIS-grade).

The Japanese standard above 1000x has become dominant worldwide in bench stones, because the Japanese are virtually the only manufacturers of fine-grit stones.

Eventually, measurement of grit size in microns will likely dominate, because it is the only system that is both rational and readily understandable by anyone, anywhere.

WHAT IS A MICRON?
A micron is one millionth of a meter. There are 25 of them in one thousandth of an inch. In more practical terms, a human hair is between 20 and 40 microns thick, and this page is about 100 microns thick.

ABRASIVE-GRADE COMPARISON

Size in Microns	U.S. Industrial Mesh	European P-Grade	Japanese JIS-Grade	Emery
100	#150	-	-	-
80	180	-	-	-
60	220	P240	#240	-
50	240	-	280	-
40	280	-	320	-
-	320	P360	360	-
-	360	P500	400	1/0
30	400	-	500	2/0
20	500	P1000	600	3/0
15	600	-	1000	-
-	800	P1200	1200	-
12	-	-	1500	-
9	-	-	2000	4/0
5	-	-	2500	-
4	-	-	3000	-
3	-	-	4000	-
2	-	-	6000	-
1	-	-	8000	-
0.3	-	-	10000	-

GLOSSARY

ABRASIVE A substance used for wearing away a surface.

BURRIS A sharp edge created by the junction of two surfaces in different planes. In short, a corner.

ATTACK ANGLE *See* Cutting angle.

BACK BEVEL A bevel ground on the clearance face of a cutting tool.

BED ANGLE The angle between the bed of a plane and its sole.

BEVEL A sloping surface. With edge tools, it is the primary part of the tool tip that is abraded to create a sharp cutting edge.

BEVEL ANGLE The angle between the face of a tool and the bevel.

BOB A small, shaped buffing head.

BOND The material holding abrasive particles together. Could be rubber, resin, fused clay (vitrified), etc.

BORT Diamonds (or diamond fragments) not of gem quality used as abrasives.

BREASTED Shaped like a breast, proud in the center. Used to describe handsaws where the line of teeth is convex.

BRUZZ Another name for a corner chisel.

BUFFING One method of polishing using cloth or felt wheels charged with compounds.

BURNISH To form or refine a surface or edge by pressure rather than abrasion.

BURR The ridge or flap of metal created at an edge during an abrading process.

CAMBER The condition of being slightly convex.

CANNEL A flute or gutter. Gouges are said to be in-cannel if the bevel is inside the flute and out-cannel if the bevel is on the outside.

CAP IRON A strip of metal reinforcing a plane blade to reduce vibration in use. Usually it is tightly fitted to the plane blade and shaped so that it causes shavings to bend sharply as they are formed. It can then also be called a chip breaker.

CHATTER The porpoising of an edge creating an uneven surface.

CHIP BREAKER *See* Cap iron.

CLEARANCE ANGLE The angle between the relief face of a cutter and the generated surface that is necessary to accommodate fiber springback. Also called the relief angle.

CROWN The amount of central projection of an edge.

CUTTING ANGLE The angle between the generated surface and the rake face of the tool. Also called the attack angle. It is always the complement of the rake angle.

DAMP To reduce the amplitude of motion.

DIG A term used in turning to describe a rapid, unplanned penetration of the tool into the work.

DOCK To shorten.

DRAW-FILE To use a file at 90° to its usual path of travel.

DRESS To restore a grinding wheel to its desired condition by selectively wearing away part of the wheel.

DUB To increase the included angle of a cutting edge beyond its effective limit. Usually done by accident.

FLEAM A beveled tooth on a saw is "fleam cut." Named after a surgeon's lancet (or fleam) for blood letting.

FLUTE A channel resembling half of a musical flute split lengthwise.

FLUTTER The degree to which a grinding wheel does not rotate in a plane at 90° to its axis.

GENERATED SURFACE The work surface created by the action of a cutting tool.

GLAZE The loading of a bench stone or wheel with metal and/or crushed abrasive.

GRAIN The direction of orientation of transportation cells in wood.

GRIND To give an edge a basic shape by rapid abrasion.

GRIT Particles of abrasive.

GULLET The hollow behind a saw tooth that provides space for chip accumulation.

GUM To deepen and enlarge the spaces (or gullets) between the teeth of a saw.

HOLLOW GRIND To grind a concave face or bevel on a tool.

HONE To refine an edge that has already been given a basic shape.

HOOK The wave-crest edge created by burnishing a tool.

HOP Lack of concentricity of a grinding wheel about its axis.

INCLUDED ANGLE The angle formed by the rake face and the clearance face of a cutter tip.

JOINT To render true by flattening or straightening.

LAND The portion of a chisel side that is vertical to the face, the unbeveled portion.

LAP A bed of material (cast iron, copper, plastic, etc.) used to hold abrasive particles to refine the surface of a tool. Also the act of using a lap.

LINISHING Freehand abrasion of tools on a belt sander to dimension the surface and/or give it a consistent surface.

MICRO-BEVEL Any small secondary (or tertiary) bevel, usually to strengthen an edge or facilitate honing.

MICRO-GRAIN Small grains. Vaguely used to describe grains of which some are one micron or less in diameter.

MICRON One millionth part of a meter.

PARING CUT Any light cut, but typically of the nature of using a kitchen paring knife.

PERIPHERAL MILLING Any milling using the periphery of a wheel or cylinder for cutting.

PITCH The angle of the leading face of a saw tooth in relation to the axis of the saw.

PLATEN The flat backing plate on a belt sander.

POLISH To refine a surface by reduction of the depth of scratches in it.

PRIMARY BEVEL *See* Bevel.

QUARTERING STROKE A honing motion where the path of travel is at 45° to the line of the edge. Most commonly used with a curved edge (like a scimitar) where a stroke at 90° to the line of the edge would create a localized flat.

QUENCH To cool by immersing in water or other liquid.

RAKE ANGLE The angle between a line drawn normal to the cut surface and the steepest part of the rake face of the cutter.

RAKER A tooth whose primary function is to remove fibers severed by another tooth.

RELIEF ANGLE *See* Clearance angle.

ROCKWELL HARDNESS Symbolized HRc or Rc. A standard measure of tool hardness on the Rockwell C scale. Other scales (A, B, etc.) are used for other materials.

ROLL CUT The rotation of a gouge around its longitudinal axis as it is being forced through wood.

SAFE-EDGE Said of files when an edge is uncut.

SECONDARY BEVEL A second bevel ground on the primary bevel of a tool. Normally done to strengthen the tool tip or to change the cutting action.

SET The deflection of metal (or other material) to another shape. Used to describe the amount of deflection of saw teeth from the plane of the blade.

SHEARING CUT The same as a skew cut.

SKATING The erratic movement of a bit tip as it moves away from the intended point of penetration.

SKEW BLADE A blade ground at an angle other than 90° to the intended path of travel.

SKEW CUT Any cut where the cutting edge is at an angle other than 90° to the path of travel.

SLICING CUT Any cut where the cutting edge is not pressed into the work at an angle 90° to the line of the edge.

SLICK Any large, long-handled chisel used to make paring cuts with body pressure only.

SPUR Usually a tooth that scores the edge of a cut on a bit or combination plane. A spur section is an outside blade of a dado set.

STROP To refine an edge with a trailing stroke.

SWAGE To spread, mold or bend with force. Also, the tool used to do it, and sometimes the item acted on.

SWARF The bits of metal and fractured abrasive created in the sharpening process.

SWEEP A measure of curvature of a gouge flute. The most gradual sweep is #1 and the tightest is #11.

TEAROUT Fibers torn from below the cutting line.

TEMPER To bring steel to a suitable degree of hardness by heating it to the required temperature and then cooling it in a controlled manner, usually by immersing (quenching) it in a liquid.

TRAILING STROKE A honing motion where the edge is trailing, not leading.

WIRE EDGE The narrow edge section that bends back rather than submit to being abraded. So called because it looks like a fine wire when removed.

WREST To twist or bend. A saw wrest is used to put set in teeth.

INDEX

EDITOR   PETER CHAPMAN

DESIGNER/LAYOUT ARTIST   HENRY ROTH

ILLUSTRATOR   LEE HOV

ART ASSISTANT   SUZANNA YANNES

PHOTOGRAPHY   LEE VALLEY TOOLS (EXCEPT WHERE NOTED)

TYPEFACE   GARAMOND

PAPER   WARREN PATINA MATTE, 70 LB., NEUTRAL pH

PRINTER   QUEBECOR PRINTING/KINGSPORT, KINGSPORT, TENNESSEE